BRITISH WOMEN WRITERS OF THE ROMANTIC PERIOD

Also by the author:

British Women Writers and the Profession of Literary Criticism, 1789–1832 (Palgrave Macmillan, 2004)

BRITISH WOMEN WRITERS OF THE ROMANTIC PERIOD

An Anthology of their Literary Criticism

Edited by
Mary A. Waters

palgrave
macmillan

First published 2009 by
PALGRAVE MACMILLAN
Houndmills, Basingstoke, Hampshire RG21 6XS and
175 Fifth Avenue, New York, N.Y. 10010
Companies and representatives throughout the world

PALGRAVE MACMILLAN is the global academic imprint of the Palgrave Macmillan division of St. Martin's Press, LLC and of Palgrave Macmillan Ltd. Macmillan® is a registered trademark in the United States, United Kingdom and other countries. Palgrave is a registered trademark in the European \Union and other countries.

ISBN-13: 978–0–230–20576–5   hardback
ISBN-10: 0–230–20576–3   hardback
ISBN-13: 978–0–230–20577–2   paperback
ISBN-10: 0–230–20577–1   paperback

This book is printed on paper suitable for recycling and made from fully managed and sustained forest sources. Logging, pulping and manufacturing processes are expected to conform to the environmental regulations of the country of origin.

A catalogue record for this book is available from the British Library.

Library of Congress Cataloging-in-Publication Data
British women writers of the Romantic period : an anthology of their
    literary criticism / edited by Mary A. Waters.
        p. cm.
    Includes bibliographical references and index.
    ISBN-13: 978-0-230-20576-5 (hbk.)
    ISBN-10: 0-230-20576-3   (hbk.)
    ISBN-13: 978-0-230-20577-2 (pbk.)
    ISBN-10: 0-230-20577-1   (pbk.)
    1. Criticism—Great Britain—History—19th century. 2. Criticism—Great Britain—History—18th century. 3. English prose literature—Women authors. 4. English prose literature—19th century. 5. English prose literature—18th century. 6. English literature—Philosophy—Sources. 7. English literature—History and criticism—Theory, etc.—Sources. 8. Women and literature—Great Britain—History—19th century. 9. Women and literature—Great Britain—History—18th century. I. Waters, Mary, A., 1954–

PR76.B75 2009
820.9'928709034–dc22   2008039120

10   9   8   7   6   5   4   3   2   1
18 17 16 15 14 13 12 11 10 09

Printed and bound in Great Britain by
CPI Antony Rowe, Chippenham and Eastbourne

Contents

List of Illustrations	viii
Acknowledgements	ix
Introduction	1
Elizabeth Moody (1737–1814)	17
Selected Reviews from the *Monthly Review*	18
Anna Letitia Barbauld (1743–1825)	23
From *The British Novelists*	24
On the Origin and Progress of Novel-Writing	24
Prefaces to Novels by:	
Clara Reeve	37
Charlotte Lennox	38
Frances Brooke	39
Elizabeth Inchbald	39
Charlotte Smith	41
Fanny Burney	42
Ann Radcliffe	46
Charlotte Turner Smith (1749–1806)	51
Preface to *Desmond*	52
Prefaces to *Elegiac Sonnets*	55
Preface to *The Letters of a Solitary Wanderer*	59
Elizabeth Inchbald (1753–1821)	60
["On Novel Writing"] from the *Artist*	61
Selected Remarks from *The British Theatre*	65
Mary Darby Robinson (1758–1800)	79
Preface to *Sappho and Phaon*	80
Mary Wollstonecraft (1759–1797)	86
["On Artificial Taste"]	88
Selected Reviews from the *Analytical Review*	92

Mary Hays (1760–1843)   107
Preface to *Memoirs of Emma Courtney*   108
Review of *A Gossip's Story, and a Legendary Tale*. By Jane West   110
["On Novel Writing"]   111

Joanna Baillie (1762–1851)   115
From the "Introductory Discourse" to *Plays on the Passions*   116
From the Preface "To the Reader" in *Plays on the Passions*, Vol. 3   129
Epistles to the Literati No. IX, "On the Character of Romiero"   133
   from *Fraser's Magazine*

Ann Ward Radcliffe (1764–1823)   136
"On the Supernatural in Poetry"   137

Lucy Aikin (1781–1864)   146
Selected Reviews from the *Annual Review*   147

Sydney Owenson (Lady Morgan; 1776?–1859)   155
Preface to *O'Donnel. A National Tale*   156
Selected Reviews from the *Athenæum*   159

Maria Jane Jewsbury (1800–1833)   164
Selected Contributions to the *Athenæum*   165
   Literary Sketches. No. I. Felicia Hemans   165
   Literary Women No. II. Jane Austen   171
   Romance and Reality by L.E.L.   174

Letitia Elizabeth Landon (1802–1838)   178
Preface to the *Venetian Bracelet*   180
Selected Essays from the *New Monthly Magazine*   181
   On the Ancient and Modern Influence of Poetry   181
   On the Character of Mrs. Hemans's Writings   186
   Female Portrait Gallery from Sir Walter Scott No. 1—"Flora   198
      MacIvor and Rose Bradwardine"

Harriet Martineau (1802–1876)   204
Selected Essays from the *Monthly Repository* and *Tait's Edinburgh*   205
   Magazine
   Female Writers on Practical Divinity. No. I. Mrs. More   205
   Female Writers on Practical Divinity. No. II. Mrs. More and   206
      Mrs. Barbauld
   "The Achievements of the Genius of Scott"   207

Appendix: Featured Periodicals   219
The Analytical Review   219
The Annual Review; or, Register of Literature   220
The Artist   220
The Athenæum   221
Fraser's Magazine for Town and Country   221

The Monthly Magazine   221
The Monthly Repository   222
The Monthly Review   222
The New Monthly Magazine and Literary Journal   223
Tait's Edinburgh Magazine   223

Selected Bibliography   225

Index   234

List of Illustrations

1. Title Page: *The British Novelists* (1810)   25
2. *The Athenæum* no. 368 (15 November 1834)   157
3. *The Athenæum* no. 368 (15 November 1834): p. 835   160

Acknowledgements

I thank the National Endowment for the Humanities for their research support through a Summer Seminar for College Teachers and Wichita State University for an Award for Research and Creative Projects in Summer. I would also like to acknowledge the following people for assistance ranging from locating texts through assisting with references to advice on how to make this volume more useful: Stephen Behrendt, Catherine Burroughs, Kari Lokke, Laura Mandell, Marjean Purinton, Brigitte Roussel, David Simpson, Gina Luria Walker, Anne Wallace, and Barbara Witucki. Staff at the libraries at University of California, Davis, University of Nebraska, and especially Wichita State University deserve acknowledgement for their untiring work. Though length restrictions sometimes prohibited making the most of them, I am grateful as well to Palgrave Macmillan's anonymous readers for their valuable suggestions on how to improve this volume. And finally, thanks to Kendra Unruh and Rebecca Timberlake for their patient transcriptions from difficult to read copies.

Introduction

In the past three decades, scholars of reading history and print culture have made impressive strides in the study of formerly neglected genres and authors, including aesthetic commentary by Romantic era women writers. Readers now widely recognize that novels, poems, and private letters all furnish passages in which women writers express views on aesthetic ideals, the value of certain literary forms, or the achievement of predecessors, male and female. The letters of Anna Seward (collected and published in 1811), Jane Austen's defense of the novel in *Northanger Abbey* (1818), and the sequence of poetic celebrations of female forebears begun by Felicia Hemans ("The Last Song of Sappho"), Letitia Landon ("Felicia Hemans") and Elizabeth Barrett Browning ("L.E.L.'s Last Question") offer only a few prominent examples.[1] These illustrations reveal much about Romantic women writers' views of literature, yet although they certainly rank as aesthetic commentary, their authors did not write them explicitly for publication as criticism. Thus even many readers who are aware of these and similar examples still retain a mistaken impression that women rarely ventured into the field of professional literary criticism during these years. By bringing together an assortment of women's texts published explicitly as criticism, this anthology challenges restrictive assumptions about the range of venues in which women's literary commentary appeared and the breadth of issues addressed. It asks us to reconsider our preconceptions about the nature of professional women's writing as we acknowledge the conscious authority of women writers' critical voices and their sense of themselves as participating in public debate. At the same time, in exploring women's views on literature and aesthetics, this collection will broaden our understanding of the nature, purposes, and principles of Romantic-era literary criticism, regardless of who may be the author.

Distinguished by shifts in literary values and practices that have long been associated with male writers, British Romanticism's defining aesthetic

---

[1] This sequence continues through the nineteenth century and beyond with contributions by poets such as Caroline Norton, Christina Rossetti, Frances Kemble, Jane Wilde, Adelaide Procter, and Michael Field.

principles emerged from Britain's growing sense of itself as a nation. With the successive incorporation of Wales, Scotland and Ireland into the single nation of Great Britain, Britons increasingly looked for the foundation of British national character to a cultural heritage that could offer common ground to this disparate populace. Standards for literary excellence derived from models originating in Greece, Rome, and more recently France declined in influence as many British critics began to proclaim the preeminence of native British writers like Chaucer, Shakespeare, and Milton over the cosmopolitan classical literary canon. A new set of literary values emphasizing originality and native genius, which critics found aplenty in these home-grown writers, came to displace classically defined correctness and recognizable faithfulness to any, but especially non-British, literary models. These changes were well underway by the mid-eighteenth century, but as Britain reacted to the French Revolution, the clash between liberatory visions on one hand and patriotic fervor to stave off fears of spreading social and political instability on the other produced a storm of controversy and innovation that reverberated in the literary realm for many years. William Wordsworth's "spontaneous overflow of emotions," Samuel Taylor Coleridge's "organic" versus "mechanical" unity, and Percy Bysshe Shelley's "unacknowledged legislators of the World" come to mind as famous examples of revisionary critical ideals, while Francis Jeffrey's "This will never do" in his 1814 review of Wordsworth's *Excursion* reminds us that aesthetic innovations were far from universally embraced.[2]

Such insistently public origins seem antithetical to the domestic privacy that we have until recently regarded as the separate sphere to which women were confined. Moreover, because it relies on faculties such as judgment and the ability to theorize that were then often associated with masculinity, many felt that criticism was beyond the abilities of most women and outside the proper domain of the few capable exceptions.[3] Yet despite this

---

[2]   *Edinburgh Review* 24 (November 1814): 1.

[3]   Such skepticism was by no means universal, however. Taste in art and literature was often regarded as an effeminate attribute, whether in a man or a woman, so a few theorists surmised that women were especially gifted in that regard. David Hume, for example, affirmed that "All men of sense, who know the world, have a great deference for [women's] judgment of such books as lie within the compass of their knowledge, and repose more confidence in the delicacy of their taste, though unguided by rules, than in all the dull labors of pedants and commentators" (*Essays Moral, Political and Literary* [London: Oxford UP, 1963] 278, qtd. in Gary Kelly, "Bluestocking Feminism," *Women, Writing and the Public Sphere, 1700–1830*, ed. Elizabeth Eger, Charlotte Grant, Clíona Ó Gallchoir, and Penny Warburton [Cambridge: Cambridge UP, 2001] 166). It is obvious, however, that Hume restricts the scope of women's literary judgment to "books as like within the compass of their knowledge" and assumes women's ignorance of systematic aesthetic theory or "rules." For further discussion, see also Robert W. Jones, *Gender and the Formation of Taste in Eighteenth-Century Britain: The Analysis of Beauty* (Cambridge: Cambridge UP, 1998).

skepticism, women writers, including women critics, contributed to the changes that define Romanticism. For example, Wordsworth's 1800 preface to *Lyrical Ballads* is considered a landmark in Romantic literary theory for its explanation of the premises behind a collection of poems that broke new ground in form and content. Yet far fewer realize that in her "Introductory Discourse" to *Plays on the Passions* (1798), Joanna Baillie articulated a number of Wordsworth's most innovative ideas while anticipating his treatise by two years. Convinced that emotions produce far more interesting psychological effects than do external events, Baillie devoted her preface and, indeed, her writing career to exploring how such powerful but shifting internal states could be conveyed in their full subtlety to a theater audience. Even earlier, Mary Wollstonecraft had voiced many of Wordsworth's views in similar language in her 1797 essay "On Artificial Taste" published in the *Monthly Magazine*, where she explores the relationship between immediate feeling and direct experience of nature on one hand and "natural," affecting poetry on the other. It diminishes none of these writers to recognize that all were concerned with finding a smooth conduit between emotional experience and literary expression. Rather, reading all three can enhance our appreciation of their concern with the relationship between emotional authenticity, communication of feeling, and literary language, one of the more significant aesthetic issues of the Romantic period. Baillie's essay, like Wordsworth's, prefaced a collection of her own work – in this case, several plays – that so differed from familiar practices that she felt readers would need a framework in order to appreciate them. And like Wordsworth's preface, Baillie's "Introductory Discourse" develops a coherent theory for a literary form – in her case closet drama – that comprises one of Romanticism's most important contributions to a major literary genre.[4] Wollstonecraft published her essay anonymously, leaving it open for readers to assume the author was male. Similarly, though Baillie joined her essay with her own work, her collection initially appeared anonymously, and most readers speculated that the author must be male. Only with subsequent editions of both publications were the authors' identities revealed. As these examples suggest, study of criticism by women may reveal that women critics were far more frequently than we now acknowledge in the vanguard of debates over literary standards that constructed Romantic aesthetics.

A milestone in literary criticism and theory, Baillie's is not the only major essay penned by a woman to revise genre theory and history. Coming a decade later, "On the Origin and Progress of Novel-Writing," Anna Barbauld's introductory essay to the fifty volume collection *The British Novelists* offered an early contribution to genre classification and literary theory as well

---

[4] See Catherine Burroughs, *Closet Stages: Joanna Baillie and the Theater Theory of British Romantic Women Writers* (Philadelphia, U of Pennsylvania P: 1997).

as a prototypical canon of British fiction.[5] Further, Barbauld's essay and her individual introductions to featured novelists revised literary history in ways that gave unprecedented attention to the contribution of women writers. At the same time, she argued that fictional literature deserved more respect than most critics were willing to grant it. Samuel Johnson served as spokesperson for many in voicing concerns about the effects of novels on the impressionable minds of the young and female, whom many believed were fiction's primary consumers. Johnson argued that, because novels "are written chiefly to the Young, the Ignorant, and the Idle," whose minds are "unfurnished with Ideas, and therefore easily susceptible of Impression," and who will regulate their behavior according to the examples they read, "Care ought to be taken, that, when the Choice is unrestrained, the best Examples only should be exhibited; and that which is likely to operate so strongly, should not be mischievous or uncertain in its Effects."[6] Johnson was so influential an authority that half a century later many critics, women included, deferred to him. Barbauld's "On the Origin and Progress of Novel-Writing," however, refuted Johnsonian dictates that novels must serve an educational and moral purpose, arguing that although these are desirable ends, entertainment is fiction's ultimate goal and the most important standard by which it should be judged. Though other women critics had recently made similar statements in less prominent venues, Barbauld offers a new twist, turning Wordsworthian concern for the dispossessed to new account by stressing the value of entertaining fiction for those isolated by hardship or illness and barred from other amusements. As the introduction to the first definitive selection of complete text British novels, the essay appeared in a context that had few rivals in either prestige or appeal to national pride since Johnson's own *Works of the English Poets* (1779–1781) over a quarter of a century earlier.

Such prominence belies several outdated generalizations about women writers – that they often hid behind anonymity to avoid the taint of immodesty associated with publication, that they were universally regarded as lacking in the judgment necessary to criticism, that they never enjoyed the kind of professional literary career that was attained by at least some men. Instead, when women's criticism enjoyed the prominence of Barbauld's

---

5   See Claudia L. Johnson, "'Let me make the novels of a country': Barbauld's *The British Novelists* (1810/1820)" *Novel: A Forum on Fiction* 34 (2001): 163–79 and Catherine E. Moore, "'Ladies … Taking the Pen in Hand': Mrs. Barbauld's Criticism of Eighteenth-Century Women Novelists," *Fetter'd or Free: British Women Novelists 1670–1815*, Ed. Mary Anne Schofield and Cecilia Macheski (Athens, OH: U of Ohio P, 1986) 383–97.

6   "The Modern Form of Romances," *Rambler* No. 4 (Saturday, 31 March 1750), *The Rambler 1750–1752* vol. 1 (London: Payne, 1752) 29, 31. See further comments from Johnson below as well as Smith's discussion in her preface to *The Letters of a Solitary Wanderer* (Chapter 3), Wollstonecraft's comments in several of her *Analytical* reviews (Chapter 6), and Hays's comments in each of her entries (Chapter 7).

"Origin and Progress of Novel-Writing," it was because of, not despite, the critic's name. By the time Barbauld's essay appeared, she had gained renown as a poet, educator, children's author, political polemicist, literary biographer, critic, and editor. The full title of the collection, boasting "with an essay, and prefaces biographical and critical, by Mrs. Barbauld," indicates the prestige and commercial appeal that the publishers hoped to gain from Barbauld's name. Barbauld enjoyed an exceptionally long literary career that included some two decades as a critic. Some of that criticism appeared anonymously in literary reviews, as was then common practice for periodical criticism. But much of it blazoned her name to augment the stature of the publications it graced.[7]

Much like Barbauld, whose work as a critic provides a counter example to preconceptions about women writers and criticism, Elizabeth Inchbald was likewise recruited to write criticism because of her celebrity as a popular actress, playwright, and novelist, yet her criticism broke new ground as well. Inchbald's prefaces to the individual plays included in *The British Theatre* (1806–1808) turned away from established models of Shakespeare criticism to emphasize staging and theatrical history, helping to shift the direction of theater criticism for decades to come. Meanwhile, although Inchbald's essays appeared first as individual installments, when brought together for the 1808 bound set, they offer, as did Baillie's "Introductory Discourse," a coherent theory of closet drama. Inchbald disliked writing criticism, but because she, like Barbauld, brought stature to the collections that bore her name, her publisher, Thomas Longman, refused to release her from her contract. The canny Inchbald discovered, however, that she need not take on further drudgery once that contract was fulfilled. Her celebrity appeal commanded a generous price from the publishers for the right to add "Selected by Mrs. Inchbald" to the title pages of *A Collection of Farces and Other Afterpieces* (1809) and *The Modern Theatre* (1811). True, as standard histories of women writers would lead us to expect, Inchbald was attacked for stepping outside the bounds of feminine competence in daring to judge the work of a man. One of the authors Inchbald discusses, George Colman the younger, displeased with her assessment, wrote a sarcastic, demeaning letter questioning her judgment and her right to invade the usually masculine domain of literary criticism. But when published, the letter was paired with Inchbald's witty but trenchant response ably defending both her role as a woman critic and her assessment of Colman's work. Meanwhile, the

---

[7] See Mary A. Waters, *British Women Writers and the Profession of Literary Criticism, 1789–1832*, Palgrave Studies in the Enlightenment, Romanticism and the Cultures of Print (Palgrave Macmillan, 2004) for discussion of literary professionalism in relation to Barbauld and several other Romantic-era women critics. Waters, "'Slovenly Monthly Catalogues': The *Monthly Review* and Anna Letitia Barbauld's Periodical Literary Criticism," *Nineteenth-Century Prose* 31 (2004): 53–81, explores Barbauld's anonymous literary reviewing for the *Monthly Review*.

success of the collection affirmed Longman's astute prediction of a strong market for literary commentary by women.

Presented in two such different contexts, Elizabeth Inchbald's series of remarks for *The British Theatre* highlights questions about the stature, influence, and audience of women's literary criticism. Like Barbauld's "Origin and Progress of Novel-Writing," the *British Theatre* bound set appealed to the burgeoning sense of British national pride and the expanding consumer market for the appurtenances of elegant sophistication, but it was priced well out of reach of all but the most affluent middle- and upper-class readers. These handsome volumes graced the library shelves of many a prosperous merchant or manufacturer, their purchase signifying the literary taste that was quickly becoming a necessary marker among the rising middle class of the cultural refinement that set them apart from more humble origins and aligned them with upper class urbanity. But if impressive collections sometimes placed women's criticism in a position of prominence, not all women's literary commentary enjoyed such prestige. Against the consumer-driven status of an attractively bound matching set stands the other form in which Inchbald's prefaces appeared – brief essays, each introducing a single recently popular play, published in inexpensive, weekly installments. Though lacking the grandeur of the costly collection, this more ephemeral form of publication could reach a wider, more diverse audience. In assessing women's contributions to Romantic-era literary culture, we must recognize what this example suggests about how widely women's literary views may have circulated.

No criticism by Romantic-era British women writers reached as many readers and yet has been as underrated as that in literary magazines, especially literary reviews. Literary periodicals, including those specializing in reviews, had long included occasional commentary by women. Isabella Griffiths, for example, is believed to have assisted her husband Ralph Griffiths with some reviews for early installments of his *Monthly Review*, the first true British literary review, founded in 1749. A few other women writers such as Eliza Haywood and Frances Brooke had written and published entire periodicals which sometimes included remarks on literature and the arts.[8] But toward the end of the eighteenth century, the number of literary magazines and reviews increased dramatically while at the same time women began to contribute to these new periodicals more frequently. As was generally the practice in periodical criticism, most of these articles were published unsigned. On one hand, editors believed that anonymity would promote

---

[8]   Haywood published her *Female Spectator* from 1744 to 1746, while Brooke's *Old Maid* lasted from November 1755 to July 1756, with a collected edition issued in 1764. See Barbauld's discussion of Frances Brooke (Chapter 2). On Griffiths, see Betty Rizzo, "Isabella Griffiths," *A Dictionary of British and American Women Writers, 1660–1800*, ed. Janet Todd (Totowa, NJ: Roan and Allanheld, 1985) 143.

objectivity. One might be less tempted to soften any censure of an acquaintance's publication when commenting anonymously. On the other hand, since the literary world regarded reviewers with little respect, many preferred obscurity. Consequently, although letters, diary entries, editors' marked copies, and the like have led to some attributions of women's periodical criticism, it is impossible to gauge how much can no longer be identified. Yet the invisibility of this work belies its importance. Broad coverage of publications on all but the most specialized subjects meant that readers of at least some literary reviews might hope to stay current in virtually all fields of knowledge. The more prestigious literary reviews and magazines were widely read, often from cover to cover, and both their indexing practices and the availability of replacements for past issues indicate that they were meant to be collected. Many were distributed to the provinces, the continent, even America. Moreover, James Basker has found that reviews not only guided reading, but by swaying the purchasing choices of both individuals and the new, popular circulating libraries, they probably helped to determine which texts still survive today. Literary journalism, Basker argues,

> introduced new, more accessible forums for critical discussion; it multiplied and diversified the opportunities for critical expression; it fostered new critical values, drew attention to new literary genres, systematized the treatment of established ones, and expanded the audience for criticism. [...I]n subtler ways it affected canon formation, reception history, the emergence of affective criticism, the assimilation of foreign influences, the segregation of 'women's literature', and ultimately the politics of culture.[9]

And if literary periodicals so dramatically influenced aesthetics and critical practice, they had a similar impact on Romantic writers' careers. It is no exaggeration to suggest that study of them has revolutionized Romantic scholarship over the quarter century since Marilyn Butler suggested that "the search for 'Romanticism' is not so much the quest for a certain literary product, as for a type of producer."[10] For Butler, the literary professional, for whom reviewing and similar literary commentary provided both income and an avenue to public authority, was the most common and the most influential kind of Romantic writer. Yet even Butler may not have anticipated the discovery of how many women writers followed this model of

---

[9] James Basker, "Criticism and the Rise of Periodical Literature," *Cambridge History of Literary Criticism* Vol. 4 The Eighteenth Century, ed. H.B. Nisbet and Claude Rawson (Cambridge: Cambridge UP, 1997) 316–32; 316.

[10] Butler, *Romantics, Rebels and Reactionaries: English Literature and Its Background 1760–1830* (Oxford: Oxford UP, 1981) 70.

professionalism. Study of their criticism offers a window onto literary culture that can redefine what writing professionally meant for both men and women.

■ The Rise of the Professional Woman Critic

Although the Romantic period saw the rise of the professional woman literary critic, women had long participated in literary culture. Norma Clarke, who documents the careers of several eighteenth-century women writers, notes that the century was one in which exceptional women writers, including some women critics, were not only accepted, but revered as public intellectuals in a developing British tradition of great literary ladies. In fact, Terry Castle has pulled together a surprisingly long list of eighteenth-century women, many of them British, who were producing and publishing literary criticism. Castle's examples include women like Aphra Behn and Susannah Centlivre, who provided critical prefaces to some of their own publications, Elizabeth Cooper, who introduced a collection of the works of others, and Judith Madan and Sarah Fielding, who published freestanding essays.[11] These studies show that the existence of British women who wrote and published literary criticism was nothing new to the Romantic period.

Clarke reminds us, however, that most of the women in her study came from the genteel classes. Unlike their lower-class counterparts, these were the women who had access to education and leisure to read and write. Further, the nature of eighteenth-century publishing explicitly emphasized the amateur or dilettante, especially in the case of women. Most women writers, critics included, emerged from an aristocratic milieu, the "country-house coterie," the most notable of which was the "bluestocking circle" of Elizabeth Montagu.[12] Much like its French counterpart, the salon, these coteries almost invariably included, and as Montagu's example shows, many were dominated by women. Through most of the century, access to publishers

---

[11]   Norma Clarke, *The Rise and Fall of the Woman Writer* (London: Pimlico, 2004); Terry Castle, "Women and Literary Criticism," *The Cambridge History of Literary Criticism* vol. 4, The Eighteenth Century, ed. H.B. Nisbet and Claude Rawson (Cambridge: Cambridge UP, 1997): 434–55. Among other examples, Castle mentions Cooper's introduction to the *Muse's Library*, Madan's "Progress of Poesy" (1731), and Fielding's anonymous *Remarks on 'Clarissa'* (1749). See the essays in Elizabeth Eger, Charlotte Grant, Clíona Ó Gallchoir, and Penny Warburton, eds, *Women, Writing and the Public Sphere, 1700–1830* (Cambridge: Cambridge UP, 2001) as well.

[12]   Sylvia Harcstark Myers provides the central study of the eighteenth-century Bluestockings (*The Bluestocking Circle: Women, Friendship, and the Life of the Mind in Eighteenth-Century England* [Oxford: Clarendon P, 1990]). For a discussion of the role of coterie culture in the dissemination of literary criticism before the Romantic period, see Paul Trolander and Zeynep Tenger, *Sociable Criticism in England, 1625–1725* (Newark, DE: U of Delaware P, 2007).

depended on these connections, either in the form of a single prestigious patron or a subscription in which acquaintances and their connections would underwrite the cost of publication. Within these networks, writing entertained one's acquaintances and displayed one's talents. Though publishing might bring much needed money to a writer patronized by the more affluent members of the circle, the ostensible purpose of bringing a work before the public was simply to expand the circle of edification and enjoyment. [13] Outside these networks, not only was publishing more difficult, but women's writing and publishing was often associated with sexual laxity. Those writers with upper-class and aristocratic connections distanced themselves where possible from perceptions that they wrote for money, even in the face of financial need. Where such distancing was impracticable, they often sacrificed class standing and respectability.

Despite the importance of coteries and patrons, though, Clarke notes that women writers were far less successful than men at exploiting the patronage system. Among other concerns, Charlotte Smith's prefaces to her *Elegiac Sonnets* illustrate some of the trials encountered even by some who succeeded at finding patrons.[14] Yet Paula McDowell has recently shown that although numbers were small, during the Restoration and early eighteenth century women participated as professionals in *"all* aspects of material literary production," including not only writing, but printing, distribution, and copyright possession as well. McDowell argues that because scholarship of early modern literary women has emphasized textual expressions of gendered subjectivity, we have remained nearsighted about "the non-élite woman" in print culture, for whom "gender was not necessarily the first category of identity."[15] McDowell references not only women writers, but printers, ballad hawkers, booksellers, and more who came not from the genteel, but from the lower and artisan classes. With little status to lose, many of these women seem to have felt the unsavory connotations of professional literary work to be beside the point. Like their upper-class counterparts, they depended on networks of support, but in contrast to female-dominated coteries and salons, their associations included male-dominated institutions such as guilds, publishing congers, and the family.

As the eighteenth century drew to a close, upper-class patronage forms of publication gave way to a more modern, professional literary culture where contracts and direct transactions between publisher and writer became paramount, where the relationship between a writer and publisher were

---

[13] It is worth noting that since new books were priced beyond the reach of most potential readers, that circle still expanded only into the upper echelons of the middle class.

[14] See Chapter 3.

[15] Paula McDowell, *The Women of Grub Street: Press, Politics, and Gender in the London Literary Marketplace, 1678–1730* (Oxford: Clarendon P, 1998) 15, 5.

usually direct and might include various types of literary work, and where a publisher might rely on writers' current specializations and expect writers to cultivate new ones. While the numbers of women publishing in all forms increased rapidly, the ever more commercialized literary world came more firmly under control of male dominated institutions like large publishing houses and heavyweight literary magazines and reviews. Among those women who best adapted to this masculine world of early professionalized literary culture, literary criticism often played a decisive role. Wollstonecraft clearly saw the significance of these changes when she exclaims to her sister Eliza that as an employee of radical bookseller Joseph Johnson, she would be "the first of a new genus."[16]

The landscape of British women's literary history would present a very different view if it were not for criticism's financial, intellectual, and even emotional impact. Criticism brought poet Elizabeth Moody, for example, into a circle of literary professionals that nudged her out of the amateur world of coterie circulation into commercial publication of both her creative and her critical work. For others such as Mary Wollstonecraft, criticism provided the financial stability to launch a literary career. Writing on demand for Johnson and especially reviewing for his new *Analytical Review* allowed Wollstonecraft to escape the lonely, taxing positions of governess and companion and establish herself in London, where she joined the most vibrant literary community in late eighteenth-century Britain. Sydney Owenson (Lady Morgan), on the other hand, possessed an independent income, but it was a modest one, and her work for *The Athenæum* seems to have smoothed financial ruts when some of her novels met with negligible success. Further, for Wollstonecraft and some other young writers such as Harriet Martineau and Letitia Landon, reading for a demanding schedule of reviewing provided intellectual training, broadening and deepening their thinking and preparing them for the creative or analytical work for which they are best known today. Since the middle class women who comprised the majority of women critics enjoyed only minimal access to systematic formal education, this reading could yield decisive benefits. And for Barbauld, criticism appears to have sustained her financially while providing her, according to her niece and first biographer, with an intellectual and emotional lifeline at the time of her husband's mental collapse and eventual suicide.[17]

---

[16] Dissenting Joseph Johnson (1738–1809), one of the most radical among London publishers, was known for his congenial manner and enthusiastic support of a wide network of writers, artists, and intellectuals. A number of women featured in this volume figured among those whom he encouraged, provided work for, or otherwise furthered their careers, including Barbauld, Smith, Inchbald, Robinson, Wollstonecraft, Hays, and Aikin.

[17] See Lucy Aikin, *The Works of Anna Lætitia Barbauld. With a Memoir by Lucy Aikin*, 2 vols. (London: Longman, *et al.*, 1825); Glennis Stephenson, *Letitia Landon: The Woman Behind L.E.L.* (Manchester: Manchester UP, 1995); and Waters, *British Women Writers and the Profession of Literary Criticism, 1789–1832*.

■ Reading Women's Criticism

There is much to discover, then, by reading literary criticism by women writers, but in order to make the most of it, we need to consider how to approach our reading. The impulse to equate criticism with literary reception can be strong, for when criticism has been republished, it has most often appeared as an appendix to an edition of an imaginative work or grouped in a collection under the name of the author it discusses. Nevertheless, in cases where criticism offers evaluations of literary works, it may reflect attempts to shape or control reader reception, but it does not equal that reception, *per se*.[18] In fact, one of the first insights that broad reading of Romantic period criticism can offer is that when critics evaluated, they usually saw their function as juridical. In the minds of some, the spread of reading and the variety of new types of publications undermined a social order where the makeup of the reading public could be known and standards of taste assumed to be shared.[19] When literary culture had been supported largely by patronage, authors often knew much of their audience, either personally or implicitly as connections of a patron or acquaintance. Mostly from the upper classes, these readers were better educated than the general run of English men and women, and their taste had usually been formed on classical literature and more recent works modeled on the classical tradition. But as the eighteenth century drew to a close, authors and critics experienced a growing sense that the makeup of the reading population had changed, and that many new readers lacked the education and hence the commonly agreed upon standards of taste that the literary world had formerly counted on. Critics saw a need to generate broader acceptance for the literary values that they regarded as desirable and began to try to police the taste of these new readers, demonstrating that aesthetic standards were far from self-evident, but were instead subject to lively debate. Meanwhile, it was not merely authors and critics who experienced anxieties about the new readers. Regarding familiarity with literature as a necessary mark of gentility, the expanding middle class that made up most of these new readers turned to criticism, especially in periodicals, for guidance in developing their literary taste. Yet evidence such as the popularity of scores of novels

---

18   See Mark Parker, *Literary Magazines and British Romanticism*, Cambridge Studies in Romanticism 45 (Cambridge: Cambridge UP, 2000) for a discussion of what has been lost as literary magazines have been read as reception. In *The Reading Nation in the Romantic Period* (Cambridge: Cambridge UP, 2004), William St. Clair documents actual reading patterns during the Romantic period, demonstrating why reviews cannot inform us about reader reception and dispelling a number of myths that have arisen from the conflation of the two.

19   See, among others, St. Clair; Frank Donaghue, *The Fame Machine: Book Reviewing and Eighteenth-Century Literary Careers* (Stanford, CA: Stanford UP, 1996); and Don Herzog, *Poisoning the Minds of the Lower Orders* (Princeton: Princeton UP, 1998).

scorned in reviews reveals a disquieting gap between the critic and an anonymous reading public with inclinations that resisted critical discipline.

If criticism failed to fully control public response to literary works, neither
did it necessarily evaluate those works according to recognized aesthetic
standards. For one, aesthetic standards change, and while the neoclassical
standards that had once held wide currency lost much favor by the end of
the eighteenth century, some of the ideals that were central at the beginning
of the nineteenth century have likewise declined in appeal since. Senti-
mentality, for example, was a hotly debated topic, and in its more florid
manifestations Romantic critics often objected – as might a critic now – that
it debased a literary work and made it suitable only for a sensation market.
But when modulated, emotional content enjoyed broad currency during the
Romantic years. Many readers and writers believed that emotional appeals
offered a route for literature to help better society by cultivating individual
sensitivity and sympathy. When literature could accomplish this softening,
it could inspire readers to sympathetic identification with the distresses of
others, forming a common bond that was regarded by many as the foundation of social conscience.[20] Thus sentiment and sensibility underlay much
of the interest in moral effect that was common to many critics during
the later years of the eighteenth century, male and female, especially when
discussing fiction. In fact, the demand for a positive moral tendency was in
itself a contested issue. Many critics, both male and female, followed Samuel
Johnson in suggesting that literature should teach moral conduct by presenting only the highest examples worthy of emulation. Yet some Romantic
women critics such as Barbauld explicitly argue that literature need not
conform to such restrictive standards, nor, indeed need it explicitly serve
a higher social purpose. They champion the central significance of other
qualities such as entertainment value, form, versification, imagery, characterization, means of creating suspense, and credibility or realism. These
concerns often supersede moral effect in importance, or combine in a new
way, such as when women such as Mary Hays argue, contra Johnson, that
realistic characters teach moral lessons better than perfectly virtuous ones
do.

Meanwhile, not only were standards shifting so that few aesthetic ideals
could claim general acceptance, but in addition, many literary reviews had
not yet acknowledged evaluation to be part of their task. Especially among
reviews that emerged from the culture of religious dissent, such as the

---

[20]   On the role of sensibility in literature, see G.J. Barker-Benfield, *The Culture of Sensibility: Sex
and Society in Eighteenth-Century Britain* (Chicago and London: U of Chicago P, 1992);
Jerome McGann, *The Poetics of Sensibility : A Revolution in Literary Style* (Oxford: Clarendon
P, 1996); John Mullan, *Sentiment and Sociability: The Language of Feeling in the Eighteenth
Century* (Oxford: Clarendon P, 1988); Adela Pinch, *Strange Fits of Passion: Epistemologies of
Emotion, Hume to Austen* (Stanford: Stanford UP, 1996); and Janet Todd, *Sensibility: An
Introduction* (London: Methuen, 1986).

Monthly Review and the *Analytical Review*, both of which employed women as regular reviewers for at least part of their histories, the imposition of the critic's own opinion was, at least during the early Romantic period, considered a corruption in the true purposes of a review. Just as dissenting worshipers read and interpreted religious text without subordinating their own understanding to priestly dogma, many critics from this subculture assumed readers to be capable of making their own judgments about literature as well. Dissenter Thomas Christie, for example, founded the *Analytical Review* explicitly to correct the fallen state of literary journalism, which he believed emerged from critics' inflated sense of their own influence. He declared that his new review would "give such an account of new publications, as may enable the reader to judge of them for himself." The *Analytical Review* would accomplish this aim by providing readers with "accounts [i.e., summaries] and extracts." Striving for encyclopedic coverage of all new publications, Christie called his reviewers "HISTORIANS of the Republic of Letters," and resisted incorporating critical evaluation. "Whether the Writers ought to add to this their own judgment," he demurs, "is with us a doubtful point."[21]

Published by radical dissenting bookseller Joseph Johnson, the *Analytical Review* constitutes a landmark in early women's periodical criticism, having employed Wollstonecraft as one of its major contributors almost from its first issue. Its example cautions us that Romantic period critics' sense of purpose may diverge from our present-day views of what a review should accomplish. At the same time, it reveals some of the shifts in critical agenda that took place during the Romantic period. Christie's democratic purpose met with an obstacle in the changing readership of the time. The original mid-eighteenth century literary reviews had taken their inspiration partly from the learned journals of the seventeenth and early eighteenth centuries. These journals could presume a highly educated and almost exclusively male audience, one where each reader was able to "judge for himself." But by the end of the century, literary reviews found much of their readership among the expanding middle class, including middle-class women. Many of these readers had only modest formal education, and in reading about literature, they sought the kind of guidance provided in the other important model for literary reviews – popular periodical papers along the lines of Joseph Addison's *Spectator* and Samuel Johnson's *Rambler*. These forebears showcased the merits of literary works in an effort to educate readers about literature and aesthetics and to help form reader taste.[22] Thus even Christie recognized that as the audience for criticism changed, so must criticism itself. About his ambition for pure objectivity, he continues: "Such was the plan [...]. But on weighing the matter more fully, a very material objection occurred to us, *viz.* that the work, though esteemed by the learned and

---

21 Thomas Christie, "To the Public," *Analytical Review* 1 (May 1788): i, iv.
22 On the origins of literary reviews, see Basker.

thinking few, would not be sufficiently adapted to the taste of the public at large, and hence fail to meet with encouragement."[23] As her reviews show, Wollstonecraft was among the *Analytical* reviewers who never wholly adhered to the objective model.

If Christie's high-minded aspirations informed part of the purpose of some criticism, entertainment often played a vital role as well. Books, even used ones, were expensive, and in order to borrow books, one had either to pay a subscription fee to a circulating library or have friends who could afford to buy books and were willing to lend them. Periodicals were comparatively more affordable. While literary magazines might publish original poetry and fiction, the extracts in reviews made it possible to be familiar with a wider variety of more extensive works as well – novels, collections of sermons, scientific discoveries, statements on major political and social questions – all sorts of publications on wide variety of subjects.[24] Further, while many articles aspired to objectivity, others strove for entertainment in the criticism itself. Some periodicals, for example, cultivated a reputation for abusive rancor as a way of drawing readers. Women critics, on the other hand, might strive for entertainment by such means as structuring a critical essay in the form of a dialog, as did Ann Radcliffe, a strategy that allows for posing multiple critical perspectives while integrating some of the diverting qualities of fiction and drama. In some cases, too, wit and irony allowed a bridge between the older cultures of coterie circulation and modern mass publication, as when Elizabeth Moody masquerades as a male writer enjoying tobacco and port with his reading.[25] While Moody's urbane, satirical tone would have amused most readers, only the few who knew that the anonymous author was a woman could have fully appreciated the humor. In other instances, articles that repeat assessments that had already become commonplace, such as Maria Jane Jewsbury's essay on Jane Austen, suggest that readers sometime cared as much for the pleasure of affirming comfortably accepted ideas as for original and rigorous criticism. Jewsbury's essay contributed to a continually circulating discourse about literature that constituted middle-class taste. The fact that some of these articles held the prestigious lead articles positions confirms that this purpose was accepted by publishers and readers alike.

Much remains to be uncovered in Romantic-era criticism by women. A few additional issues have already emerged, however, that are worth noting. For one, Romantic-era women critics used commentary on literature

---

[23] "To the Public" iv. See Wollstonecraft's reviews in Chapter 6.

[24] See St. Clair and Daniel Reiss, "Laetitia Landon and the Dawn of English Post-Romanticism," *SEL: Studies in English Literature* 36 (1996): 807–27 for discussions of readers relying on reviews and literary magazines as an important source of new literature.

[25] See Jan Wellington's discussion of Moody's reviews in *The Poems and Prose of Elizabeth Moody* (Diss. University of New Mexico, 1997).

to participate in wide-ranging debates on topics of public concern. In the course of talking about literature, women often comment on public events or call attention to the ways their work or the work of others affects public issues. Their comments on British character or the British literary heritage, for example, demonstrate that they understood national identity and character as historically and culturally determined constructs even at the time these concepts were first taking shape. When women critics speak of literature's influence on individual virtue, for instance, they frequently do so in terms of growing Romantic interest in the ways literature shapes national character. Moreover, women critics show strong interest in women writers. Male critics during these years were often patronizing toward women writers, nudging them toward acceptably "feminine" subject matter and literary forms while holding their productions to a lower standard of quality than similar works by male writers. By writing criticism at all, women critics had already broken out of these constraints, for most readers, writers, and publishers regarded this sort of work as beyond the purview of women. But examining the commentary of a number of women critics on women writers reveals new insights about women's views of other women writers. Barbauld's revisions to literary history and her inclusion of women in a proposed canon of British fiction represent only one instance of women's promotion of other women writers. Not only do women critics frequently praise other women writers, but they sometimes capitalize on the occasion of reviewing one female writer to promote other women writers, as when Jewsbury endorses Caroline Bowles while writing on Jane Austen. Yet as Wollstonecraft's reviews of Charlotte Smith's novels show, women critics seem to hold their female contemporaries to exacting standards, refusing to follow the example of feigned tolerance that provided a thin veneer for their male contemporaries' clubby assurance of feminine literary inferiority. It is to be hoped that the present volume will encourage study of Romantic period literary criticism by women as a body of work that will yield new insights in Romantic aesthetics, journalism, and literary professionalism that may even revolutionize our understanding of Romantic-era print culture.

■ A Note on Texts:

The first consideration in choosing texts has been immediate relevance to teachers and scholars today. The selections emphasize women critics whose creative work increasingly appears on syllabi and in the titles of conference papers and scholarly articles and books. It pays particular attention to critical discussions of canonical writers, male or female, and of women writers, especially, again, women writers who are frequently taught and studied. A number of selections feature discussion of writers important to the Romantic tradition, whether through their own work, as, for example, Wordsworth, or through Romantic commentary on their work, as with Shakespeare and Milton.

All of the selections were written specifically for publication. Thus, private letters and diaries have not been included even when the letters were later edited for the press. Instead, this collection includes reviews, published essays, and prefaces either to the writer's own work or that of others. While major essays comprise much of this collection, short reviews and articles from more obscure periodicals make a broader range of commentary accessible for a more comprehensive representation of the Romantic aesthetic scene.

Few of these selections appeared in more than one edition, but where multiple versions exist, I have, unless otherwise noted, relied on the earliest published version for copy text. Where spelling and punctuation differ from modern practice, I have retained the original.

Elizabeth Moody (1737–1814)

Born Elizabeth Greenly, daughter of a wealthy lawyer residing near Kingston, southwest of London, Elizabeth Moody grew up surrounded by a fashionable set that included lawyers, politicians, courtiers, and literary dilettantes. A book lover from an early age, she also attained unusual fluency in French and Italian, and with access to several fine libraries among neighbors and relatives, she was well read in English, French, and Italian literature. For many years, she composed and privately circulated verse within a small literary coterie that included poets Edward Lovibond (1724–1775) and George Hardinge (1744–1816). She remained unmarried until 1777, when she wedded dissenting clergyman Christopher Lake Moody, a versatile literary professional. Soon after, Elizabeth Moody began publishing her poetry, first in the *General Evening Post* and the *Gentleman's Magazine*. The following year, Christopher Moody and publisher Ralph Griffiths joined resources to found the *St. James's Chronicle*, with the poetry of Elizabeth Moody, now sometimes called the "Muse of Surbiton," as one of the cornerstones of the new journal's success.

The connection with Griffiths proved fruitful in another way as well. Griffiths was editor of the most prestigious literary periodical of the time, the *Monthly Review*, where Christopher Moody frequently reviewed arts and letters publications. In 1789, Elizabeth Moody also began to contribute, becoming the *Monthly Review*'s first regular woman reviewer. In addition to her husband's connection with the *Monthly Review*, Moody's own unusual skill with French and her status as an experienced poet in her own right must explain this unusual opportunity. Her first article reviewed L.R. Lafaye's *Le Paradis Reconquis* (1789), a French imitation of Milton's poem. Indeed, French and Italian literature, translated or not, makes the bulk of Moody's twenty-six reviews between the years 1789 and 1808. Moody turns reviewer anonymity to ironic purpose by facetious emphasis on and subtle critique of the presumed masculinity of reviewers and the plural "we" of uniform corporate critical judgments. Her amusingly pointed criticisms coexist with analysis, especially of French literature, that finds in cultural products a mirror to national character.

In 1798, Moody published *Poetic Trifles*, containing a selection of her periodical verse as well as many new poems. While the collection includes several affecting lyrics, the poems are overwhelmingly social, commemorating occasions or addressing figures as various as Erasmus Darwin, Joseph Priestley, Samuel Johnson, and politician John Wilkes. Several show her satirical bent,

such as "Sappho, Tempted by the Prophesy, Burns Her Books and Culti-
vates the Culinary Arts." To evade a loveless future, the poet heroine aban-
dons her literary vocation "To salt the ham, to mix the pie." The poem takes
on additional irony when we remember that Moody occasionally signed herself "Sappho."

Other than an occasional review, Moody published little after 1800, but
she retained a circle of correspondents that included novelist and playwright Elizabeth Inchbald. At her death she left behind a body of poems
and literary articles that, though not large, merits attention for its characteristics of good-humored warmth, witty urbanity, learned reference, and
pointed critique.

■ Selected Reviews from the *Monthly Review*

Art. VII. *The Denial*; or, The Happy Retreat. By the Rev. James Thomson.[1]

Of the various species of composition that in course come before us, there
are none in which *our* writers of the male sex have less excelled, since the
days of Richardson and Fielding, than in the arrangement of a novel. Ladies
seem to appropriate to themselves an exclusive privilege in this kind of
writing; witness the numerous productions of romantic tales to which female
authors have given birth. The portraiture of the tender passions, the delicacy of sentiment, and the easy flow of style, may, perhaps, be most adapted
to the genius of the softer sex: but however that may be, politeness, certainly, will not suffer us to dispute this palm with our fair competitors. We,
though of the harder sex, as men, and of a still harder *race as critics*, are no
enemies to an affecting well-told story: but as we are *known* not to be very
easily pleased, it may be imagined that those performances only will obtain
the sanction of our applause, which can stand the test of certain criteria of
excellence.

The story of a novel should be formed of a variety of interesting incidents; a knowlege of the world, and of mankind, are essential requisites in
the writer; the characters should be always natural; the personages should
talk, think, and act, as becomes their respective ages, situations, and characters; the sentiments should be moral, chaste, and delicate; the language
should be easy, correct, and elegant, free from affectation, and unobscured
by pedantry; and the narrative should be as little interrupted as possible by
digressions and episodes of every kind: yet if an author chuses to indulge,
occasionally, in moral reflections, in the view of blending instruction with
amusement, we would not wish, altogether, to frustrate so good a design:—
but, that his precepts may obtain the utmost efficacy, we would recommend

---

[1]   *Monthly Review* 2nd Series 3 (December 1790): 400–2.

them to be inserted in those periods of the history, where the reader's curiosity can most patiently submit to suspense. [...][2]

Art. 25. *Rimualdo; or,* The Castle of Badajos. A Romance. By W.H. Ireland.[3]

The title of romance still invigorates our spirits. Old as we are, it recalls to our recollection the stories in which our youth delighted, of wandering knights, tilts, tournaments, enchanted castles, formidable giants, sea monsters, distressed damsels, tremendous fights, and impossible valour. We forget, however, that "the days of chivalry are gone;" and that, in the *present-day romance*, we must expect little other amusement than the oglio of the modern novel supplies: consisting of unnatural parents,—persecuted lovers,—murders,—haunted apartments,—winding sheets, and winding stair-cases,—subterraneous passages,—lamps that are dim and perverse, and that always go out when they should not,—monasteries,—caves,—monks, tall, thin, and withered, with lank abstemious cheeks,—dreams,—groans,—and spectres.

Such is the outline of the *modern* romance; and Mr. Ireland's copy is not unworthy of its numerous prototypes. We have here, in the personages of the drama, a parent and a husband in the Marquis of Badajos, as wicked and as unnatural as any with whom we have before had the honor of being acquainted.—We have a son in the Condé Rimualdo, as eminent for filial piety as Æneas himself.—We have patient suffering innocence in the fair Constanza, equalling if not transcending any of our novel heroines.—We have *very good* haunted towers,—and a *spectre* that stands supremely eminent over the whole race of ghosts.—Hamlets and Banquos were no more than *mawkins* in a cherry-tree, compared with that terrific vision which Rimualdo encounters on entering the old ruined chapel in the forest.—Though familiarized very much, lately, to these apparitions, we did not feel inclined to go to bed, till we had puffed away the recollection of this spectre in a whiff of tobacco, and re-animated our fleeting spirits by a double draught of old October: which will not be matter of surprise to the reader, when he learns that the hero himself, the brave Rimualdo, dropped down in a swoon immediately on seeing it!

Murder is in this romance too much *the order of the day*. We have murders in castles, in forests, and in cottages; and, to borrow a word from the author, we are too frequently *enhorrored*.—*Raw head and bloody bones* is continually at our heels, through a long journey of 926 pages; and we were therefore happy to get rid of him, and to leave our terrified fellow-travellers calmly settled in the unhaunted Castilio di Montalvan.

Mr. Ireland's language is animated and flowing, when it is *not inflated* with pomposity. The Escurial (for the scene of action is in Spain) is well and minutely described; and the Castle of Badajos is a pleasing picture: but, like

---

2   Extracts from the novel omitted.
3   *Monthly Review* 2nd Series 34 (February 1801): 203–4.

some sister *Novelists*, he deals too profusely in poetic description, and the common operations of Nature are never detailed in common language. Morning never appears without 'Aurora's tints that crown the summits of the distant mountains.'—The sun never rises but 'as the imperial charioteer of day, hast'ning his car of blazing light towards green ocean's occidental flood-gate.' The moon is always full orb'd, yet never looks *full* at us, but peeps behind fleecy clouds.—Night never forgets to assume the appropriate dignity of her sable mantle, with which (when she is not in a good humour) 'she overspreads heaven's countless luminaries;'—and if the hero and heroine are in a storm, God alone can help them,—for then 'impetuous winds blow from *every direction* (*all at once*), flakey lightning emblazons night's ebon robe, and full charged clouds *discharge* tremendous explosions.'

Thus is poetic imagery blended with prose detail; producing a medley of heterogeneous language totally destructive of good writing, by violating those principles of harmonious congruity which form the basis of a correct and uncontaminated diction.

ART. XIII. *The Rival Mothers, or Calumny*. Translated from the French of Madame de Genlis.[4]

$$[...].^5$$

Though often a charming *human creature*, this lady is but too apt to degenerate into a *French court lady;* one moment, we admire her; the next, we despise the formal painted wooden doll. We turn with disgust from the allegoric garden, the romantic machinery, and the theatrical personifications; and we would also gladly erase the many unnatural events that crowd her novel: yet let us remember that French and English *Nature* differs, and that the author is acquainted only with the former;—whom we consider as a degenerate goddess.

The style of these letters is sprightly and animated, bidding defiance to the foul fiend *Ennui*.—The translator of a work of this kind finds it almost impossible to transfuse into another language that spirit and vivacity, with that beautiful and elegant *tour de phrase*, which so peculiarly characterize the French writers of eminence; and mere fidelity produces flatness and insipidity. In many passages, however, the present translator is successful in catching a ray of the author's illuminated pencil; and the version of the ingenious lines with the *double sens*, found in the oratory, is extremely well executed.

---

4   *Monthly Review* 2nd Series 36 (October 1801): 186–8.
5   Moody remarks on the inconsistent moral sentiments and "pleasing and interesting" plot before discussing characterization.

ART. IX. *Les Amours Épiques*, &c. *i.e.* **Love Epics, an Heroic Poem, in six Cantos, containing a Translation of Episodes on Love, composed by the best Epic Poets. By** PARSEVAL GRANDMAISON.[6]

[…].

With a stroke of his wand, the poet conjures up six of the most celebrated bards, whom he orders to the Elysian grove; and there seated, each with his lyre in this hand, they rehearse, by turns, one of their own favorite songs. This band is composed of Homer, Virgil, Tasso, Ariosto, Milton, and Camoens. […]. It is the natural propensity of the human mind to grasp every ideas of pleasure that presents itself; and though conscious of the impracticability of any version doing complete justice to a transcendently beautiful original, we unwarily participate in the enthusiasm of this poet: who, like a true knight-errant in literature, shrinks from no enterprize, though he himself acknowleges its magnitude, and almost insurmountable difficulties. We, therefore, jump with him into the enchanting and enchanted scenery of Armida's bower:—but we confess that we looked as blue as the bill of the Italian warbler, when we hear the pretty song which he sings in Tasso's grove imitated by the pert chirping of a little French cock-sparrow […].[7]

The same critical remarks apply equally to Ariosto; namely, that it is impossible to give an adequate idea of the beauty of his episodes by a French translation. Hitherto, we keep our temper, and are rather pleased than angry at the hardihood of our literary knight: but when he sets his foot on the hallowed ground of the most sublime of our English bards, Milton, we *could* be indignant:—still, however, we forbear. M. GRANDMAISON, from not understanding the majestic march of our blank verse, is unable to perceive the ludicrous effect produced by the change into paltry diminutive rhiming couplets: but to us the scene exhibits a dwarf supporting the train of a giant […].

ART. XII. *Le Divorce*, & c; *i.e.* **The Divorce, the False Revolutionist, and the Heroism of Women; Three Novels. By M.** FIÉVÉE.[8]

OF all the absurd and capricious institutions which France, under either her old or her new *Régime*, has dignified by the name of *Law*, the modern divorce claims the pre-eminence for cruelty and injustice;—at least, if Madame *Dormeuil*'s relation is to be accredited.—Mme. *Dormeuil* was a beautiful and accomplished young woman, and married to a handsome and well-informed young man. Six years of perfect happiness they enjoyed together, and perhaps Hymen thought this was as large a portion of felicity as he commonly allows; for after this period, a degree of languor and insipidity is

---

6   *Monthly Review* 2ⁿᵈ Series 45 (September–December 1804, Foreign Appendix): 511–15.
7   Extracts omitted here and below.
8   *Monthly Review* 2ⁿᵈ Series 46 (Foreign Appendix, January–April 1805): 539–41.

too often found consequent on a state of uninterrupted tranquility. Mons. *Dormeuil* required variety, and sought it in the scenes of dissipation; and hence proceeded those vicious and libertine pursuits which never fail to undermine the conjugal affection. Among other depravities, the *French Husband* had a mistress whom he wished to marry; and, as the Legislature had so easily and so conveniently devised the means of breaking old chains, and forging new, he resolved on availing himself of so desirable a privilege, and being divorced from his amiable and most affectionate wife. Madame *Dormeuil* protests against the divorce, with an obstinacy as inflexible as was that of Catherine of Arragon:[9]—she protested against all the formalities necessary to ascertain the separation, and she insisted on keeping the name and arms of *Dormeuil*, and on being the true and lawful wife of the old Régime:—she was, however, divorced against her consent, and Monsieur married his new Love.

Of this connection, also, the inconstant husband grew tired; and he felt the same inclination to be emancipated from the second captivity, which had induced him to break the first. The matter being so easily adjusted, and the remedy for matrimonial ennui so immediately at hand, *Dormeuil* is a second time *divorced*; and with his first wife he became once more desperately in love. Her affections were never alienated from him, but stood the brunt of all his cruelties with the most persevering affection:—but the same firmness, which had directed her conduct in opposing the divorce, now supported her in refusing to renew the *ci-devant* nuptial vow; since that act would have been acknowleging *the legality of the divorce*, which she had with so much pertinacity refused to sanction. The situation of Monsieur and Madame now becomes whimsically laughable; they love each other to distraction: but they must not live together, and renew the conjugal endearments, because she *is not his wife*, and would be liable to be considered as his mistress; and it would be a breach of good morality, which would necessarily implicate her reputation on the ground of decorum, were they again to inhabit the same house. We leave the reader to Mme. *Dormeuil*'s own description of the caprices of her destiny; which she details with refined and romantic sentiments of prudery, truly *French, and extremely artificial and unnatural* […].

---

[9]   Daughter of Ferdinand and Isabella of Spain, Catherine of Aragon married Henry VIII of England in 1509. When in 1533, after the death of several children had dashed Henry's hopes of an heir with Catherine, Anne Boleyn, one of Catherine's ladies-in-waiting, became pregnant by Henry, Catherine found herself faced with an annulment which she refused until the end of her life to acknowledge as legal. Henry's break with the Roman Catholic Church in the course of these events ultimately led to the establishment of the Church of England.

Anna Letitia Barbauld
(1743–1825)

By the end of her long career, Anna Letitia Barbauld was esteemed as a poet, essayist, educator, author of children's literature and educational materials, devotional writer, political pamphleteer, and finally literary critic. Born into a family of religious dissenters, Anna Aikin benefited from the position of her clergyman father, John Aikin, as a noted theologian and classics tutor at the highly respected Warrington Academy for dissenters. Her unusually rigorous home education included modern languages, Latin, and Greek. At Warrington, she was welcomed into a convivial and vibrant intellectual and social circle that included some of the leading figures in eighteenth-century dissent, among whom she circulated her early literary efforts, culminating in the publication of *Corsica: An Ode* (1768), *Poems* (1773), and *Miscellaneous Pieces in Prose* (1773), a volume produced in collaboration with her brother John.

In 1774 Anna Aikin married Rochemont Barbauld, a former Warrington pupil, who for the next ten years managed a boys' school in Palgrave, Suffolk, with Anna teaching composition. The childless couple adopted one of Anna's nephews, for whom she developed innovative educational materials and children's literature, including *Lessons for Children* (1787–1788) and *Hymns in Prose for Children* (1781). Meanwhile she formed friendships with numerous other notable women writers including Hannah More, Fanny Burney, and Joanna Baillie, eventually becoming particularly close to Maria Edgeworth.

During the turbulent 1790s, Anna Barbauld contributed to the pamphlet war supporting progressive dissenting causes such as the repeal of the discriminatory religious Test Acts and the abolition of the slave trade. She continued collaborating with her brother John on *Evenings at Home, or, The Juvenile Budget Opened* (1792). Around this time, too, Barbauld began publishing essay criticism and literary reviews, an occupation she continued until at least the mid 1810s, contributing anonymously to *The Analytical Review*, *The Annual Review*, *The Gentlemen's Magazine*, and *The Monthly Review*, for which her identified reviews number well over three hundred. Her first major critical essay introduced a 1795 edition of Mark Akenside's *The Pleasures of Imagination*, and was soon followed by a critical introduction to *The Poetical Works of Mr. William Collins* (1797). In 1804 her edition of *The Correspondence of Samuel Richardson*, until recently the standard edition of Richardson's letters, appeared with a critical biography in which Barbauld assessed Richardson's work on such issues at artistic coherence, style, entertainment value, and moral and emotional effect. The same year her *Selections from the Spectator, Tatler, Guardian, and Freeholder* included a critical preface arguing the cultural significance of these popular publications.

Meanwhile, Barbauld's husband showed increasing signs of mental instability, ultimately necessitating confinement, from which he escaped to commit suicide. Barbauld's niece, Lucy Aikin, believed that Barbauld took up the work on *The British Novelists*, a 50 volume novel collection, in part to fill the void left by this loss. The introductory essay, "On the Origin and Progress of Novel Writing," provides a critical history of fiction that places women writers on a near-equal par with men. In addition to this essay, Barbauld provided critical biographies to introduce each of the twenty-five novels in the series.

In 1812 Barbauld published *Eighteen Hundred and Eleven*, a long prophetic poetic critique of British military expansionism. The reactionary climate of the early nineteenth century contrasted sharply with the more freethinking early 1790s, and the poem received some harsh reviews, partly for what were regarded as its anti-patriotic sentiments, but even more for Barbauld's presumption in writing on national political affairs. Barbauld continued a rigorous schedule of reviewing for several more years, and occasionally published poems and short prose pieces in periodicals. Her final edited volume, *The Female Speaker; or, Miscellaneous Pieces in Prose and Verse, Selected from the Best Writers*, an imitation of William Enfield's *Speaker*, appeared in 1816.

■ From *The British Novelists*

On the Origin and Progress of Novel-Writing.[1]

A COLLECTION of Novels has a better chance of giving pleasure than of commanding respect. Books of this description are condemned by the grave, and despised by the fastidious; but their leaves are seldom found unopened, and they occupy the parlour and the dressing-room while productions of higher name are often gathering dust upon the shelf. It might not perhaps be difficult to show that this species of composition is entitled to a higher rank than has been generally assigned it. Fictitious adventures, in one form or other, have made a part of the polite literature of every age and nation. These have been grafted upon the actions of their heroes; they have been interwoven with their mythology; they have been moulded upon the manners of the age,—and, in return, have influenced the manners of the succeeding gen-

---

[1]   *The British Novelists; with an Essay, and Prefaces Biographical and Critical, by Mrs. Barbauld,* 50 vols. (London: Printed for F.C. and J. Rivington, 1810) 1: 1–62.

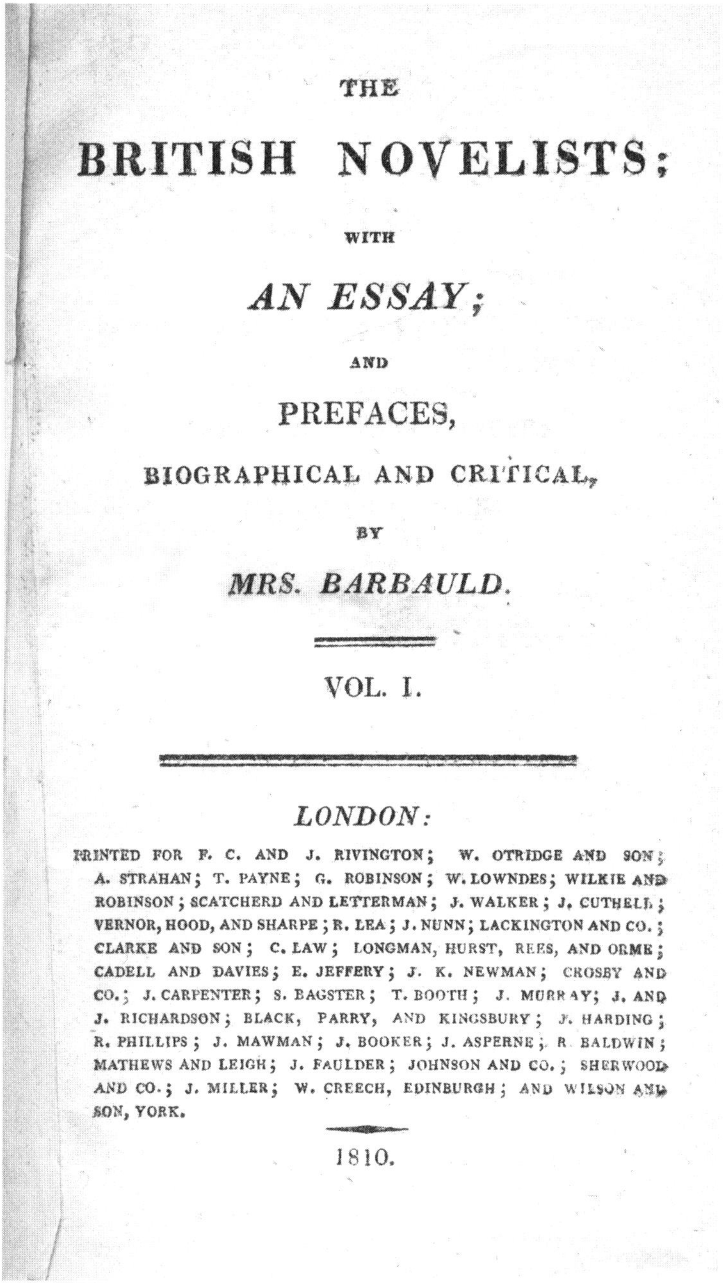

THE

BRITISH NOVELISTS;

WITH

AN ESSAY;

AND

PREFACES,

BIOGRAPHICAL AND CRITICAL,

BY

MRS. BARBAULD.

VOL. I.

LONDON:

PRINTED FOR F. C. AND J. RIVINGTON; W. OTRIDGE AND SON;
A. STRAHAN; T. PAYNE; G. ROBINSON; W. LOWNDES; WILKIE AND
ROBINSON; SCATCHERD AND LETTERMAN; J. WALKER; J. CUTHELL;
VERNOR, HOOD, AND SHARPE; R. LEA; J. NUNN; LACKINGTON AND CO.;
CLARKE AND SON; C. LAW; LONGMAN, HURST, REES, AND ORME;
CADELL AND DAVIES; E. JEFFERY; J. K. NEWMAN; CROSBY AND
CO.; J. CARPENTER; S. BAGSTER; T. BOOTH; J. MURRAY; J. AND
J. RICHARDSON; BLACK, PARRY, AND KINGSBURY; J. HARDING;
R. PHILLIPS; J. MAWMAN; J. BOOKER; J. ASPERNE; R. BALDWIN;
MATHEWS AND LEIGH; J. FAULDER; JOHNSON AND CO.; SHERWOOD
AND CO.; J. MILLER; W. CREECH, EDINBURGH; AND WILSON AND
SON, YORK.

1810.

Fig. 2.1   Title Page: *The British Novelists* (1810)

eration by the sentiments they have infused and the sensibilities they have excited.

Adorned with the embellishments of Poetry, they produce the epic; more concentrated in the story, and exchanging narrative for action, they become dramatic. When allied with some great moral end, as in the *Telemaque* of Fenelon, and Marmontel's *Belisaire*, they may be termed didactic. They are often made the vehicles of satire, as in Swift's *Gulliver's Travels*, and the *Candide* and *Babouc* of Voltaire.[2] They take a tincture from the learning and politics of the times, and are made use of successfully to attack or recommend the prevailing systems of the day. When the range of this kind of writing is so extensive, and its effect so great, it seems evident that it ought to hold a respectable place among the productions of genius; nor is it easy to say, why the poet, who deals in one kind of fiction, should have so high a place allotted him in the temple of fame; and the romance-writer so low a one as in the general estimation he is confined to. To measure the dignity of a writer by the pleasure he affords his readers is not perhaps using an accurate criterion; but the invention of a story, the choice of proper incidents, the ordonnance of the plan, occasional beauties of description, and above all, the power exercised over the reader's heart by filling it with the successive emotions of love, pity, joy, anguish, transport, or indignation, together with the grave impressive moral resulting from the whole, imply talents of the highest order, and ought to be appretiated accordingly. A good novel is an epic in prose, with more of character and less (indeed in modern novels nothing) of the supernatural machinery [...].[3]

At the head of writers of this class stands the seductive, the passionate Rousseau,—the most eloquent writer in the most eloquent modern language: whether his glowing pencil paints the strong emotions of passion, or the enchanting scenery of nature in his own romantic country, or his peculiar cast of moral sentiment,—a charm is spread over every part of the work, which scarcely leaves the judgement free to condemn what in it is dangerous or reprehensible. His are truly the "Thoughts that breathe and

---

[2]   As tutor for Louis XIV's grandson, François Fénelon (1651–1715) wrote *Les Avantures de Télémaque, fils d'Ulysse* (1699) for his pupil's instruction; *Candide; ou, L'optimisme* (1759) and *Le Monde Comme Il Va, Vision De Babouc* (1748) by Voltaire (1694–1778) both satirize naïve optimism. *Gulliver's Travels* (1726) is the best-known work of Jonathan Swift (1667–1745).

[3]   Barbauld alludes to Henry Fielding's (1707–1754) description of his comic novel *The History of the Adventures of Joseph Andrews* (1742) as a "comic Epic-Poem in Prose," a formula that he later extended to other novels in *The History of Tom Jones, a Foundling* (1749). The omitted section of Barbauld's essay provides a history of fiction beginning with the Greeks, continuing through the Roman empire, the Norman Conquest, and the Crusades up through the rise of romance fiction in continental Europe. In turning to Jean-Jacques Rousseau (1712–1778), Barbauld continues a discussion of French sentimental fiction.

words that burn."[4] He has hardly any thing of story; he has but few figures upon his canvass; he wants them not; his characters are drawn more from a creative imagination than from real life, and we wonder that what has so little to do with nature should have so much to do with the heart. Our censure of the tendency of this work will be softened, if we reflect that Rousseau's aim, as far as he had a moral aim, seems to have been to give a striking example of fidelity in the *married* state, which, it is well known, is little thought of by the French; though they would judge with the greatest severity the more pardonable failure of an unmarried woman. But Rousseau has not reflected that *Julie* ought to have considered herself as indissolubly united to *St. Preux*; her marriage with another was the infidelity. […] For the expression of sentiment in all its various shades, for the most delicate tact, and a refinement and polish, the fruit of high cultivation, the French writers are superior to those of every other nation […].

Writings like these cooperated powerfully with the graver labours of the encyclopedists in diffusing sentiments of toleration, a spirit of free inquiry, and a desire for equal laws and good government over Europe. Happy, if the mighty impulse had permitted them to stop within the bounds of justice and moderation! The French language is well calculated for eloquence. The harmony and elegance of French prose, the taste of their writers, and the grace and amenity which they know how to diffuse over every subject, give great effect to compositions of this kind […].

There is one objection to be made to these romances founded on history, which is, that if the personages are not judiciously selected, they are apt to impress false ideas on the mind. […] Where history says little, fiction may say much: events and men that are dimly seen through the obscurity of remote periods and countries, may be illuminated with these false lights; but where history throws her light steady and strong, no artificial colouring should be permitted. Impressions of historical characters very remote from the truth, often remain on the mind from dramatic compositions. If we examine into our ideas of the Henries and Richards of English history, we shall perhaps find that they are as much drawn from Shakespear as from Hume or Rapin[5] […].

The celebrated daughter of Necker is one whose name cannot be passed over in this connexion.[6] Her *Delphine* exhibits great powers: some of the situations are very striking; and the passion of love is expressed in such a

---

4   Thomas Gray (1716–1771), "The Progress of Poesy, A Pindaric Ode" (1754).
5   David Hume (1711–1776) and Paul de Rapin (1661–1725) both authored histories of England.
6   Anne Louise Germaine Necker de Staël (1766–1817). *Delphine* (1803) was popular among British women readers, while *Corinne, ou l'Italie* (1807) influenced Romantic women's conceptions of the female artist.

variety of turns and changes, and with so many refined delicacies of sentiment, that it is surprising how any language could, and surely no language
could but the French, find a sufficient variety of phrases in which to dress
her ideas.—Yet this novel cannot be called a pleasing one. One monotonous
colour of sadness prevails through the whole, varied indeed with deeper or
lighter shades, but no where [sic] presenting the cheerful hues of content-
ment and pleasure. A heavier accusation lies against this work from its tendency, on which account it has been said that the author was desired by the
present sovereign of France to leave Paris; but we may well suspect that a
scrupulous regard to morality had less share than political motives in such
a prohibition. *Corinne*, by the same author, is less exceptionable, and has
less force. It has some charming descriptions, and a picture of English country manners which may interest our curiosity, though it will not greatly
flatter our vanity.

[… I]t must not be disguised, that besides the more respectable French
novels, there are a number of others, which having passed no licence of
press, were said to be sold *sous le manteau*,[7] and were not therefore the less
read. These are not merely exceptionable, they are totally unfit to enter a
house where the morals of young people are esteemed an object. They are
generally not coarse in language, less so perhaps than many English ones
which aim at humour; but gross sensual pleasure is the very soul of them.
The awful frown with which the better part of the English public seem disposed to receive any approaches, either in verse or prose, to the French
voluptuousness, does honour to the national character.

The Germans, formerly remarkable for the laborious heaviness and
patient research of their literary labours, have, within this last century, cultivated with great success the field of polite literature. Plays, tales, and novels of all kinds, many of them by their most celebrated authors, were at first
received with avidity in this country, and even made the study of their language popular. The tide has turned, and they are now as much depreciated
[sic]. The *Sorrows of Werter*, by Goethe, was the first of these with which we
were familiarized in this country: we received it through the medium of a
French translation.[8] It is highly pathetic, but its tendency has been severely,
perhaps justly, censured; yet the author might plead that he has given
warning of the probable consequences of illicit and uncontrolled passions
by the awful catastrophe. It is certain, however, that the impression made
is of more importance than the moral deduced; and if Schiller's fine play

---

7   Literally, "under the cloak." Royal censorship of literature reached a peak in France under
    Louis XIV, producing a strong underground market in prohibited texts. Libertine literature
    often hid a surreptitious political message as well.

8   Johann Wolfgang von Goethe (1749–1832) anonymously published *Die Leiden des jungen
    Werthers* in 1774.

of *The Robbers*[9] has had, as we are assured it has, the effect of leading some well-educated young gentlemen to commit depredations on the public, allured by the splendour of the principal character, we may well suppose that Werter's delirium of passion will not be less seducing […]. The Germans abound in materials for works of the imagination; for they are rich in tales and legends of an impressive kind, which have perhaps amused generation after generation as nursery stories, and lain like ore in the mine, ready for the hand of taste to separate the dross and polish the material: for it is infinitely easier, when a nation has gained cultivation, to polish and methodize than to invent […].

The first author amongst us who distinguished himself by natural painting, was that truly original genius De Foe. His *Robinson Crusoe* is to this day an *unique* in its kind, and he has made it very interesting without applying to the common resource of love. At length, in the reign of George the Second, Richardson, Fielding, and Smollet, appeared in quick succession; and their success raised such a demand for this kind of entertainment, that it has ever since been furnished from the press, rather as a regular and necessary supply, than as an occasional gratification.[10] Novels have indeed been numerous "as leaves in Vallombrosa"[11] […].

About fifty years ago a very singular work appeared, somewhat in the guise of a novel, which gave a new impulse to writings of this stamp; namely, *The Life and Opinions of Tristram Shandy* [1760–1767], followed by *The Sentimental Journey* [1768], by the rev. Mr. Sterne, a clergyman of York.[12] They exhibit much originality, wit, and beautiful strokes of pathos; but a total want of plan or adventure, being made up of conversations and detached incidents. It is the peculiar characteristic of this writer, that he affects the heart, not by long drawn tales of distress, but by light electric touches which thrill the nerves of the reader who possesses a correspondent sensibility of frame. His characters, in like manner, are struck out by a few masterly touches. He resembles those painters who can give expression to a figure by two or three strokes of bold outline, leaving the imagination to fill up the sketch; the feelings are awakened as really by the story of *Le Fevre*, as by the narrative of *Clarissa*. The indelicacies of these volumes are very reprehensible, and indeed in a clergyman scandalous, particularly in the first publication, which however has the richest vein of humour. The two *Shandys*,

---

[9]   Published anonymously in 1781, *Die Räuber* was by Friedrich von Schiller (1759–1805).

[10] Daniel Defoe (1660–1731) had already enjoyed a long writing career when he published his first novel, *The Life and Strange Surprizing Adventures of Robinson Crusoe*, in 1719. Works by Samuel Richardson (1689–1761), including *Clarissa: or, The History of a Young Lady* (1747–1748; below), and Tobias Smollet (1721–1771) appear in *The British Novelists*.

[11] In *Paradise Lost* (1667), Satan's fallen legions lie on the lake of fire, "Thick as Autumnal Leaves that strow the Brooks/ in *Vallombrosa*" (Bk. I, 302–3).

[12] The two novels by Laurence Sterne (1713–1768) constituted landmarks in sentimental and experimental fiction.

Trim, Dr. Slop, are all drawn with a masterly hand. It is one of the merits of Sterne that he has awakened the attention of his readers to the wrongs of the poor negroes, and certainly a great spirit of tenderness and humanity breathes throughout the work. It is rather mortifying to reflect how little the power of expressing these feelings is connected with moral worth; for Sterne was a man by no means attentive to the happiness of those connected with him: and we are forced to confess that an author may conceive the idea of "brushing away flies without killing them," and yet behave ill in every relation of life.

It has lately been said that Sterne has been indebted for much of his wit to *Burton's Anatomy of Melancholy*.[13] He certainly exhibits a good deal of reading in that and many other books out of the common way, but the wit is in the application, and that is his own. This work gave rise to the vapid effusions of a crowd of sentimentalists, many of whom thought they had seized the spirit of Sterne, because they could copy him in his breaks and asterisks. The taste spread, and for a while, from the pulpit to the playhouse, the reign of sentiment was established [...].

Many tears have been shed by the young and tender-hearted over *Sidney Biddulph*, the production of Mrs. Sheridan, the wife of Mr. Thomas Sheridan the lecturer, an ingenious and amiable woman:[14] the sentiments of this work are pure and virtuous, but the author seems to have taken pleasure in heaping distress upon virtue and innocence, merely to prove, what no one will deny, that the best dispositions are not always sufficient to ward off the evils of life. Why is it that women when they write are apt to give a melancholy tinge to their compositions? Is it that they suffer more, and have fewer resources against melancholy? Is it that men, mixing at large in society, have a brisker flow of ideas, and, seeing a greater variety of characters, introduce more of the business and pleasures of life into their productions? Is it that humour is a scarcer product of the mind than sentiment, and more congenial to the stronger powers of man? Is it that women nurse those feelings in secrecy and silence, and diversify the expression of them with endless shades of sentiment, which are more transiently felt, and with fewer modifications of delicacy, by the other sex? [...].

If the end and object of this species of writing be asked, many no doubt will be ready to tell us that its object is,—to call in fancy to the aid of reason [...] with such-like reasons equally grave and dignified. For my own part, I scruple not to confess that, when I take up a novel, my end and object is entertainment; and as I suspect that to be the case with most readers,

---

13   *The Anatomy of Melancholy* (1621) by Robert Burton (1577–1640).

14   Playwright and novelist, author of *Memoirs of Miss Sidney Bidulph* (1761–1767) Frances Sheridan (1724–1766) was wife to actor, theater manager, and occasional lecturer Thomas Sheridan and mother of Richard Brinsley Sheridan, one of the eighteenth century's foremost playwrights, who was influenced by his mother's work.

I hesitate not to say that entertainment is their legitimate end and object.[15] To read the productions of wit and genius is a very high pleasure to all persons of taste, and the avidity with which they are read by all such shows sufficiently that they are calculated to answer this end. Reading is the cheapest of pleasures: it is a domestic pleasure. Dramatic exhibitions give a more poignant delight, but they are seldom enjoyed in perfection, and never without expense and trouble. Poetry requires in the reader a certain elevation of mind and a practised ear. It is seldom relished unless a taste be formed for it pretty early. But the humble novel is always ready to enliven the gloom of solitude, to soothe the languor of debility and disease, to win the attention from pain or vexatious occurrences, to take man from himself, (at many seasons the worst company he can be in,) and, while the moving picture of life passes before him, to make him forget the subject of his own complaints […].

It is sufficient therefore as an end, that these writings add to the innocent pleasures of life; and if they do no harm, the entertainment they give is a sufficient good. We cut down the tree that bears no fruit, but we ask nothing of a flower beyond its scent and its colour. The unpardonable sin in a novel is dullness: however grave or wise it may be, if its author possesses no powers of amusing, he has no business to write novels; he should employ his pen in some more serious part of literature.

But it is not necessary to rest the credit of these works on amusement alone, since it is certain they have had a very strong effect in infusing principles and moral feelings. It is impossible to deny that the most glowing and impressive sentiments of virtue are to be found in many of these compositions, and have been deeply imbibed by their youthful readers. They awaken a sense of finer feelings than the commerce of ordinary life inspires. Many a young woman has caught from such works as *Clarissa* or *Cecilia*, ideas of delicacy and refinement which were not, perhaps, to be gained in any society she could have access to.[16] Many a maxim of prudence is laid up in the memory from these stores, ready to operate when occasion offers.

The passion of love, the most seductive of all the passions, they certainly paint too high, and represent its influence beyond what it will be found to be in real life; but if they soften the heart they also refine it. They mix with the natural passions of our nature all that is tender in virtuous affection; all that is estimable in high principle and unshaken constancy; all that grace,

---

[15] In arguing for entertainment as a legitimate purpose and for middle-class readers as an important audience, Barbauld joins several other women writers who refute arguments against novels advanced by the genre's hostile critics. See Johnson's remarks in the Introduction as well as Smith's discussion in her preface to *The Letters of a Solitary Wanderer* (Chapter 3), Wollstonecraft's comments in several of her *Analytical* reviews (Chapter 6), and Hays's comments in each of her entries (Chapter 7).

[16] See Barbauld's essay on Fanny Burney, author of *Cecilia* (1782).

delicacy, and sentiment can bestow of touching and attractive. Benevolence and sensibility to distress are almost always insisted on in modern works of this kind; and perhaps it is not too much to say, that much of the softness of our present manners, much of that tincture of humanity so conspicuous amidst all our vices, is owing to the bias given by our dramatic writings and fictitious stories. A high regard to female honour, generosity, and a spirit of self-sacrifice, are strongly inculcated. It costs nothing, it is true, to an author to make his hero generous, and very often he is extravagantly so; still, sentiments of this kind serve in some measure to counteract the spirit of the world, where selfish considerations have always more than their due weight. In what discourse from the pulpit are religious feelings more strongly raised than in the prison sermon of *The Vicar of Wakefield*, or some parts of *The Fool of Quality*?[17]

But not only those splendid sentiments with which, when properly presented, our feelings readily take part, and kindle as we read; the more severe and homely virtues of prudence and œconomy have been enforced in the writings of a Burney and an Edgeworth.[18] Writers of their good sense have observed, that while these compositions cherished even a romantic degree of sensibility, the duties that have less brilliancy to recommend them were neglected. Where can be found a more striking lesson against unfeeling dissipation than the story of the *Harrels*?[19] Where have order, neatness, industry, sobriety, been recommended with more strength than in the agreeable tales of Miss Edgeworth? If a parent wishes his child to avoid caprice, irregularities of temper, procrastination, coquetry, affectation,—all those faults and blemishes which undermine family happiness, and destroy the every-day comforts of common life,—whence can he derive more impressive morality than from the same source? When works of fancy are thus made subservient to the improvement of the rising generation, they certainly stand on a higher ground than mere entertainment, and we revere while we admire.

Some knowledge of the world is also gained by these writings, imperfect indeed, but attained with more ease, and attended with less danger, than by mixing in real life. If the stage is a mirror of life, so is the novel, and perhaps a more accurate one, as less is sacrificed to effect and representation. There are many descriptions of characters in the busy world, which a young woman in the retired scenes of life hardly meets with at all, and many whom it is safer to read of than to meet; and to either sex it must be desirable that the

---

[17]   Henry Brooke (1703–1783) authored *The Fool of Quality* (1765–1770).

[18]   Maria Edgeworth (1768–1849), novelist and children's writer, is best remembered for *Castle Rackrent* (1800). Her *Belinda* (1801) featured in *The British Novelists*. In addition to *Cecilia*, Frances, or more commonly, Fanny Burney (1752–1840), later Mme. D'Arblay, authored *Evelina*, which featured in *The British Novelists* (see Barbauld's essay on Burney).

[19]   The Harrels appear in *Cecilia*.

first impressions of fraud, selfishness, profligacy and perfidy should be connected, as in good novels they always will be, with infamy and ruin. At any rate, it is safer to meet with a bad character in the pages of a fictitious story, than in the polluted walks of life; but an author solicitous for the morals of his readers will be sparing in the introduction of such characters.—It is an aphorism of Pope,

> "Vice is a monster of such frightful mien
> As to be hated, needs but to be seen."

But he adds,

> "But seen too oft, familiar with her face,
> We first endure, then pity, then embrace."[20]

Indeed the former assertion is not true without considerable modifications. If presented in its naked deformity, vice will indeed give disgust; but it may be so surrounded with splendid and engaging qualities, that the disgust is lost in admiration. Besides, though the selfish and mean propensities are radically unlovely, it is not the same with those passions which all have felt, and few are even desirous to resist. To present these to the young mind in the glowing colours of a Rousseau or a Madame de Stael is to awaken and increase sensibilities, which it is the office of wise restraint to calm and to moderate. Humour covers the disgust which the grosser vices would occasion; passion veils the danger of the more seducing ones.

After all, the effect of novel-reading must depend, as in every other kind of reading, on the choice which is made. If the looser compositions of this sort are excluded, and the sentimental ones chiefly perused, perhaps the danger lies more in fixing the standard of virtue and delicacy too high for real use, than in debasing it. Generosity is carried to such excess as would soon dissipate even a princely fortune; a weak compassion often allows vice to escape with impunity; an overstrained delicacy, or regard to a rash vow, is allowed to mar all the prospects of a long life: dangers are despised, and self is annihilated, to a degree that prudence does not warrant, and virtue is far from requiring. The most generous man living, the most affectionate friend, the most dutiful child, would find his character fall far short of the perfections exhibited in a highly-wrought novel.

Love is a passion particularly exaggerated in novels. It forms the chief interest of, by far, the greater part of them. In order to increase this interest, a false idea is given of the importance of the passion. It occupies the serious hours of life; events all hinge upon it; every thing gives way to its influence,

---

[20]   Alexander Pope (1688–1744), *An Essay on Man*, Epistle II.5.217–220, slightly altered.

and no length of time wears it out. When a young lady, having imbibed these notions, comes into the world, she finds that this formidable passion acts a very subordinate part on the great theatre of the world; that its vivid sensations are mostly limited to a very early period; and that it is by no means, as the poet sings,

"All the colour of remaining life."[21]

She will find but few minds susceptible of its more delicate influences. Where it is really felt, she will see it continually overcome by duty, by prudence, or merely by a regard for the show and splendour of life; and that in fact it has a very small share in the transactions of the busy world, and is often little consulted even in choosing a partner for life. In civilized life both men and women acquire so early a command over their passions, that the strongest of them are taught to give way to circumstances, and a moderate liking will appear apathy itself, to one accustomed to see the passion painted in its most glowing colours. Least of all will a course of novels prepare a young lady for the neglect and tedium of life which she is perhaps doomed to encounter. If the novels she reads are virtuous, she has learned how to arm herself with proper reserve against the ardour of her lover; she has been instructed how to behave with the utmost propriety when run away with, like *Miss Byron*, or locked up by a cruel parent, like *Clarissa*; but she is not prepared for indifference and neglect.[22] Though young and beautiful, she may see her youth and beauty pass away without conquests, and the monotony of her life will be apt to appear more insipid when contrasted with scenes of perpetual courtship and passion.

It may be added with regard to the knowledge of the world, which, it is allowed, these writings are calculated in some degree to give, that, let them be as well written and with as much attention to real life and manners as they can possibly be, they will in some respects give false ideas, from the very nature of fictitious writing. Every such work is a *whole*, in which the fates and fortunes of the personages are brought to a conclusion, agreeably to the author's own preconceived idea. Every incident in a well written composition is introduced for a certain purpose, and made to forward a certain plan. A sagacious reader is never disappointed in his forebodings. If a prominent circumstance is presented to him, he lays hold on it, and may be very sure it will introduce some striking event; and if a character has strongly engaged his affections, he need not fear being obliged to withdraw

---

21   Matthew Prior (1664–1721), *Solomon on the Vanity of the World* (1718), Book II, 235.
22   The eponymous hero of Richardson's *History of Sir Charles Grandison* (1753–1754) rescues the heroine, Harriet Byron, after she has been abducted by an iniquitous nobleman. Clarissa is locked up by parents attempting to compel her marriage to a repulsive neighboring landowner.

them: the personages never turn out differently from what their first appearance gave him a right to expect; they gradually open, indeed; they may surprise, but they never disappoint him. Even from the elegance of a name he
may give a guess at the amenity of the character. But real life is a kind of
chance-medley, consisting of many unconnected scenes. The great author of
the drama of life has not finished his piece; but the author must finish his;
and vice must be punished and virtue rewarded in the compass of a few
volumes; and it is a fault in *his* composition if every circumstance does not
answer the reasonable expectations of the reader. But in real life our reasonable expectations are often disappointed; many incidents occur which
are like "passages that lead to nothing,"[23] and characters occasionally turn
out quite different from what our fond expectations have led us to expect.

In short, the reader of a novel forms his expectations from what he sup-
poses passes in the mind of the author, and guesses rightly at his intentions,
but would often guess wrong if he were considering the real course of
nature. It was very probable, at some periods of his history, that *Gil Blas*, if
a real character, would come to be hanged; but the practised novel-reader
knows well that no such event can await the hero of the tale. Let us suppose
a person speculating on the character of *Tom Jones* as the production of an
author, whose business it is pleasingly to interest his readers. He has no
doubt but that, in spite of his irregularities and distresses, his history will
come to an agreeable termination. He has no doubt but that his parents
will be discovered in due time; he has no doubt but that his love for *Sophia*
will be rewarded sooner or later with her hand; he has no doubt of the constancy of that young lady, or of their entire happiness after marriage.[24] And
why does he foresee all this? Not from the real tendencies of things, but
from what he has discovered of the author's intentions. But what would
have been the probability in real life? Why, that the parents would either
never have been found, or have proved to be persons of no consequence
—that *Jones* would pass from one vicious indulgence to another, till his natural good disposition was quite smothered under his irregularities—that
Sophia would either have married her lover clandestinely, and have been
poor and unhappy, or she would have conquered her passion and married
some country gentleman with whom she would have lived in moderate
happiness, according to the usual routine of married life. But the author
would have done very ill so to have constructed his story […].

Though a great deal of trash is every season poured out upon the public
from the English presses, yet in general our novels are not vicious; the food
has neither flavour nor nourishment, but at least it is not poisoned. Our

---

23   Thomas Gray, "A Long Story" (1753) 8.
24   Gil Blas is the picaresque hero of *Histoire de Gil Blas de Santillane* (1715–1735) by Alain Rene
     Le Sage (1668–1747). In Fielding's *Tom Jones*, the hero eventually marries Sophia Western,
     his true love.

national taste and habits are still turned towards domestic life and matrimonial happiness, and the chief harm done by a circulating library is occasioned by the frivolity of its furniture, and the loss of time incurred. Now
and then a girl perhaps may be led by them to elope with a coxcomb; or, if
she is handsome, to expect the homage of a *Sir Harry* or *My lord*, instead of
the plain tradesman suitable to her situation in life; but she will not have
her mind contaminated with such scenes and ideas as Crebillon, Louvet,
and others of that class have published in France.[25]

And indeed, notwithstanding the many paltry books of this kind published in the course of every year, it may safely be affirmed that we have
more good writers in this walk living at the present time, than at any period
since the days of Richardson and Fielding. A very great proportion of these
are ladies; and surely it will not be said that either taste or morals have been
losers by their taking the pen in hand. The names of D'Arblay, Edgeworth,
Inchbald, Radcliffe, and a number more will vindicate this assertion.[26]

No small proportion of modern novels have been devoted to recommend,
or to mark with reprobation, those systems of philosophy or politics which
have raised so much ferment of late years. Mr. Holcroft's *Anna St. Ives* is of this
number: its beauties, and beauties it certainly has, do not make amends for its
absurdities. What can be more absurd than to represent a young lady gravely
considering, in the disposal of her hand, how she shall promote the greatest
possible good of the system? Mr. Holcroft was a man of strong powers, and
his novels are by no means without merit, but his satire is often partial, and his
representations of life unfair. On the other side may be reckoned *The modern
Philosophers* [*sic*], and the novels of Mrs. West. In the war of systems these
light skirmishing troops have been often employed with great effect; and,
so long as they are content with fair, general warfare, without taking aim at
individuals, are perfectly allowable[27] […].

Some perhaps may think that too much importance has been already given
to a subject so frivolous, but a discriminating taste is no where more called
for than with regard to a species of books which every body reads. It was said
by Fletcher of Saltoun, "Let me make the ballads of a nation, and I care not

---

25 Claude-Prosper Jolyot de Crébillon, fils (1707–1777), noted for satirical and lascivious nov-
    els. Jean-Baptiste Louvet (1760–1797) authored the licentious *Les Amours du Chevalier de
    Faublas* (1786–1791).
26 See Barbauld's essays on Elizabeth Inchbald (1753–1821) and Ann Radcliffe (1764–1823)
    and these writers' own criticism, selections of which appear in the present volume
    (Inchbald, Chapter 4; Radcliffe Chapter 9).
27 Novelist, playwright, journalist, translator, and critic, radical Thomas Holcroft (1745–1809),
    one of the most radical members of Joseph Johnson's circle, authored *Anna St. Ives* (1792)
    in response to Edmund Burke's (1729–1797) *Reflections on the Revolution in France* (1790).
    Many, including Hays herself, believed that Elizabeth Hamilton (1758–1816) composed the
    anonymously published *Memoirs of Modern Philosophers* (1800) to satirize London's radical
    circle, particularly author Mary Hays. The novels and poems of Jane West (1758–1832) tended
    toward conservative didacticism. See Hays's review of West's *A Gossip's Story* (Chapter 7).

who makes the laws."[28] Might it not be said with as much propriety, Let me make the novels of a country, and let who will make the systems?

"Clara Reeve."[29]

THE Old English Baron, though a novel of but a moderate degree of merit, has been always a great favourite with the novel-reading public, and as such is here introduced; for, though subsequent publications of more elegance and more invention have caused it to slide down from the place it once held; it is still generally agreeable to young people who are fond of the serious and the wonderful; and as it inspires none but noble and proper sentiments, it can do them no harm, except it should make them afraid to go up stairs to bed, by themselves, on a winter's night […].

With regard to the wonderful part of the story, the writer does not, like the author of *The Castle of Otranto*, give unlimited play to her imagination in the supernatural means she employs.[30] She says in her preface, "We can conceive and allow for the appearance of a ghost." The appearances she has introduced are therefore such as, till lately, coincided with the belief, perhaps, of the generality of readers; haunted rooms, presaging dreams, groans, clanking of chains, and apparitions of murdered persons; such ornaments as, the author seems to think, come within the verge—the utmost verge of probability; and to those whose minds are thus properly imbued, the story will be striking. At present we should require these appearances to be more artful, or more singular.

The chief fault of it is, that we foresee the conclusion before we have read twenty pages: but this is not the case with the young and unpractised reader; and those who have read *The Old English Baron* at an early time of life are generally conscious at a much later period of the impression it once made upon their youthful fancy […].[31]

---

28 Andrew Fletcher, Laird of Saltoun (1655–1716) recounts an acquaintance's view that "if a man were permitted to make all the ballads, he need not care who should make the laws of a nation" in *An Account of a Conversation concerning a Right Regulation of Government for the Common Good of Mankind in a Letter to the Marquiss of Montrose, the Earls of Rothes, Roxburg and Haddington*. From London the first of December, 1703 (Edinburgh 1704), rpt. in *Andrew Fletcher: Political Works*, ed. John Robertson (Cambridge: Cambridge UP, 1997) 179. See also Baillie's reference in her "Introductory Discourse" (Chapter 8).

29 *The British Novelists*, 22: i–iii, prefacing the *Old English Baron* (1778, originally published in 1777 as *The Champion of Virtue. A Gothic Story*), by Clara Reeve (1729–1807).

30 *The Castle of Otranto* (1764) by Horace Walpole (1717–1797) is regarded as the first Gothic novel. Reeve follows while improving on Walpole's model.

31 Most of Barbauld's prefaces incorporate plot summary and biographical sketches. Where they are not combined with pertinent criticism, they are here omitted.

"Mrs. Lennox."[32]

[…]

The Female Quixote, published in 1752, is an agreeable and ingenious satire upon the old romances; not the more ancient ones of chivalry, but the languishing love romances of the Calprenédes and Scuderis.[33] Arabella, the heroine, is supposed to have been brought up in the country, and secluded, during the life of her father, from all society, but allowed to amuse herself in an old library furnished with the works of those voluminous authors. Of course she imbibes their sentiments, and at her father's death she comes out into the world, possessed of beauty and fortune, but with a profound ignorance of every circumstance of real life and manners […].

The falsification of history in these romances, which was the fault Boileau chiefly exposed in his satire,[34] is agreeably ridiculed by the incident of a conversation which passes between the heroine and a gentleman who is introduced to her as one who possesses a great knowledge of history and of the ancients, and whom she strangely perplexes by questions and anecdotes of Cyrus, and Cletia, and Horatius Cocles, which he cannot explain or answer by any information his reading has furnished him with. The young lady's cousin is represented as more patient of her extravagancies than most modern lovers would be; but she is painted as amiable, and, like Don Quixote, rational in every respect where her particular whim is not touched.

The work is rather spun out too much, and not very well wound up. The grave moralizing of a clergyman is not the means by which the heroine should have been cured of her reveries. She should have been recovered by the sense of ridicule; by falling into some absurd mistake, or by finding herself on the brink of becoming the prey of some romantic footman, like the ladies in Moliere's piece of *Les Précieuses Ridicules*, the ridicule of which has pretty much the same bearing.[35]

The performance of Mrs. Lennox is the best of the various *Quixotes* which have been written in imitation of the immortal Cervantes, and forms a fair

---

[32] *The British Novelists*, 24: i–iv, prefacing *The Female Quixote* (1752), an imitation and parody of Cervantes's *Don Quixote* (1605) by Charlotte Lennox (1729?–1804).

[33] Playwright and fiction writer Gautier de Costes La Calprénede (1610–1663) and novelist and salonnière Madeleine de Scudéry (1607–1701) were known for aesthetics of delicate refinement exalting chivalric virtues in long works of romance fiction classed as *Roman de longue haleine*, literally "long-winded novel."

[34] Most famous for his *L'Art poétique* (1674), Nicolas Boileau-Despréaux (1636–1711) also authored satires developing neoclassical literary standards.

[35] In *Les Précieuses Ridicules* (The Affected Young Ladies, 1660), an early play by Molière (1622–1673), two rejected suitors send their disguised valets to court the pretentious provincial girls who scorned them.

counterpart to it, as it presents a similar extravagance, yet drawn from a later class of authors, and more adapted to female reading […].

"Mrs. Brooke."[36]

FRANCES BROOKE […]wrote a periodical paper entitled *The Old Maid*, and some pieces for the theatre. […] The two novels by which she is best known are *Emily Montague* and *Lady Julia Mandeville*.[37] The latter is a simple, well connected story, told with elegance and strong effect. It is a forcible appeal to the feelings against the savage practice of duelling. *Emily Montague* is less interesting in the story, which serves but as a thread to connect a great deal of beautiful description of the manners and scenery of Canada, which country the author had visited. Mrs. Brooke was perhaps the first female novel-writer who attained a perfect purity and polish of style. The whole is correct and easy, and many passages are highly beautiful […].

"Mrs. Inchbald."[38]

TO readers of taste it would be superfluous to point out the beauties of Mrs. Inchbald's novels. The *Simple Story* has obtained the decided approbation of the best judges. There is an originality both in the characters and the situations which is not often found in similar productions. To call it a *simple story* is perhaps a misnomer, since the first and second parts are in fact two distinct stories, connected indeed by the character of Dorriforth, which they successively serve to illustrate.

Dorriforth is introduced as a Roman priest of a lofty mind, generous, and endued with strong sensibilities, but having in his disposition much of sternness and inflexibility. His being in priest's orders presents an apparently insurmountable obstacle to his marriage; but it is got over, without violating probability, by his becoming heir to a title and estate, and on that account receiving a dispensation from his vows. Though slow to entertain thoughts of love, as soon as he perceives the partiality of his ward, it enters his breast like a torrent when the flood-gates are opened. The perplexities in which he is involved by Miss Milner's gay unthinking conduct bring them to the very brink of separating for ever; and very few scenes in any novel

---

36 *The British Novelists*, 27: i–ii, prefacing *The History of Lady Julia Mandeville* (1763), by Frances Brooke (1724–1789).

37 Modeled on Addison's *Spectator*, the *Old Maid*, ran from November 1955–July 1956. Like *Julia Mandeville*, the *History of Emily Montague* (1769) was published anonymously.

38 *The British Novelists*, 28: i–iv, prefacing *A Simple Story* (1791). Actor, playwright, and novelist, Elizabeth Inchbald also authored criticism, selections from which appear in the present volume (see Chapter 4).

have a finer effect than the intended parting of the lovers, and their sudden, immediate, unexpected marriage.

It is impossible not to sympathize with the feelings of Miss Milner, when she sees the corded trunks standing in the passage; or again, when after their reconciliation she sees the carriage, which was to take away her lover, drive empty from the door. The character of the ward of Dorriforth is so drawn as to excite an interest such as we seldom feel for more faultless characters. Young, sprightly, full of sensibility, gay and thoughtless, we feel such a tenderness for her as we should for a child who is playing on the brink of a precipice. The break between the first and second parts of the story has a singularly fine effect. We pass over in a moment a large space of years, and find every thing changed: scenes of love and conjugal happiness are vanished; and for the young, gay, thoughtless, youthful beauty, we see a broken-hearted penitent on her death-bed.

This sudden shifting of the scene has an effect which no continued narrative could produce; an effect which even the scenes of real life could not produce; for the curtain of futurity is lifted up only by degrees, and we must wait the slow succession of months and years to bring about events which are here presented close together. The death-bed letter of Lady Milner is very solemn, and cannot be perused without tears.

Dorriforth in these latter volumes is become, from the contemplation of his injuries, morose, unrelenting, and tyrannical. How far it was possible for a man to resist the strong impulse of nature, and deny himself the sight of his child residing in the same house with him, the reader will determine; but the situation is new and striking.

It is a particular beauty in Mrs. Inchbald's compositions, that they are thrown so much into the dramatic form. There is little of mere narrative, and in what there is of it, the style is careless; but all the interesting parts are carried on in dialogue:—we see and hear the persons themselves; we are but little led to think of the author, and it is only when we have done feeling that we being to admire.

The only other novel which Mrs. Inchbald has given to the public is *Nature and Art* [1796]. It is of a slighter texture than the former, and put together without much attention to probability; the author's object being less to give a regular story than to suggest reflections on the political and moral state of society. For this purpose two youths are introduced, one of whom is educated in all the ideas and usages of civilized life; the other (the child of Nature) without any knowledge of or regard to them. This is the frame which has been used by Mr. Day and others for the same purpose, and naturally tends to introduce remarks more lively than solid, and strictures more epigrammatic than logical, on the differences between rich and poor, the regard paid to rank, and such topics, on which it is easy to dilate with an appearance of reason and humanity; while it requires a much profounder philosophy to suggest any alteration in the social system, which would not be rather Utopian than beneficial.

There is a beautiful stroke in this part of the work, where Henry, who, according to Rousseau's plan, had not been taught to pray till he was of an age to know what he was doing, kneels down for the first time with great emotion; and on being asked if he was not afraid to speak to God, says, "To be sure I trembled very much when I first knelt, but when I came to the words 'Our Father who art in heaven,' they gave me courage, for I know how kind a father is."

But by far the finest passage in this novel is the meeting between Hannah and her seducer, when he is seated as judge upon the bench, and, without recollecting the former object of his affection, pronounces sentence of death upon her. The shriek she gives, and her exclamation, "Oh, not from you!" electrifies the reader, and cannot but stir the coldest feelings.

Judgement and observation may sketch characters, and often put together a good story; but strokes of pathos, such as the one just mentioned, or the dying-scene in Mrs. Opie's *Father and Daughter*,[39] can only be attained by those whom nature has endowed with her choicest gifts […].

"Mrs. Charlotte Smith."[40]

AMONG those writers who have distinguished themselves in the polite literature of the present day, the late Mrs. CHARLOTTE SMITH well deserves a place, both from the number and elegance of her publications […].

Possessed of a fine imagination, an ear and a taste for harmony, an elegant and correct style, the natural bent of Mrs. Smith's genius seems to have been more to poetry than to any other walk of literature. Her *Sonnets*, which was the first publication she gave to the world, were universally admired.[41] That species of verse, which in this country may be reckoned rather an exotic, had at that time been but little cultivated. For plaintive, tender, and polished sentiment the Sonnet forms a proper vehicle, and Mrs. Smith's success fixed at once her reputation as a poet of no mean class […].

Poets are apt to complain, and often take a pleasure in it; yet they should remember that the pleasure of their readers is only derived from the elegance and harmony with which they do it. The reader is a selfish being, and seeks only his own gratification. But for the language of complaint in plain

---

39 Amelia Alderson Opie (1769–1853) authored *The Father and Daughter* (1801).
40 *The British Novelists*, 36: i–viii, prefacing *The Old Manor House* (1793) by Charlotte Smith (1749–1806). See Smith's critical prefaces in the present volume (Chapter 3).
41 Smith's *Elegiac Sonnets, and Other Essays*, originally published in 1784, which was repeatedly expanded and republished up through 1800, helped inspire the Romantic sonnet revival.

prose, or the exasperations of personal resentment, he has seldom much sympathy […].

Mrs. Smith is most known to readers in general by her novels; yet they seem to have been less the spontaneous offspring of her mind than her poems. She herself represents them as being written to supply money for those emergencies, which, from the perplexed state of her affairs, she was often thrown into; but, though not of the first order, they hold a respectable rank among that class of publications. They are written in a style correct and elegant; they show a knowledge of life, and of genteel life; and there is much beauty in the descriptive scenery, which Mrs. Smith was one of the first to introduce. Descriptions, of whatever beauty, are but little attended to in a novel of high interest, particularly if introduced, as they often are, during a period of anxious suspense for the hero or heroine; but are very properly placed, at judicious intervals, in compositions of which variety rather than deep pathos, and elegance rather than strength, are the characteristics […].

The *Old Manor-House* is said to be the most popular of the author's productions. The best drawn character in it is that of a wealthy old lady who keeps all her relations in constant dependence, and will not be persuaded to name her heir. This was written during the war with America; and the author takes occasion, as also in many other of her publications, to show the strain of her politics.

She also wrote *Desmond* [1792], *The Wanderings of Warwick* [1794], *Montalbert* [1795], and many others, to the number of thirty-eight volumes. They all show a knowledge of life, and facility of execution, without having any very strong features, or particularly aiming to illustrate any moral truth. The situations and the scenery are often romantic; the characters and the conversations are from common life.

Her later publications would have been more pleasing, if the author, in the exertions of fancy, could have forgotten herself; but the asperity of invective and the querulousness of complaint too frequently cloud the happier exertions of her imagination […].

"Miss Burney."[42]

SCARCELY any name, if any, stands higher in the list of novel-writers than that of Miss BURNEY, now Mrs. D'ARBLAY […].

Evelina became at once a fashionable novel: there are even those who still prefer it to *Cecilia*, though that preference is probably owing to the partiality inspired by a first performance. Evelina is a young lady, amiable and

---

[42]   *The British Novelists*, 38: i–xi, prefacing *Evelina; or the History of a Young Lady's Introduction to the World* (1778) by Fanny Burney.

inexperienced, who is continually getting into difficulties from not knowing or not observing the established etiquettes of society, and from being unluckily connected with a number of vulgar characters, by whom she is involved in a series of adventures both ludicrous and mortifying. Some of these are certainly carried to a very extravagant excess, particularly the tricks played upon the poor Frenchwoman; but the fondness for humour, and low humour, which Miss Burney discovered in this piece, runs through all her subsequent works, and strongly characterizes, sometimes perhaps blemishes, her genius. Lord Orville is a generous and pleasing lover; and the conclusion is so wrought, as to leave upon the mind that glow of happiness which is not found in her subsequent works. The meeting between Evelina and her father is pathetic. The agonizing remorse and perturbation of the man who is about to see, for the first time, his child whom he had deserted, and whose mother had fallen a sacrifice to his unkindness; the struggles between the affection which impels him towards her, and the dread he feels of seeing in her the image of his injured wife; are described with many touches of nature and strong effect.—Other characters in the piece are, Mrs. Selwyn, a wit and an oddity; a gay insolent baronet; a group of vulgar cits; a number of young bucks, whose coldness, carelessness, rudeness, and impertinent gallantry, serve as a foil to the delicate attentions of Lord Orville.

Upon the whole, *Evelina* greatly pleased; and the interest the public took in the young writer was rewarded with fresh pleasure by the publication of *Cecilia*, than which it would be difficult to find a novel with more various and striking beauties. Among these may be reckoned the style, which is so varied, according to the characters introduced, that, without any information from the names, the reader would readily distinguish the witty loquacity of Lady Honoria Pemberton, the unmeaning volubility of Miss Larolles, the jargon of the captain, the affected indifference of Meadows, the stiff pomposity of Delville senior, the flighty heroics of Albany, the innocent simplicity if Miss Belfield, the coarse vulgarity of her mother, the familiar address and low comic of Briggs, and the cool finesse of the artful attorney, with many others,—all expressed in language appropriate to the character, and all pointedly distinguished from the elegant and dignified style of the author herself. The character of the miser Briggs is pushed, perhaps, to a degree of extravagance, though certainly not more so than Moliere's Harpagon;[43] but it is highly comic, and it is not the common idea of a miser half-starved, sullen and morose; an originality is given to it by making him jocose, good-humoured, and not averse to enjoyment when he can have it for nothing. All the characters are well discriminated, from the skipping Morrice, to the artful Monckton, and the high-toned feeling of Mrs. Delville. The least natural character is Albany. An idea prevailed at the

---

[43] Character in *L'Avare* (*The Miser*, 1669).

time, but probably without the least foundation, that Dr. Johnson had supplied the part.

Cecilia herself is an amiable and dignified character. She is brought into situations distressful and humiliating, by the peculiarity of her circumstances, and a flexibility and easiness readily pardoned in a young female. The restriction she is laid under of not marrying any one who will not submit to assume her name is a new circumstance, and forms, very happily, the plot of the piece. Love appears with dignity in Cecilia; with fervour, but strongly combated by pride as well as duty, in young Delville; with all the helplessness of unrestrained affection in Miss Belfield, whose character of simplicity and tenderness much resembles that of Emily in *Sir Charles Grandison*. If resemblances are sought for, it may also be observed that the situation of Cecilia with Mrs. Delville is similar to that of Marivaux's Marianne with the mother of Valville.[44]

Miss Burney possesses equal powers of pathos and of humour. The terrifying voice of the unknown person who forbids the banns has an electrifying effect upon the reader; and the distress of Cecilia seeking her husband about the streets, in agony for his life, till her reason suddenly fails, is almost too much to bear. Indeed we lay down the volumes with rather a melancholy impression upon our minds; there has been so much of distress that the heart feels exhausted, and there are so many deductions from the happiness of the lovers, that the reader is scarcely able to say whether the story ends happily or unhappily. It is true that in human life things are generally so balanced; but in fictitious writings it is more agreeable, if they are not meant to end tragically, to leave on the mind the rainbow colours of delight in their full glow and beauty.

But the finest part of these volumes is the very moral and instructive story of the *Harrels*. It is the high praise of Miss Burney, that she has not contented herself with fostering the delicacies of sentiment, and painting in vivid colours those passions which nature has made sufficiently strong. She has shown the value of economy, the hard-heartedness of gaiety, the mean rapacity of the fashionable spendthrift. She has exhibited a couple, not naturally bad, with no other inlet to vice, that appears on the face of the story, than the inordinate desire of show and splendour, withholding his hard-earned pittance from the poor labourer, and lavishing it on every expensive trifle. She has shown the wife trifling and helpless, vain, incapable of serious thought or strong feeling; and has beautifully delineated the gradual extinction of an early friendship between two young women whom youth and cheerfulness alone had assimilated, as the two characters diverged in after-life,—a circumstance that frequently happens. She has shown the husband fleecing his guest and his

---

[44] Characters in *La vie de Marianne* (1731–1742), a novel by Pierre Carlet de Marivaux (1688–1763) translated as *The Virtuous Orphan* (1736–1742).

ward by working on the virtuous feelings of a young mind, and has conducted him by natural steps to the awful catastrophe. The last scene at Vaux-
hall is uncommonly animated; every thing seems to pass before the reader's
eyes. The forced gaiety, the starts of remorse, the despair, the bustle and glare
of the place, the situation of the unprotected females in such scene of horror,
are all most forcibly described. We almost hear and feel the report of the
pistol.—In the uncommon variety of characters which this novel affords, there
are many others deserving of notice; that, for instance, of the high-minded
romantic Belfield may give a salutary lesson to many a youth who fancies his
part in life *ill cast*, who wastes life in projects, and does nothing because he
things every thing beneath his ambition and his talents.

Such are the various merits of *Cecilia*, through the whole of which it is
evident that the author draws from life, and exhibits not only the passions
of human nature, but the manners of the age and the affectation of the
day […].

[H]er third publication, entitled *Camilla* [(1796); …] is inferior to *Cecilia* as a
whole, but it certainly exhibits beauties of as high an order. The character of Sir
Hugh is new and striking. There is such an unconscious shrewdness in his
remarks, that they have all the effect of the sharpest satire without his intending any malice; while, at the same time, his complaints are so meek, his self-
humiliation so touching, his benevolence so genuine and overflowing, that
the reader must have a bad heart who does not love while he laughs at
him. The incidents of the piece show much invention, particularly that
which induces Sir Hugh to adopt Eugenia instead of his favourite. How
charmingly is Camilla described! "Every look was a smile, every step was
a spring, every thought was a hope, and the early felicity of her mind was
without alloy."

Camilla, in the course of the work, falls, like Cecilia, into pecuniary difficulties. They are brought on partly by milliners' bills, which unaware and
through the persuasion of others she has suffered to run up, but chiefly from
being drawn in to assist an extravagant and unprincipled brother. The character of the brother, Lionel, is drawn with great truth and spirit, and presents but
too just a picture of the manner in which many deserving females have been
sacrificed to the worthless part of the family. The author appears to have
viewed with a very discerning eye the manners of those young men who
aspire to lead the fashion; and in all three of her novels has bestowed a good
deal her satire upon the affected apathy, studied negligence, coarse slang,
avowed selfishness, or mischievous frolic, by which they often distinguish
themselves, and through which they contrive to be vulgar with the advantages of rank, mean with those of fortune, and disagreeable with those of
youth.

A very original character in this work is that of Eugenia. Her surprise and
sorrow when, at the age of fifteen, she first discovers her deformity, and her
deep, gentle, dignified sorrow for the irremediable misfortune, it is impossible to peruse without sympathy; and in the incident which follows, when

her father, after a discourse the most rational and soothing, brings her to the sight of a beautiful idiot, the scene is one of the most striking and sublimely moral any where to be met with.

As well as great beauties there are great faults in *Camilla*. It is blemished by the propensity which the author has shown in all her novels, betrayed into it by her love of humour, to involve her heroines not only in difficult but in degrading adventures. The mind may recover from distress, but not from disgrace; and the situations Camilla is continually placed in with the Dubsters and Mrs. Mittin are of a nature to degrade. Still more, the overwhelming circumstance of her father's being sent to prison for her debts, seems to preclude the possibility of her ever raising her head again. It conveys a striking lesson; and no doubt Mrs. D'Arblay, in her large acquaintance with life, must have often seen the necessity of inculcating, even upon *young* ladies, the danger of running up bills on credit; but the distress becomes too deep, too humiliating, to admit of a happy conclusion. The mind has been harassed and worn with excess of painful feeling. At the conclusion of *Clarissa*, we are dismissed in calm and not unpleasing sorrow; but on the winding up of *Cecilia* and *Camilla* we are somewhat tantalized with imperfect happiness. It must be added, that the interest is more divided in *Camilla* than in the author's former work, and the adventures of Eugenia become at length too improbable.

Among the new characters in this piece is Mrs. Arlberry, a woman of fashion, with good sense and taste, but fond of frivolity through *désœuvrement*,[45] and amusing herself with a little court about her of fashionable young men, whom she at the same time entertains and despises.

In short, Mrs. D'Arblay has observed human nature, both in high and low life, with the quick and penetrating eye of genius. Equally happy in seizing the ridiculous, and in entering into the finer feelings, her pictures of manners are just and interesting, and the highest value is given to them by the moral feelings they exercise, and the excellent principles they inculcate […].

"Mrs. Radcliffe."[46]

THOUGH every production which is good in its kind entitles its author to praise, a greater distinction is due to those which stand at the head of a class; and such are undoubtedly the novels of Mrs. Radcliffe,—which exhibit a genius of no common stamp. She seems to scorn to move those passions which form the interest of common novels: she alarms the soul with terror; agitates it with suspense, prolonged and wrought up to the most intense feeling, by mysterious hints and obscure intimations of unseen danger. The

---

[45] Idleness; want of occupation.
[46] *The British Novelists*, 43: i–viii, prefacing *The Romance of the Forest* (1791) by Ann Radcliffe. See Radcliffe's essay in the present volume (Chapter 9).

scenery of her tales is in "time-shook towers,"[47] vast uninhabited castles, winding staircases, long echoing aisles; or, if abroad, lonely heaths, gloomy forests, and abrupt precipices, the haunt of banditti;—the canvass and the figures of Salvator Rosa.[48] Her living characters correspond to the scenery:—their wicked projects are dark, singular, atrocious. They are not of English growth; their guilt is tinged with a darker hue than that of the bad and profligate characters we see in the world about us; they seem almost to belong to an unearthly sphere of powerful mischief. But to the terror produced by the machinations of guilt, and the perception of danger, this writer has had the art to unite another, and possibly a stronger feeling. There is, perhaps, in every breast at all susceptible of the influence of imagination, the germ of a certain superstitious dread of the world unknown, which easily suggests the ideas of commerce with it. Solitude, darkness, low-whispered sounds, obscure glimpses of objects, flitting forms, tend to raise in the mind that thrilling, mysterious terror, which has for its object the "powers unseen and mightier far than we."[49] But these ideas are suggested only; for it is the peculiar management of this author, that though she gives, as it were, a glimpse of the world of terrible shadows, she yet stops short of any thing really supernatural: for all the strange and alarming circumstances brought forward in the narrative are explained in the winding up of the story by natural causes; but in the mean time the reader has felt their full impression.

The first production of this lady, in which her peculiar genius was strikingly developed, is *The Romance of the Forest*, and in some respects it is perhaps the best.[50] It turns upon the machinations of a profligate villain and his agent against an amiable and unprotected girl, whose birth and fortunes have been involved in obscurity by crime and perfidy. The character of La Motte, the agent, is drawn with spirit. He is represented as weak and timid, gloomy and arbitrary in his family, drawn by extravagance into vice and atrocious actions; capable of remorse, but not capable of withstanding temptation. There is a scene between him and the more hardened marquis, who is tempting him to commit murder, which has far more nature and truth than the admired scene between King John and Hubert, in which the writer's imagination has led him rather to represent the action to which the King is endeavouring to work his instrument, as it would be seen by a person who had a great horror of its guilt, than in the manner in which he

---

47 Elizabeth Carter (1717–1806), "Ode to Wisdom" 3 (1747).
48 Italian painter Salvator Rosa's (1615–1673) wild, dramatic landscapes and battle scenes inspired many Romantic period evocations of the sublime.
49 Alexander Pope, *Essay on Man* III, 251–2, slightly altered.
50 Barbauld seems unaware of Radcliffe's two novels that preceded *The Romance of the Forest*, *The Castles of Athlin and Dunbayne* (1789) and *A Sicilian Romance* (1790), or she may confuse the latter with *The Italian; or The Confessional of the Black Penitents* (1797). See below.

ought to represent it in order to win him to his purpose […].[51] What must be the effect of such imagery, but to infuse into the mind of Hubert that horror of the crime with which the spectator views the deed, and which it was the business, indeed, of Shakespear to impress upon the mind of the spectator, but not of King John to impress upon Hubert? In the scene referred to, on the other hand, the marquis, whose aim is to tempt La Motte to the commission of murder, begins by attempting to lower his sense of virtue, by representing it as the effect of prejudices imbibed in early youth; reminds him that in many countries the stiletto is resorted to without scruple; treats as trivial his former deviations from integrity; and, by lulling his conscience and awakening his cupidity, draws him to his purpose.

There are many situations in this novel which strike strongly upon the imagination. Who can read without a shudder, that Adeline in her lonely chamber at the abbey hardly dared to lift her eyes to the glass, lest she should see another face than her own reflected from it? or who does not sympathize with her feelings, when, thinking she has effected her escape with Peter, she hears a strange voice, and finds herself on horseback in a dark night carried away by an unknown ruffian?

The next work which proceeded from Mrs. Radcliffe's pen was *The Mysteries of Udolpho* [1795]. Similar to the former in the turn of its incidents, and the nature of the feelings it is meant to excite, it abounds still more with instances of mysterious and terrific appearances, but has perhaps less of character, and a more imperfect story. It has been the aim in this work to assemble appearances of the most impressive kind, which continually present the idea of supernatural agency, but which are at length accounted for by natural means. They are not always, however, *well* accounted for; and the mind experiences a sort of disappointment and shame at having felt so much from appearances which had nothing in them beyond "this visible diurnal sphere."[52] The moving of the pall in the funereal chamber is of this nature. The curtain which no one dares to undraw, interests us strongly; we feel the utmost stings and throbs of curiosity; but we have been affected so repeatedly, the suspense has been so long protracted, and expectation raised so high, that no explanation can satisfy, no imagery of horrors can equal the vague shapings of our imagination.

The story of *Udolpho* is more complicated and perplexed than that of *The Romance of the Forest*; but it turns, like that, on the terrors and dangers of a young lady confined in a castle. The character of her oppressor, Montoni, is less distinctly marked than that of La Motte; and it is a fault in the story, that its unravelling depends but little on the circumstances that have previously engaged our attention. Another castle is introduced; wonders are multiplied

---

51 Barbauld quotes (deleting a few lines) from Shakespeare's *King John* III.iii.37–50, a portion of which serves an epigraph to Chapter 14 of *The Romance of the Forest*.

52 Milton, *Paradise Lost* Bk. VII, 22.

upon us; and the interest we had felt in the castle of Udolpho in the Appenines, is suddenly transferred to Chateau le Blanc among the Pyrenees.

The Mysteries of Udolpho is the most popular of this author's performances, and as such has been chosen for this Selection; but perhaps it is exceeded in strength by her next publication, *The Sicilian*.[53] Nothing can be finer than the opening of this story. An Englishman on his travels, walking through a church, sees a dark figure stealing along the aisles. He is informed that he is an assassin. On expressing his astonishment that he should find shelter there, he is told that such adventures are common in Italy. His companion then points to a confessional in an obscure aisle of the church. "There," says he, "in that cell, such a tale of horror was once poured into the ear of a priest as overwhelmed him with astonishment, nor was the secret ever disclosed." This prelude, like the tuning of an instrument by a skilful hand, has the effect of producing at once in the mind a tone of feeling correspondent to the future story. In this, as in the former productions, the curiosity of the reader is kept upon the stretch by mystery and wonder. The author seems perfectly to understand that obscurity, as Burke has asserted, is a strong ingredient in the sublime:—a face shrouded in a cowl; a narrative suddenly suspended; deep guilt half revealed; the untold secrets of a prison-house; the terrific shape, "if shape it might be called, that shape had none distinguishable;"[54]—all these affect the mind more powerfully than any regular or distinct images of danger or of woe.

But this novel has also high merit in the character of Schedoni, which is strikingly drawn, as is his personal appearance [...].[55] A striking figure for the painter to transfer to the canvass; perhaps some picture might originally have suggested it. The scene where this singular character is on the point of murdering his own daughter, as she then appears to be, is truly tragical, and wrought up with great strength and pathos. It is impossible not to be interested in the situation of Ellen, in the convent, when her lamp goes out while she is reading a paper on which her fate depends; and again when, in making her escape, she has just got to the end of the long vaulted passage, and finds the door locked, and herself betrayed. The scenes of the Inquisition are too much protracted, and awaken more curiosity than they fully gratify; perhaps than any story can gratify.

In novels of this kind, where the strong charm of suspense and mystery is employed, we hurry through with suspended breath, and in a kind of agony

---

[53] Barbauld describes *The Italian*.

[54] Edmund Burke's *A Philosophical Enquiry into the Origin of Our Ideas of the Sublime and Beautiful* (1757) helped inspire the late eighteenth-century vogue for Gothic fiction and became a standard in British aesthetics through the Romantic period and beyond. The quotation comes from Milton's description of Death in *Paradise Lost* Bk. II, 667, and serves Burke as one of his most powerful examples of the effect of obscurity in producing ideas of the sublime.

[55] Barbauld includes the description of Schedoni from Chapter 2 of *The Italian*.

of expectation; but when we are come to the end of the story, the charm is dissolved, we have no wish to read it again; we do not recur to it as we do to the characters of Western in *Tom Jones*, or the Harrels in *Cecilia*; the interest is painfully strong while we read, and when once we have read it, it is nothing; we are ashamed of our feelings, and do not wish to recall them.

There are beauties in Mrs. Radcliffe's volumes, which would perhaps have more effect if our curiosity were less excited,—for her descriptions are rich and picturesque. Switzerland, the south of France, Venice, the valleys of Piedmont, the bridge, the cataract, and especially the charming bay of Naples, the dances of the peasants, with the vine-dressers and the fishermen, have employed her pencil. Though love is but of a secondary interest in her story, there is a good deal of tenderness in the parting scenes between Emily and Valancourt in *The Mysteries of Udolpho*, when she dismisses him, who is still the object of her tenderness, on account of his irregularities.

It ought not to be forgotten that there are many elegant pieces of poetry interspersed through the volumes of Mrs. Radcliffe; among which are to be distinguished as exquisitely sweet and fanciful, the *Song to a Spirit*, and *The Sea Nymph*, "Down down a hundred fathom deep!"[56] They might be sung by Shakespear's Ariel. The true lovers of poetry are almost apt to regret its being brought in as an accompaniment to narrative, where it is generally neglected; for not one in a hundred, of those who read and can judge of novels, are at all able to appreciate the merits of a copy of verses, and the common reader is always impatient to get on with the story.

The Sicilian is the last of Mrs. Radcliffe's performances. Some have said that, if she wishes to rise in the horrors of her next, she must place her scene in the infernal regions. She would not have many steps to descend thither from the courts of the Inquisition.

[…][57]

---

[56] "Song of a Spirit" appeared in *The Romance of the Forest*, while "The Sea-Nymph" is from *The Mysteries of Udolpho*. Line 1 of the latter poem reads "Down, down a thousand fathom deep."

[57] *The British Novelists* also includes Maria Edgeworth's *Belinda* beginning in volume 49, but presumably because of her friendship with Edgeworth, Barbauld's brief preface contains little evaluation.

Charlotte Turner Smith
(1749–1806)

Charlotte Smith was born into privilege, but at an early age found herself faced with a life of pain, penury, and isolation. Her father, Nicholas Turner, owned estates in Sussex and Surrey, and Charlotte spent much of her childhood in the country. After her mother died when she was three years old, her father traveled abroad for several years, leaving Charlotte consigned to the care of an aunt. At age six, she was sent to school, where she attained some distinction in the usual feminine accomplishments, and became known as an avid reader and composer of verse.

Soon after Charlotte reached her teens, Nicholas Turner, his finances apparently rather drained, married a woman of substantial property, and in 1765 a marriage was arranged for Charlotte, now age fifteen and disinclined to submit to her new stepmother. The groom, twenty-one year old Benjamin Smith, was the son of a West Indian merchant and director of the East India Company. Smith proved dissipated, unfaithful, and violent, and the family was perpetually in debt. Benjamin's father, Richard Smith, clearly understood his son's nature; when he died in 1776, he left a fortune of £36,000 specifically for his daughter-in-law and grandchildren. The will was so complex, however, and Benjamin Smith's legal representative so tenacious, that the money was never made available until after both Benjamin and Charlotte were dead and the children matured. By 1783 Benjamin Smith was imprisoned for debt. Leaving the children with a relative, Charlotte spent seven months with her husband in King's Bench prison advocating for his release and composing poetry for the literary market. *Elegiac Sonnets, and Other Essays* (1784) was published at Smith's own expense and achieved immediate success, with Smith enlarging it for new editions several times during her life. Its preface defending her deviations from strict sonnet form sparked a debate about sonnet form that engaged Anna Seward, William Lisle Bowles, Mary Robinson, and Samuel Taylor Coleridge.

On release from prison, Benjamin Smith was almost immediately embroiled again in financial difficulties, and in 1784 he fled to France with his wife, now pregnant with their twelfth child. In France, Charlotte Smith first tried translating, but this proved burdensome and not particularly lucrative. In 1787 she separated from her husband, though she continued to provide him some financial assistance from the proceeds of her publications. In 1788 she published her first novel, *Emmeline, the Orphan of the Castle*, soon followed by *Ethelinde; or, The Recluse of the Lake* (1789), *Celestina* (1791), and *Desmond* (1792). The first three are sentimental tales, but *Desmond*, set against the backdrop of the French Revolution, explicitly raises political questions. Smith continues this same theme in *The Emigrants: A Poem, in Two Books* (1793), a verse narrative that criticizes France's absolute monarchy while urging compassion for the French aristocrats and clergy exiled to Britain in the wake of the revolution. Her next novel, *The Old Manor House* (1793), appeared that same year. Set during the war over American independence, it narrates a Gothic story of an elderly spinster who mistreats a sentimentally portrayed lovely young orphan while tyrannizing over relatives whom she keeps in uncertainty over who will inherit her magnificent estate. Other novels followed in continued rapid succession, as well as several books for children, more poetry, and even a play. Of these, *The Banished Man* (1794) expresses Smith's horror over the atrocities of the French Reign of Terror, while *Marchmont* (1796) contains her most scathing condemnation of the English legal system.

Publisher Richard Phillips commissioned *The History of England, from the Earliest Records to the Peace of Amiens, in a Series of Letters to a Young Lady at School* (1806), but progressing illness prevented Smith from completing it, and Phillips turned the project over to Mary Hays. Smith's final volume of poetry, *Beachy Head: With Other Poems*, was published posthumously in 1807. By the time of her death at age fifty-seven, Smith had authored at least ten novels, most well received. Her *Elegiac Sonnets*, along with its preface, helped spawn the Romantic period sonnet revival that was to include Mary Robinson, William Wordsworth, Coleridge, and a host of other writers as well.

■ Preface to *Desmond*[1]

IN sending the world a work so unlike those of my former writings, which have been honored by its approbation, I feel some degree of that apprehension which an Author is sensible of on a first publication.

This arises partly from my doubts of succeeding so well in letters as in narrative; and partly from a supposition, that there are Readers, to whom the fictitious occurrences, and others to whom the political remarks in these volumes may be displeasing.

To the first I beg leave to suggest, that in representing a young man, nourishing an ardent but concealed passion for a married woman; I certainly do not mean to encourage or justify such attachments; but no delineation

---

[1]   London: G.G.J. and J. Robinson, 1792.

of character appears to me more interesting, than that of a man capable of such a passion so generous and disinterested as to seek only the good of its object; nor any story more moral, than one that represents the existence of an affection so regulated.

As to the political passages dispersed through the work, they are for the most part, drawn from conversations to which I have been a witness, in England, and France, during the last twelve months. In carrying on my story in those countries, and at a period when their political situation (but particularly that of the latter) is the general topic of discourse in both; I have given to my imaginary characters the arguments I have heard on both sides; and if those in favor of one party have evidently the advantage, it is not owing to my partial representation but to the predominant power of truth and reason, which can neither be altered nor concealed.

But women it is said have no business with politics.—Why not?—Have they no interest in the scenes that are acting around them, in which they have fathers, brothers, husbands, sons, or friends engaged?—Even in the commonest course of female education, they are expected to acquire some knowledge of history; and yet, if they are to have no opinion of what *is* passing, it avails little that they should be informed of what *has passed*, in a world where they are subject to such mental degradation; where they are censured as affecting masculine knowledge if they happen to have any understanding; or despised as insignificant triflers if they have none.

Knowledge, which qualifies women to speak or to write on any other than the most common and trivial subjects, is supposed to be of so difficult attainment, that is cannot be acquired but by the sacrifice of domestic virtues, or the neglect of domestic duties.—*I* however, may safely say, that it was in the *observance*, not in the *breach* of duty, *I* became an Author; and it has happened, that the circumstances which have compelled me to write, have introduced me to those scenes of life, and those varieties of character which I should otherwise never have seen: Tho' alas! it is from thence, that I am too well enabled to describe from *immediate* observation,

"The proud man's contumely, th' oppressors wrong;
The laws delay, the insolence of office."[2]

But, while in consequence of the affairs of my family being most unhappily in the power of men who *seem to exercise all these with impunity*, I am become

---

[2] Shakespeare, *Hamlet*, III.i.70–2.

an *Author by profession*, and feel every year more acutely, *"that hope delayed maketh the heart sick."*[3] I am sensible also (to use another quotation) that

> ——————— "Adversity—
> Tho' like a toad ugly and venomous,
> Wears yet a precious jewel in its head."[4]

For it is to my involuntary appearance in that character, that I am indebted, for all that makes my continuance in the world desirable; all that softens the rigor of my destiny and enables me to sustain it: I mean friends among those, who, while their talents are the boast of their country, are yet more respectable for the goodness and integrity of their hearts.

Among these I include a female friend, to whom I owe the beautiful little Ode in the last volume; who having written it for this work, allows me thus publicly to boast of a friendship, which is the pride and pleasure of my life.[5]

If I may be indulged a moment longer in my egotism, it shall be only while I apologize for the typographical errors of the work, which may have been in some measure occasioned by the detached and hurried way, in which the sheets were sometimes sent to the press when I was at a distance from it; and when my attention was distracted by the troubles, which it seems to be the peculiar delight of the persons who are concerned in the management of my children's affairs, to inflict upon me. With all this the Public have nothing to do: but were it proper to relate all the disadvantages from anxiety of mind and local circumstances, under which these volumes have been composed, such a detail might be admitted as an excuse for more material errors.

For that asperity of remark, which will arise on the part of those whose political tenets I may offend, I am prepared; those who object to the matter, will probably arraign the manner, and exclaim against the impropriety of making a book of entertainment the vehicle of political discussion. I am however conscious that in making these slight sketches, of manners and opinions, as they fluctuated around me; I have not sacrificed truth to any party—Nothing appears to me more respectable than national pride; nothing so absurd as national prejudice—And in the faithful representation of the manners of other countries, surely Englishmen many find abundant reason to indulge the one, while they conquer the other. To those however who still cherish the idea of our having a *natural* enemy in the French

---

3   Proverbs 13:12.
4   Shakespeare, *As You Like It* II.i.13–14.
5   Antje Blank and Janet Todd identify this Ode as "Ode to the Poppy" by Henrietta O'Neill (1753–1793), first published in *Desmond* (*Desmond*, ed. Antje Blank and Janet Todd [Peterborough, ON: Broadview P, 2001] 415 n. 6).

nation; and that they are still more *naturally* our foes, because they have dared to be freemen, I can only say, that against the phalanx of prejudice kept in constant pay, and under strict discipline by interest, the slight skirmishing of a novel writer can have no effect: we see it remains hitherto unbroken against the powerful efforts of learning and genius—though united in that cause which *must* finally triumph—the cause of truth, reason, and humanity.

■ Prefaces to *Elegiac Sonnets*[6]

PREFACE to the FIRST AND SECOND EDITIONS

THE little poems which are here called Sonnets, have, I believe, no very just claim to that title: but they consist of fourteen lines, and appear to me no improper vehicle for a single Sentiment. I am told, and I read it as the opinion of very good judges, that the legitimate Sonnet is ill calculated for our language. The specimen [*sic*] Mr. Hayley has given, though they form a strong exception, prove no more, than that the difficulties of the attempt vanish before uncommon powers.

Some very melancholy moments have been beguiled by expressing in verse the sensations those moments brought. Some of my friends, with partial indiscretion, have multiplied the copies they procured of several of these attempts, till they found their way into the prints of the day in a mutilated state; which, concurring with other circumstances, determined me to put them into their present form. I can hope for readers only among the few, who, to sensibility of heart, join simplicity of taste.

PREFACE to the THIRD AND FOURTH EDITIONS

THE reception given by the public, as well as my particular friends, to the two first editions of these poems, has induced me to add to the present such other Sonnets as I have written since, or have recovered from my acquaintance, to whom I had given them without thinking well enough of them at the time to preserve any copies myself. A few of those last written, I have attempted on the Italian model; with what success I know not; but I am persuaded that, to the generality of readers, those which are less regular will be more pleasing.

---

[6] Smith first published *Elegiac Sonnets, and Other Essays by Charlotte Smith of Bignor Park* in 1784 with the assistance of her neighbor, poet William Hayley (1745–1820). She continued to expand the volume in subsequent editions up through 1800. The third edition appeared in 1786, the sixth in 1792 and the two volume eighth edition in 1797. While the fifth edition does include a preface, it simply conveys gratitude for the support of friends and patrons, and so is omitted here. Copytext for all prefaces is the eighth edition, (*Elegiac Sonnets and other Poems* [Cadell and Davies, 1797]), which includes the earlier prefaces as well as its own prefaces. The earlier ones are there slightly altered from their original versions.

As a few notes were necessary, I have added them at the end. I have there quoted such lines as I have borrowed; and even where I am conscious the ideas were not my own, I have restored them to the original possessors.

From the PREFACE TO THE SIXTH EDITION

WHEN a sixth Edition of these little Poems was lately called for, it was proposed to me to add such Sonnets, or other pieces, as I might have written since the publication of the fifth—Of these, however, I had only a few; and on shewing them to a friend, of whose judgment I had an high opinion, he remarked that some of them, particularly "The Sleeping Woodman," and "The Return of the Nightingale," resembled in their subjects, and still more in the plaintive tone in which they are written, the greater part of those in the former Editions—and that, perhaps, some of a more lively cast might be better liked by the Public—"Toujours perdrix," said my friend—"Toujours perdrix," you know, "ne vaut rien."—I am far from supposing that *your* compositions can be neglected or disapproved, on whatever subject: but perhaps "toujours Rossignols, toujours des "chansons tristes," may not be so well received as if you attempted, what you would certainly execute as successfully, a more cheerful style of composition. "Alas! replied I, "Are grapes gathered from thorns, or figs from thistles?"[7] Or can the *effect* cease, while the *cause* remains? *You know* that when in the Beech Woods of Hampshire, I first struck the chords of the melancholy lyre, its notes were never intended for the public ear! It was unaffected sorrows drew them forth: I wrote mournfully because I was unhappy—And I have unfortunately no reason yet, though nine years have since elapsed, to *change my tone* […].[8]

[N]otwithstanding I am thus frequently appearing as an Authoress, and have derived from thence many of the greatest advantages of my life, (since it has procured me friends whose attachment is most invaluable,) I am well aware that for a woman—"The Post of Honor is a Private Station."

From the PREFACE to Volume II

IT so rarely happens that a second attempt in any species of writing equals the first, in the public opinion, when the first has been remarkably successful; that I send this second volume of small Poems into the world with a considerable degree of diffidence and apprehension.

---

7   Matthew 7:16. The French expressions, which appear to consist of a commonplace saying now archaic and a twist on the same idea, translate to "Always partridges, Always partridges, is not worth anything" followed by "always nightingales, always sad songs." Idiosyncratic placing of quotation marks follows the source text.

8   Omitted section alludes more specifically to the legal entanglements surrounding her father-in-law's estate that prevented her children from receiving the inheritance he intended for them.

Whatever inferiority may be adjudged to it, I cannot plead want of *time* for its completion, if I should attempt any excuse at all; for I do not forget that more than three years have elapsed since I reluctantly yielded to the pressing instances of some of my friends[9]; and accepted their offers to promote a subscription to another volume of Poems—I say, accepted the offers of my friends, because (with a single exception) I have never made any application myself.

Having once before had recourse to the indulgence of the public, in publishing a book by subscription, and knowing that it had been so often done by persons with whom it is honourable to be ranked, it was not pride that long withheld my consent from this manner of publication; and, certainly, the pecuniary inconveniences I had been exposed to for so many years, never pressed upon me *more* heavily than at the moment this proposal was urged by my friends; if then I declined it, it was because I even at *that* period doubted, whether from extreme depression of spirit, I should have the power of fulfilling (so as to satisfy myself) the engagement I must feel myself bound by, the moment I had accepted subscriptions […].[10]

I am well aware that the present is not a time when the complaints of individuals against private wrong are likely to be listened to; nor is this an opportunity fit to make those complaints; but I know so much has been said (so much more than so trifling a matter could be worth) of the *delay* of this publication, that it becomes in some measure a matter of self-defence, to account for that delay. Those who have expressed such impatience for it, were apprehensive (indeed they owned they were) of the loss of the half guinea they had paid. I have more than once thought of returning their money, rather than have remained under any obligation to persons who could suspect me of a design to accumulate, by gathering subscriptions for a work I never meant to publish, a sum, which no contrivance, no success, was likely to make equal to one year of the income I ought to possess. Surely, any who have entertained and *expressed* such an opinion of me, must either never have understood, *or must have forgotten*, what I was, what I am, or what I ought to be […].

> Some degree of pride which
>   "Still travels on, nor leaves us till we die,"[11]

makes me somewhat solicitious to account for the visible difference in point of numbers between the subscribers to this and the former volume. If I were willing to admit that these Poems are inferior to those that preceded them, I know that such a supposition would not have withheld a single subscription—but I also know, that as party can raise prejudices against the colour

---

[9]   Particularly those of Joseph Cooper Walker, Esq. of Dublin, by whose friendly and successful applications in Ireland I am particularly obliged [Smith's note].

[10] Smith explains in detail the personal and financial hardships she has endured as a result of the legal complications tying up her father-in-law's estate.

[11] Paraphrasing Pope's *Essay on Man* 274.

of a ribband, or the cut of a cape, it generates still stranger antipathies, even in regard so things almost equally trifling. And *there are*, who can never forgive an author that has, in the story of a Novel, or the composition of a Sonnet, ventured to hint at any opinions different from those which these liberal-minded personages are determined to find the best.

I know, therefore, perfectly well, how I have sinned against some ci-devant,[12] I was going to say friends, but I check myself, and change the word for acquaintance,

"Since friendship should be made of stronger stuff,"[13]

who when my writing first obtained popularity, erected themselves into patrons and patronesses. To the favour they *then* conferred I am not insensible; and I hope they will accept it as a proof of my perfectly understanding the extent of the obligation, that I have so silently acquiesced in not expecting it to be repeated, and have never suffered them to be put under the painful necessity of avowing their dereliction in 1797, of the writer whom they affected so warmly to patronize in 1787. Ten years do indeed operate most wonderful changes in this state of existence […].

I am at length enabled to send it into the world—and have certainly omitted nothing that was in my power to make it not intirely unworthy the general favor, and of the particular kindness of *those* without whose support I believe it would have been impossible for me to have prepared the few verses I had by me, or to have composed others. That these are gloomy, none will surely have a right to complain; for I never engaged they should be gay. But I am unhappily exempt from the suspicion of *feigning* sorrow for an opportunity of showing the pathos with which it can be described—a suspicion that has given rise to much ridicule, and many invidious remarks, among certain critics, and others, who carry into their closets the same aversion to any thing tragic, as influences, at the present period, their theatrical taste.

It is, indeed, a melancholy truth, that at this time there is so much tragedy in real life, that those who have escaped private calamity, can withdraw their minds a moment from that which is general, very naturally prefer to melancholy books, or tragic representations, those lighter and gayer amusements, which exhilarate the senses, and throw a transient veil over the extensive and still threatening desolation, that overspreads this country, and in some degree, every quarter of the world.

CHARLOTTE SMITH

May 15th , 1797.

---

[12]   Former.
[13]   Paraphrasing Shakespeare, *Julius Caesar* III.ii.92.

▪ Preface to *The Letters of a Solitary Wanderer*[14]

SINCE I began this Work almost two years have elapsed, and the two first volumes have been printed nearly half that time. My original intention was to publish six volumes, each containing a single Narrative, which the Solitary Wanderer is supposed to collect in the countries he visits.

Books of entertainment, usually described as Novels, are supposed to be, if not exclusively, principally read by young persons; and much has been said of the inutility and the danger of that species of reading.[15]

Of the danger I mean not to speak, except to remark, that a young woman who is so weak as to become in imagination the Heroine of a Novel, would have been a foolish, frivolous, and affected character, though she had never heard of a circulating library.

That Novels are at least useless where they are not pernicious I cannot allow: if they do not instruct, they may awaken a wish for useful knowledge; and young persons, who have not taste for any thing but narrative, may sometimes, by the local descriptions of a Novel, learn what they would never have looked for in books of Geography or Natural History.—The dangers and distresses that are expected to form the greater part of the story in every Work of this kind, may be imagined amidst the most interesting period of history, without, however, falsifying or misinterpreting any material or leading fact. I have endeavoured to construct these volumes in some degree on this plan. It is my present purpose to prepare the remaining part of the Work for publication early in the ensuing summer.

---

[14] London: Longman and Rees, 1802.
[15] See Samuel Johnson's comments quoted in the Introduction. Other statements on this issue can be found in several of Wollstonecraft's *Analytical* reviews (Chapter 6), and Hays's comments in each of her entries (Chapter 7).

Elizabeth Inchbald (1753–1821)

Actor, playwright, novelist, and literary critic, Elizabeth Inchbald offers the best example of canny professionalism among her female literary contemporaries. Born into a family of theater enthusiasts, Elizabeth Simpson received only an informal education, but reading and attending plays comprised much of the family's recreation. Her brother acted in a Norwich theater company, and, determined to follow suit, Elizabeth tried unsuccessfully during her teen years to join the company as well. Failing there, she packed her bags for London, where she soon married the much older established actor, Joseph Inchbald. Together they toured with a Bristol theater company, where Elizabeth made her stage debut as Shakespeare's Cordelia. After her husband's early death, Elizabeth Inchbald returned to London to continue her stage career. Never ranked among top actors, she still achieved notable success, performing with, among others, the famed John Kemble and Sarah Siddons.

Still acting but in need of additional income, Inchbald began to write for the theater, eventually authoring twenty plays, some original, others translations or adaptations, but the majority comedies or farces. She turned her knowledge of stagecraft to effect in pleasing her audiences by prompting their laughter and tears. Her plays often contain hints of double entendre and occasionally compromised propriety. *Lovers' Vows* (1798), an adaptation of German playwright August von Kotzebue's *Das Kind der Liebe* (1790), is best remembered today as the play that threw Jane Austen's Bertram family into chaos in *Mansfield Park* (1814). Nevertheless, Inchbald found playwriting profitable, and her astute management of both her finances and her personal life allowed her to live in reasonable comfort and decorum as a single woman while attached to a profession that was not always lucrative and frequently cast shadows on the reputations of its female affiliates, especially those without male protection.

Besides her plays, Inchbald authored two novels, *A Simple Story* (1791) and *Nature and Art* (1796), both well received. Between acting and writing, Inchbald had by the early 1800s achieved a name with both the reading and play-going public. When Thomas Longman, one of London's most successful booksellers, decided to publish a series of popular, recently staged plays, he approached Inchbald to pen the introductions. Initially published in weekly installments over two years, the one hundred twenty-five introductions that Inchbald provided for *The British Theatre* stand as the first instance of ongoing signed criticism by a woman writer. George Colman the younger, one of the writers whose work appeared in the collection, attacked Inchbald on the grounds that she stepped outside the bounds of accepted feminine discourse by entering the masculine territory of literary criticism, to which Inchbald offered a richly ironic reply.

Though annoying Colman, Inchbald's introductions pleased her publisher enough that he approached her for more criticism. She declined, however, after realizing that she could command nearly the same price for lending her name to a volume of selections as for the labor of composing essays. The loss is ours, for Inchbald's prefaces draw on her stage experience to develop a critical formula based on fresh standards that often depart from established authorities and featuring anecdotes about actors and performances that make an amusing contribution to British theater history. Her only other identified criticism is the ironic essay "On Novel Writing."

■ ["On Novel Writing"][1]

TO THE ARTIST.

SIR,

IF the critical knowledge of an art was invariably combined with the successful practice of it, I would here proudly take my rank among artists, and give instructions on the art of writing Novels.—But though I humbly confess that I have not the slightest information to impart, that may tend to produce a good novel; yet it may not be wholly incompatible with the useful design of your publication, if I show—how to avoid writing a very bad one.

Observe, that your hero and heroine be neither of them too bountiful. The prodigious sums of money which are given away every year in novels, ought, in justice, to be subject to the property tax; by which regulation, the national treasury, or every such book, would be highly benefited.

Beware how you imitate Mrs. Radcliffe, or Maria Edgeworth; you cannot equal them; and those readers who most admire their works, will most despise yours.

Take care to reckon up the many times you make use of the words "Amiable," "Interesting," "Elegant," "Sensibility," "Delicacy," "Feeling." Count each of these words over before you send your manuscript to be printed, and be sure to erase half the number you have written;—you may erase again

---

[1]   *The Artist* 1 (13 June 1807): 9–19, from the 1810 bound edition.

when your first proof comes from the press—again, on having a revise—and then mark three or four, as mistakes of the printer, in your Errata.

Examine likewise, and for the same purpose, the various times you have made your heroine blush, and your hero turn pale—the number of times he has pressed her hand to his "trembling lips," and she his letters to her "beating heart"—the several times he has been "speechless" and she "all emotion," the one "struck to the soul;" the other "struck dumb."

The lavish use of "tears," both in "showers" and "floods," should next be scrupulously avoided; though many a gentle reader will weep on being told that others are weeping, and require no greater cause to excite their compassion.

Consider well before you introduce a child into your work. To maim the characters of men and women is no venial offence; but to destroy innocent babes is most ferocious cruelty: and yet this savage practice has, of late, arrived at such excess, that numberless persons of taste and sentiment have declared—they will never read another novel, unless the advertisement which announces the book, adds (as in advertisements for letting Lodgings) *There are no children.*

When you are contriving that incident where your heroine is in danger of being drowned, burnt, or her neck broken by the breaking of an axle-tree—for without perils by fire, water, or coaches, your book would be incomplete—it might be advisable to suffer her to be rescued from impending death by the sagacity of a dog, a fox, a monkey, or a hawk; any one to whom she cannot give her hand in marriage; for whenever the deliverer is a fine young man, the catastrophe of your plot is foreseen, and suspense extinguished.

Let not your ambition to display variety cause you to produce such a number of personages in your story, as shall create perplexity, dissipate curiosity, and confound recollection. But if, to show your powers of invention, you are resolved to introduce your reader to a new acquaintance in every chapter, and in every chapter snatch away his old one; he will soon have the consolation to perceive—they are none of them worth his regret.

Respect virtue—nor let her be so warm or so violent as to cause derision:—nor vice so enormous as to resemble insanity. No one can be interested for an enthusiast—nor gain instruction from a madman.

And when you have written as good a novel as you can—compress it into three or four short volumes at most; or the man of genius, whose moments are precious, and on whose praise all your fame depends, will not find time to read the production, till you have committed suicide in consequence of its ill reception with the public.

There are two classes of readers among this public, of whom it may not be wholly from the purpose to give a slight account. The first are all hostile to originality. They are so devoted to novel-reading, that they admire one novel because it puts them in mind of another, which they admired a few days before. By them it is required, that a novel should be like a novel; that is, the majority of those compositions; for the minor part describe fictitious characters and events merely as they are in real life:—ordinary represent-ations, beneath the concern of a true voracious novel-reader.

Such an one (more especially of the female sex) is indifferent to the fate of nations, or the fate of her own family, whilst some critical situation in a romance agitates her whole frame! Her neighbour might meet with an acci-dental death in the next street, the next house, or the next room, and the shock would be trivial, compared to her having just read—"that the ami-able Sir Altamont, beheld the interesting Eudocia, faint in the arms of his thrice happy rival."

Affliction, whether real or imaginary, must be refined,—and calamity ele-gant, before this novel-reader can be roused to "sympathetic sensation." Equally unsusceptible is her delicate soul to vulgar happiness. Ease and content are mean possessions! She requires transport, rapture, bliss, extatic [*sic*] joy, in the common occurrences of every day.

She saunters pensively in shady bowers, or strides majestically through brilliant circles. She dresses by turns like a Grecian statue and a pastoral nymph: then fancies herself as beautiful as the undone heroine in "*Barbarous Seduction*;" and has no objection to become equally unfortunate.

To the healthy, that food is nourishment, which to the sickly proves their poison. Such is the quality of books to the strong, and to the weak of under-standing.—Lady Susan is of another class of readers, and has good sense. —Let her therefore read certain well-written novels, and she will receive intimation of two or three foibles, the self-same as those, which, adhering to her conduct, cast upon all her virtues a degree of ridicule.—These failings are beneath the animadversions of the pulpit. They are so trivial yet so awkward, that neither sermons, history, travels, nor biography, could point them out with propriety. They are ludicrous, and can only be described and reformed by a humourist.

And what book so well as a novel, could show to the enlightened Lord Henry——the arrogance of his extreme condescension? Or insinuate to the judgment of Lady Eliza——the wantonness of her excessive reserve?

What friend could whisper so well to Lady Autumnal—that affected sim-plicity at forty, is more despicable than affected knowledge at fifteen?— And by what better means could the advice be conveyed to Sir John Egotist—to pine no more at what the world may say of him; for that men like himself are too insignificant for the world to know.

A novel could most excellently represent to the valiant General B—, that though he can forgive the miser's love of gold, the youth's extravagance and even profligacy; that although he has a heart to tolerate all female faults, and to compassionate human depravity of every kind; he still exempts from this his universal clemency—the poor delinquent soldier.

The General's wife, too, forgives all injuries done to her neighbours: those to herself are of such peculiar kind, that it would be encouragement to offenders, not to seek vengeance.—The lovely Clarissa will pardon every one—except the mantua-maker who spoils her shape.—And good Sir Gormand never bears malice to a soul on earth—but to the cook who spoils his dinner.

That Prebendary is merciful to a proverb—excluding negligence towards holy things—of which he thinks himself the holiest. Certain novels might make these people think a second time.

Behold the Countess of L——! Who would presume to tell that once celebrated beauty—that she is now too wrinkled for curling hair; and her complexion too faded for the mixture of blooming pink? Should her husband convey such unwelcome news, he would be more detested than he is at present! Were her children or her waiting-maid to impart such intelligence, they would experience more of her peevishness than ever!—A novel assumes a freedom of speech to which all its readers must patiently listen; and by which, if they are wise, they will know how to profit.

The Novelist is a free agent. He lives in a land of liberty, whilst the Dramatic Writer exists but under a despotic government.—Passing over the subjection in which an author of plays is held by the Lord Chamberlain's office,[2] and the degree of dependence which he has on his actors—he is the very slave of the audience. He must have their tastes and prejudices in view, not to correct, but to humour them. Some auditors of a theatre, like some aforesaid novel-readers, love to see that which they have seen before; and originality, under the opprobrious name of innovation, might be fatal to a drama, where the will of such critics is the law, and execution instantly follows judgment.

In the opinion of these theatrical juries, Virtue and Vice attach to situations, more than to characters: at least, so they will have the stage represent. The great moral inculcated in all modern plays constantly is—for the rich to love the poor. As if it was not much more rare, and a task by far more difficult—for the poor to love the rich.—And yet, what author shall presume to expose upon the stage, certain faults, almost inseparable from the indigent? What dramatic writer dares to expose in a theatre, the consummate vanity of a certain rank of paupers, who boast of that wretched state as a sacred honour, although it be the result of indolence or criminality? Who dares to show an audience, the privilege, of poverty debased into the instrument of ingratitude?—"I am poor and therefore slighted"—cries the unthankful beggar; whilst his poverty is his sole recommendation to his friends; and for which alone, they pay him much attention, and some respect.

What dramatist would venture to bring upon the stage—that which so frequently occurs in real life—a benefactor living in awe of the object of his bounty; trembling in the presence of the man whom he supports, lest by one inconsiderate word, he should seem to remind him of the predicament

---

[2]   The official censor of dramatic productions until that function was abolished in 1968.

in which they stand with each other; or by an involuntary look, seem to glance at such and such obligations?

Who, moreover, dares to exhibit upon the stage, a benevolent man, provoked by his crafty dependant—for who is proof against ungratefulness?—to become that very tyrant, which he unjustly had reported him?

Again.—The giver of alms, as well as the alms-receiver, must be revered on the stage.—That rich proprietor of land, Lord Forecast, who shall dare to bring him upon the boards of a theatre, and show—that, on the subject of the poor, the wily Forecast accomplishes two most important designs? By keeping the inhabitants of his domain steeped in poverty, he retains his vast superiority on earth; then secures, by acts of charity, a chance for heaven.

A dramatist must not speak of national concerns, except in one dull round of panegyrick. He must not allude to the feeble minister of state, nor to the ecclesiastical coxcomb.

Whilst the poor dramatist is, therefore, confined to a few particular provinces; the novel-writer has the whole world to range, in search of men and topics. Kings, warriors, statesmen, churchmen, are all subjects of his power. The mighty and the mean, the common-place and the extraordinary, the profane and the sacred, all are prostrate before his muse. Nothing is forbidden, nothing is withheld from the imitation of a novelist, except—other novels.

E. I.

■ Selected Remarks from *The British Theatre*[3]

From Remarks on *A Comedy of Errors* by William Shakspeare.

[...] Of all improbable stories, this is the most so. The Ghost in "Hamlet," Witches in "Macbeth," and Monster in "The Tempest," seem all like events in the common course of nature, when compared to those which take place in this drama. Its fable verges on impossibility, but the incidents which arise from it could never have occurred.

Granting that the two Antipholises and the two Dromios were as like, as twins often are, would their clothes, even the fashion of their habits, have been so exactly alike, that mistakes could have been carried to such

---

[3] London: Longman, Hurst, Rees & Orme, 1806–1808. The initial periodical publication of Inchbald's *British Theatre* essays produces some discrepancies in the form of the series. Collections bound for the bookseller do not present the plays in the order of publication. In addition, some extant copies were assembled and bound by private collectors. As a result, bound copies vary, not always presenting their contents in the same order, and sometimes lacking some feature such as one or two of Inchbald's essays or some of the illustrative frontispiece engravings. Pagination extends not through entire volumes, but only through single plays, each play beginning its own pagination anew. I thank Cecilia Macheski for explaining this discrepancy between copies in *Remarks for the British Theatre (1806–1809) by Elizabeth Inchbald* (Delmar, NY: Scholars' Facsimiles & Reprints, 1990).

extremities? Nay, one brother comes purposely to Ephesus, in search of his twin brother, his own perfect resemblance, and yet, when every accident he encounters tells him directly, that his brother being resident in that very place is the cause of them all, this is an inference he never once draws, but rather chuses to believe the people of the town are all mad, than that the person whom he hoped to find there is actually one of its inhabitants […].

In most of the old comedies, there is seemingly a great deal of humour designed in the beating of servants:—this is a resource for mirth, of which modern authors are deprived, because the custom is abolished, except in the West Indies; and, even there, not considered of humorous tendency. As far as the usage was ever known to produce comic effect, this play may boast of being comical […].

Romeo and Juliet.

[…] Shakspeare has produced, from this "Tragical History," one of his most admirable plays: Yet, had the subject fallen to Otway's pen, though he would have treated it less excellently, he would have rendered it more affecting.[4]

"Romeo and Juliet" is called a pathetic tragedy, but it is not so in reality. It charms the understanding, and delights the imagination, without melting, though it touches, the heart.

The reason that an auditor or reader cannot feel a powerful sympathy in the sorrows of these fervent lovers is, because they have witnessed the growth of their passion from its birth to its maturity, and do not honour it with that warmth of sentiment as if they had conceived it to have been of longer duration; fixed by time, and rendered more tender by familiarity.

The ardour of the youthful pair, like the fervency of children, gives high amusement, without much anxiety that their wishes should be accomplished—they have been so suddenly enamoured of each other, that it seems matter of doubt whether they would not as quickly have fallen in love a second time, or as soon have become languid through satiety, if all obstacles to their bliss had been removed […].

Henry IV, Pt 1.

THIS is a play which all men admire, and which most women dislike. Many revolting expressions in the comic parts, much boisterous courage in some of the graver scenes, together with Falstaff's unwieldy person, offend every female auditor; and whilst a facetious Prince of Wales is employed in taking purses on the highway, a lady would rather see him stealing hearts at a ball, though the event might produce more fatal consequences.

---

[4]   Works by Thomas Otway (1652–1685), playwright and satirist, appeared in *The British Theatre*.

The great Percy, they confess, pays some attention to his wife, but still more to his horse: and, as the king was a rebel before he mounted the throne, and all women are naturally loyal, they shudder at a crowned head with a traitor's heart.

With all these plausible objections, infinite entertainment and instruction may be received from this drama, even by the most delicate readers. They will observe the pen of a faithful historian, as well as of a great poet; and they ought, surely, to be charmed with every character, as a complete copy of nature; admiring even the delinquency of them all, far beyond that false display of unsullied virtue, so easy for a bard to bestow upon the creatures of his fancy, when truth of description is sacrificed to brilliant impossibilities.

The reader who is too refined to laugh at the wit of Sir John, must yet enjoy Hotspur's picture of a coxcomb; and receive high delight from those sentences of self-reproach, and purpose of amendment, which occasionally drop from the lips of the youthful and royal profligate.

If the licentious faults of old-fashioned dialogue should here too frequently offend the strictly nice, they must, at least, confer the tribute of their praises upon every soliloquy. It is impossible for puritanism not to be merry, when Falstaff is ever found talking to himself; or holding discourse over the honoured dead. It is nearly impossible for stupidity to be insensible of the merit of those sentiments delivered by the prince, over the same extended corse; or to be unmoved by various other beauties with which this work abounds […].

Merchant of Venice.

[…] Probability is, indeed, continually violated in "The Merchant of Venice;" but so it should ever be in plays, or not at all—one improbable incident only, among a train of natural occurrences, revolts an audience; but where all is alike extravagant, comparison is prevented, and extravagance becomes familiar.

Boldness of design, strength of character, excellence of dialogue, with pre-possession in favour of the renowned author of this work, shield every fault from observation, or from producing an ill effect by its intrusion.

Refinement is honourable to our nation; and the delicacy of the English stage at present is the best characteristic of that elegant propriety, with which the public shrink from all savage indecorum of principles or manners, however excited by passions, or by debased sentiments. Yet, with due respect for refined notions, they would indisputably, in Shakspeare's days, have limited and impaired his mighty genius.

The knife to cut—the scales to weigh—and what? part of an enemy's body! […].

Henry V

[…] Fiction, from the pen of genius, will often appear more like nature, than nature will appear like herself. The admired speech invented by the author for

King Henry, in a beautiful soliloquy just before battle, seems the exact effect of the place and circumstances with which he was then surrounded, and to be, as his very mind stamped on the dramatic page; and yet perhaps his majesty, in his meditations, had no such thoughts as are here provided for him […].

Much Ado About Nothing.

[…] Claudio and Hero are said to be in love, but they say so little about it themselves, that no strong sympathy is created, either by their joys, or their sorrows, their expectations or disappointments;—though, such is the reverence for justice implanted in humankind, that every spectator feels a degree of delight in the final vindication of her innocence, and the confusion of her guilty accusers.

Those persons, for whom the hearts of the audience are most engaged, have, on the contrary, scarce one event to aid their personal interest; every occurrence, which befalls them, depends solely on the pitiful act of private listening. If Benedick or Beatrice had possessed perfect good manners, or just notions of honour and delicacy, so as to have refused to have become eves-droppers, the action of the play must have stood still, or some better method have been contrived—a worse hardly could—to have imposed on their mutual credulity […].

But, in whatever failings the ill-bred custom of Messina may have involved the said Benedick and Beatrice, they are both highly entertaining, and most respectable personages. They are so witty, so jocund, so free from care, and yet so sensible of care in others, that the best possible reward is conferred on their merit—marriage with each other […].

Shakspeare has given such an odious character of the bastard, John, in this play, and of the bastard, Edmund, in King Lear, that, had those dramas been written in the time of Charles the Second, the author must have been suspected of disaffection to half the court.

Measure for Measure.

[…] Had Shakspeare been the inventor of the fable of the present play, he would assuredly have avoided the incredible occurrences here inserted. Allowing that the Duke's disguise, as a friar, could possible conceal him from the knowledge of his intimate friends, and that Angelo should be so blind a lover, as not to distinguish, in closest conference, her he loved from her he hated (for these are stage inconsistencies permitted for stage accommodation,) there still remains a most disgraceful improbability, in representing the deputy of Angelo, a monster, instead of a man. The few lines he speaks in a soliloquy, offer a plea too weak for his enormity, in giving orders for the death of Claudio, after the supposed ransom paid by his sister. This plea is besides reduced in part from all show of reason, by a sentence which precedes it in the very same speech.—In that sentence, Angelo says—"He rests satisfied Isabella will not reveal her dishonour"—yet he has ordered the brother's execution, lest she should disclose this dishonour to him, and that he should proclaim it to all the world by taking his revenge […].

The Winter's Tale.

[…] "The Winter's Tale" was very successful at Drury Lane Theatre a few years ago; and yet it seems to class among those dramas that charm more in perusal than in representation. The long absence from the scene of the two most important characters, Leontes and his wife, and the introduction of various other persons to fill their places, divert, in some measure, the attention of an audience; and they do not so feelingly unite all they see and all they hear into a single story, as he who, with the book in his hand, and neither his eye nor ear distracted, combines and enjoys the whole grand variety.

Besides the improbability of exciting equal interest by the *plot* of this drama in performance as in the closet, some of the poetry is less calculated for that energetic delivery which the stage requires, than for the quiet contemplation of one who reads. The conversations of Florizel and Perdita have more of the tenderness than the fervour of love; and consequently their passion has not the force of expression to animate a multitude, though it is properly adapted to steal upon the heart of an individual.

Shakspeare has said, in his tragedy of Othello, that a man is "jealous, because he is jeallous [*sic*]." This conceit of the poet seems to be the only reason that can possibly be alleged for the jealousy of the hero of the present work; for the unfounded suspicion of Leontes, in respect to the fidelity of Hermione, is a much greater fault, and one with which imagination can less accord, than with the hasty strides of time, so much censured by critics, between the third and fourth acts of the play. It is easier for fancy to overleap whole ages, than to overlook one powerful demonstration of insanity in that mind which is reputed sane.

The mad conduct of Leontes is however the occasion of such noble, yet such humble and forbearing demeanour on the part of his wife, that his phrensy is rendered interesting by the sufferings which it draws upon her: and the extravagance of the first is soon forgotten, through the deep impression made by the last […].

King Lear.

[…] Lear is not represented much more affectionate to his daughters by Shakspeare, than James the Second is by Hume. James's daughters were, besides, under more than ordinary obligations to their king and father, for the tenderness he had evinced towards their mother, in raising her from a humble station to the elevation of his own; and thus preserving these two princesses from the probable disgrace of illegitimate birth […].

Lear, exposed on a bleak heath, suffered not more than James, at one of our sea-ports, trying to escape to France. King Lear was only pelted by a storm, King James by his merciless subjects […].

Macbeth.

IN this grand tragic opera is combined that which is terrific, sublime, infernal. Spirits are called from the bottomless pit, to give additional horror to the crimes which are here perpetrated. Yet supernatural agency is produced and conducted by such natural means, that spectators return again to their childish credulity, and tremble, as in the nursery, at a witch and a goblin […].

[T]o those who are unacquainted with the effect wrought by theatrical action and decoration, it may not be superfluous to say—the huge rocks, the enormous caverns, and blasted heaths of Scotland, in the scenery;—the highland warrior's dress, of centuries past, worn by the soldiers and their generals;—the splendid robes and banquet at the royal court held at Fores;—the awful, yet inspiring music, which accompanies words assimilated to each sound;—and, above all—the fear, the terror, the remorse;—the agonizing throbs and throes, which speak in looks, whispers, sudden starts, and writhings, by Kemble and Mrs. Siddons, all tending to one great precept—*Thou shalt not murder,*—render this play one of the most impressive moral lessons which the stage exhibits […].[5]

Julius Caesar.

[… I]t has been thought adviseable, for some years past, that this tragedy should not appear upon the stage.

When men's thoughts are deeply engaged on public events, historical occurrences, of a similar kind, are only held proper for the contemplation of such minds as know how to distinguish, and to appreciate, the good and the evil with which they abound. Such discriminating judges do not compose the whole audience of a play-house; therefore, when the circumstances of certain periods make certain incidents of history most interesting, those are the very seasons to interdict their exhibition.

Till the time of the world's repose, then, the lovers of the drama will, probably, be compelled to accept of real conspiracies, assassinations, and the slaughter of war, in lieu of such spectacles, ably counterfeited […].

Coriolanus.

[…] With all their faults, this mother [Volumnia] and son produce scenes the most affecting, because the most natural, that were ever, perhaps, written, for persons of their elevated rank in life. Here, in the part on Coriolanus, human nature, in the likeness of a stubborn schoolboy, as well as of the obstinate general of an army, is so exquisitely delineated, that every

---

[5]   Sarah Siddons (1755–1831), the most revered female actor of her day, was born into a theatrical family that included two actor brothers, Charles (1775–1854) and John Philip (1757–1823) Kemble. She debuted in the theatrical company of actor, playwright, and manager David Garrick (1717–1779).

mental trait of the one can be discerned in the propensities of the other, so as forcibly to call to the recollection, that children are the originals of men.

Volumnia, too, with all her seeming heroism, so dazzling to common eyes, is woman to the very heart. One whose understanding is by no means ordinary; but which extends no further than the customary point of woman's sense—to do mischief. She taught her son to love glory, but to hate his neighbors; and thus made his skill in arms a scourge to his own country. But, happily, her feminine spirit did not stop here; for, terrified at the peril which threatened Rome from the hand of this darling son, she averted the frightful danger of a city in flames, by the careless sacrifice of his life to the enemy.

All these inconsistencies in Volumnia do not, however, make that great woman less admired or beloved. The frailties of her and her son constitute the pathetic parts of this tragedy, which are wonderfully moving. These personages talk so well, and at times act so well, that their pitiable follies, couched beneath such splendid words and deeds, raise a peculiar sympathy in the heart of frail man; who, whilst he beholds this sorrowful picture of human weakness, discerns along with it his own likeness, and obtains an instructive lesson.

This novel drama, in which Mr. Kemble reaches the utmost summit of the actor's art, has been withdrawn from the theatre of late years, for some reasons of state. When the lower order of people are in good plight, they will bear contempt with cheerfulness, and even with mirth; but poverty puts them out of humour at the slightest disrespect. Certain sentences in this play are therefore of dangerous tendency at certain times, though at other periods they are welcomed with loud applause.

As "Coriolanus" is now once more brought upon the stage, and the voice of the public has hailed its return; this circumstance may be received as a joyful evidence—that the multitude at present are content in their various stations; and can therefore, in this little dramatic history, amuse themselves with beholding, free from anger and resentment, that vainglory, which presumes to despise them.

Othello.

[…] There is in the love of Othello and Desdemona such a rational apology, such a description of gradual passion taking possession of her heart, through pity and admiration; rooted in his, from gratitude and tenderness; that no sooner has he delivered that speech of natural eloquence to the senate, in the first act, than every auditor feels himself agitated with interest for the fate of the enamoured and newly-wedded pair.

So vast is the power of the author's skill in delineating the rise and progress of sensations in the human breast, that a young and elegant female is here represented, by his magic pen, as deeply in love with a Moor,—a man different in complexion and features from her and her whole race,—and yet without the slightest imputation of indelicacy resting upon her taste: —whilst the Moor, in his turn, dotes on her with all the transport of the most impassioned lover, yet without the smallest abatement of the rough and rigid cast of his nature.—The mutual affection of these two characters seems most forcibly to be inspired by the very opposite qualities which they each possess.

There is a second contrast in this play more impressive than the foregoing. The consummate art and malignant spirit of Iago are so reverse from the generous mind and candid manners of Othello, that it appears like the highest point, the very zenith, of the poet's genius, to have conceived two such personages, not only for the same drama, but to have brought them on the stage together in almost every scene […].

The Tempest.

[… *The Tempest*] would never have become a favourite on the stage without the aid of Dryden's alteration. The human beings in the original drama had not business enough on the scene to make human beings anxious about them: and the preternatural characters were more wonderful than pleasing; for, whilst an auditor or a reader pours forth his praise before the creator of Caliban, he loathes the creature.

Ariel, opposed to this monster, is one of those happy contrasts which Shakspeare deals in; yet this airy and mild spirit cannot charm an audience, except by singing. Nor could the love scenes produce much sympathy, but from the artlessness of the objects concerned. Ignorance of what their own sensations mean is the charm which alone elevates those pleasing characters above the common order of insipid lovers.

"The Tempest" contains some of the author's best poetry […].

Twelfth Night

[…] Those readers, who can receive entertainment from a fictitious, or from a real fool, will find much humorous amusement in the parts of both the Clown, and Sir Andrew; and they will possibly, also, enjoy the ridicule which arises from an imposition that is practised upon a presumptuous upper servant of a woman of quality. But the dramatis personæ of higher interest are those, with whom Viola is concerned in the serious, more than in the comic occurrences, which befall her; for, with them, she speaks a language that enchants both the ear and the understanding; and produces a happy contrast to the less refined dialogue.

It is said that King Charles the First, whose admiration of Shakspeare was a crime with the Puritans, gave this play the title of "Malvolio." Had his Majesty seen Mrs. Jordan perform in it, he, no doubt, would have called it "Viola." The former character is, however, suited to former times […].

Although the mirth, which is excited at the expense of Malvolio, is impeded by the ungenerous stratagem, through which he has been deceived; yet it is gratifying to observe the skill, by which he is made, as soon as his vanity is caught, to interpret every event that occurs, every word that is uttered, to the purpose, on which his wishes are bent.—Other gratifications, of a more exalted kind, will be derived from the more exalted characters. The meeting of the brother and sister will produce a sympathy, that every reader will sensibly feel;—and the following lines, delivered by Fabian, in the original edition, ought to mollify criticism upon some of the most extraordinary incidents contained in this work: for in these lines Shakspeare alludes, perhaps, to other extravagant circumstances in "Twelfth Night" as well as to that, exhibited in the scene where they are spoken; and meant thus indirectly, to plead guilty.

Fabian. "If this were played upon a stage now, I could condemn it as an improbable fiction."

The Rival Queens by Nathaniel Lee.[6]

[…] This tragedy is calculated for representation rather than the amusement of the closet; for, though it is graced with some beautiful poetry, it is likewise deformed by an extravagance, both in thought and in language, that at times verges upon the ludicrous. Actors, eminent in their art, know how to temper those failings in a tragic author: they give rapidity to their utterance in the mock sublime, and lengthen their cadence upon every poetic beauty […].

All For Love by Dryden.[7]

[…] The burning bosom, throbbing heart, the enchanting sensations, which the author, in his odes and poems, inspires, are rarely excited by his dramatic works. The stage, which exalts the muse of many an author, humbles that of the present great poet; and he ranks as a dramatist beneath those rivals who can move the passions by a more judicious adherence to nature and simplicity […].

Oroonoko by Thomas Southerne.[8]

[…] The tragedy of "Oroonoko" is never acted in Liverpool, for the very reason why it ought to be acted there oftener than at any other place—The merchants of that great acquire their riches by the slave trade […].

---

[6] Tragedian Nathaniel Lee (c. 1645–1692), was known for blank verse drama. *The Rival Queens*, his most popular play, was first performed at the Theatre Royal in Drury Lane on March 17, 1677.

[7] Satirist, dramatist, poet, translator, and essayist John Dryden (1631–1700) became Poet Laureate in 1668. The first known performance of *All for Love*, his blank verse tragedy about Mark Anthony and Cleopatra, occurred at Drury Lane on December 12, 1677.

[8] Thomas Southerne (1660–1746) was noted for moving female characters. *Oroonoko*, a tragedy dramatizing the barbarity of slavery, first opened at Drury Lane in late 1695.

The Distressed Mother by Ambrose Philips.[9]

[…] The French and the English stages differ so essentially, that every drama requires great alteration, before it can please a London audience, although it has previously charmed the audience of Paris.

The gloomy mind of a British auditor demands a bolder and more varied species of theatrical amusement, than the lively spirits of his neighbours in France. The former has no attention, no curiosity, till roused by some powerful fable, intricate occurrences, and all the interest which variety creates— whilst the latter will quietly sit, absorbed in their own glowing fancy, to hear speeches after speeches, of long narration, nor wish to see any thing performed, so they are but told, that something has been done […].

The Careless Husband by Colley Cibber.[10]

[…] The dialogue is so brilliant, at the same time, so very natural, that its force will admit of no augmentation, even from the delivery of the best actors: nor is this admirable work, according to the present demand for perpetual incident, so well calculated to please on the stage, as in the closet.

The occurrences, which take place in this drama, are of that delicate, as well as probable kind, that their effect is not sufficiently powerful in the representation—whereas, in reading, they come to the heart with infinitely more force, for want of that extravagance, which public exhibition requires. The smaller avenues to the mind and bosom are often the surest passages to convey sensations of pain or delight; and the connoisseur in all the little touches of refined nature may here indulge his taste, whilst, as an auditor, he might possibly be deprived of his enjoyment, by the vain endeavour of performers, to display, by imitation, that, which only real life can show, or imagination pourtray […].

The Wonder!: A Woman Keeps a Secret by Susannah Centlivre.[11]

Mrs Centlivre, […] ranks in the first class of our comic dramatists: for though she does not possess the repartee of Congreve or Wycherly, and her dialogue, in general, is not equal even to Farquhar's, yet she discovers such happy invention in her plots, incidents, and characters; such skill in conducting the intrigues of a comedy; such art in exciting the curiosity, the anxiety, or the mirth of her auditors, that she foils both the scholar and the wit when the comparison is limited to theatrical effect […].

---

[9]   Ambrose Philips (1675–1749) was ridiculed in Pope's *Dunciad*. *The Distressed Mother*, a translation of *Andromaque* (1668) by French poet and playwright Jean Racine (1639–1699), was first staged at Drury Lane on March 17, 1712.

[10] *The Careless Husband* was first staged on December 7, 1704 at Drury Lane, where its author, actor Colley Cibber (1671–1757), later served as manager.

[11] A prolific and popular playwright, Susannah Centlivre (1667?–1723) authored lively plays that attracted large audiences long after her death. Among them, *The Wonder: A Woman Keeps a Secret* opened at Drury Lane on April 27, 1714.

This comedy is by far her best work. In excellence of fable, strength of character, and intricacy of occurrence, it forms one of the most entertaining exhibitions the theatre can boast […].

Most comic writers of the present time accomplish the tedious labour of a five act drama by having recourse, alternately, to sentiment and drollery: here a long play is sustained without excursions to either and yet its consistency, in adhering to one fixed point of entertainment, never creates satiety, nor shows a languor of invention in the author, which for a moment leaves the expectation of the auditor unemployed, or leaves that expectation in one single instance disappointed […].

The Man of the World by Charles Macklin.[12]

This play […] first appeared in Dublin, where it was well received; but reasons of a political nature advised a delay in bringing it before a London audience, that events might perhaps arise in the administration of public affairs, so as to favour, rather than injure, its reception.

The elevation of Mr. Pitt to the high office of prime minister—from which occurrence it was confidently expected, that all ancient failings in that hazardous department would cease, and ministerial regeneration ensue—this seemed the happy era for "The Man of the World" to be introduced on the stage of the metropolis.[13] To hold up to detestation vices, now no longer to be tolerated, could give offence to none—at least to none in power to resent the affront […].

Yet the opposition on the first night of its appearance was so violent in some scenes, whilst the followers of the new minister were such enthusiastic admirers of those very parts which gave displeasure that plaudits and counter-plaudits lengthened the time of performance nearly to midnight, before the ayes and the noes became all of one mind […].

The Brothers by Richard Cumberland.[14]

[…] To give blunt repartee, or other humorous dialogue, to characters in low life; to produce variety of comic accidents, by which a petty tradesman, a sailor, or a country clown, shall raise a peal of laughter, is the easy

---

12 Actor, playwright, and theater manager Charles Macklin (1699–1797) was admired as an acting instructor as well, in which capacity he helped foster naturalism in eighteenth-century acting style. *The Man of the World*, a revision of Macklin's *The True-Born Scotsman* (1764), opened in London at Covent Garden on May 10, 1781 with Macklin gaining lasting fame in the satirical role of Sir Pertinax Macsycophant.

13 William Pitt "the Younger" (1759–1806) offered a refreshing change from moral and political corruption that had reigned during several of his predecessor's terms, but he did not become prime minister until 1783. Inchbald's chronology appears confused in this instance.

14 Richard Cumberland (1732–1811) specialized in sentimental works, as exemplified by the melodramatic comedy *The Brothers*, first performed at Covent Garden on December 2, 1769.

attainment of every whimsical writer; but to exhibit the weak side of wisdom, the occasional foibles which impede the full exertion of good sense; the chance awkwardness of the elegant, and mistakes of the correct; to bestow wit on beauty, and to depict the passions visible in the young as well as in the aged;—these are efforts of intellect required in the production of a good comedy, and can alone confer the title of a good comic author […].

The West Indian by Richard Cumberland.[15]

[… A]lthough it may bestow no small degree of entertainment in the closet, its proper region is the stage.—Many of the characters require the actor's art, to fill up the bold design, where the author's pen has not failed, but wisely left the perilous touches of a finishing hand to the judicious comedian […].

A Bold Stroke for a Husband by Hannah Cowley.[16]

Although "The Bold Stroke for a Husband," by Mrs Cowley, does not equal "The Bold Stroke for a Wife," by Mrs Centlivre, either in originality of design, wit, or humour, it has other advantages more honourable to her sex, and more conducive to the reputation of the stage.

Here is contained no oblique insinuation, detrimental to the cause of morality—but entertainment and instruction unite, to make a pleasant exhibition at a theatre, or give an hour's amusement in the closet […].

The Dramatist by Frederick Reynolds.[17]

Plays of former times were written to be read, not seen. Dramatic authors succeeded in their aim; their works were placed in libraries, and the theatres were deserted.—Now, plays are written to be seen, not read—and present authors gain their views; for they and the managers are enriched, and the theatres crowded.

To be both seen and read at the present day, is a degree of honour, which, perhaps, not one comic dramatist can wholly boast, except Shakspeare. Exclusive of his, scarcely any of the very best comedies of the best of former bards will now attract an audience: yet the genius of ancient writers was assisted by various tales, for plots, of which they have deprived the moderns; they had, besides, the privilege to write without either political or moral restraint. Uncurbed by law or delicacy, they wrote at random; and at random wrote some pages worthy posterity—but along with these, they produced others, which disgrace the age that reprints and circulates them.

---

15 First performed at Drury Lane on January 19, 1771.
16 Actor and playwright Hannah Cowley (1743–1809) was known for lively comedies. *A Bold Stroke for a Husband* opened at Covent Garden on February 25, 1783.
17 *The Dramatist, or, Stop him who can!*, a comedy by Frederick Reynolds (1764–1841), opened at Covent Garden on May 15, 1789.

It might be deemed suspicious to insinuate, that those persons, perhaps, who so vehemently exclaim against modern dramas, give up with reluctance the old prerogative of listening to wit and repartee, which would make the refined hearer of the present day blush, and the moral auditor shudder […].

The Road to Ruin by Thomas Holcroft.[18]

This comedy ranks among the most successful of modern plays. There is merit in the writing, but much more in that dramatic science, which disposes character, scenes, and dialogue, with minute attention to theatric exhibitions, for the author has nicely considered, that it is only by passing the ordeal of a theatre with safety, that a drama has the privilege of being admitted to a library.

The nice art, with which the conversations in this play are written, will, by a common reader, pass unadmired and unnoticed. Some of the most important speeches consist of no more than one line. The grand skill has been to make no skill evident—to force a reader to forget the author, but to remember his play, and each distinct character.

To produce this effect, both on the stage and in the closet, the whole comedy is perfectly natural. Paternal and filial affection are described with infinite power, and yet without one inflated or poetic sentence. The scenes between Dornton and his son are not like scenes in a play, but like occurrences in the house of a respectable banker, who has a dissipated, though a loving and beloved, son […].

De Monfort by Joanna Baillie.[19]

AMONGST the many female writers of this and other nations, how few have arrived at the elevated character of a woman of genius!

The authoress of "De Monfort" received that rare distinction, upon this her first publication.

There was genius in the novelty of her conception, in the strength of her execution; and though her play falls short of dramatic excellence, it will ever be rated as a work of genius.

Joanna Baillie, in her preface to her first publication, displays knowledge, taste, and judgment, upon the subject of the drama, to a very high degree: still, as she observes, "theory and practice are very different things;" and, perhaps, so distinct is the art of criticism, from the art of producing plays, that no one critic so good as herself, has ever written a play half so good as the following tragedy.

---

[18] Holcroft, a staunch radical, was Inchbald's close friend. *The Road to Ruin*, Holcroft's satire on the morals of affluent Britons, opened at Covent Garden on February 18, 1792.

[19] Opening at Drury Lane on April 29, 1800, *De Monfort* was among the few of Baillie's works to be staged during her lifetime.

Authors may think too profoundly, as well as too superficially—and if a dramatic author, with the most accurate knowledge of the heart of a man, probe it too far, the smaller, more curious, and new-created passions, which he may find there, will be too delicate for the observation of those who hear and see in a mixed, and, sometimes, riotous, company.[20]

The spirit, the soul, the every thought and sensation of the first character in this piece, De Monfort, is clearly discerned by the reader, and he can account for all the events to which they progressively lead: but the most attentive auditor, whilst he plainly beholds effects, asks after causes; and not perceiving those diminutive seeds of hatred, here described, till, swollen, they extend to murder, he conceives the hero of the tragedy to be more a pitiable maniac, than a man acting under the dominion of natural propensity.

Even to the admiring reader of this work, who sees the delineation of nature in every page, it may perchance occur, that disease must have certain influence with hate so rancorous; for rooted antipathy, without some more considerable provocation than is here adduced, is very like the first unhappy token of insanity [...].

On Jane De Monfort she has bestowed some of her very best poetic descriptions; and, from the young Page's first account of the "queenly" stranger, has given such a striking resemblance of both the person and mien of Mrs. Siddons, that it would almost raise a suspicion she was, at the time of the writing, designed for the representation of this noble female.

This drama, of original and very peculiar formation, plainly denotes that the authoress has studied theatrical productions as a reader more than a spectator; and it may be necessary to remind her—that Shakspeare gained his knowledge of the effect produced from plays upon an audience, and profited, through such attainment, by his constant attendance on dramatic representations, even with the assiduity of a performer [...].

---

[20]   See Baillie's discussion on the effect of theater size in "To the Reader."

Mary Darby Robinson
(1758–1800)

Poet, novelist, actor, and periodical editor, Mary Robinson, née Darby, enjoyed a short but apparently tranquil rural childhood before her father, a Bristol merchant, sustained heavy losses on his investment in an unsuccessful whaling venture. Insolvent and accompanied by a mistress, Mr. Darby brought his family to London, where he separated from his wife, establishing her and the children in Chelsea. Mary's education included several boarding schools, most notably first at the Bristol school run by Hannah More's sisters, and later with a Mrs. Lorrington, a talented but alcoholic woman who encouraged Mary's penchant for literature and experiments in composing verse. By the time Mary reached fourteen, finances had become so strained that her mother established her own boarding school with Mary assisting in teaching grammar and literature. Mr. Darby soon broke up this project, and Mary was sent to a finishing school. There her dancing master introduced her to actor, playwright, and theater manager David Garrick (1717–1779), who later helped launch her acting career.

Mary's good looks attracted a number of suitors, including Thomas Robinson, the illegitimate son of a Welsh landowner, who somehow convinced Mrs. Darby and her daughter that he was a good match. They married in 1774, when Mary was fifteen. Though Thomas Robinson neglected both his wife and profession, the couple nevertheless lived a fashionable life, he gambling and womanizing, she attracting the attention of several gallants of property, until creditors' demands forced an escape to Wales. On returning to London the following year, Mary arranged publication of her *Poems* (1775). The book's proceeds did not prevent Thomas Robinson from being arrested for debt. The volume did, however, attract the patronage of Georgiana, Duchess of Devonshire, but not until Mary and her infant daughter had remained with her husband some ten months in King's Bench Prison. Inspired by the experience, Mary composed *Captivity, a Poem, and Celadon and Lydia, a Tale* (1777).

In December 1776 Mary Robinson made her acting debut as Shakespeare's Juliet under the patronage of Garrick and Richard Brinsley Sheridan. From that point she ascended rapidly if somewhat scandalously in the London fashionable scene, establishing a separate residence from her husband, attracting numerous prominent admirers, and eventually becoming the subject for painters such as Sir Joshua Reynolds and Thomas Gainsborough. In December of 1779, King George, Queen Charlotte, and their eldest son attended a performance of *A Winter's Tale* with Robinson playing Perdita. The Prince of Wales was so taken with Robinson that he began sending her letters signed "Florizel." Although the relationship lasted less than a year, the resulting scandal effectively put an end to Robinson's stage career, leaving her largely dependent on an irregularly paid £500 royal annuity.

After a sojourn in Paris as part of Marie Antoinette's court circle, Robinson returned to London to begin a long relationship with Colonel Banastre Tarleton, who shared her taste for fashionable life. In 1783, attempting to join Tarleton in France, where he had fled from creditors, Robinson, then pregnant, miscarried. The subsequent complications left her legs almost completely paralyzed. Soon after Tarleton returned to London they were again in debt, and in 1784 they returned to France, remaining until 1788. Back in London, Robinson began, under the pseudonym "Laura Maria," composing sentimentally delicate Della Cruscan poetry for *The World*. Eventually collected in *Poems* (1791), these pieces definitively established her reputation as a poet. Other publications quickly followed, including *Sappho and Phaon* (1796). The preface, outlining the current place of the sonnet in English literature, helped inaugurate the sonnet revival during the romantic period.

Though primarily a poet, Robinson was truly a versatile and professional woman of letters. Her numerous novels, the most noteworthy of which include *Vancenza* (1792), *The Widow* 1792), *Angelina* (1796), *Hubert de Sevrac* (1796), *Walsingham* (1797), *The False Friend* (1799), and *The Natural Daughter* (1799), did the most toward improving her financial stability. Under the names Tabitha Bramble and Laura, she contributed poetry and for a time edited the poetry section of *The Morning Post*. *A Letter to the Women of England, on the Cruelties of Mental Subordination* (1799, later *Thoughts on the Condition of Women*) published under the pseudonym Anne Frances Randall, articulates eighteenth-century championing of the woman writer through both the language of Mary Wollstonecraft's *A Vindication of the Rights of Woman* and Robinson's own embittering experiences with male protectors. *Lyrical Tales* (1800), the last volume published in her lifetime, appeared only a few days before her death.

■ Preface to *Sappho and Phaon*[1]

IT must strike every admirer of poetical compositions, that the modern sonnet, concluding with two lines, winding up the sentiment of the whole, confines the poet's fancy, and frequently occasions an abrupt termination of a beau-

---

[1]   *Sappho and Phaon, in a Series of Legitimate Sonnets* (London: Hookham & Carpenter, 1796).

tiful and interesting picture; and that the ancient, or what is generally denominated, the LEGITIMATE SONNET, may be carried on in a series of sketches, composing, in parts, one historical or imaginary subject, and forming in the whole a complete and connected story.

With this idea, I have ventured to compose the following collection; not presuming to offer them as imitations of PETRARCH,[2] but as specimens of that species of sonnet writing, so seldom attempted in the English language; though adopted by that sublime Bard, whose Muse produced the grand epic of Paradise Lost, and the humbler effusion, which I produce as an example of the measure to which I allude, and which is termed by the most classical writers, the *legitimate sonnet*.

O Nightingale, that on yon bloomy spray
　　Warblest at eve, when all the woods are still,
　　Thou with fresh hope the lover's heart dost fill,
While the jolly hours lead on propitious May.
Thy liquid notes that close the eye of day
　　First heard before the shallow cuccoo's bill,
　　Portend success in love; O if Jove's will
Have link'd that amorous power to thy soft lay,
　　Now timely sing, ere the rude bird of hate
Foretel my hopeless doom in some grove nigh,
　　As thou from year to year hast sung too late
For my relief, yet hadst no reason why:
　　Whether the Muse, or Love call thee his mate,
Both them I serve, and of their train am I.[3]

To enumerate the variety of authors who have written sonnets of all descriptions, would be endless; indeed few of them deserve notice: and where, among the heterogeneous mass of insipid and laboured efforts, sometimes a bright gem sheds lustre on the page of poesy, it scarcely excites attention, owing to the disrepute in which sonnets are fallen. So little is rule attended to by many, who profess the art of poetry, that I have seen a composition of more than thirty lines, ushered into the world under the name of Sonnet, and that, from the pen of a writer, whose classical taste ought to have avoided such a misnomer.

Doctor Johnson describes a Sonnet, as "a short poem, consisting of fourteen lines, of which the rhymes are adjusted by a particular rule."

---

[2]　Francesco Petrarca (1304–1374), known for his *Canzoniere* series of love sonnets to the woman they immortalized as "Laura."
[3]　Milton, Sonnet I, "O Nightingale!."

He further adds, "It has not been used by any man of eminence since MILTON."[4]

Sensible of the extreme difficulty I shall have to encounter, in offering to the world a little wreath, gathered in that path, which, even the best poets have thought it dangerous to tread; and knowing that the English language is, of all others, the least congenial to such an undertaking, (for, I believe, that the construction of this kind of sonnet was originally in the Italian, where the vowels are used almost every other letter,) I only point out the track where more able pens may follow with success; and where the most classical beauties may be adopted, and drawn forth with peculiar advantage.

Sophisticated sonnets are so common, for every rhapsody of rhyme, from six lines to sixty comes under that denomination, that the eye frequently turns from this species of poem with disgust. Every school-boy, every romantic scribbler, thinks a sonnet a task of little difficulty. From this ignorance in some, and vanity in others, we see the monthly and diurnal publications abounding with ballads, odes, elegies, epitaphs, and allegories, the nondescript ephemera from the heated brains of self-important poetasters, all ushered into notice under the appellation of SONNET!

I confess myself such an enthusiastic votary of the Muse, that any innovation which seems to threaten even the least of her established rights, makes me tremble, lest that chaos of dissipated pursuits which has too long been growing like an overwhelming shadow, and menacing the lustre of

---

[4]   Since the death of Doctor Johnson a few ingenious and elegant writers have composed sonnets, according to the rules described by him: of their merits the public will judge, and the *literati* decide. The following quotations are given as the opinions of living authors, respecting the legitimate sonnet.

The little poems which are here called Sonnets, have, I believe, no very just claim to that title: but they consist of fourteen lines, and appear to me no improper vehicle for a single sentiment. I am told, and I read it as the opinion of very good judges, that the legitimate sonnet is ill calculated for our language. The specimens Mr. Hayley has given, though they form a strong exception, prove no more, than that the difficulties of the attempt vanish before uncommon powers.

Mrs. C. Smith's Preface to her Elegiac Sonnets

Likewise in the preface to a volume of very charming poems, (among which are many *legitimate sonnets*) by Mr. William Kendall, of Exeter, the following opinion is given of the Italian rythm [*sic*], which constitutes the legitimate sonnet: he describes it as—

A chaste and elegant model, which the most enlightened poet of our own country disdained not to contemplate. Amidst the degeneracy of modern taste, if the studies of a Milton have lost their attraction, legitimate sonnets, enriched by varying pauses, and an elaborate recurrence of rhyme, still assert their superiority over those tasteless and inartificial productions, which assume the name, without evincing a single characteristic of distinguishing modulation [Robinson's note].

Samuel Johnson defined the sonnet in his *Dictionary of the English Language* (1755). On Smith, see the entry in the present volume.

intellectual light, should, aided by the idleness of some, and the profligacy of others, at last obscure the finer mental powers, and reduce the dignity of talents to the lowest degradation.

As poetry has the power to raise, so has it also the magic to refine. The ancients considered the art of such importance, that before they led forth their heroes to the most glorious enterprizes, they animated them by the recital of grand and harmonious compositions. The wisest scrupled not to reverence the invocations of minds, graced with the charm of numbers: so mystically fraught are powers said to be, which look beyond the surface of events, that an admired and classical writer,[5] describing the inspirations of the MUSE, thus expresses his opinion:

> So when remote futurity is brought
> Before the keen inquiry of her thought,
> A terrible sagacity informs
> The Poet's heart, he looks to distant storms,
> He hears the thunder ere the tempest low'rs,
> And, arm'd with strength surpassing human pow'rs,
> Seizes events as yet unknown to man,
> And darts his soul into the dawning plan.
> Hence in a Roman mouth the graceful name
> Of Prophet and of Poet was the same,
> Hence British poets too the priesthood shar'd,
> And ev'ry hallow'd druid—was a bard.

That poetry ought to be cherished as a national ornament, cannot be more strongly exemplified than in the simple fact, that, in those centuries when the poets' laurels have been most generously fostered in Britain, the minds and manners of the natives have been most polished and enlightened. Even the language of a country refines into purity by the elegance of numbers: the strains of WALLER[6] have done more to effect that, than all the labours of monkish pedantry, since the days of druidical mystery and superstition.

Though different minds are variously affected by the infinite diversity of harmonious effusions, there are, I believe, very few that are wholly insensible to the powers of poetic compositions. Cold must that bosom be, which can resist the magical versification of Eloisa to Abelard;[7] and torpid to all the more exalted sensations of the soul is that being, whose ear is not

---

5   Cowper [Robinson's note]. William Cowper (1731–1800); the quoted lines are from *Table Talk* 492–503.
6   Edmund Waller (1606–1687), known for the polished sweetness of his verse, was credited as one of the poets who ushered in the Augustan age of British literature.
7   Peter Abelard (1079–1142) and his pupil, Héloïse, fell in love and were separated by her family. Their impassioned correspondence inspired Alexander Pope's *Eloisa to Abelard* (1717).

delighted by the grand and sublime effusions of the divine Milton! The romantic chivalry of Spencer vivifies the imagination; while the plaintive sweetness of Collins soothes and penetrates the heart.[8] How much would Britain have been deficient in a comparison with other countries on the scale of intellectual grace, had these poets never existed! yet it is a melancholy truth, that here, where the attributes of genius have been diffused by the liberal hand of nature, almost to prodigality, there has not been, during a long series of years, the smallest mark of public distinction bestowed on literary talents. Many individuals, whose works are held in the highest estimation, now that their ashes sleep in the sepulchre, were, when living, suffered to languish, and even to perish, in obscure poverty: as if it were the peculiar fate of genius, to be neglected while existing, and only honoured when the consciousness of inspiration is vanished for ever.

The ingenious mechanic has the gratification of seeing his labours patronized, and is rewarded for his invention while he has the powers of enjoying its produce. But the Poet's life is one perpetual scene of warfare: he is assailed by envy, stung by malice, and wounded by the fastidious comments of concealed assassins. The more eminently beautiful his compositions are, the larger is the phalanx he has to encounter; for the enemies of genius are multitudinous.

It is the interest of the ignorant and powerful, to suppress the effusions of enlightened minds: when only monks could write, and nobles read, authority rose triumphant over right; and the slave, spell-bound in ignorance, hugged his fetters without repining. It was then that the best powers of reason lay buried like the gem in the dark mine; by a slow and tedious progress they have been drawn forth, and must, ere long, diffuse an universal lustre: for that era is rapidly advancing, when talents will tower like an unperishable column, while the globe will be strewed with the wrecks of superstition.

As it was the opinion of the ancients, that poets possessed the powers of prophecy, the name was consequently held in the most unbounded veneration. In less remote periods the bard has been publicly distinguished; princes and priests have bowed before the majesty of genius: Petrarch was crowned with laurels, the noblest diadem, in the Capitol of Rome: his admirers were liberal; his contemporaries were just; and his name will stand upon record, with the united and honourable testimony of his own talents, and the generosity of his country.

It is at once a melancholy truth, and a national disgrace, that this Island, so profusely favored by nature, should be marked, of all enlightened countries, as the most neglectful of literary merit! and I will venture to believe, that there are both POETS and PHILOSOPHERS, now living in Britain, who, had

---

[8]   William Collins (1721–1759) authored *Odes on Several Descriptive and Allegorical Subjects* (1746). Edmund Spenser (c. 1552–1599) authored *The Faerie Queene* (1590–1596) among numerous other works.

they been born in any *other* clime, would have been honoured with the proudest distinctions, and immortalized to the latest posterity.

I cannot conclude these opinions without paying tribute to the talents of my illustrious countrywomen; who, unpatronized by courts, and unprotected by the powerful, persevere in the paths of literature, and ennoble themselves by the unperishable lustre of MENTAL PRE-EMINENCE!

Mary Wollstonecraft
(1759–1797)

Britain's first known truly professional woman literary critic, Wollstonecraft was born into a London middle-class family headed by a profligate and tyrannical father who squandered the family's money on a series of unsuccessful business ventures. Her childhood was dominated by the family's frequent moves, her father's drunkenness and domestic violence, and her own haphazard education. At age eighteen Wollstonecraft accepted employment as a lady's companion, but returned home after two years to nurse her mother through a fatal illness. Soon after, her sister Eliza suffered from a post-partum depression. Convinced that Eliza was being maltreated, Wollstonecraft persuaded her to abandon her husband and their baby, who died a year later. To support herself, Eliza, another sister, and a close friend, Fanny Blood, Wollstonecraft established a marginally successful girls' school at Newington Green. The school's location brought Wollstonecraft into contact with some of England's most prominent religious dissenters, and though she never converted to dissent, her ties with this community remained strong throughout her life.

This period of Wollstonecraft's life ended when Fanny Blood married and moved with her husband to Portugal, where Wollstonecraft later attended her death in childbirth. When Wollstonecraft returned to England, their school had failed, so she accepted a governess position with the family of the Irish Lord Kingsborough. Dismissed from this position in 1787, Wollstonecraft returned to London carrying the manuscript of her first novel, *Mary* (1788), which she took to bookseller Joseph Johnson, who had recently published her *Thoughts on the Education of Daughters* (1787). Johnson, a prominent dissenting publisher and a convivial and generous man, engaged to publish Wollstonecraft's novel, offered her steady literary work, and put her up at his own rooms until she could get on her feet. Under Johnson's employ, Wollstonecraft translated French and German texts, authored children's literature, edited collections, and became one of the most important contributors to his literary review, *The Analytical Review*, launched in 1788. In this capacity, Wollstonecraft penned hundreds of reviews, and evidence suggests that she took on editorial functions for Johnson as well.

With Johnson, Wollstonecraft grew rapidly as a thinker and a writer. When Edmund Burke published his antirevolutionary *Reflections on the Revolution in France* (1790), Wollstonecraft retorted with *A Vindication of the Rights of Men* (1790), one of the first and most vehement of the many rebuttals to Burke's reactionary text. Wollstonecraft's next major publication, *A Vindication of the Rights of Woman* (1792), the work for which she is best known, critiques the superficial education and constricted roles available to women, advocating an education equal to that of men as well as some access to careers and the professions. The work stands as a landmark in the history of feminism.

In 1792, the year of the September Massacres, Wollstonecraft moved to France to witness revolutionary events firsthand. She published *An Historical and Moral View of the Origins and Progress of the French Revolution; and the Effect It Has Produced in Europe* (1794) partly to explain the revolution's violent turn as a backlash from the tyranny of the French monarchy. In France Wollstonecraft met and lived with American businessman Gilbert Imlay, with whom she bore a daughter, Fanny. In 1795 Wollstonecraft followed Imlay to London, where his neglect and infidelity drove her to attempt suicide. On her recovery Imlay engaged her to travel to Scandinavia as his representative for some difficult and apparently shady business matters. Johnson published Wollstonecraft's letters to Imlay as *Letters Written during a Short Residence in Sweden, Norway, and Denmark* (1796).

Returning to London, Wollstonecraft hoped to reunite with Imlay, but instead found him living with another woman. She again attempted suicide, but this time when she recovered she reconciled herself to living without him. Resuming her writing and editing for Johnson, she soon became attracted to William Godwin, author of *An Enquiry concerning Political Justice and its Influence on Morals and Happiness* (1793). Wollstonecraft became pregnant, and she and Godwin married in March 1797. On August 30 Wollstonecraft gave birth to a daughter who, under her married name, Mary Shelley, eventually became the author of *Frankenstein* (1818). Probably because her physician failed to follow aseptic medical practices, post-partum complications escalated into systemic infection, and ten days later Wollstonecraft died of puerperal fever. Godwin published her unfinished novel *Maria; or, The Wrongs of Woman* along with his own *Memoirs of the Author of A Vindication of the Rights of Woman* in *Posthumous Works of the Author of A Vindication of the Rights of Woman* (1798). Rather than producing understanding and respect for this controversial writer as Godwin had hoped, the frank nature of both Wollstonecraft's novel and the memoir shocked the public so deeply that even many sympathizers dissociated themselves from Wollstonecraft's ideas, and her works failed to receive the attention they deserve until revived by feminist readers in the twentieth century.

■ ["On Artificial Taste"]

To the Editor of the Monthly Magazine[1]
SIR,

A TASTE for rural scenes, in the present state of society, appears to me to be very often an artificial sentiment, rather inspired by poetry and romances, than a real perception of the beauties of nature; but, as it is reckoned a proof of refined taste to praise the calm pleasure which the country affords, the theme is exhausted; yet, it may be made a question, whether this romantic kind of declamation has much effect on the conduct of those who leave, for a season, the crowded cities in which they were bred.

I have been led into these reflections by observing, when I have resided for any length of time in the country, how few people seem to contemplate nature with their own eyes. I have "brushed the dew away"[2] in the morning; but, pacing over the printless grass, I have wondered that, in such delightful situations, the sun was allowed to rise in solitary majesty, whilst my eyes alone hailed its beautifying beams. The webs of the evening have still been spread across the hedged path, unless some labouring man, trudging to work, disturbed the fairy structure; yet, in spite of this supineness, on joining the social circle, every tongue rang changes on the pleasures of the country.

Having frequently had occasion to make the same observation, in one of my solitary rambles, I was led to endeavour to trace the cause, and likewise to enquire why the poetry, written in the infancy of society, is most natural: which, strictly speaking (for natural is a very indefinite expression) is merely to say, that it is the transcript of immediate emotions, when fancy, awakened by the view of interesting objects, in all their native wildness and simplicity, was most actively at work. At such moments, sensibility quickly furnishes similes, and the sublimated spirits combine with happy facility —images, which spontaneously bursting on him, it is not necessary coldly to ransack the understanding or memory, till the laborious efforts of judgment exclude present sensations and damp the fire of enthusiasm.

---

[1] This essay first appeared in the *Monthly Magazine* (3 [April 1797]: 279–82). After Wollstonecraft's death, William Godwin (1756–1836) revised and then republished it under the title "On Poetry" in *Posthumous Works of the Author of A Vindication of the Rights of Woman*, 4 vols., ed. William Godwin (London: Joseph Johnson and G.G. & J. Robinson, 1798). The version published by Wollstonecraft herself, this one reflects somewhat more of characteristic Wollstonecraft concerns than the more frequently reprinted one published under Godwin's hand.

[2] Though the idea is commonplace, appearing in several early Celtic chronicles and in Milton and Shakespeare, Wollstonecraft may draw her quote from *Reflections on Death* (1763) by William Dodd, L.L.D (1729–1777), a clergyman, biblical commentator, and literary critic who had been convicted and executed for forgery. The book was popular enough to go through numerous editions and reprintings, including one the year before Wollstonecraft's essay.

The effusions of a vigorous mind will, nevertheless, ever inform us how far the faculties have been enlarged by thought, and stored with knowledge. The richness of the soil even appears on the surface; and the result of profound thinking often mixing with playful grace in the reveries of the poet, smoothly incorporates with the ebullitions of animal spirits, when the finely-fashioned nerve vibrates acutely with rapture, or when relaxed by soft melancholy, a pleasing languor prompts the long-drawn sigh, and feeds the slowly falling tear.

The poet, the man of strong feelings, only gives us a picture of his mind when he was actually alone, conversing with himself, and marking the impression which nature made on his own heart. If, during these sacred moments, the idea of some departed friend—some tender recollection, when the soul was most alive to tenderness, intrudes unawares into his mind, the sorrow which it produces is artlessly, but poetically, expressed; and who can avoid sympathizing?

Love of man leads to devotion. Grand and sublime images strike the imagination. God is seen in every floating cloud, and comes from the misty mountain to receive the noblest homage of an intelligent creature—praise. How solemn is the moment, when all affections and remembrances fade before the sublime admiration which the wisdom and goodness of God inspires, when he is worshipped in a temple not made with hands, and the world seems to contain only the mind that formed and contemplates it! These are not the weak responses of ceremonial devotion; nor to express them would the poet need another poet's aid. No: his heart burns within him, and he speaks the language of truth and nature, with resistless energy.

Inequalities, of course, are observable in his effusions; and a less vigorous imagination, with more taste, would have produced more elegance and uniformity. But as passages are softened or expunged, during the cooler moments of reflection, the understanding is gratified at the expense of those involuntary sensations which like the beauteous tints of an evening sky, are so evanescent that they melt into new forms before they can be analyzed. For, however eloquently we may boast of our reason, man must often be delighted he cannot tell why, or his blunt feelings are not made to relish the beauties which nature, poetry, or any of the imitative arts afford.

The imagery of the ancients appears naturally to have been borrowed from the surrounding objects, and their mythology. When a hero is to be transported from one place to another, across pathless wastes, is any vehicle so natural as one of the fleecy clouds, on which he has often gazed, scarcely conscious that he wished to make it his chariot? Again; when nature seems to present obstacles to his progress at almost every step, when the tangled forest and steep mountain stand as barriers, to pass over which, the mind longs for supernatural aid; and interposing deity, created by love or fear, who walks on the waves, and rules the storm, severely felt in the first attempts to cultivate a country, will receive from the impassioned fancy a local habitation and the name.

It would be a philosophical inquiry, and throw some light on the history of the human mind, to trace, as far as our information will allow us, the spontaneous feelings and ideas which have produced the images that now frequently appear unnatural, because they are remote, and disgusting, because they have been servilely copied by poets, whose habits of thinking and views of nature must have been different; for the understanding seldom disturbs the current of our present feelings without dissipating the gay clouds which fancy has been embracing; yet, it silently gives the colour to the whole tenor of them, and the reverie is over when the truth is grossly violated, or imagery introduced, selected from books, and not from local manners, or popular prejudices.

In a more advanced state of civilization, a poet is rather a creature of art than nature; the books that he peruses in his youth, become a hot-bed, in which artificial fruits are produced, beautiful to a common eye, though they want the true hue and flavour. His images do not flow from his imagination, but are servile copies; and, like the works of the painters who copy ancient statues when they draw men and women of their own times, we acknowledge that the features are fine, and the proportions just, but still they are men of stone: insipid figures, that never convey to the mind the idea of a portrait taken from the life, where the soul gives spirit and homogeneity to the whole form. The silken wings of fancy are shriveled by rules, and a desire of attaining elegance of diction occasions an attention to words, incompatible with sublime impassioned thoughts.

A boy of abilities, who has been taught the structure of verse at school, and been roused by emulation to compose rhymes whilst he was reading works of genius, may, by practice, produce pretty verses, and even become what is often termed an elegant poet; though his readers, without knowing well where the fault lies, do not find themselves warmly interested. In the productions of the poets who fasten on their affections, they see grosser defects, and the very images and allusions which shocked their taste; yet they do not appear as puerile or extrinsic in one as the other. Why? Because they did not appear so to the author.

It may sound paradoxical, after observing that those productions want vigour that are the work of imitation, in which the understanding violently directed, if not extinguished, the blaze of fancy, to assert, that though genius be allowed to be only another word for a strong imagination, the first observers of nature exercised their judgment much more than their imitators. But they exercised it to discriminate things, whilst their followers were busy borrowing sentiments and arranging words.

Boys who have received a classical education load their memory with words, and the correspondent ideas are, perhaps, never distinctly comprehended. As a proof of this assertion I must mention as a fact, that I have known many young people who could write tolerably smooth verses, and string epithets prettily together, when their prose themes showed the barrenness of their minds; or, more justly speaking, how superficial the cultivation must have been, which their understanding had received.

Dr. Johnson, I know, has taken some pains to prove, that a strong mind, accidentally led to some particular study in which it excels, is a genius.[3] Not to stop to investigate the causes which produced this happy strength of mind, it is sufficient to remark, that the world has agreed to denominate those men of genius, who have pursued a particular art or science, after the bent of nature has been displayed in obstinate perseverance or fond attachment to a favourite study. Dr. Johnson, in fact, appears sometimes to be of the same opinion; especially when he observes "that Thomson looked on nature with the eye which she only gives to a poet."

But though it should be allowed that books conned at school may lead some youths to write poetry, I fear they will never be the poets who charm our cares to sleep, or extort admiration. They may diffuse taste, and polish the language, but I am apt to conclude that they will seldom have the energy to rouse the passions which amend the heart.

And, to return to the first object of discussion, the reason why most people are more interested by a scene described by a poet than by a view of nature, probably arises from the want of a lively imagination. The poet contrasts the prospect, and selecting the most picturesque parts in his camera, the judgment is directed, and the whole attention of the languid faculty turned towards the objects which excited the most forcible emotions in the poet's heart, firing his imagination; the reader consequently feels the enlivened description, though he was not able to receive a first impression from the operations of his own mind.

Besides, it may be farther observed, that uncultivated minds are only to be moved by forcible representations. To rouse the thoughtless, objects must be contrasted, calculated to excite tumultuous emotions. The unsubstantial picturesque forms which a contemplative man gazes on, and often follows with ardour till mocked by a glimpse of unattainable excellence, appear to them the light vapours of a dreaming enthusiast, who gives up the substance for the shadow. It is not within that they seek amusement—their eyes are rarely turned back on themselves; of course, their emotions, though sometimes fervid, are always transient, and the nicer perceptions which distinguish the man of taste are not felt, or make such a slight impression as scarcely to excite any pleasurable sensations. Is it surprising, then, that fine scenery is often overlooked by those who yet may be delighted by the same imagery concentrated and contrasted by the poet? But even this numerous class is exceeded by witlings, who, anxious to appear to have wit and taste, do not allow their understandings, or feelings, any liberty; for instead of cultivating their faculties, and reflecting on their operations, they are busy collecting prejudices, and are pre-determined to admire what the suffrage of time announces excellent; not to store up a fund of amusement for themselves, but to enable them to talk.

---

3   Altered from Samuel Johnson's "Life of [Abraham] Cowley" in *Works of the English Poets* (1779). The quote on Thomson below is from the same series, "Life of [James] Thomson."

These hints will assist the reader to trace some of the causes why the beauties of nature are not forcibly felt, when civilization and its canker-worm, luxury, have made considerable advances. Those calm emotions are not sufficiently lively to serve as a relaxation to the voluptuary, or even for the moderate pursuers of artificial pleasures. In the present state of society, the understanding must bring back the feelings to nature, or the sensibility must have attained such strength, as rather to be sharpened than destroyed by the strong exercise of passions.

That the most valuable things are liable to the greatest perversion, is, however, a trite as true. For the same sensibility, or quickness of senses, which makes a man relish the charms of nature, when sensation, rather than reason, imparts delight, frequently makes a libertine of him, by leading him to prefer the tumult of love, a little refined by sentiment, to the calm pleasure of affectionate friendship, in whose sober satisfactions reason, mixing her tranquilizing convictions, whispers that content, not happiness, is the reward, or consequence, of virtue in this world.

W.Q.[4]

■ Selected Reviews from the *Analytical Review*[5]

ART. XIII. EMMELINE, *the Orphan of the Castle*. By Charlotte Smith.[6]

[...]

FEW of the numerous productions termed novels, claim any attention; and while we distinguish this one, we cannot help lamenting that it has the same tendency as the generality, whose preposterous sentiments our young females imbibe with such avidity. Vanity thus fostered, takes deep root in the forming mind, and affectation banishes natural graces, or at least obscures them. We do not mean to confound affectation and vice, or allude

---

[4]   As in this example, literary and general interest magazines that published letters and unsolicited essays usually did so signed with either initials or pseudonyms. See Hays's article in the *Monthly Magazine* (Chapter 7) and Martineau's contributions to the *Monthly Repository* (Chapter 17).

[5]   Like most periodical reviews, Wollstonecraft's reviews were published anonymously, signed, if at all, with letters that only sometimes refer to parts of her name. With a few emendations, the canon of Wollstonecraft's reviews has been established by Janet Todd and Marilyn Butler in *The Works of Mary Wollstonecraft* Vol. 5 (London: William Pickering, 1989). An overview of identification controversies can be found in their introduction with additional comments in Waters, *British Women Writers and the Profession of Literary Criticism, 1789–1832.*

[6]   *AR* 1 (July 1788): 327–33. *The Analytical Review* was founded with the plan "to give such an account of new publications, as may enable the reader to judge of them for himself." The review would accomplish this aim by providing readers with "accounts [i.e., summaries] and extracts," avoiding pronouncements of judgment (Thomas Christie, editor, "To the Public," *AR* 1 [1788]: i. See Introduction). Reviews therefore often included several pages of direct extract, as was the case with the opening of this review.

to those pernicious writings that obviously vitiate the heart, while they lead the understanding astray. But we must observe, that the false expectations these wild scenes excite, tend to debauch the mind, and throw an insipid kind of uniformity over the moderate and rational prospects of life, consequently *adventures* are fought for and created, when duties are neglected, and content despised.[7]

We will venture to ask any young girl if Lady Adelina's theatrical contrition did not catch her attention, while Mrs. Stafford's rational resignation escaped her notice? Lady Adelina is indeed a character as absurd as dangerous. Despair is not repentance, nor is contrition of any use when it does not serve to strengthen resolutions of amendment. The being who indulges useless sorrow, instead of fulfilling the duties of life, may claim our pity, but should never excite admiration; for in such characters there is no true greatness of soul, or just sentiments of religion; indeed this kind of sorrow is rather the offspring of romantic notions and false refinement, than of sensibility and a nice sense of duty. Mrs. Stafford, when disappointed in her husband, turned to her children. We mention this character because it deserves praise.

We have not observed many touches of nature in the delineation of the passions, except the emotions which the descriptions of romantic views gave rise to; in them the poetical talents of the author appear, as well as in some sonnets interspersed in the work. Indeed some of the descriptions are so interesting and beautiful that we would give a specimen, if they could be separated from the woven web without injuring them, and if we had not already exceeded the bounds prescribed. M.

ART. XLIX. *Letters on the Works and Character of J.J. Rousseau. To which are added, a Letter from the Countess Alexandre de Vassy, to the Baroness de Stael, with the Baroness's Answer, and an Account of the last Moments of Rousseau.* By Mademoiselle Necker, Baroness de Stael [*sic*].[8]

THESE remarks on Rousseau, consist of warm panegyrics, and answers to a few well known objections. The author in an easy genteel style, describes the effect his various writings produced on her own mind; dwelling particularly on Eloisa, Emilius, and the private character of their parent, deduced from his confessions and accidental information.[9] These observations are written with timid caution, to steer clear of censure, while contending for a

---

[7] Here and in several other locations Wollstonecraft refers to views about the effects of novels popularized by Samuel Johnson (see Introduction). For other views, see Smith's discussion in her preface to *Letters of a Solitary Wanderer* (Chapter 3) and Hays's comments in each of her entries (Chapter 7).

[8] *AR* 4 (July 1789): 360–2.

[9] Eloisa and Emilius appear in, respectively, Rousseau's *Julie, ou la nouvelle Héloïse* (1761) and *Emilius and Sophia; or, The Solitaries*, the 1763 English translation of his *Emile, ou de l'éducation* (1762).

literary wreath, and sometimes so superficial, that indiscriminate admiration appears like the blind homage of ignorance to a great name.

Rousseau's literary station has long been settled by time on a firm basis; his genius spreads flowers over the most barren tract, yet his profound sagacity and paradoxical caprice, his fascinating eloquence and specious errors, may be seen by their own light; a lamp is an officious twinkler when the sun has diffused his beams […].

The praises lavished, throughout, on M. Necker, are so extravagant, that they appear to be dictated rather by the head than the heart; nay, they are indelicate, when we consider that they probably met his eye before their publication; nor can we pay great deference to the Baroness's judgment after reading her opinion of her father, written in the bombast language of pride, instead of appearing to be the simple effusion of gratitude or tenderness […]. M.

ART. XXI. *Ethelinde, or the Recluse of the Lake.* By Charlotte Smith.[10]

THE ingenious Mrs. Smith very quickly presents her fair countrywomen with another novel, and the pleasure her last must have afforded will naturally lead them to peruse it with avidity; yet we cannot help lamenting, that this elegant writer neglects her talent for poetry, though we perceive in her novel that she looks at nature with a poet's eye. The same quick sensibility which enabled her to produce such apt similies in her sonnets, led her to catch all those alluring charms of nature, which form such enchanting back grounds to the historical part of the pictures she displays in these volumes, and gives them sentiment and interest.

Her picturesque views of the Lake claim the warmest praise; indeed, all her landscapes are drawn by the pencil of taste, that can feel and describe the evanescent graces, which are so profusely scattered around us, and escape the notice of common, blunt organs, or only affect them, when seen through the medium of lively descriptions. We may likewise emphatically add, that Mrs. S. writes like a gentlewoman: if she introduce ladies of quality, they are transcribed from life, and not the sickly offspring of a distempered imagination, that looks up with awe to the sounding distinctions of rank, and the gay delights which riches afford. Her delineations of local manners are equally skilful. The characters of lady Newenden, Miss Newenden, captain Chesterville, Tom Davenant, &c. &c. are forcibly represented in many amusing scenes; but her ideal forms have not the same fair proportion. She faithfully follows nature as far as she can see, and brings forward each latent grace, or tint, which discriminates the characters. There is a charming simplicity in some of her groups, which made us recollect Gainsborough's

---

10   *AR* 5 (December 1789): 484–6.

pictures;[11] but she does not always keep within her sphere: when she attempts to combine without a model, she is lost; and theatrical attitudes are exhibited instead of impassioned expressions. To say the truth, there is very little passion in the tale; and the attention of the reader is called to slight circumstances, and seldom engrossed by the main features: ingenious, forcible hints, are not thrown out to engage the imagination to finish the sketch, and give those interesting touches which leave a lasting impression on the mind. We were rather amused than interested by the story: every thing is described with that minute exactness, which distinguishes a mind more inclined to observe the various shades of manners than the workings of passion, or the inconsistencies of human nature.

We shall not attempt to analyze this complicated tale. It has the faults and beauties so obvious in Emmeline, and the two heroines might be taken for twin sisters. The story wants a grand point of interest; and innumerable misfortunes are so entangled together, that sympathy must be worn out, and give place to sheer curiosity, long before the close of the fifth volume. Many of the incidents are very novel-like, or rather introduced for effect;—mere stage tricks. The heroine is too often sick, and rather inspires love than respect. Though we are told, in express words, that she is all perfection—nature's masterpiece—she appears a frail woman, with none of those supernatural charms, which an impassioned fancy spreads round a deified mortal, as a lambent flame is represented encircling the heads of men become saints. Besides, we cannot help wishing that Mrs. S. had considered how many females might probably read her pleasing production, whose minds are in a ductile state; she would not then have cherished their delicacy, or, more properly speaking, weakness, by making her heroine so very beautiful, and so attentive to preserve her personal charms, even when grief, beauty's cankerworm, was at work […].

ART. IV. *Seconde Partie des Confessions de* J. J. Rousseau. **Second Part of the Confessions of J. J. Rousseau.**[12]

ROUSSEAU'S fate is the fate of a genius—he is either enthusiastically admired, or sneeringly allowed to have some force of diction, by those who fear to have their taste called in question, yet have not an heart formed to beat in unison with his virtuous energetic sentiments. To speak of the literary character of a man, whose works have long since received the sanction of fame, would be impertinent in a review, that rather wishes to enable the public

---

[11]   Thomas Gainsborough (1727–1788) was one of England's most respected portrait painters. His work introduced a more Romantic style of painting through emphasis on naturalistic settings and direct observation of nature.

[12]   *AR* 6 (April 1790): 385–91.

to form its own opinion of a production, than, in a dictatorial style, to say, which is good or bad [...].[13]

It is true the former volumes of the confessions have been treated with great contempt, and with that supercilious compassion, that affectation of candour and reason with which good sort of people are often puffed up, who have a little smattering of learning, and dabble in literature more through vanity than taste. Reading the effusions of a warm heart, cold critics have termed them the ravings of a madman, and the honest man has been pitied and ridiculed in the same breath [...]. However, those who admire Rousseau as a writer, respect his integrity, and love the foundation of his singular character, will not be extreme to mark the shades which throw it forward;—in short, without screening himself behind the pronoun WE, the reviewer's *phalanx*, the writer of this article will venture to say, that he should never expect to see that man do a generous action, who could ridicule Rousseau's interesting account of his feelings and reveries—who could, in all the pride of wisdom, falsely so called, despise such a heart when naked before him.[14]

Without considering whether Rousseau was right or wrong, in thus exposing his weaknesses, and shewing himself just as he was, with all his imperfections on his head, to his frail fellow-creatures, it is only necessary to observe, that a description of what has actually passed in a human mind must ever be useful; yet, men who have not the power of concentering seeming contradictions, will rudely laugh at inconsistencies as if they were absurdities; but their laugh is the crackling of thorns, the empty noise of insensible ignorance. M.

ART. LVII. *Julia, a Novel: interspersed with some poetical Pieces*. By Helen Maria Williams.[15]

MISS W. is already known to the literary world as a poet, and though it may require more knowledge of the human heart, and comprehensive views of life, to write a good novel than to tell a pretty story in verse, or write a little plaintive lay—yet, from her, calm domestic scenes were to be expected—and in this novel they abound. Her landscapes are highly finished in water colours, and her characters delineated with a degree of truth and

---

13 Wollstonecraft occasionally calls attention to her deviations from the *Analytical* plan to "enable the reader to judge [...] for himself."

14 Reviews were presumed to reflect the homogenous editorial position of the publication as a whole, and the plural pronoun reinforced this perspective. Wollstonecraft's unusual departure from custom declares her opinion to be personal rather than corporate.

15 *AR* 7 (May 1790): 97–100. Poet, translator, and travel writer, Williams (1761–1827), a friend of Wollstonecraft, spent several years living in France during the height of the revolutionary period. Her sympathetic accounts exerted a powerful influence on British opinion regarding the tumultuous events.

proportion, which instantly insinuates that they were drawn from nature; particularly when filial affection is exhibited, for then there is a degree of winning tenderness glowing in the picture, that silently reaches the heart. Indeed, there is a simplicity and ease reigning throughout, which renders many detached passages very interesting; yet, considered as a whole, the tale is not sufficiently dramatic to excite lively sympathy or interest; nor complex enough to rouse a kind of restless curiosity as a substitute. Miss W. is, probably, a warm admirer of Mrs. Smith's novels; but if, in descriptions of nature, and lively characteric [*sic*] conversations, she falls far short of her model, the reader of taste will never be disgusted with theatrical attitudes, artificial feelings, or a display of studied unimpassioned false grace. This lady seems to be an exception to Pope's rule, 'that every woman is at heart a rake'[16]—and that two passions divide the sex—love of pleasure and sway; for no scenes of dissipation are here sketched by the dancing spirits of an intoxicated imagination; nor dresses described with the earnest minuteness of vanity. In short, her mind does not seem to be *debauched*, if we may be allowed the expression, by reading novels; but every sentiment is uttered in an original way, which proves that it comes directly from her heart with the artless energy of feeling, that rather wishes to be understood than admired. Without any acquaintance with Miss W. only from the perusal of this production, we should venture to affirm, that sound principles animate her conduct, and that the sentiments they dictate are the pillars instead of being the fanciful ornaments of her character.

There is such feminine sweetness in her style and observations—such modesty and indulgence in her satire—such genuine unaffected piety in her effusions and remarks, that we warmly recommend her novel to our young female readers, who will here meet with refinement of sentiment, without a very great alloy of romantic notions:—if the conclusion, that love is not to be conquered by reason, had been omitted, this would be an unexceptionable book for young people […].

But a reader, with the least discernment, must soon perceive that Julia's principles are so fixed that nothing can tempt her to act wrong; and as she appears like a rock, against which the waves vainly beat, no anxiety will be felt for her safety:—she is viewed with respect, and left very tranquilly to quiet her feelings, because it cannot be called a contest. A good tragedy or novel, if the criterion be the effect which it has on the reader, is not always the most moral work, for it is not the reveries of sentiment, but the struggles of passion—of those *human passions*, that too frequently cloud the reason, and lead *mortals* into dangerous errors, if not into absolute guilt, which raise the most lively emotions, and leave the most lasting

---

[16] Alexander Pope, *Of The Characters of Women: An Epistle To A Lady* (Martha Blount) (1735) 216.

impression on the memory; an impression rather made by the heart than the understanding; for our affections are not quite so voluntary as the suffrage of reason […].

Art. xliii. *Euphemia.* By Mrs. Charlotte Lennox.[17]

As a great number of pernicious and frivolous novels are daily published, which only serve to heat and corrupt the minds of young women, and plunge them (by co-operating with their amusements) into that continual dissipation of thought which renders all serious employment irksome, we open a novel with a certain degree of pleasure, when a respectable name appears in the title-page. This was the case with the present work; but as we advanced, so many cold romantic flights struck us in the main story, and still more in the episodes, that we could not avoid ranking it with those novels, which, perhaps, tend to lead the female mind further astray from nature and common sense, than even the tales of chivalry to which Mrs. L. has allowed no quarter.[18] Her notions of female delicacy and reserve are carried as far as any sentimental French writer ever pushed them; and though this prudery might arise from a different cause, yet it may be equally baneful in its effects, and banish true frankness and delicacy of mind, to make room for that false enervating refinement, which eradicates not only simplicity, but all dignity of character. We will appeal to any of our readers whether they would not think woman very affected, or *ridiculously* squeamish, who could promise to give her hand to her lover one moment, and the next scruple to admit him to a tête-à-tête breakfast. But if the ladies are to be cold and *indisposed to the marriage state*, the gentlemen are sufficiently ardent; weep, kneel and faint in the most impassioned manner. With respect to Mr. Harley, who is termed a hero for acting as any man would have done, that had the least spark of honour in his soul, to say nothing of religion, we think no knight of ancient days ever cherished a more *refined* passion, or more accidentally gained his bride. If the ladies, for such artificial beings must not be familiarly called women, are something like the cherubim under the organ-loft, soft, simple, and good, the gentlemen, and more particularly the poor husbands, are painted in stronger colours, and several of them appear to be drawn from the life by a faithful feminine pencil: the maternal affection and solicitude, which takes place of every other, is much of the same cast, blind and weak; but the virtue of Mrs. Freeman towers above her sex—Lucretia was a washerwoman to her! […]. T.

---

[17]   *AR* 8 (October 1790): 222–4.
[18]   Wollstonecraft refers to Lennox's *Female Quixote* (1752).

Art. xvi. *Letters written in France, in the Summer, 1790, to a Friend in England; containing various Anecdotes relative to the French Revolution; and Memoirs of Mons. and Madame Du F——* . **By Helen Maria Williams.**[19]

Women have been allowed to possess, by a kind of prescription, the knack of epistolary writing; the talent of chatting on paper in that easy immethodical manner, which render letters dear to friends, and amusing to strangers. Who that has read Madame Sevigne's and Pope's letters, with an unprejudiced eye, can avoid giving the preference to the artless elegance of the former; interested by the eloquence of her heart, and the unstudied sallies of her imagination; whilst the florid periods of the latter appear, like state robes, grand and cumbersome, and his tenderness vapid vanity.[20]

The interesting unaffected letters which this pleasing writer has now presented to the public, revived these reflections, and gave new force to them, at the same time that they confirmed the very favourable opinion we have entertained of the goodness of the writer's heart.

Her reflections on the French Revolution are truly feminine, and such an air of sincerity runs through the descriptive part of her letters, as leads us to hope that they may tend to remove from some polite circles, a *few* of the childish prejudices that have the *insignia* of raw-head and bloody-bones to sink them deeper in the vacant mind […].

As the destruction of the Bastille was an event that affected every heart—even hearts not accustomed to the melting mood, it was natural to suppose that it would particularly touch a tender one—and every page of Miss W.'s book tells us, in an unequivocal tone, that her's is true to every soft emotion […]. T.

Art. xxiv. *Stanzas of Woe, addressed from the Heart on a Bed of Illness, to Levi Eames, Esq. late mayor of the City of Bristol.* **By Ann Yearsley, a Milk-woman of Clifton, near Bristol.**[21]

It has been the fate of several poets, whom *good-luck* has pushed forward, to see their blooming honours fade, and to find by painful experience, that premature fame, though sweet to the taste, becomes bitter in digestion. We

---

[19]   *AR* 8 (December 1790): 431–5.

[20]   Collected in 1726, translated as *Letters of Madame de Rabutin Chantal, marchioness de Sévigné, to the Comtess of Grignan Her Daughter* in 1727, and enjoyed by great writers into the twentieth century, the letters of Mme. de Sévigné (1626–1696) place her among the most significant letter writers of the seventeenth and eighteenth centuries.

[21]   *AR* 9 (April 1791): 447–8. Under the patronage of Hannah More (1745–1833), Yearsley (1753–1806) enjoyed a period of celebrity as a working-class literary phenomenon. More herself was a versatile writer, authoring poetry, drama, novels, and non-fiction prose, but it was her evangelical tracts that made her one of the most financially successful woman authors of the Romantic period.

scruple not to rank Mrs. Y. among the number; for the praise which she has received has been, in our opinion, much warmer than she ever merited. But the pleasure of exalting a wonder, till puffed up by the breath of popular applause, it grows most wonderful, intoxicates the public of the day, and the ephemeral buzz is mistaken for the awful sanction which time gives to the general voice. Mrs. Y. certainly has abilities; but instead of 'native wood-notes wild,' stale allusions obscure her poems, in which, however, we discover an independent mind and feeling heart […].

A second poem is addressed to William Cromartie Yearsley, on his becoming a pupil to Mr. ***. We now expected to have heard the simple effusions of maternal fondness; but the trite illustrations from classical lore, which we have already noticed, met our view in every page; and the sense is rendered still more intricate by that confusion of thought, which shews struggling energy not sufficiently strong to cultivate itself, and give a form to a chaotic mass […]. M.

ART. LXIII. *A Simple Story.* By Mrs. Inchbald.[22]

THE plan of this novel is truly dramatic, for the rising interest is not broken, or even interrupted, by any episode, nor is the attention so divided, by a constellation of splendid characters, as to make the reader at a loss to say which is the hero of the tale.

Mrs. I. had evidently a very useful moral in view, namely to show the advantage of a good education; but it is to be lamented that she did not, for the benefit of her young readers, inforce it by contrasting the characters of the mother and daughter, whose history must warmly interest them. It were to be wished, in fact, in order to insinuate a useful moral into thoughtless unprincipled minds, that the faults of the vain, giddy miss Milner had not been softened, or rather gracefully withdrawn from notice by the glare of such splendid, yet fallacious virtues, as flow from sensibility. And to have rendered the contrast more useful still, her daughter should have possessed greater dignity of mind. Educated in adversity she should have learned (to prove that a cultivated mind is a real advantage) how to bear, nay, rise above her misfortunes, instead of suffering her health to be undermined by the trials of her patience, which ought to have strengthened her understanding. Why do all female writers, even when they display their abilities, always give a sanction to the libertine reveries of men? Why do they poison the minds of their own sex, by strengthening a male prejudice that makes women systematically weak? We alluded to the absurd fashion that prevails of making the heroine of a novel boast of a delicate constitution; and the still more ridiculous and deleterious custom of spinning the most picturesque scenes out of fevers, swoons, and tears.

---

22   *AR* 10 (May 1791): 101–3.

The characters in the Simple Story are marked with a discriminating out-line, and little individual traits are skilfully brought forward, that produce some natural and amusing scenes. Lively conversations abound, and they are, in general, written with the spirited vivacity and the feminine ease that characterizes the conversation of an agreeable well-bred woman. The author has even the art to render dialogues interesting that appear to have only the evanescent spirit, which mostly evaporates in description, to rec-ommend them […].

ART. VII. *Celestina. A Novel.* By Charlotte Smith.[23]

THIS ingenious writer's invention appears to be inexhaustible; yet we are sorry to observe that it is still fettered by her respect for some popular mod-ern novels. For in the easy elegant volumes before us, she too frequently, and not very happily, copies, we can scarcely say imitates, some of the dis-tressing encounters and ludicrous embarrassments, which in Evelina, &c. lose their effect by breaking the interest.

As a whole, Mrs. S.'s amusing production is certainly very defective and unnatural; but many lucid parts are scattered with negligent grace, and amidst the entanglement of wearisome episodes, interesting scenes, and prospects, seen with a poetic eye, start to relieve the reader, who would turn, knowing something of the human heart, with disgust from the romantic adventures, and artificial passions, that novel reading has suggested to the author. It were indeed to be wished, that with Mrs. S.'s abilities, she had sufficient courage to think for herself, and not view life through the medium of books: some-times, it is true, she has given us portraits forcibly sketched from nature: we shall only particularize Mr. and Mrs. Elphinstone. The extracts that we mean to give, display the easy flow of her style, and render praise super-fluous; and after selecting them, it is almost impertinent to add, that there is a degree of sentiment in some of her delicate tints, that steals on the heart, and made us *feel* the exquisite taste of the mind that guided the pencil […]. M.

ART. IX. *Earl Goodwin, an Historical Play.* By Ann Yearsley, Milkwoman of Clifton, near Bristol.[24]

MRS. YEARSLEY, taking Shakspeare for her model, has copied like most copyists, and despising method, supposed she imitated the wild notes of nature's darling child. But vast, in life and poetry, is the gulph that sep-arates the negligent disorderly parts, produced by indolent weakness, from the bold flights of genius […].

---

23   *AR* 10 (August 1791): 409–15.
24   *AR* 11 (December 1791): 427–8.

The tragedy before us is equally defective in the plot and characters; yet it contains some interesting scenes, and many sentiments happily conceived and vigorously expressed […].T.

ART. XXXVII. *Anna St. Ives. A Novel.* By Thomas Holcroft[25]

THIS novel appears to be written as a vehicle to convey what are called democratical sentiments. Be that as it may, it contains many interesting scenes, which forcibly illustrate what the author evidently wished to inculcate. Young people, it is true, might catch from the highly-wrought pictures a spice of romance, and even affectation, and attempt to stride on *stilts* before they had learned to walk steadily; yet, truth and many just opinions are so strongly recommended, that what they must read with interest, will not fail to leave some seeds of thought in their minds.

The story is not entangled with episodes, yet, simple as it is, it carries the reader along, and makes him patiently swallow not a few improbabilities […].

Some of the characters are rather over-charged, but the *moral* is assuredly a good one. It is calculated to strengthen despairing virtue, to give fresh energy to the cause of humanity, to repress the pride and insolence of birth, and to shew that true nobility which can alone proceed from the head and the heart, claims genius and virtue for its armorial bearings, and possessed of these, despises all the foppery of either ancient of modern heraldry […]. M.

ART. XXX. *Desmond. A Novel.* By Charlotte Smith.[26]

MRS. SMITH quickly presents the public with another novel, written with her usual flow of language and happy discrimination of manners. The subordinate characters are sketched with that peculiar dexterity which shoots folly as it flies; and the tale, not encumbered with episodes, is a more interesting, as well as a more finished production than any of her former ones.

The hero, who leaves England to avoid the society of an amiable woman, married unhappily, naturally introduces the French Revolution, and the present state of France, into his correspondence; and in it the cause of freedom is defended with warmth, whilst shrewd satire and acute observations back the imbodied arguments […].

The letters, written with great ease, exhibit, as do all Mrs. S.'s productions, more knowledge of the world than of the human heart; yet, they contain many just remarks pointedly expressed, and some picturesque views of nature, with characteristic figures, to give life to the landscapes […]. M.

---

25   *AR* 13 (May 1792): 72–6.
26   *AR* 13 (August 1792): 428–35.

ART. XXIV. *Angelina. A Novel. In a Series of Letters.* **By Mrs. Mary Robinson.**[27]

OUR readers, we doubt not, will be pleased to see, that we are indebted for Angelina to the elegant pen of Mrs. R. To the merit of the author, as a poet and a novelist, we have already, on several occasions, born our testimony; and we conceive that the production, which is now before us, will in no respect detract from her well-earned reputation. Unwilling by anticipation to diminish the pleasure which our readers may receive from the perusal of these volumes, we forbear to enter on the subject of the piece. We shall only observe, that it's [*sic*] principal object is to expose the folly and the iniquity of those parents who attempt to compel the inclinations of their children into whatever conjugal connections their mercenary spirit may choose to prescribe, and to hold forth to just detestation the cruelty of those, who scruple not to barter a daughter's happiness, perhaps through life, for a founding title or a glittering coronet. The characters in the piece are in general naturally pourtrayed and distinctly marked [...]. In the portrait of Angelina we behold an assemblage of almost every excellence which can adorn the female mind, beaming mildly through clouds of affliction and melancholy. Her situation will interest the feelings of the reader, and the disclosure of her history and character forms an agreeable and important scene in the catastrophe. The sentiments contained in these volumes are just, animated and rational. They breathe a spirit of independence, and a dignified superiority to whatever is unessential to the true respectability and genuine excellence of human beings. The story, though it will not greatly rouse or deeply agitate, is yet sufficiently interesting to excite and prolong the attention of the reader; and the phraseology is at once correct and appropriate [...].

ART. X. *Nature and Art.* **By Mrs. Inchbald.**[28]

THE present novel, though written with a more philosophical spirit than the simple story, has not, on that very account, perhaps, an equally lively interest to keep the attention awake. The reason may be easily traced, without derogating from the abilities of the author. Virtuous prejudices produce the most violent passions; and, consequently, are the powerful engines to be employed in depicting the adventures, that become interesting in proportion as they exhibit the conflicts of feeling and duty, truly or falsely estimated.

This work abounds with judicious satirical sallies, and with those artless strokes which go directly to the heart. In fact, were we to characterize Mrs. I.'s peculiar talent, we should unhesitatingly say *naïveté*. The story of Hannah Primrose we found particularly affecting: the catastrophe giving point to a benevolent system of morality. The transitions, however, from one

---

[27]   *AR* 23 (February 1796): 293–4.
[28]   *AR* 23 (May 1796): 511–14.

period of the history to another, are too abrupt; for the incidents, not being shaded into each other, sometimes appear improbable. This we think is the principal defect of the work on the whole. The chapters conclude with a degree of laboured conciseness, which seems to disconnect them, or rather snaps the thread of the fiction. The reader jumps with reluctance over eighteen years; and is forced to reason about the fate of the favourite hero, which was before a matter of feeling.

The making a young modest woman, with some powers of mind, acknowledge herself the mother of a child that she humanely fostered, in the presence of the man she loved, is also highly improbable, not to say unnatural.

Some of the conversations are written with dramatic spirit […]. M.

ART. VI. *Camilla: or, A Picture of Youth.* By the Author of Evelina and Cecilia.[29]

THE celebrity which miss Burney has so deservedly acquired by her two former novels, naturally roused the expectation of the public for the promised production of madame d'Arblay [*sic*].

A mind like hers could not be supposed to stand still, and new combinations of character are continually ripening to court the fickle.

As a whole, we are in justice bound to say, that we think it inferiour to the first fruits of her talents, though we boldly assert, that Camilla contains parts superiour to anything she has yet produced.

In her former works dramatical exhibitions of manners of the comic cast certainly excel the displays of passion; and the remark may with still more propriety be applied to the volumes before us.

The incidents, which are to mark out the errours of youth, are frequently only perplexities, forcibly brought forward merely to be disentangled; yet, there are many amusing, and some interesting incidents, though they have not a plot of sufficient importance to bind them together.

The illustrating sentiments are often excellent, and expressed with great delicacy, evincing the sagacity and rectitude of the author's mind, reflecting equal credit on her heart and understanding. In the style, it is true, there are some indications of haste; but it would be almost invidious to point them out, when so large a proportion is written so well […]. M.

ART. XXII. *The Italian, or the Confessional of the Black Penitents. A Romance.* By Ann Radcliffe.[30]

MRS. Radcliffe's uncommon talent for exhibiting, with the picturesque touches of genius, the vague and horrid shapes which imagination bodies

---

[29]   *AR* 24 (August 1796): 142–8. The author is Fanny Burney, by this time Mme. d'Arblay.
[30]   *AR* 25 (May 1797): 516–20.

forth, has rendered her so deservedly celebrated, that any new work of hers must be peculiarly dear to curiosity and taste. Her mode, it is true, of accounting in a natural manner for supernatural appearances, now the secret has gotten vent, lessens the effect, and the interest of the story is interrupted by the reader's attention to guard against the delusions of the imagination, which he knows to be glistening bubbles, blown up in air, only to evaporate more conspicuously; leaving the aching sight searching after the splendid nothing.

The confession, the object of curiosity, is of the same kind, but not so terrible, as one in the Adventures of a Guinea.[31] It is not, however, as a whole, but for particular parts, that this admirable production demands the warmest praise.

The first scenes in which Schedoni, the italian, is introduced, are boldly drawn; and throughout, the passions of fear, anger, pride, and ambition, with their numerous train, are more happily delineated, than those of love, grief, or despair.

The picturesque views of the varying charms of nature, drawn by an animated imagination, are less diffuse than in the former productions of this writer; and the reflections, which oftener occur, give strong proofs likewise of an improving judgment. The nature of the story obliges us to digest improbabilities, and continually to recollect that it is a romance, not a novel, we are reading; especially as the restless curiosity it excites is too often excited by something like stage trick.—We are made to wonder, only to wonder; but the spell, by which we are led, again and again, round the same magic circle, is the spell of genius. Pictures and scenes are conjured up with happy exuberance; and reason with delight resigns the reins to fancy, till forced to wipe her eyes and recollect, with a sigh, that it is but a dream […]. M.

Art. xxiv. *Marchmont: A Novel.* By Charlotte Smith.[32]

[…] The present novel is certainly spun out in the beginning, and wound up too hastily at the conclusion; still the design of showing the misery, which unprincipled men of the law may bring on the innocent, is well imagined. The family pride of the Marchmonts is made to assume the most amiable form, and the victim of it, the hero of the tale, is a very interesting example of filial piety. The story is founded on the difficulties a young man of family has to encounter in consequence of the thoughtless extravagance of his father, and the rapacity of the men to whom he applied for assistance.

---

31 *Chrysal; or, The Adventures of a Guinea* (1760–1765) by Charles Johnstone (1719–1800) professed to record the travels of a golden guinea while offering a satirical glimpse into the sordid lives of Johnstone's fictional and actual contemporaries.

32 *AR* 25 (May 1797): 523.

In the description of the mansion house we find Mrs. Smith alive to the scene she is pourtraying; and observe in her landscapes the delicate strokes of a pencil, from which we have frequently received pleasure.

ART. xxv. *Hubert de Sevrac, a Romance of the eighteenth century.* By Mary Robinson.[33]

MRS. Robinson writes so rapidly, that she scarcely gives herself time to digest her story into a plot, or to allow those incidents gradually to grow out of it, which are the fruit of matured invention. She certainly possesses considerable abilities; but she seems to have fallen into an errour, common to people of lively fancy, and to think herself so happily gifted by nature, that her first thoughts will answer her purpose. The consequence is obvious; her sentences are often confused, entangled with superfluous words, half-expressed sentiments, and false ornaments.

In writing the present romance Mrs. Radcliffe appears to be her model; and she deserves to rank as one of her most successful imitators: still the characters are so imperfectly sketched, the incidents so unconnected, the changes of scene so frequent, that interest is seldom excited, and curiosity flags.

After this account we shall not be expected to give the outlines of such an imperfect tale; the object of it is apparently benevolent, but it has no centre out of which the moral, that the vices of the rich produce the crimes of the poor, could naturally emanate.

It is but just, however, to observe, before dismissing the article, that some of the descriptions are evidently sketched by a poet, and irradiations of fancy flash through the surrounding perplexity, sufficient to persuade us, that she could write better, were she once convinced, that the writing of a good book is no easy task. M.

---

[33]   *AR* 25 (May 1797): 523.

Mary Hays (1760–1843)

Mary Hays's wide-ranging literary career included writing on feminism, philosophy, biography, education, social and political reform, fiction, history, and literary criticism. Born to a middle-class family in the Southwark suburb of London, Hays received the usual superficial education for women of her class. In her teens she became engaged to religious dissenter John Eccles, and the letters they exchanged show the influence of late eighteenth century ideals of sensibility, in which sympathy and delicate sentiments are understood to reflect personal refinement and virtue. Shortly before their wedding, Eccles died suddenly, leaving Hays emotionally devastated. Nevertheless, she remained close to Eccles's circle of dissenting intellectuals, and began a course of self-improving reading under their guidance.

Given her modest intellectual background, Hays's first major publication is surprisingly bold. Under the pseudonym Eusebia, she published *Cursory Remarks on an Enquiry into the Expediency and Propriety of Public or Social Worship: Inscribed to Gilbert Wakefield* (1791) as a reply to Wakefield's *An Enquiry into the Expediency and Propriety of Public or Social Worship* (1791). Wakefield, a leading dissenter, argued that worship should be a private, personal experience. Hays defended the propriety of communal religious expression, and both reviewers and Wakefield himself praised the work.

Soon after, Hays was galvanized by reading Mary Wollstonecraft's *A Vindication of the Rights of Woman* (1792). She wrote to Wollstonecraft, beginning a friendship that was to last until Wollstonecraft's death in 1797. Wollstonecraft advised Hays on *Letters and Essays, Moral and Miscellaneous* (1793), and obtained literary work for Hays with her own publisher, Joseph Johnson, including some reviewing for the *Analytical Review*. The same year, Hays also wrote to William Godwin lauding his *Enquiry Concerning Political Justice* (1793), and Godwin too became one of Hays's intellectual mentors. Soon Hays reintroduced Wollstonecraft to Godwin, whom Wollstonecraft had known slightly, and the couple began the relationship that was to result in their marriage, the birth of the child who would become author Mary Shelley, and Wollstonecraft's death from post-partum sepsis ten days later. Hays authored the *Monthly Magazine*'s September 1797 obituary of Wollstonecraft.

During these years Hays became enamoured with dissenter William Frend, and under Godwin's influence, offered herself as Frend's mistress. Frend declined, and Godwin suggested Hays work through her distraught feelings by writing a novel. The result, *Memoirs of Emma Courtney* (1796), criticizes the political order and moral double standard, and reviewers responded according to their political stance. Meanwhile, Hays had begun reviewing for the *Critical Review,* and this same year she also began sending articles on the social determinism of philosopher Claude-Arien Hélvetius (1715–1771), to the *Monthly Magazine.* Hays's essay "On Novel Writing" continues her relationship with this literary magazine.

For the next few years Hays published frequently. *Appeal to the Men of Great Britain in Behalf of Women* appeared anonymously in 1798, followed by her next novel, *The Victim of Prejudice* in 1799, another critique of sexual constraints on women. Raped by a socially prominent man, the heroine is driven into prostitution and imprisoned. By the time it was published, antifeminist backlash was gathering force, and this novel received more reviewer censure than had her last.

Hays continued to publish for some years. Her most noted publication after *The Victim of Prejudice* was *Female Biography; or, Memoirs of Illustrious and Celebrated Women, of all Ages and Countries* (1803), which features entries on notable women writers as well as historical figures. She assisted Charlotte Smith with *A History of England, from the Earliest Records, to the Peace of Amiens: In a Series of Letters to a Young Lady at School* (1806) when illness halted Smith's work. Hays's last major publication was *Memoirs of Queens, Illustrious and Celebrated* (1821), which capitalized on renewed attention to the status of women following the rancorous divorce between George IV and Queen Caroline.

Though sidelined from the literary scene, Hays lived well into the Victorian period. Her known criticism coincides with her other work in its anti-authoritarianism, interest in the coexistence of virtue with imperfection, and concern for women.

■ Preface to *Memoirs of Emma Courtney*[1]

THE most interesting, and the most useful, fictions, are, perhaps, such, as delineating the progress, and tracing the consequences, of one strong, indulged, passion, or prejudice, afford materials, by which the philosopher may calculate the powers of the human mind, and learn the springs which set it in motion—— "Understanding, and talents," says Helvetius, "being nothing more, in men, than the produce of their desires, and particular situations."[2] Of the passion of terror Mrs. Radcliffe has made admirable use in her ingenious

---

[1]   London: G.G. and J. Robinson, 1796.
[2]   See Hélvetius, *Treatise on Man: His Intellectual Faculties and His Education,* 2 vols., trans. W. Hooper (1777), improved edition (1810) II, 406.

romances.—In the novel of Caleb Williams, curiosity in the hero, and the love of reputation in the soul-moving character of Falkland, fostered into ruling passions, are drawn with a masterly hand.

For the subject of these Memoirs, a more universal sentiment is chosen —a sentiment hackneyed in this species of composition, consequently more difficult to treat with any degree of originality;—yet, to accomplish this, has been the aim of the author; with what success, the public will, probably, determine.

Every writer who advances principles, whether true of false, that have a tendency to set the mind in motion, does good. Innumerable mistakes have been made, both moral and philosophical:—while covered with a sacred and mysterious veil, how are they to be detected? From various combinations and multiplied experiments, truth, only, can result. Free thinking, and free speaking, are the virtue and the characteristics of a rational being:— there can be no argument which militates against them in one instance, but what equally militates against them in all; every principle must be doubted, before it will be examined and proved.

It has commonly been the business of fiction to pourtray characters, not as they really exist, but, as, we are told, they ought to be—a sort of *ideal perfection*, in which nature and passion are melted away, and jarring attributes wonderfully combined.[3]

In delineating the character of Emma Courtney, I had not in view these fantastic models: I meant to represent her, as a human being, loving virtue while enslaved by passion, liable to the mistakes and weaknesses of our fragile nature.—Let those readers, who feel inclined to judge with severity the extravagance and eccentricity of her conduct, look into their own hearts; and should they there find no record, traced by an accusing spirit, to soften the asperity of their censures—yet, let them bear in mind, that the errors of my heroine were the offspring of sensibility; and that the result of her hazardous experiment is calculated to operate as a *warning*, rather than as an example.—The philosopher—who is not ignorant, that light and shade are more powerfully contrasted in minds rising above the common level; that, as rank weeds take strong root in fertile soil, vigorous powers not unfrequently produce fatal mistakes and pernicious exertions; that character is the produce of a lively and constant affection—may, possibly, discover in these Memoirs traces of reflection, and of some attention to the phænomena of the human mind.

Whether the incidents, or the characters, are copied from life, is of little importance—The only question is, if the *circumstances*, and situations, are

---

3   Hays refers to views about the novel popularized by Samuel Johnson (see Introduction). Other statements by Hays can be found below, and related comments appear in Smith's preface to *Letters of a Solitary Wanderer* (Chapter 3) and several of Wollstonecraft's *Analytical* reviews (Chapter 6).

altogether improbable? If not—whether the consequences *might* not have followed from the circumstances?—This is a grand question, applicable to all the purposes of education, morals, and legislation—*and on this I rest my moral*—"Do men gather figs of thorns, or grapes of thistles?" asked a moralist and reformer.[4]

Every *possible* incident, in works of this nature, might, perhaps, be rendered *probable*, were a sufficient regard paid to the more minute, delicate, and connecting links of the chain. Under this impression, I chose, as the least arduous, a simple story—and, even in that, the fear of repetition, of prolixity, added, it may be, to a portion of indolence, made me, in some parts, neglectful of this rule:—yet, in tracing the character of my heroine from her birth, I had it in view. For the conduct of my hero, I consider myself less responsible—it was not *his* memoirs that I professed to write.

I am not sanguine respecting the success of this little publication. It is truly observed, by the writer of a late popular novel[5]—"That an author, whether good or bad, or between both, is an animal whom every body is privileged to attack; for, though all are not able to write books, all conceive themselves able to judge them. A bad composition carries with it its own punishment—contempt and ridicule:—a good one excites envy, and (frequently) entails upon its author a thousand mortifications."

To the feeling and the thinking few, this production of an active mind, in a season of impression, rather than of leisure, is presented.

■ ART. IV. *A Gossip's Story, and a Legendary Tale* [by Jane West, 1796][6]

IT requires but little knowledge of the human mind to discover, that the most effectual method of giving instruction, is by interesting the imagination and engaging the affections. Reason conveys the knowledge of truth and falsehood, but, while it shows us the *means* of attaining happiness and avoiding misery, it must awaken sentiment and feeling before it can operate as a motive to action. If novels, romances, and fables, be held as an inferiour and insignificant species of literary composition, it must be by those who have paid little attention to the human heart: principles are disseminated and propagated, by writings of this nature, with peculiar facility and effect: they fall into the hands of the young, whose minds, unoccupied by previous impression, are ductile, and whose feelings are susceptible and ardent. Superiour writers begin to be aware of this truth, and seem inclined to rescue, from the hands of the illiterate and the interested, this obvious and

---

4   Matthew 7:16.
5   The Monk [Hays's note]. The quotation appears Volume 2, in Chapter 2 of the lurid 1796 Gothic novel by Matthew Lewis (1775–1818).
6   *Analytical Review* 25 (January 1797): 25–6.

popular method of influencing the sentiments and opinions of the rising generation, by whom reform, whether moral or political, must be effected.

The writer of the present production, without attempting those higher investigations of principle and action, which exercise the understanding, and stimulate it's [*sic*] dormant faculties, is yet entitled to praise.

In a simple, interesting, and well-written story, are exemplified the unhappy consequences, which result from false views of life, in a mind, though amiable and ingenuous, yet destitute of vigour or stability; solicitous to excel, and desirous to be happy, but sinking under fancied evils, and destroying it's [*sic*] own peace, by the very means which it takes to secure it.

[...][7]

■ ["On Novel Writing"]

To the Editor of the Monthly Magazine.[8]

SIR,

I WAS led into a train of reflections, a few days since, from perusing a paper in Dr. Johnson's Rambler,[9] respecting the works of fiction, in which he sanctions an opinion, which appears to have been generally received: that in narratives where historical veracity has no place, the most perfect models of virtue ought only to be exhibited. The arguments adduced in support of this notion, are those which regard the prevalence of example, the respect due to the innocence of youth, and the moral advantages which may be expected to result from engaging the affections on the side of virtue.

Notwithstanding the authority of so respectable a moralist, I am, I confess, inclined to suspect this reasoning to be fallacious. The greater proportion of modern novelists, from the incomparable Richardson, down to the humble purveyors for the circulating libraries, appear to have aimed at proceeding upon this principle: to calculate the effects produced by their labours upon the morals and manners of the age, might, perhaps, be an unpleasant and an invidious task. In the exquisite novel of Clarissa, impressed by its various excellencies, and carried away by the magic powers of a sovereign genius, we almost lose sight of the false and pernicious principles, the violations of truth and nature, the absurd superstitions and ludicrous prejudices with which, notwithstanding the author's rectitude of intension, it abounds. The character of Clarissa, a beautiful superstructure upon a false

---

7   Short extracts and summary comments omitted.
8   *Monthly Magazine* 4 (September 1797): 180–1.
9   *Rambler* No. 4 (see Introduction, note 6). Quotes below appear in the same paper.

and airy foundation, can never be regarded as a model for imitation. It is the portrait of an ideal being, placed in circumstances equally ideal, far removed from common life and human feelings.

There has been much declamation respecting the beauty of truth, and yet we are continually supposing it necessary to veil her simple and majestic charms, to adorn her with the robe of falsehood, or, in her stead, solicitously to impose upon the minds of youth a semblance, a deceptive appearance, a magic lantern of shadows, which can answer little other purpose than to amuse the imagination, and to bewilder and mislead the judgment. In fitting beings for human society, why should we seek to deceive them, by illusive representations of life?—Why should we not rather paint it as it really exists, mingled with imperfection, and discoloured by passion? "Familiar histories (justly observes Dr. Johnson) may be made of greater use than the solemnities of professed morality.—When an adventurer is made to act in such scenes of the universal drama, as may be the lot of any other man, young spectators fix their eyes upon him with attention, and hope, by observing his behaviour, to regulate their own practice when they shall be engaged in the like part." "But vice (it is added) should always disgust wherever it appears, it should raise hatred by the malignity of its practices, and contempt by the meanness of its stratagems; nor should any grace or excellence be so united with it, as to reconcile it with the mind." Would such delineations be consistent with truth and fact? Human nature seems to be at an equal distance from the humiliating descriptions of certain ascetic moralists, and the exaggerated eulogiums of enthusiasts. Gradations, almost imperceptible, of light and shade, must mingle in every true portrait of the human mind. Few persons are either wholly or disinterestedly virtuous or vicious; he who judges of mankind in masses, and praises or censures without discrimination, will foster innumerable prejudices, and be betrayed into perpetual mistakes: upon the most superficial appearances, he will yield himself up to excessive admiration and boundless confidence, or indulge in bitterness of invective, and the acrimony of contempt. The consequences of judgments so erroneous, are too obvious to be insisted upon, or to require pointing out. "If the world be promiscuously described (says my author) I cannot see of what use it can be to read the account, or why it may not be as safe to turn the eye immediately upon mankind, as upon a mirror, which impartially shows all that presents itself." Were we about to travel, or to settle in a new country, should we conceive it useless to acquire previous information of the difficulties to which we might be exposed, the accommodations which might be procured, the dispositions of the inhabitants, their laws, their usages, and their manners? Should we think it wise to reject the advantages which might be derived from availing ourselves of the experience of our predecessors, and to rush, at once, without knowledge or precaution, on untried situations, and hazards, equally unexpected as explored. If the persons to whom we applied for information, far from representing circumstances as they really existed, should seek to beguile our imaginations, and amuse themselves by fanciful and Utopian descriptions of the country and its inhabitants; what opinions, when we discovered the deception, must we form of their kindness and integrity, and what effects would be likely to ensue to ourselves? This statement needs no application.

The business of familiar narrative should be to describe life and manners in real or probable situations, to delineate the human mind in its endless varieties, to develop the heart, to paint the passions, to trace the springs of action, to interest the imagination, exercise the affections, and awaken the powers of the mind. A good novel ought to be subservient to the purposes of truth and philosophy: such are the novels of Fielding and Smollet.

The beauty of romance consists principally in the display of a picturesque fancy, and the creative powers of a fertile and inventive genius. The excellence of a novel is of a distinct nature, and must be the result of an attentive observance of mankind, acute discernment, exquisite moral sensibility, and an intimate acquaintance with human passions and powers. A luxuriant and poetic style of composition accords with the legends of romance. The language of the novelist should be simple, unaffected, perspicuous, yet energetic, touching, and impressive. It is not necessary that we should be able to deduce from a novel, a formal and didactic moral; it is sufficient if it has a tendency to raise the mind by elevated sentimens [*sic*], to warm the heart with generous affections, to enlarge our views, or to increase our stock of useful knowledge. A more effectual lesson might perhaps be deduced from tracing the pernicious consequences of an erroneous judgment, a wrong step, an imprudent action, an indulged and intemperate affection, a bad habit, in a character in other respects amiable and virtuous, than in painting chimerical perfection and visionary excellence, which rarely, if ever existed. How deep is our regret, how touching our sympathy, how generous our sorrow, while we contemplate the noble mind blasted by the ravages of passion, or withered by the canker of prejudice! Such examples afford an affecting and humiliating lesson of human frailty, they teach us to soften the asperity of censure, to appreciate the motives and actions of our fellow-beings with candour, to distrust ourselves, and to watch with diffidence lest we should, even by the excess of our most amiable and laudable qualities, be precipitated into folly, or betrayed into vice. It is such examples that are the most calculated to be useful; they affect every heart, they are consistent with truth, for they do not calumniate the species. Our sympathy is faint with beings whose virtues, or whose crimes, are out of the sphere of our activity. "A God, an animal, a plant (says Lavater) are not companions for man; nor are the faultless."[10] Among novelists of the present day, the author of Caleb Williams has afforded the best illustration of what I mean to inculcate. The development and struggles of the passions, in the

---

10   Johann Kaspar Lavater (1741–1801) *Aphorisms on Man* number 630. Joseph Johnson printed Henry Fuseli's translation with a frontispiece by William Blake in 1788.

character of Ferdinando Faulkland, is perhaps the most masterly performance of its kind. By the predominance of one strong, habitual, and fostered
prejudice, the finest qualities are perverted, and the most fatal calamities
involved. "He imbibed the poison of chivalry with his earliest youth—he
was the fool of honour and of fame; a man, whom, in the pursuit of reputation, nothing could divert; who would have purchased the character of a
true, a gallant, and undaunted hero, at the expense of worlds; and who
thought every calamity nominal, but a stain upon his honour."[11]

Fictitious histories, in the hands of persons of talents and observation,
might be made productive of incalculable benefit; by interesting curiosity,
and addressing the common sympathies of our nature, they pervade all
ranks; and, judiciously conducted, would become a powerful and effective
engine of truth and reform.

M. H.[12]

---

[11]   William Godwin, *Things as They Are; or, the Adventures of Caleb Williams* (1794), Ch. 12.
[12]   On the signature, see Wollstonecraft Chapter 6, note 4.

Joanna Baillie (1762–1851)

The most significant Romantic period British woman playwright with Elizabeth Inchbald the only possible challenger, Joanna Baillie stands as one of the foremost women critics as well. Born in Scotland, Baillie evinced an early antipathy to her studies, and her late mastery of reading seems an unpromising beginning for a literary career. Yet her passion for mathematics and creativity in storytelling proclaimed a strong intellect and vigorous imagination. Her teen years disrupted by the death of her father, Baillie endured with her mother and sisters several years of transitory housing and financial dependency before her brother inherited his uncle's London medical practice and they all moved to London. When the brother married in 1791, Baillie, her mother, and her sister moved to Hampstead, where Baillie remained for the rest of her life, and where she enjoyed an active social life among the circle of Hampstead literary figures, including her aunt, poet Anne Hunter, and Anna Letitia Barbauld. Her broadening circle of literary friends eventually came to include Samuel Rogers, Henry MacKenzie, Maria Edgeworth, and Walter Scott, among others.

Hampstead is where Baillie's literary career began, first with her publication of a volume of poems. The volume received little attention, but some of the poems reappeared in *Fugitive Verses* (1840). In 1798 the anonymous publication of the first volume of *A Series of Plays: in which it is attempted to delineate the stronger passions of the mind—each passion being the subject of a tragedy and a comedy*, better known as *Plays on the Passions*, drew immediate applause and aroused animated speculation about who might be the author. Though several prominent male writers were posed as possibilities, some readers noticed the strong, intellectual, female characters, and suggested that the author might be a woman. Not until the third edition of the volume did Baillie disclose her identity, sparking nearly as much conjecture about this new figure on the literary scene as did the initial anonymity.

Intending to produce a comedy and a tragedy on each of the human passions, Baillie added additional volumes to the *Plays* in 1802 and 1812. Though she meant her work for the stage, the dramas were widely read, but only *De Monfort* was much staged. Nevertheless, Baillie continued her project, adding more plays and extending some of those already published until 1836, when her three volume collection *Dramas* appeared. Meanwhile, she tried her hand at narrative poetry, returning to her own ancestors in Britain's feudal past for the subject of *Metrical Legends of Exalted Characters* (1821). *Ahalya Baee*, another narrative poem, appeared in 1849. She also published a theological tract, *A View of the General Tenour of the New Testament regarding the nature and dignity of Jesus Christ* (1831). Finally she agreed to the Longmans' request to collect and edit her entire opus for *The Dramatic and Poetical Works of Joanna Baillie, complete in one volume*, published in 1851, the year she died.

In addition to dramatic genre theory and classification, Baillie's "Introductory Discourse" to her first volume of *Plays* can be compared with Wordsworth's preface to *Lyrical Ballads*, which it preceded. Both provide theoretical background to enable an audience to appreciate the respective literary experiments, and similar principles underlie the explanations. Both stress the return to a native British literary heritage, the natural idioms of everyday language, and realistic characterization of ordinary individuals as the means of recuperating British literature from a slide toward decadent sensationalism, substituting instead authentic emotion as the foundation for moral behavior. The preface "To the Reader" from the third volume and her defense of her tragedy *Romiero* continue Baillie's work of theorizing her dramatic innovations.

■ Introductory Discourse[1]

[…]

Our desire to know what men are in the closet as well as the field, by the blazing hearth, and at the social board, as well as in the council and the throne, is very imperfectly gratified by real history; romance writers, therefore, stepped boldly forth to supply the deficiency; and tale writers, and novel writers, of many descriptions, followed after. If they have not been very skilful in their delineations of nature; if they have represented men and women speaking and acting as men and women never did speak or act; if they have caricatured both our virtues and our vices; if they have given us such pure unmixed, or such heterogeneous combinations of character as real life never presented, and yet have pleased and interested us, let it not be imputed to the dulness of man in discerning what is genuinely natural in himself. […] In a work abounding with the marvellous and unnatural, if the author has any how stumbled upon an unsophisticated genuine stroke of nature, we will immediately perceive and be delighted with it, though

---

[1]   This essay introduced the first volume of Baillie's *A Series of Plays* Vol. 1 (London: Cadell and Davies, 1798) 1–72. In the omitted opening pages, Baillie explains her purpose in supplying a preface and outlines how sympathy naturally inclines human beings toward interest in the ways others behave in situations of strong emotion, an inclination, she argues, that all tragic drama addresses.

we are foolish enough to admire at the same time, all the nonsense with which it is surrounded. After all the wonderful incidents, dark mysteries, and secrets revealed, which eventful novel so liberally presents to us; after the beautiful fairy ground, and even the grand and sublime scenes of nature with which descriptive novel so often enchants us; those works which most strongly characterize human nature in the middling and lower classes of society, where it is to be discovered by stronger and more unequivocal marks, will ever be the most popular. For though great pains have been taken in our higher sentimental novels to interest us in the delicacies, embarrassments, and artificial distresses of the more refined part of society, they have never been able to cope in the publick opinion with these. The one is a dressed and beautiful pleasure-ground, in which we are enchanted for a while, amongst the delicate and unknown plants of artful cultivation; the other is a rough forest of our native land; the oak, the elm, the hazle, and the bramble are there; and amidst the endless varieties of its paths we can wander for ever. Into whatever scenes the novelist may conduct us, what objects soever he may present to our view, still is our attention most sensibly awake to every touch faithful to nature; still are we upon the watch for every thing that speaks to us of ourselves.

The fair field of what is properly called poetry, is enriched with so many beauties, that in it we are often tempted to forget what we really are, and what kind of beings we belong to. Who in the enchanted regions of simile, metaphor, allegory and description, can remember the plain order of things in this every-day world? From heroes whose majestick forms rise like a lofty tower, whose eyes are lightening, whose arms are irresistible, whose course is like the storms of heaven, bold and exalted sentiments we will readily receive; and will not examine them very accurately by that rule of nature which our own breast prescribes to us. A shepherd whose sheep, with fleeces of the purest snow, browze the flowery herbage of the most beautiful vallies; whose flute is ever melodious, and whose shepherdess is ever crowned with roses; whose every care is love, will not be called very strictly to account for the loftiness and refinement of his thoughts. The fair Nymph, who sighs out her sorrows to the conscious and compassionate wilds; whose eyes gleam like the bright drops of heaven; whose loose tresses stream to the breeze, may say what she pleases with impunity. I will venture, however, to say, that amidst all this decoration and ornament, all this loftiness and refinement, let one simple trait of the human heart, one expression of passion genuine and true to nature, be introduced, and it will stand forth alone in the boldness of reality, whilst the false and unnatural around it, fades away upon every side, like the rising exhalations of the morning. With admiration, and often with enthusiasm we proceed on our way through the grand and the beautiful images, raised to our imagination by the lofty Epic muse; but what even here are those things that strike upon the heart; that we feel and remember? Neither the descriptions of war, the sound of the trumpet, the clanging of arms, the combat of heroes, nor the death of the mighty, will interest our minds like the fall of the feeble stranger, who simply expresses the anguish of his soul, at the thoughts of that far-distant home which he must never return to again, and closes his eyes amongst the ignoble and forgotten; like the timid stripling goaded by the shame of reproach, who urges his trembling steps to the fight, and falls like a tender flower before the first blast of winter. How often will some simple picture of this kind be all that remains upon our minds of the terrifick and magnificent battle, whose description we have read with admiration! How comes it that we relish so much the episodes of an heroick poem? It cannot merely be that we are pleased with a resting-place, where we enjoy the variety of contrast; for were the poem of the simple and familiar kind, and an episode after the heroick style introduced into it, ninety readers out of an hundred would pass over it altogether. Is it not that we meet such a story, so situated, with a kind of sympathetick good will, as in passing through a country of castles and of palaces, we should pop unawares upon some humble cottage, resembling the dwellings of our own native land, and gaze upon it with affection. The highest pleasures we receive from poetry, as well as from the real objects which surround us in the world, are derived from the sympathetick interest we all take in beings like ourselves […].

If the study of human nature then, is so useful to the poet, the novelist, the historian, and the philosopher, of how much greater importance must it be to the dramatick writer? To them it is a powerful auxiliary, to him it is the centre and strength of the battle. If characteristick views of human nature enliven not their pages, there are many excellencies with which they can, in some degree, make up for the deficiency, it is what we receive from them with pleasure rather than demand. But in his works no richness of invention, harmony of language, nor grandeur of sentiment will supply the place of faithfully delineated nature. The poet and the novelist may represent to you their great characters from the cradle to the tomb. They may represent them in any mood or temper, and under the influence of any passion which they see proper, without being obliged to put words into their mouths, those great betrayers of the feigned and adopted. They may relate every circumstance however trifling and minute, that serves to develop their tempers and dispositions. They tell us what kind of people they intend their men and women to be, and as such we receive them. If they are to move us with any scene of distress, every circumstance regarding the parties concerned in it, how they looked, how they moved, how they sighed, how the tears gushed from their eyes, how the very light and shadow fell upon them, is carefully described, and the few things that are given them to say along with all this assistance, must be very unnatural indeed if we refuse to sympathize with them. But the characters of the drama must speak directly for themselves. Under the influence of every passion, humour, and impression; in the artificial veilings of hypocrisy and ceremony, in the openness of freedom and confidence, and in the lonely hour of mediation they speak. He who made us hath placed within our breast a judge that judges instantaneously of every thing they say. We expect to find them creatures like ourselves; and if they are untrue to nature, we feel that we are imposed upon; as though the poet had introduced to us for brethren, creatures of a different race, beings of another world.

As in other works deficiency in characteristick truth may be compensated by excellencies of a different kind, in the drama characteristick truth will compensate every other defect. Nay, it will do what appears a contradiction; one strong genuine stroke of nature will cover a multitude of sins even against nature herself. When we meet in some scene of a good play a very fine stroke of this kind, we are apt to become so intoxicated with it, and so perfectly convinced of the author's great knowledge of the human heart, that we are unwilling to suppose that the whole of it has not been suggested by the same penetrating spirit […].

In whatever age or country the Drama might have taken its rise, tragedy would have been the first-born of its children. For every nation has its great men, and its great events upon record; and to represent their own forefathers struggling with those difficulties, and braving those dangers, of which they have heard with admiration, and the effects of which they still, perhaps, experience, would certainly have been the most animating subject for the poet, and the most interesting for his audience, even independently of the natural inclination we all so universally shew for scenes of horrour and distress, of passion and heroick exertion. Tragedy would have been the first child of the Drama, for the same reasons that have made heroick ballad, with all its battles, murders, and disasters, the earliest poetical compositions of every country.

We behold heroes and great men at a distance, unmarked by those small but distinguishing features of the mind, which give a certain individuality to such an infinite variety of similar beings, in the near and familiar intercourse of life. […]To Tragedy it belongs to lead them forward to our nearer regard, in all the distinguishing varieties which nearer inspection discovers; with the passions, the humours, the weaknesses, the prejudices of men. It is for her to present to us the great and magnanimous hero, who appears to our distant view as a superior being, as a God, softened down with those smaller frailties and imperfections which enable us to glory in, and claim kindred to his virtues. […] But above all, to her, and to her only it belongs to unveil to us the human mind under the dominion of those strong and fixed passions, which, seemingly unprovoked by outward circumstances, will from small beginnings brood within the breast, till all the better dispositions, all the fair gifts of nature are borne down before them. […] For who hath followed the great man into his secret closet, or stood by the side of his nightly couch, and heard those exclamations of the soul which heaven alone may hear, that the historian should be able to inform us? and what form of story, what mode of rehearsed speech will communicate to us those feelings, whose irregular bursts, abrupt transitions, sudden pauses, and half-uttered suggestions, scorn all harmony of measured verse, all method and order of relation?

On the first part of this task her Bards have eagerly exerted their abilities: and some amongst them, taught by strong original genius to deal immediately with human nature and their own hearts, have laboured in it successfully. But in presenting to us those views of great characters, and of the human mind in difficult and trying situations which peculiarly belong to Tragedy, the far greater proportion, even of those who may be considered as respectable dramatick poets, have very much failed. From the beauty of those original dramas to which they have ever looked back with admiration, they have been tempted to prefer the embellishments of poetry to faithfully delineated nature. They have been more occupied in considering the works of the great Dramatists who have gone before them, and the effects produced by their writings, than the varieties of human character which first furnished materials for those works, or those principles in the mind of man by means of which such effects were produced. Neglecting the boundless variety of nature, certain strong outlines of character, certain bold features of passion, certain grand vicissitudes, and striking dramatick situations have been repeated from one generation to another; whilst a pompous and solemn gravity, which they have supposed to be necessary for the dignity of tragedy, has excluded almost entirely from their works those smaller touches of nature, which so well develope the mind; and by showing men in their hours of state and exertion only, they have consequently shewn them imperfectly. Thus, great and magnanimous heroes, who bear with majestick equanimity every vicissitude of fortune; who in every temptation and trial stand forth in unshaken virtue, like a rock buffeted by the waves; who encompast with the most terrible evils, in calm possession of their souls, reason upon the difficulties of their state; and, even upon the brink of destruction, pronounce long eulogiums on virtue, in the most eloquent and beautiful language, have been held forth to our view as objects of imitation and interest; as though they had entirely forgotten that it is only from creatures like ourselves that we feel, and therefore, only from creatures like ourselves that we receive the instruction of example. [...] Thus, also, tyrants are represented as monsters of cruelty, unmixed with any feelings of humanity; and villains as delighting in all manner of treachery and deceit, and acting upon many occasions for the very love of villainy itself; though the perfectly wicked are as ill fitted for the purposes of warning, as the perfectly virtuous are for those of example.[2] [...]

---

2   I have said nothing here in regard to female character, though in many tragedies it is brought forward as the principal one of the piece, because what I have said of the above characters is likewise applicable to it. I believe there is no man that ever lived, who has behaved in a certain manner, on a certain occasion, who has not had amongst women some corresponding spirit, who on the like occasion, and every way similarly circumstanced, would have behaved in the like manner. With some degree of softening and refinement, each class of the tragick heroes I have mentioned has its corresponding one amongst the heroines. The tender and pathetick no doubt has the most numerous, but the great and magnanimous is not without it, and the passionate and impetuous boasts of one by no means inconsiderable in numbers, and drawn sometimes to the full as passionate and impetuous as itself [Baillie's note].

But the last part of the task which I have mentioned as peculiarly belonging to tragedy, unveiling the human mind under the dominion of those strong and fixed passions, which seemingly unprovoked by outward circumstances, will from small beginnings brood within the breast, till all the better dispositions, all the fair gifts of nature are borne down before them, her poets in general have entirely neglected, and even her first and greatest have but imperfectly attempted. They have made use of the passions to mark their several characters, and animate their scenes, rather than to open to our view the nature and portraitures of those great disturbers of the human breast, with whom we are all, more or less, called upon to contend. With their strong and obvious features, therefore, they have been presented to us, stripped almost entirely of those less obtrusive, but not less discriminating traits, which mark them in their actual operation. To trace them in their rise and progress in the heart, seems but rarely to have been the object of any dramatist. We commonly find the characters of a tragedy affected by the passions in a transient, loose, unconnected manner; or if they are represented as under the permanent influence of the more powerful ones, they are generally introduced to our notice in the very height of their fury, when all that timidity, irresolution, distrust, and a thousand delicate traits, which make the infancy of every great passion more interesting, perhaps, than its full-blown strength, are fled. The impassioned character is generally brought into view under those irresistible attacks of their power, which it is impossible to repell; whilst those gradual steps that led him into this state, in some of which a stand might have been made against the foe, are left entirely in the shade. These passions that may be suddenly excited, and are of short duration, as anger, fear, and oftentimes jealousy, may in this manner be fully represented; but those great masters of the soul, ambition, hatred, love, every passion that is permanent in its nature, and varied in progress, if represented to us in but one stage of its course, is represented imperfectly. It is a characteristick of the more powerful passions that they will encrease and nourish themselves on very slender aliment; it is from within that they are chiefly supplied with what they feed on; and it is in contending with opposite passions and affections of the mind that we least discover their strength, not with events. But in tragedy it is events more frequently than opposite affections which are opposed to them; and those often of such force and magnitude that the passions themselves are almost obscured by the splendour and importance of the transactions to which they are attached. But besides being thus confined and mutilated, the passions have been, in the greater part of our tragedies, deprived of the very power of making themselves known. Bold and figurative language belongs peculiarly to them. Poets, admiring those bold expressions which a mind, labouring with ideas too strong to be conveyed in the ordinary forms of speech, wildly throws out, taking earth, sea, and sky, every thing great and terrible in nature to image forth the violence of its feelings, borrowed them gladly, to adorn the calm sentiments of their premeditated song. It has therefore been thought that the less animated parts of tragedy

might be so embellished and enriched. In doing this, however, the passions
have been robbed of their native prerogative; and in adorning with their
strong figures and lofty expressions the calm speeches of the unruffled, it
is found that, when they are called upon to raise their voice, the power of
distinguishing themselves has been taken away. […]

From this general view, which I have endeavoured to communicate to my
reader, of tragedy, and those principles in the human mind upon which the
success of her efforts depends, I have been led to believe, that an attempt to
write a series of tragedies, of simpler construction, less embellished with
poetical decorations, less constrained by that lofty seriousness which has so
generally been considered as necessary for the support of tragick dignity,
and in which the chief object should be to delineate the progress of the
higher passions in the human breast, each play exhibiting a particular passion, might not be unacceptable to the publick. And I have been the more
readily induced to act upon this idea, because I am confident, that tragedy,
written upon this plan, is fitted to produce stronger moral effect than upon
any other. I have said that tragedy in representing to us great characters
struggling with difficulties, and placed in situations of eminence and danger, in which few of us have any chance of being called upon to act, conveys
its moral efficacy to our minds by the enlarged views which it gives to us of
human nature, by the admiration of virtue, and execration of vice which it
excites, and not by the examples it holds up for our immediate application.
But in opening to us the heart of man under the influence of those passions
to which all are liable, this is not the case. Those strong passions that, with
small assistance from outward circumstances, work their way in the heart,
till they become the tyrannical masters of it, carry on a similar operation in
the breast of the Monarch, and the man of low degree. It exhibits to us the
mind of man in that state when we are most curious to look into it, and is
equally interesting to all. Discrimination of character is a turn of mind, tho'
more common than we are aware of, which every body does not possess;
but to the expressions of passion, particularly strong passion, the dullest
mind is awake; and its true unsophisticated language the dullest understanding will not misinterpret. To hold up for our example those peculiarities in disposition, and modes of thinking which nature has fixed upon us,
on which long and early habit has incorporated with our original selves, is
almost desiring us to remove the everlasting mountains, to take away the
native land-marks of the soul; but representing the passions brings before
us the operation of a tempest that rages out its time and passes away. We
cannot, it is true, amidst its wild uproar, listen to the voice of reason, and
save ourselves from destruction; but we can foresee it coming, we can mark
its rising signs, we can know the situations that will most expose us to its
rage, and we can shelter our heads from the coming blast. To change a certain disposition of mind which makes us view objects in a particular light,
and thereby, oftentimes, unknown to ourselves, influences our conduct and
manners, is almost impossible; but in checking and subduing those visita-

tions of the soul, whose causes and effects we are aware of, every one may make considerable progress, if he proves not entirely successful. Above all, looking back to the first rise, and tracing the progress of passion, points out to us those stages in the approach of the enemy, when he might have been combated most successfully; and where the suffering him to pass may be considered as occasioning all the misery that ensues.

Comedy presents to us men as we find them in the ordinary intercourse of the world, with all the weaknesses, follies, caprice, prejudices, and absurdities which a near and familiar view of them discovers. It is her task to exhibit them engaged in the busy turmoil of ordinary life, harassing and perplexing themselves with the endless pursuits of avarice, vanity, and pleasure; and engaged with those smaller trials of the mind, by which men are most apt to be overcome, and from which he, who could have supported with honour the attack of greater occasions, will oftentimes come off most shamefully foiled. It belongs to her to shew the varied fashions and manners of the world, as, from the spirit of vanity, caprice, and imitation, they go on in swift and endless succession; and those disagreeable or absurd peculiarities attached to particular classes and conditions in society. It is for her also to represent men under the influence of the stronger passions; and to trace the rise and progress of them in the heart, in such situations, and attended with such circumstances as take off their sublimity, and the interest we naturally take in a perturbed mind. It is hers to exhibit those terrible tyrants of the soul, whose ungovernable rage has struck us so often with dismay, like wild beasts tied to a post, who growl and paw before us, for our derision and sport. In pourtraying the characters of men she has this advantage over tragedy, that the smallest traits of nature, with the smallest circumstances which serve to bring them forth, may by her be displayed, however ludicrous and trivial in themselves, without any ceremony. And in developing the passions she enjoys a similar advantage; for they often most strongly betray themselves when touched by those small and familiar occurrences which cannot, consistently with the effect it is intended to produce, be admitted into tragedy.

As tragedy has been very much cramped in her endeavours to exalt and improve the mind, by that spirit of imitation and confinement in her successive writers, which the beauty of her earliest poets first gave rise to, so comedy has been led aside from her best purposes by a different temptation. Those endless changes in fashions and in manners, which offer such obvious and ever-new subjects of ridicule; that infinite variety of tricks and manœuvers by which the ludicrous may be produced, and curiosity and laughter excited: the admiration we so generally bestow upon satirical remark, pointed repartee, and whimsical combinations of ideas, have too often led her to forget the warmer interest we feel, and the more profitable lessons we receive from genuine representations of nature. The most interesting and instructive class of comedy, therefore, the real characteristick, has been very much neglected, whilst satirical, witty, sentimental, and, above all, busy or circumstantial comedy have usurped the exertions of the far greater proportion of Dramatick Writers.

In Satirical Comedy, sarcastick and severe reflections on the actions and manners of men, introduced with neatness, force, and poignancy of expression into a lively and well supported dialogue, of whose gay surface they are the embossed ornaments, make the most important and studied part of the work: Character is a thing talked of rather than shewn. The persons of the drama are indebted for the discovery of their peculiarities to what is said to them, rather than to any thing they are made to say or do for themselves. Much incident being unfavourable for studied and elegant dialogue, the plot is commonly simple, and the few events that compose it neither interesting nor striking. It only affords us that kind of moral instruction which an essay or a poem could as well have conveyed, and, though amusing in the closet, is but feebly attractive in the Theatre.[3]

In what I have termed Witty Comedy, every thing is light, playful, and easy. Strong decided condemnation of vice is too weighty and material to dance upon the surface of that stream, whose shallow currents sparkle in perpetual sun-beams, and cast up their bubbles to the light. Two or three persons of quick thought, and whimsical fancy, who perceive instantaneously the various connections of every passing idea, and the significations, natural or artificial, which single expressions, or particular forms of speech can possible convey, take the lead thro' the whole, and seem to communicate their own peculiar talent to every creature in the play. The plot is most commonly feeble rather than simple, the incidents being numerous enough, but seldom striking or varied. To amuse, and only to amuse, is its aim: it pretends not to interest nor instruct. It pleases when we read, more than when we see it represented; and pleases still more when we take it up by accident, and read but a scene at a time.

Sentimental Comedy treats of those embarrassments, difficulties, and scruples, which, though sufficiently distressing to the delicate minds who entertain them, are not powerful enough to gratify the sympathetick desire we all feel to look into the heart of man in difficult and trying situations, which is the sound basis of tragedy, and are destitute of that seasoning of the lively and ludicrous, which prevents the ordinary transactions of comedy from becoming insipid. In real life, those who, from the peculiar frame of their minds, feel most of this refined distress, are not generally communicative upon the subject; and those who do feel and talk about it at the same time, if any such there be, seldom find their friends much inclined to listen to them. It is not to be supposed, then, long conversations upon the

---

3   These plays are generally the work of men, whose judgment and acute observation, enable
     them admirably well to generalize, and apply to classes of men the remarks they have
     made upon individuals; yet know not how to dress up, with any natural congruity, an
     imaginary individual in the attributes they have assigned to those classes [Baillie's note].

stage about small sentimental niceties, can be generally interesting. I am afraid plays of this kind, as well as works of a similar nature, in other departments of literature, have only tended to encrease amongst us a set of sentimental hypocrites; who are the same persons of this age that would have been the religious ones of another; and are daily doing morality the same kind of injury, by substituting the particular excellence which they pretend to possess, for plain simple uprightness and rectitude.

In Busy or Circumstantial Comedy, all those ingenious contrivances of lovers, guardians, governantes and chamber-maids; that ambushed bush-fighting amongst closets, screens, chests, easy-chairs, and toilet-tables, form a gay varied game of dexterity and invention; which, to those who have played at hide-and-seek, who have crouched down, with beating heart, in a dark corner, whilst the enemy groped near the spot; who have joined their busy school-mates in many a deep-laid plan to deceive, perplex, and torment the unhappy mortals deputed to have the charge of them, cannot be seen with indifference. Like an old hunter, who pricks up ears at the sound of the chace, and starts away from the path of his journey, so, leaving all wisdom and criticism behind us, we follow the varied changes of the plot, and stop not for reflection. […]

But Charateristick Comedy, which represents to us this motley world of men and women in which we live, under those circumstances of ordinary and familiar life most favourable for the discovery of the human heart, offers to us a wide field of instruction, adapted to general application. We find in its varied scenes an exercise of the mind analogous to that which we all, less or more, find out for ourselves, amidst the mixed groupes of people whom we meet with in society; and which I have already mentioned as an exercise universally pleasing to man. As the distinctions which it is its high-est aim to discriminate, are those of nature and not situation, they are judged of by all ranks of men; for a peasant will very clearly perceive in the char-acter of a peer, those native peculiarities which belong to him as a man, though he is entirely at a loss in all that regards his manners and address as a nobleman. [… C]haracters who are to speak for themselves, who are to be known by their own words and actions, not by the accounts that are given of them by others, cannot well be developed without considerable variety of judicious incident; a smile that is raised by some trait of undisguised nature, and a laugh that is provoked by some ludicrous effect of passion, or clashing of opposite characters, will be more pleasing to the generality of men, than either the one or the other when occasioned by a play upon words, or a whimsical combination of ideas; and to behold the operation and effects of the different propensities and weaknesses of men, will nat-urally call up in the mind of the spectator moral reflections more applicable, and more impressive, than all the high-sounding sentiments, with which the graver scenes of Satirical and Sentimental Comedy are so frequently inter-larded. It is much to be regretted, however, that the eternal introduction of love as the grand business of the Drama, and the consequent necessity for making the chief persons in it such, in regard to age, appearance, manners, dispositions, and endowments, as are proper for interesting lovers, has occasioned so much insipid similarity in the higher characters. It is chiefly, therefore, on the second and inferiour characters, that the efforts, even of our best poets, have been exhausted; and thus we are called upon to be interested in the fortune of one man, whilst our chief attention is directed to the character of another, which produces a disunion of ideas in the mind, injurious to the general effect of the whole. From this cause, also, those characteristick varieties have been very much neglected, which men present to us in the middle stages of life; when they are too old for lovers or the confidents of lovers, and too young to be the fathers, uncles, and guardians, who are contrasted with them; but when they are still in full vigour of mind, eagerly engaged with the world, joining the activity of youth to the providence of age, and offer to our attention objects sufficiently interesting and instructive. It is to be regretted that strong contrasts of character are too often attempted, instead of those harmonious shades of it, which nature so beautifully varies, and which we so greatly delight in, whenever we clearly distinguish them […].

In comedy, the stronger passions, love excepted, are seldom introduced but in a passing way. We have short bursts of anger, fits of Jealousy and impatience; violent passion of any continuance we seldom find. […] Yet we all know from our own experience in real life, that, in certain situations, and under certain circumstances, the stronger passions are fitted to produce scenes more exquisitely comick than any other; and one well-wrought scene of this kind, will have a more powerful effect in repressing similar intemperance in the mind of a spectator, than many moral cautions, or even, perhaps, than the terrifick examples of tragedy […].

But a complete exhibition of passion, with its varieties and progress in the breast of man has, I believe, scarcely ever been attempted in comedy. Even love, though the chief subject of almost every play, has been pourtrayed in a loose, scattered, and imperfect manner. The story of the lovers is acted over before us, whilst the characteristicks of that passion by which they are actuated, and which is the great master-spring of the whole, are faintly to be discovered. We are generally introduced to a lover after he has long been acquainted with his mistress, and wants but the consent of some stubborn relation, relief from some embarrassment of situation, or the clearing up some mistake or love-quarrel occasioned by malice or accident, to make him completely happy. To overcome these difficulties, he is engaged in a busy train of contrivance and exertion, in which the spirit, activity and ingenuity of the man is held forth to view, whilst the lover, comparatively speaking, is kept out of sight […].

From this view of the Comick Drama I have been induced to believe, that, as companions to the forementioned tragedies, a series of comedies on a similar plan, in which bustle of plot, brilliancy of dialogue, and even the bold and striking in character, should, to the best of the authour's judgment, be kept in due subordination to nature, might likewise be acceptable to the publick. I am confident that comedy upon this plan is capable of being made as interesting, as entertaining, and superiour in the moral tendency to any other. For even in ordinary life, with very slight cause to excite them, strong passions will foster themselves within the breast; and what are all the evils which vanity, folly, prejudice, or peculiarity of temper lead to, compared with those which such unquiet inmates produce? […].

It was the saying of a sagacious Scotchman, 'let who will make the laws of a nation, if I have the writing of its ballads.'[4] Something similar to this may be said in regard to the Drama. Its lessons reach not, indeed, to the lowest classes of labouring people, who are the broad foundation of society, which can never be generally moved without endangering everything that is constructed upon it, and who are our potent and formidable ballad readers; but they reach to the classes next in order to them, and who will always have over them no inconsiderable influence. The impressions made by it are communicated, at the same instant of time, to a greater number of individuals, than those made by any other species of writing; and they are strengthened in every spectator, by observing their effects upon those who surround him […].

This idea has prompted me to begin a work in which I am aware of many difficulties. In plays of this nature the passions must be depicted not only with their bold and prominent features, but also with those minute and delicate traits which distinguish them in an infant, growing, and repressed state; which are the most difficult of all to counterfeit, and one of which falsely imagined, will destroy the effect of a whole scene. The characters over whom they are made to usurp dominion, must be powerful and interesting, exercising them with their full measure of opposition and struggle; for the chief antagonists they contend with must be the other passions and propensities of the heart, not outward circumstances and events. Though belonging to such characters, they must still be held to view in their most baleful and unseductive light; and those qualities in the impassioned which are necessary to interest us in their fate, must not be allowed, by any lustre borrowed from them, to diminish our abhorrence of guilt. The second and even the inferiour persons to each play, as they must be kept perfectly distinct from the great impassioned one, should generally be represented in a calm unagitated state, and therefore more pains is necessary than in other dramatick works, to mark them by appropriate distinctions of character, lest they should appear altogether insipid and insignificant. As the great object here is to trace passion through all its varieties, and in every stage, many of which are marked by shades so delicate, that in much bustle of events they would be little attended to, or entirely overlooked, simplicity of plot is more necessary, than in those plays where only occasional bursts of passion are introduced, to distinguish a character, or animate a scene. But where

---

[4]   See note Barbauld, Chapter 2, note 29.

simplicity of plot is necessary, there is a very great danger of making a piece appear bare and unvaried, and nothing but great force and truth in the delineations of nature will prevent it from being tiresome […].[5] Soliloquy, or those overflowings of the perturbed soul, in which it unburthens itself of those thoughts which it cannot communicate to others, and which in certain situations is the only mode that a Dramatist can employ to open us to the mind he would display, must necessarily be often, and to considerable length, introduced. Here, indeed, as it naturally belongs to passion, it will not be so offensive as it generally is in other plays, when a calm unagitated person tells over to himself all that has befallen him, and all his future schemes of intrigue or advancement; yet to make speeches of this kind sufficiently natural and impressive, to excite no degree of weariness nor distaste, will be found to be no easy task […].

It may, perhaps, be supposed from my publishing these plays, that I have written them for the closet rather than the stage. If upon perusing them with attention, the reader is disposed to think they are better calculated for the first than the last, let him impute it to want of skill in the authour, and not to any previous design. A play, but of small poetical merit, that is suited to strike and interest the spectator, to catch the attention of him who will not, and of him who cannot read, is a more valuable and useful production than one whose elegant and harmonious pages are admired in the libraries of the tasteful and refined. To have received approbation from an audience of my country men, would have been more pleasing to me than any other praise. A few tears from the simple and young would have been, in my eyes, pearls of great price; and the spontaneous, untutored plaudits of the rude and uncultivated would have come to my heart as offerings of no mean value. I should, therefore, have been better pleased to have introduced them to the world from the stage than from the press. I possess, however, no likely channel to the former mode of publick introduction; and upon further reflection it appeared to me that by publishing them in this way, I have an opportunity afforded me of explaining the design of my work and enabling the publick to judge, not only of each play by itself, but as making a part likewise of the whole; an advantage which, perhaps, does more than overbalance the splendour and effect of theatrical representation […].

*Shakspeare, more than any of our poets, gives peculiar and appropriate distinction to the characters of his tragedies. The remarks I have made, in regard to the little variety of character to be met with in tragedy, apply not to him. Neither has he, as other Dramatists generally do, bestowed pains on the chief persons of his drama only, leaving the second and inferiour ones insignificant and spiritless. He never wears out our capacity to feel, by eternally pressing upon it. His tragedies are agreeably checquered with variety of scenes, enriched with good sense, nature, and vivacity, which relieve our

---

[5]   Baillie's note on ceremonial interruptions in dramatic performances here omitted.

minds from the fatigue of continued distress. If he sometimes carries this so far as to break in upon that serious tone of mind, which disposes us to listen with effect to the higher scenes of tragedy, he has done so chiefly in his historical plays, where the distresses set forth are commonly of that publick kind, which does not, at any rate, make much impression upon the feelings [Baillie's note].

■ To the Reader[6]

[…]

   With the exception of a small piece, in two acts, at the end of the book, this volume is entirely occupied with different representations of one passion; and a passion, too, which has been supposed to be less adapted to dramatic purposes than any other—Fear. It has been thought that, in Tragedy at least, the principal character could not possibly be actuated by this passion, without becoming so far degraded as to be incapable of engaging the sympathy and interest of the spectator or reader. I am, however, inclined to think, that even Fear, as it is under certain circumstances and to a certain degree a universal passion (for our very admiration of Courage rests upon this idea), is capable of being made in the tragic drama, as it often is in real life, very interesting, and consequently not abject.
   The first of these plays is a Tragedy of five acts, the principal character of which is a woman, under the dominion of Superstitious Fear; and that particular species of it, (the fear of ghosts, or the returning dead,) which is so universal and inherent in our nature, that it can never be eradicated from the mind, let the progress of reason or philosophy be what it may […]. Those, I believe, who possess strong imagination, quick fancy, and keen feeling, are most easily affected by this species of Fear: I have, therefore, made Orra a lively, cheerful, buoyant character, when not immediately under its influence; and even extracting from her superstitious propensity a kind of wild enjoyment, which tempts her to nourish and cultivate the enemy that destroys her. The catastrophe is such as Fear, I understand, does more commonly produce than any other passion. […].
   But if it has been at all necessary to offer any apology for exhibiting Fear as the actuating principle of the heroine of the first play, what must I say in defence of a much bolder step in the one that follows it? in which I have made Fear, and the fear of Death too, the actuating principle of a hero of Tragedy. I can only say, that I believed it might be done, without submitting

---

6   Joanna Baillie, *A Series of Plays: in which It Is Attempted to Delineate the Stronger Passions of the Mind–each passion being the subject of a tragedy and a comedy* [*Plays on the Passions*] Vol 3 (1812) iii–xxxi. This volume contained the plays *Orra, The Dream* (featuring the character Osterloo), *The Siege*, and *The Beacon*.

him to any degradation that would affect the sympathy and interest I intended to excite. I must confess, however, that, being unwilling to appropriate this passion in a serious form to my own sex entirely, when the subjects of all the other passions, hitherto delineated in this series, are men, I have attempted what did indeed appear at first sight almost impracticable. This *esprit de corps* must also plead my excuse for loading the passion in question with an additional play. The fear of Death is here exhibited in a brave character, placed under such new and appalling circumstances as might, I supposed, overcome the most courageous; and as soon as he finds himself in a situation like those in which he has been accustomed to be bold, *viz.* with arms in his hand and an enemy to encounter, he is made immediately to resume all his wonted spirit. Even after he believes himself to be safe, he returns again to attack, in behalf of his companion, who beseeches him to fly, and who is not exposed to any personal danger, a force so greatly superior to his own as to leave himself scarcely a chance for redemption.

[... I]t is not want of fortitude to bear bodily sufferings, or even deliberately inflicted death, under the circumstances commonly attending it, that the character of Osterloo exhibits. It is the horror he conceives on being suddenly awakened to the imagination of the awful retributions of another world, from having the firm belief of them forced at once upon his mind by extraordinary circumstances, which so miserably quells an otherwise undaunted spirit. [...].

It may be objected that the fear of Death is in him so closely connected with Superstitious Fear, that the picture traced in this play bears too near a resemblance to that which is shewn in the foregoing. But the fears of Orra have nothing to do with apprehension of personal danger, and spring solely from a natural horror of supernatural intercourse: while those of Osterloo arise, as I have already noticed, from a strong sense of guilt, suddenly roused within him by extraordinary circumstances; and the prospect of being plunged, almost immediately by death, into an unknown state of punishment and horror. Not knowing by what natural means his guilt could be brought to light, in a manner so extraordinary, a mind the least superstitious, in those days, perhaps I may even say in these, would have considered it to be supernatural; and the dreadful consequences, so immediately linked to it, are surely sufficiently strong to unhinge the firmest mind, having no time allowed to prepare itself for the tremendous change. If there is any person, who, under such circumstances, could have remained unappalled, he does not belong to that class of men, who, commanding the fleets and armies of their grateful and admiring country, dare every thing by blood and by field that is dangerous and terrific for her sake; but to one far different, whom hard drinking, opium, or impiety have sunk into a state of unmanly and brutish stupidity. It will probably be supposed that I have carried the consequences of his passion too far in the catastrophe to be considered as natural; but the only circumstance in the piece that is not entirely invention, is the catastrophe. The idea of it I received from a story told to me by my mother, many years ago, of a man condemned to the block, who died in the same manner; and since the play has been written, I have had the satisfaction of finding it confirmed by a circumstance very similar, related in Miss Plumtre's [*sic*] interesting account of the atrocities committed in Lions by the revolutionary tribunals[7] […].

Contrary to our established laws of Tragedy, this Play consists only of three acts, and is written in prose. I have made it short, because I was unwilling to mix any lighter matter with a subject so solemn; and in extending it to the usual length without doing so, it would have been in danger of becoming monotonous and harrassing. I have written it in prose, that the expressions of the agitated person might be plain though strong, and kept as closely as possible to the simplicity of nature […].

A Comedy on Fear, the chief character being a man, is not liable to the objections I have supposed might be made to a Tragedy under the same circumstances. But a very great degree of constitutional cowardice would have been a picture too humiliating to afford any amusement, or even to engage the attention for any considerable time. The hero of my third Play,[8] therefore, is represented as timid indeed, and endeavouring to conceal it by a boastful affectation of gallantry and courage; but at the same time, worked upon by artful contrivances to believe himself in such a situation as would have miserably overcome many a one, who, on ordinary occasions of danger, would have behaved with decorum. Cowardice in him has been cultivated by indulgence of every kind: and self-conceit and selfishness are the leading traits of his character, which might have been originally trained to useful and honourable activity […].

The last Play in the volume is a drama of two acts, the subject of which is Hope.[9] This passion, when it acts permanently, loses the character of a passion, and when it acts violently is like Anger, Joy, or Grief, too transient to become the subject of a piece of any length. It seemed to me, in fact, neither fit for Tragedy nor Comedy; and like Anger, Joy, or Grief, I once thought to have left it out of my Series altogether. However, what it wanted in strength it seemed to have in grace; and being of a noble, kindly and engaging nature, it drew me to itself; and I resolved to do every thing for it that I could, in spite of the objections which had at first deterred me […].

As this passion, though more pleasing, is not so powerfully interesting as those that are more turbulent, and was therefore in danger of becoming languid and tiresome, if long dwelt upon without interruption; and at the same time of being sunk into shade or entirely overpowered, if relieved from it by variety of strong marked characters in the inferior persons of the

---

7   Plumtre's Residence in France, vol. i. p. 339. [Baillie's Note]. The author of *A Narrative of a Three Years' Residence in France* (1810) is Anne Plumptre (1760–1818).

8   *The Siege.*

9   *The Beacon.*

drama, I have introduced into the scenes several songs. So many indeed, that I have ventured to call it a Musical Drama. I have, however, avoided one fault so common, I might say universal, in such pieces, viz. making people sing in situations in which it is not natural for them to do so: and creating a necessity for either having the first characters performed by those, who can both act and sing, (persons very difficult to find,) or permitting them to be made entirely insipid and absurd. For this purpose, the songs are all sung by those who have little or nothing to act, and introduced when nothing very interesting is going on. They are also supposed not to be spontaneous expressions of sentiment in the singer, but (as songs in ordinary life usually are) compositions of other people, which have been often sung before, and are only generally applicable to the present occasion […].

The Series of Plays was originally published in the hope that some of the pieces it contains, although first given to the Public from the press, might in time make their way to the stage, and there be received and supported with some degree of public favour. But the present situation of dramatic affairs is greatly against every hope of this kind; and should they ever become more favourable, I have now good reason to believe, that the circumstance of these plays having been already published, would operate strongly against their being received upon the stage. I am therefore strongly of opinion that I ought to reserve the remainder of the work in manuscript, if I would not run the risk of entirely frustrating my original design […].

The Public have now to chuse between what we shall suppose are well-written and well-acted Plays, the words of which are not heard, or heard but imperfectly by two thirds of the audience, while the finer and more pleasing traits of the acting are by a still greater proportion lost altogether, and splendid pantomime, or pieces whose chief object is to produce striking scenic effect, which can be seen and comprehended by the whole. […].

The size of our theatres, then, is what I chiefly allude to, when I say, present circumstances are unfavourable for the production of these Plays.[10] While they continue to be of this size, it is a vain thing to complain either of want of taste in the Public, or want of inclination in Managers to bring forward new pieces of merit, taking it for granted that there are such to produce. Nothing can be truly relished by the most cultivated audience that is not distinctly heard and seen, and Managers must produce what will be relished. Shakespeare's Plays, and some of our other old Plays, indeed, attract full houses, though they are often repeated, because, being familiar to the

---

[10]   Though lacking modern lighting and acoustics to compensate for often noisy audiences, theater size had recently increased dramatically, leaving many playgoers unable to see or hear much of the production. The Theatre Royal in Drury Lane, for example, had been rebuilt after a recent fire to seat well over 3,000, roughly half again its present capacity of 2,200. Similarly, the Theatre Royal in Covent Garden, also destroyed by fire, was rebuilt to seat 3,000, up from its original capacity of just under 1,900. As the Royal Opera House, it holds 2,268 today.

audience, they can still understand and follow them pretty closely, though but imperfectly heard; and surely this is no bad sign of our public taste […].

Our great tragic actress, Mrs. Siddons, whose matchless powers of expression have so long been the pride of our stage, and the most admired actors of the present time, have been brought up in their youth in small theatres, where they were encouraged to enter thoroughly into the characters they represented; and to express in their faces that variety of fine fleeting emotion which nature, in moments of agitation, assumes, and the imitation of which we are taught by nature to delight in.[11] But succeeding actors will only consider expression of countenance as addressed to an audience removed from them to a greater distance; and will only attempt such strong expression as can be perceived and have effect at a distance. It may easily be imagined what exaggerated expression will then get into use […].

But the department of acting that will suffer most under these circumstances, is that which particularly regards the gradually unfolding of the passions, and has, perhaps, hitherto been less understood than any other part of the art—I mean Soliloquy. What actor in his senses will then think of giving to the solitary musing of a perturbed mind that muttered, imperfect articulation which grows by degrees into words; that heavy, suppressed voice as of one speaking through sleep; that rapid burst of sounds which often succeeds the slow languid tones of distress; those sudden untuned exclamations which, as if frightened at their own discord, are struck again into silence as sudden and abrupt, with all the corresponding variety of countenance that belongs to it;—what actor, so situated, will attempt to exhibit all this? No; he will be satisfied, after taking a turn or two across the front of the stage, to place himself directly in the middle of it, and there, spreading out his hands as if he were addressing some person whom it behoved him to treat with great ceremony, to tell to himself, in an audible uniform voice, all the secret thoughts of his own heart. When he has done this, he will think, and he will think rightly, that he has done enough […].[12]

■ From *Fraser's Magazine*

EPISTLES TO THE LITERATI.[13]

No. IX.

"ON THE CHARACTER OF ROMIERO."

When any reasonable and specific fault is found with a work, and by a very friendly and able critic, it behoves [*sic*] the author to consider well how

---

11   On Siddons and her talented family, see Inchbald Chapter 4, note 5.

12   Baillie examines further obstacles to effective acting technique and staging presented by the period's extremely large theaters and concludes with a note describing the deleterious effects of contemporary stage lighting.

13   *Fraser's Magazine for Town and Country* 14 (December 1836): 748–9. Baillie responds to a review of *Dramas* (1836) in *The Quarterly Review* 55 (February 1836): 487–513.

far it may really deserve the censure laid upon it, and also how far it may be vindicated from that censure. The *Quarterly Review* for January last, so discriminating in the observations, and liberal in the praises bestowed upon the new dramas, &c. says, regarding the first play, *Romiero,*

"The passion of jealousy may co-exist with the noblest qualities of our nature; but a jealous disposition—and such seems that of Romiero—is something mean and degrading: it is almost impossible to make it assume that dignity which is necessary to great tragic interest."

I am not presumptuous enough to suppose that I can altogether vindicate Romiero; but, in simply laying before the reader my own intentions in delineating this character, something very near a vindication may, perhaps, be found. I have endeavoured to represent him as a man fastidiously delicate in every thing connected with the affections of the heart. This is shewn by his former concealed attachment to a lady, which was only discovered after her death—by his being so distressed at the ideas of Zorada's love having passed from him to another, that he at first thinks the further personal criminality is scarcely worth considering—by his not enduring, when that criminality is, from circumstances, made to appear probable or presumptive, even in his aggravated agony, to have her name coupled with any gross epithet. This, it appears to me, is a jealousy dealing particularly with the affections of the heart, not being afraid or suspicious of more ignoble wrongs; and therefore a jealousy which (as its frailty, indeed) might belong to a noble nature. Does not a lover, whether man or woman, feel pleased with tokens of this refined jealousy in the object beloved, and receive it as a proof of the value set upon the hidden treasure of the heart? The idea of its arising from an over anxiety to retain unimpaired and exclusively what is held so precious, does not *degrade* the character of the lover, though it may give cause to fear much for his future happiness. The tragedy of *Othello* is a work of so much genius and interest, that it seems to be established as a pattern for the passion of jealousy to all succeeding writers, without considering what was the real design of our immortal bard when he wrote the play. He had no design, I truly believe, but to represent to his audience the story of the Moor of Venice, instigated to murder his wife by the falsehoods of a diabolical villain: and, as it appears to me, revenge against her for the grossest infidelity is more manifested through the whole of the piece than what is termed jealousy. Shakespeare does all that he, probably, intended to do with exquisite understanding of nature, and with unrivalled beauty and force of expression; but had no idea that he was thereby to fascinate men's minds so much as to bind them over to follow his steps for ever on the subject connected with the story of his play. He goaded his hero to the fatal catastrophe by the machinations of a villain, whose falsehoods he never, or but very slightly, at any time distrusts; and, with such strong faith in Iago, he does conceive that his wife has been grossly false, and, in his rage, calls her by the vile name he believes her to deserve. But must every man, to be entitled to our sympathy when jealous, have his jealousy fastened upon him from without, by the evil agency of another? I thought not; and was not aware that, in representing this passion as suspicious and watchful over small indications of change in the affections of a beloved object, I should make it unworthy of human sympathy.

Romiero is likewise charged with taking up one cause of suspicion, as soon as another has been proved to be unfounded; which has been considered as breaking the unity of action, as well as testifying too strongly the natively suspicious character of the man. The circumstance of Zorada's unhappy father and Romiero's oath I considered as the continuous story of the piece; the love-matters of Don Maurice and Beatrice only as auxiliaries to it. And when the causes of Zorada's altered behaviour to him can no longer be accounted for by a supposed love for Maurice, and new circumstances arise, fitted naturally to create suspicion, and to bring the former unaccountable ones fresh to his mind, the story, as I apprehended the matter, proceeds without being broken. We sympathise with suspicion, as with all other emotions, according to its object. To suspect that another would circumvent, or endeavour to deprive you of your gold or worldly wealth, would not readily come into a noble mind; but a fear lest the affections of the heart may be estranged from us, and a suspicious watchfulness for indications of this misfortune, may be weak, indeed, but cannot be called mean. We sympathise with the anger of Achilles for the loss of his beautiful captive; but had a herd of beeves been taken from him with equal injustice, we should be less susceptible on his behalf.

In the usual courtesy of writing, I ought to say that I produce this attempted vindication of *Romiero* with diffidence: but I do not; contrariwise, I do it with considerable confidence. It is, however, a confidence that is more than equalled by that which I feel in the natural disposition of my friendly critic. He will not, I am certain, continue to think me in the wrong, for want of a good hearty inclination to think me in the right: and I trust that many of my readers will receive this attempted defence of the character with similar candour and indulgence.

Ann Ward Radcliffe
(1764–1823)

One of the most popular and imitated novelists of her day, yet reticent about publicity, Ann Radcliffe was admired by celebrated literary contemporaries such as Austen, Scott, Coleridge, Shelley, Byron, and Keats. Born Ann Ward, she spent much of her girlhood with relatives who enjoyed strong contacts within the major circles of religious dissent. She probably received little formal education but enjoyed reading, and her later journals show her appreciation for nature and some knowledge of art, recent literature, and the major aesthetic theories. Family connections may have brought her into contact with such notable literary women as Hester Thrale, Elizabeth Montagu, and Anna Barbauld. In 1784 she married William Radcliffe, an Oxford graduate trained for the bar but turned journalist with republican sympathies. The couple settled in London, where they enjoyed the pleasures of urban life varied with travels to picturesque destinations in England and abroad.

Ann Radcliffe appeared on the literary scene at the beginning of the revolutionary last decade of the eighteenth century. After the 1789 publication of *The Castles of Athlin and Dunbayne*, she followed with *A Sicilian Romance* (1790), *The Romance of the Forest* (1791), *The Mysteries of Udolpho* (1794), and *The Italian, or The Confessional of the Black Penitents* (1797). Her travel narrative, *A Journey Made in the Summer of 1794 through Holland and the Western Frontier of Germany with a Return down the Rhine: To Which Are Added Observations during a Tour to the Lakes of Lancashire, Westmoreland and Cumberland*, also appeared in 1795. *Gaston de Blondeville, or The Court of Henry III Keeping Festival in Ardenne. A Romance* was written in 1802, though it was not published until after her death, when it appeared with *St. Albans Abbey. A Metrical Tale* (1826). Readers have remarked on her novels' poetic descriptions of nature as well as their inclusion of lyrical poetry that often celebrates the emotional or psychological effects of sublime or picturesque settings. But Radcliffe's most characteristic literary technique is to sustain suspense by avoiding the explicit grotesqueries of horror, instead exploiting obscurity and the unknown to produce more subtle sensations of terror. Exploring theories that Edmund Burke had popularized in his essay on the sublime,[1] Radcliffe's "On the Supernatural in Poetry," her only known critical essay, takes the form of a dialogue, a form that had often been used for literary criticism, including by Clara Reeve in *The Progress of Romance* (1785).

■ On the Supernatural in Poetry. By the Late Mrs. Radcliffe[2]

ONE of our travelers began a grave dissertation on the illusions of the imagination. "And not only on frivolous occasions," said he, "but in the most important pursuits of life, an object often flatters and charms at a distance, which vanishes into nothing as we approach it; and 'tis well if it leave only disappointment in our hearts. Sometimes a severer monitor is left there."

These truisms, delivered with an air of discovery by Mr. S— , who seldom troubled himself to think upon any subject, except that of a good dinner, were lost upon his companion, who, pursuing the airy conjectures which the present scene, however humbled, had called up, was following Shakspeare into unknown regions. "Where is now the undying spirit," said he, "that could so exquisitely perceive and feel?—that could inspire itself with the various characters of this world, and create worlds of its own; to which the grand and the beautiful, the gloomy and the sublime of visible Nature, up-called not only corresponding feelings, but passions; which seemed to perceive a soul in everything: and thus, in the secret workings of its own characters, and in the combinations of its incidents, kept the elements and local scenery always in unison with them, heightening their effect. So the conspirators at Rome pass under the fiery showers and sheeted lightning of the thunder-storm, to meet, at midnight, in the porch of Pompey's theatre. The streets being then deserted by the affrighted multitude, that place, open as it was, was convenient for their council; and, as to the storm, they felt it not; it was not more terrible to them than their own passions, nor so terrible to others as the dauntless spirit that makes them, almost unconsciously, brave its fury. These appalling circumstances, with others of supernatural import, attended the fall of the conqueror of the world—a

---

[1] *A Philosophical Enquiry into the Origin of our Ideas of the Sublime and Beautiful* (1757).

[2] Having been permitted to extract the above eloquent passages from the manuscripts of the author of the "Mysteries of Udolpho," we have given this title to them, though certainly they were not intended by the writer to be offered as a formal or deliberate essay, under this, or any other denomination. They were, originally, part of an INTRODUCTION to the Romance, or Phantasie, which is about to appear. The discussion is supposed to be carried on by two travelers in Shakspeare's native county, Warwickshire [*New Monthly Magazine* note]. The "Romance, or Phantasie, which is about to appear" would be the posthumously published *Gaston de Blondeville* (1826). This essay appeared posthumously in the *New Monthly Magazine* 16 (February 1826): 145–52.

man, whose power Cassius represents to be dreadful as this night, when the sheeted dead were seen in the lightning to glide along the streets of Rome. How much does the sublimity of these attendant circumstances heighten our idea of the power of Cæsar, of the terrific grandeur of his character, and prepare and interest us for his fate. The whole soul is roused and fixed, in the full energy of attention, upon the progress of the conspiracy against him; and, had not Shakspeare wisely withdrawn him from our view, there would have been no balance of our passions."[3]—"Cæsar was a tyrant," said Mr. S——. W—— looked at him for a moment, and smiled, and then silently resumed the course of his own thoughts. No master ever knew how to touch the accordant springs of sympathy by small circumstances like our own Shakspeare. In Cymbeline, for instance, how finely such circumstances are made use of, to awaken, at once, solemn expectation and tenderness, and, by recalling the softened remembrance of a sorrow long past, to prepare the mind to melt at one that was approaching, mingling at the same time, by means of a mysterious occurrence, a slight tremour of awe with our pity. Thus, when Belarius and Arviragus return to the cave where they had left the unhappy and worn-out Imogen to repose, while they are yet standing before it, and Arviragus, speaking of her with tenderest pity, as "the poor sick Fidele," goes out to enquire for her,—solemn music is heard from the cave, sounded by that harp of which Guiderius says, "*Since the death of my dearest mother, it did not speak before. All solemn things should answer solemn accidents.*" Immediately Arviragus enters with Fidele senseless in his arms:

"The bird is dead, that we have made so much of.
——How found you him?
Stark, as you see, thus smiling.
——I thought he slept, and put
My clouted brogues from off my feet, whose rudeness
Answered my steps too loud."—"Why he but sleeps!"
      *   *   *   *   *
      "With fairest flowers
While the summer lasts, AND I LIVE HERE, FIDELE,
I'll sweeten thy sad grave———."[4]

Tears alone can speak the touching simplicity of the whole scene. Macbeth shows, by many instances, how much Shakspeare delighted to heighten the effect of his characters and his story by correspondent scenery: there

[3]   The speaker refers to Shakespeare's *Julius Caesar* I.iii and II.i.
[4]   *Cymbeline* IV.ii.189–220.

the desolate heath, the troubled elements, assist the mischief of his malignant beings. But who, after hearing Macbeth's thrilling question——

         ——"What are these,
So withered and so wild in their attire,
That look not like the inhabitants o' the earth,
And yet are on't?"—— [5]

who would have thought of reducing them to mere human beings, by attir-
ing them not only like the inhabitants of the earth, but in the dress of a particular country, and making them downright Scotch-women? thus not only
contradicting the very words of Macbeth, but withdrawing from these cruel
agents of the passions all that strange and supernatural air which had made
them so affecting to the imagination, and which was entirely suitable to the
solemn and important events they were foretelling and accomplishing.
Another *improvement* on Shakspeare is the introducing a crowd of witches
thus arrayed, instead of the three beings "so withered and so wild in their
attire."

About the latter part of this sentence, W——, as he was apt to do, thought
aloud, and Mr. S—— said, "I, now, have sometimes considered, that it was
quite suitable to make Scotch witches on the stage, appear like Scotch
women. You must recollect that, in the superstition concerning witches,
they lived familiarly upon the earth, mortal sorcerers, and were not always
known from mere old women; consequently they must have appeared in
the dress of the country where they happened to live, or they would have
been more than suspected of witchcraft, which we find was not always the
case."

"You are speaking of old women, and not of witches," said W—— laughing, "and I must more than suspect you of crediting that obsolete superstition which destroyed so many wretched, yet guiltless persons, if I allow
your argument to have any force. I am speaking of the only real witch—the
witch of the poet; and all our notions and feelings connected with terror
accord with his. The wild attire, the look *not of this earth*, are essential traits
of supernatural agents, working evil in the darkness of mystery. Whenever
the poet's witch condescends, according to the vulgar notion, to mingle
mere ordinary mischief with her malignity, and to become familiar, she is
ludicrous, and loses her power over the imagination; the illusion vanishes.
So vexatious is the effect of the stage-witches upon my mind, that I should
probably have left the theatre when they appeared, had not the fascination
of Mrs. Siddons's influence so spread itself over the whole play, as to overcome my disgust, and to make me forget even Shakspeare himself; while
all consciousness of fiction was lost, and his thoughts lived and breathed

---

[5]   *Macbeth* I.iii.38–42.

before me in the very form of truth. Mrs. Siddons, like Shakspeare, always disappears in the character she represents, and throws an illusion over the whole scene around her, that conceals many defects in the arrangements of the theatre. I should suppose she would be the finest Hamlet that ever appeared, excelling even her own brother in that character; she would more fully preserve the tender and refined melancholy, the deep sensibility, which are the peculiar charm of Hamlet, and which appear not only in the ardour, but in the occasional irresolution and weakness of his character— the secret spring that reconciles all his inconsistencies.[6] A sensibility so profound can with difficulty be justly imagined, and therefore can very rarely be assumed. Her brother's firmness, incapable of being always subdued, does not so fully enhance, as her tenderness would, this part of the character. The strong light which shows the mountains of a landscape in all their greatness, and with all their rugged sharpnesses, gives them nothing of the interest with which a more gloomy tint would invest their grandeur; dignifying, though it softens, and magnifying, while it obscures."

"I still think," said Mr. S——, without attending to these remarks, "that, in a popular superstition, it is right to go with the popular notions, and dress your witches like the old women of the place where they are supposed to have appeared."

"As far as these notions prepare us for the awe which the poet designs to excite, I agree with you that he is right in availing himself of them; but, for this purpose, every thing familiar and common should be carefully avoided. In nothing has Shakspeare been more successful than in this; and in another case somewhat more difficult—that of selecting circumstances of manners and appearance for his supernatural beings, which, though wild and remote, in the highest degree, from common apprehension, never shock the understanding by incompatibility with themselves—never compel us, for an instant, to recollect that he has a license for extravagance. Above every ideal being is the ghost of Hamlet, with all its attendant incidents of time and place. The dark watch upon the remote platform, the dreary aspect of the night, the very expression of the officer on guard, 'the air bites shrewdly; it is very cold;' the recollection of a star, an unknown world, are all circumstances which excite forlorn, melancholy, and solemn feelings, and dispose us to welcome, with trembling curiosity, the awful being that draws near; and to indulge in that strange mixture of horror, pity, and indignation, produced by the tale it reveals. Every minute circumstance of the scene between those watching on the platform, and of that between them and Horatio, preceding the entrance of the apparition, contributes to excite some feeling of dreariness, or melancholy, or solemnity, or expectation, in unison with, and leading on toward that high curiosity and

---

6   On Sarah Siddons, see Inchbald, Chapter 4, note 5.

thrilling awe with which we witness the conclusion of the scene. So the first question of Bernardo, and the words in reply, 'Stand and unfold yourself.' But there is not a single circumstance in either dialogue, not even in this short one, with which the play opens, that does not take its secret effect upon the imagination. It ends with Bernardo desiring his brother-officer, after having asked whether he has had 'quiet watch,' to hasten the guard, if he should chance to meet them; and we immediately feel ourselves alone on dreary ground.

"When Horatio enters, the challenge—the dignified answers, 'Friends to this ground, and liegemen to the Dane,'—the question of Horatio to Bernardo, touching the apparition—the unfolding of the reason why 'Horatio has consented to watch with them the minutes of this night'—the sitting down together, while Bernardo relates the particulars of what they had seen for two nights; and, above all, the few lines with which he begins his story, 'Last night of all,' and the distinguishing, by the situation of 'yon same star,' the very point of time when the spirit had appeared—the abruptness with which he breaks off, 'the bell then beating one'—the instant appearance of the ghost, as though ratifying the story for the very truth itself—all these are circumstances which the deepest sensibility only could have suggested, and which, if you read them a thousand times, still continue to affect you almost as much as at first.[7] I thrill with delightful awe, even while I recollect and mention them, as instances of the exquisite art of the poet."

"Certainly you must be very superstitious," said Mr. S—— , "or such things could not interest you thus."

"There are few people less so than I am," replied W—— , "or I understand myself and the meaning of superstition very ill."

"That is quite paradoxical."

It appears so, but so it is not. If I cannot explain this, take it as a mystery of the human mind."

"If it were possible for me to believe the appearance of ghosts at all," replied Mr. S—— , "it would certainly be the ghost of Hamlet; but I never can suppose such things; they are out of all reason and probability."

"You would believe the immortality of the soul," said W—— , with solemnity, "even without the aid of revelation; yet our confined faculties cannot comprehend *how* the soul may exist after separation from the body. I do not absolutely know that spirits are permitted to become visible to us on earth; yet that they may be permitted to appear for very rare and important purposes, such as could scarcely have been accomplished without equal suspension, or a momentary change, of the laws prescribed to what we call *Nature*—that is, without one more exercise of the same CREATIVE POWER of

---

[7]   The incidents and quotes are from *Hamlet*, Act I, mostly the first scene.

which we must acknowledge so many millions of existing instances, and by which alone we ourselves at this moment breathe, think, or disquisite at all, cannot be impossible, and, I think, is probable. Now, probability is enough for the poet's justification, the ghost being supposed to have come for an important purpose. Oh, I should never be weary of dwelling on the perfection of Shakspeare, in his management of every scene connected with that most solemn and mysterious being, which takes such entire possession of the imagination, that we hardly seem conscious we are beings of this world while we contemplate 'the extravagant and erring spirit.' The spectre departs, accompanied by natural circumstances as touching as those with which he had approached. It is by the strange light of the glow-worm, which 'gins to pale his ineffectual fire;' it is at the first scent of the morning air—the living breath, that the apparition retires. There is, however, no little vexation in seeing the ghost of Hamlet *played*. The finest imagination is requisite to give the due coloring to such a character on the stage; and yet almost any actor is thought capable of performing it. In the scene where Horatio breaks his secret to Hamlet, Shakspeare, still true to the touch of circumstances, makes the time evening, and marks it by the very words of Hamlet, 'Good even, sir,' which Hammer and Warburton changed, without any reason, to 'good morning,' thus making Horatio relate his most interesting and solemn story by the clear light of the cheerfullest part of the day; when busy sounds are stirring, and the sun itself seems to contradict every doubtful tale, and lessen every feeling of terror. The discord of this must immediately be understood by those who have bowed the willing soul to the poet."

"How happens it then," said Mr. S—— , "that objects of terror sometimes strike us very forcibly, when introduced into scenes of gaiety and splendour, as, for instance, in the Banquet scene in Macbeth?"[8]

"They strike, then, chiefly by the force of contrast," replied W—— ; "but the effect, though sudden and strong, is also transient; it is the thrill of horror and surprise, which they then communicate, rather than the deep and solemn feelings excited under more accordant circumstances, and left long upon the mind. Who ever suffered for the ghost of Banquo, the gloomy and sublime kind of terror, which that of Hamlet calls forth? though the appearance of Banquo, at the high festival of Macbeth, not only tells us that he is murdered, but recalls to our minds the fate of the gracious Duncan, laid in silence and death by those who, in this very scene, are reveling in his spoils. There, though deep pity mingles with our surprise and horror, we experience a far less degree of interest, and that interest too of an inferior kind. The union of grandeur and obscurity, which Mr. Burke describes as a sort of tranquility tinged with terror, and which causes the sublime, is to be

---

[8]   *Macbeth* III.iv.

found only in Hamlet; or in scenes where circumstances of the same kind prevail."[9]

"That may be," said Mr. S—— , "and I perceive you are not one of those who contend that obscurity does not make any part of the sublime." "They must be men of very cold imaginations," said W—— , "with whom certainty is more terrible than surmise. Terror and horror are so far opposite, that the first expands the soul, and awakens the faculties to a high degree of life; the other contracts, freezes, and nearly annihilates them. I apprehend, that neither Shakspeare nor Milton by their fictions, nor Mr. Burke by his reasoning, anywhere looked to positive horror as a source of the sublime, though they all agree that terror is a very high one; and where lies the great difference between horror and terror, but in the uncertainty and obscurity, that accompany the first, respecting the dreaded evil?"

"But what say you to Milton's image—
"On his brow sat horror plumed."[10]

"As an image, it is certainly sublime; it fills the mind with an idea of power, but it does not follow that Milton intended to declare the feeling of horror to be sublime; and after all, his image imparts more of terror than of horror; for it is not distinctly pictured forth, but is seen in glimpses through obscuring shades, the great outlines only appearing, which excite the imagination to complete the rest; he only says, 'sat horror plumed;' you will observe, that the look of horror and the other characteristics are left to the imagination of the reader; and according to the strength of that, he will feel Milton's image to be either sublime or otherwise. Milton, when he sketched it, probably felt, that not even his art could fill up the outline, and present to other eyes the countenance which his 'mind's eye' gave to him. Now, if obscurity has so much effect on fiction, what must it have in real life, when to ascertain the object of our terror, is frequently to acquire the means of escaping it. You will observe, that this image, though indistinct or obscure, is not confused."

"How can anything be indistinct and not confused?" said Mr. S—— .

"Ay, that question is from the new school," replied W.; "but recollect, that obscurity, or indistinctness, is only a negative, which leaves the imagination to act upon the few hints that truth reveals to it; confusion is a thing as positive as distinctness, though not necessarily so palpable; and it may, by mingling and confounding one image with another, absolutely counteract

---

9   In *A Philosophical Enquiry*, Burke proposes that obscurity is key to the terror that constitutes the sublime. Radcliffe's essay and her own novelistic technique often put Burke's ideas into practice.
10 Milton, *Paradise Lost* IV.988–9. Milton's epic supplies Burke with several examples of the sublime.

the imagination, instead of exciting it. Obscurity leaves something for the imagination to exaggerate; confusion, by blurring one image into another, leaves only a chaos in which the mind can find nothing to be magnificent, nothing to nourish its fears or doubts, or to act upon in any way; yet confusion and obscurity are terms used indiscriminately by those, who would prove, that Shakspeare and Milton were wrong when they employed obscurity as a cause of the sublime, that Mr. Burke was equally mistaken in his reasoning upon the subject, and that mankind have been equally in error, as to the nature of their own feelings, when they were acted upon by the illusions of those great masters of the imagination, at whose so potent bidding, the passions have been awakened from their sleep, and by whose magic a crowded Theatre has been changed to a lonely shore, to a witch's cave, to an enchanted island, to a murderer's castle, to the ramparts of an usurper, to the battle, to the midnight carousal of the camp or the tavern, to every various scene of the living world."

"Yet there are poets, and great ones too," said Mr. S——, "whose minds do not appear to have been very susceptible of those circumstances of time and space—of what you, perhaps, would call the picturesque in feeling—which you seem to think so necessary to the attainment of any powerful effect on the imagination. What say you to Dryden?"

"That he had a very strong imagination, a fertile wit, a mind well prepared by education, and great promptness of feeling; but he had not—at least not in good proportion to his other qualifications—that delicacy of feeling, which we call taste; moreover, that his genius was overpowered by the prevailing taste of the court, and by an intercourse with the world, too often humiliating to his morals, and destructive of his sensibility. Milton's better morals protected his genius, and his imagination was not lowered by the world."

"Then you seem to think there may be great poets, without a full perception of the picturesque; I mean by picturesque, the beautiful and grand in nature and in art—and with little susceptibility to what you would call the accordant circumstances, the harmony of which is essential to any powerful effect upon your feelings."

"No; I cannot allow that. Such men may have high talents, wit, genius, judgment, but not the soul of poetry, which is the spirit of all these, and also something wonderfully higher—something too fine for definition. It certainly includes an instantaneous perception, and an exquisite love of whatever is graceful, grand, and sublime, with the power of seizing and combining such circumstances of them, as to strike and interest a reader by the representation, even more than a general view of the real scene itself could do. Whatever this may be called, which crowns the mind of a poet, and distinguishes it from every other mind, our whole heart instantly acknowledges it in Shakspeare, Milton, Gray, Collins, Beattie, and a very few others, not excepting Thomson, to whose powers the sudden tear of delight and admiration bears at once both testimony and tribute. How deficient Dryden was of a poet's feelings in the fine province of the beautiful and the graceful, is apparent from his alteration of the Tempest, by which he has not only lessened the interest by incumbering the plot, but has absolutely disfigured the character of Miranda, whose simplicity, whose tenderness and innocent affections, might, to use Shakspeare's own words in another play, 'be shrined in crystal.' A love of moral beauty is as essential in the mind of a poet, as a love of picturesque beauty. There is as much difference between the tone of Dryden's moral feelings and those of Milton, as there is between their perceptions of the grand and the beautiful in nature. Yet, when I recollect the 'Alexander's Feast,' I am astonished at the powers of Dryden, and at my own daring opinions upon them; and should be ready to unsay much that I have said, did I not consider this particular instance of the power of music upon Dryden's mind, to be as wonderful as any instance he has exhibited of the effect of that enchanting art in his sublime ode. I cannot, however, allow it to be the finest ode in the English language, so long as I remember Gray's Bard, and Collin's Ode on the Passions.[11]—— But, to return to Shakspeare, I have sometimes thought, as I walked in the deep shade of the North Terrace of Windsor Castle, when the moon shone on all beyond, that the scene must have been present in Shakspeare's mind, when he drew the night-scenes in Hamlet; and, as I have stood on the platform, which there projects over the precipice, and have heard only the measured step of a sentinel or the clink of his arms, and have seen his shadow passing by moonlight, at the foot of the high Eastern tower, I have almost expected to see the royal shade armed cap-a-pee standing still on the lonely platform before me. The very star—'yon same star that's westward from the pole' —seemed to watch over the Western towers of the Terrace, whose high dark lines marked themselves upon the heavens. All has been so still and shadowy, so great and solemn, that the scene appeared fit for 'no mortal business nor any sounds that the earth owns.'[12] Did you ever observe the fine effect of the Eastern tower, when you stand near the Western end of the North terrace, and its tall profile rears itself upon the sky, from nearly the base to the battled top, the lowness of the parapet permitting this? It is most striking at night, when the stars appear, at different heights, upon its tall dark line, and when the sentinel on watch moves a shadowy figure at its foot."

---

[11] In 1667, the same year he published *Alexander's Feast; or, the Power of Musique,* John Dryden also published an adaptation of *The Tempest* that remained popular through the eighteenth century. Thomas Gray authored *The Bard* (1757) while *The Passions: An Ode to Music,* one of the *Odes on Several Descriptive and Allegorical Subjects* (1746), was published by William Collins. James Beattie (1735–1803) and James Thomson (1700–1748) both helped pave the way for the British Romantic poets through affecting depictions of nature, with Thomson's *The Seasons* (1726–1730) exerting particular influence.

[12] *The Tempest* I.ii.407–8, slightly altered.

Lucy Aikin (1781–1864)

Daughter of one prolific writer, editor, and literary critic and niece to another, Lucy Aikin was born into the world of letters. At the time of her birth, her father, physician John Aikin, was tutor of classics at the renowned Warrington Academy for Dissenters. Later forced from his medical practice by the combination of religious discrimination and his own weak health, he became an astonishingly fruitful writer, critic, and editor, producing biographies, histories, essays, fiction, and volumes of criticism, and operating several literary reviews. Under his guidance, Lucy received a home education of far greater breadth and rigor than that available to most English youth, boy or girl. Lucy's aunt, Anna Letitia Barbauld, one of the most revered women writers of her day, was also a productive literary critic and editor whose essay on fiction appears in the present volume. Lucy's brother Arthur was not only known for his scientific writing, but himself operated a literary review, *The Annual Review*.

With such a background, it is not surprising that before Lucy Aikin was out of her teens she was already publishing articles in reviews and magazines. By age twenty she had begun a career as both an editor and a children's writer with a collection of poems for children that proved popular enough to go through several editions. Her first major work of her own authorship was *Epistles on Women, Exemplifying Their Character and Condition in Various Ages and Nations: With Miscellaneous Poems* (1810), a forward-looking piece that advocated placing women on a more equal footing with men. In years following, she published poetry, fiction, children's literature, history, memoirs, biographies, correspondence, translations, adaptations, and edited collections. Works of note include her gothic novel *Lorimer* (1816), several biographies and histories of the fifteenth- and sixteenth-century English courts, a biography of Joseph Addison, and memoirs of her much-admired aunt, *The Works of Anna Laetitia Barbauld, edited, with a memoir, by Lucy Aikin* (1825), and her father, *Memoir of John Aikin, M.D.* (1823). As a biographer, Aikin stands out as one of the earliest to make significant use of primary materials such as letters and journals, and her work often met with considerable success, both critical and popular.

Most literary reviews were published anonymously during this period, and those by Lucy Aikin were no exception. Though the articles have not been identified, she is believed to have contributed to Joseph Johnson's *Analytical Review*, a speculation that seems plausible considering the dates of her known reviews and the friendships between several members of her family and Johnson. Along with her father and aunt, Lucy Aikin contributed reviews to her brother's *Annual Review*, a few of which appear below. Her Wordsworth review below has sometimes been cited as an instance of women's mistaken critical judgment, but it is no harsher than some reviews by male critics, including some of the best known critics of the day. Rather, it shows that many of the aesthetics now most closely associated with Romanticism were by no means universally accepted at the time.

■ Selected Reviews from the *Annual Review*

ART. XVI. *Popular Tales. By* MARIA EDGEWORTH, *Author of Practical Education, Belinda, Castle Rackrent, Irish Bulls, & c.*[1]

THE title of Popular Tales, which appears somewhat ambiguous, is explained in the preface, as having been chosen, not from a presumptuous and premature claim to popularity, but from the wish that they may be current beyond circles which are sometimes exclusively considered as polite. In pursuance of this design, the heroes and heroines of the stories before us, are judiciously selected from the middling and lower classes of life: instead of my lord and my lady, the baronet and the colonel, we have farmer Gray and his pretty daughter Rose, the glover and the tanner, the house-steward and the Cornish miner; what is better still we have *Soft Simon O'Dougherty*, Mr. Brian O'Neill, Barney O'Grady, and Paddy M'Cormack, the hay-maker, all true born Irishmen! and in Hibernian portraits, comic or pathetic, who may contend with the author of Castle Rackrent?[2] To touch or to amuse is not however the greatest merit of these tales, touching and amusing as they are; they are adapted to a still nobler end, to teach

"That useful science—to be good."[3]

Had not Miss Edgeworth anticipated the title, these might, with emphatic propriety, have been called "Moral Tales," such a pure love of virtue, such a just and discriminating judgment of right and wrong pervades them, set off by such sagacious observation, such variety of useful knowledge, such acute remarks on life, and delicate touches of nature, that few readers, we

---

[1]   *Annual Review* 3 (1804): 461–3.
[2]   Edgeworth's *Castle Rackrent* (1800) constitutes a landmark in both Irish and regional fiction.
[3]   Alexander Pope, "The Temple of Fame" 108.

really believe, will rise from the perusal, without feeling themselves, temporarily at least, both wiser and better. There is nothing here of romance, either in character or incident; every thing has been reduced within the compass of probability, by the scrutinizing eye of good sense.—Love, instead of reigning here triumphant over reason, duty, and interest, finds his power as transient, as much divided, and as straitly limited, as in real life. "Duty first, and love afterwards," is the maxim of one of the most amiable females.[4] Prudence, industry, fidelity, punctuality, kind heartedness, and domestic affections, are the calm and humble virtues most strongly inculcated; whilst extravagance, thoughtlessness, procrastination, dissipated habits, a love of scheming, and that presumptuous confidence in talents, or in good fortune, which precludes circumspection and steady application, are held up to view in their most despicable form and ruinous consequences.

Miss Edgeworth's style in this, as in all her former works, is distinguished by extreme perspicuity and an elegant simplicity, combined with strength and spirit, always correct and never mean: it is frequently brilliant with simile or allusion, dignified wherever dignity is required, and, above all, characterized by that inimitable ease which renders it the best possible vehicle of humorous and familiar dialogue. The conversation pieces of this author are conversation itself: the same exquisite talent of observation which enables her by a thousand delicate touches, to give to her narratives the stamp of truth, has taught her the very difficult, though apparently simple art, of talking on paper, in the very style really employed by such characters as those that she so naturally represents. The history of "Lame Jervas" is told, we think, with too much prolixity, and detail of things little interesting to the common reader; Mrs. Dolly's accident is not well managed; she would be more likely to go out in a stage-coach than on horseback. The story entitled "The Grateful Negro" is the only one to the moral of which we have any objection to make; it seems to us by no means clear, that even gratitude could justify Cæsar in betraying his friends and countrymen into the hands of their oppressors. Gratitude ought, indeed, to have induced him to use his utmost efforts for the preservation of his benefactor; but his fellow slaves were bound by no such obligations, and what right had he to prevent them from accomplishing that just vengeance in which he had before been so willing to join? We are ready to allow that the case was a difficult one, and that possibly, however Cæsar had been made to act, we should not have felt perfectly satisfied with his conduct; but why should these difficult cases be brought forward in works of fiction? When they occur in real life, an honest mind will commonly be enabled, by its own intuitive or habitual feelings of right, quickly to decide even amid a choice of evils; but by general rules these nice points never can be decided. To bring them forward unnecessarily is, therefore, to incur, without any

---

4   Patty Frankland, a farmer's daughter in "The Contrast," one of the *Popular Tales*.

adequate advantage, the risk of confounding, and thus blunting the moral sense. A note informs us that "whatever merit the heads of chapters, in the following stories, may have, it must be attributed to the editor," that is to Mr. Edgeworth. We really feel glad to have Miss Edgeworth exculpated from the imputation of having prefixed to her chapters such trite obvious maxims as "The passionate and capricious are often unjust." "Hasty conclusions are but seldom just." "Surmise is often partly true and partly false," and "The end of vice is shame and misery." Several errors have crept into these volumes, "caused by the author's absence from the press." We must present our readers with an extract from the beautiful tale of "Rosanna," merely to whet their curiosity. The remark with which it begins is equally new and judicious, and the Irish cabin is drawn from nature [...].[5]

ART. II. *Poems in two volumes, by* WILLIAM WORDSWORTH, *Author of the Lyrical Ballads.*[6]

MR. Wordsworth is a writer whose system and practice of poetry are both so entirely his own, that in order to appreciate as fairly as we wish to do, the value of these volumes, it will be necessary for us to enter somewhat at length into a discussion of the theory of the art. His own theory of it the author has given in the preface to a former work, published before this review existed; and as we do not perceive that his style of writing has since undergone any material alteration, we shall refer to it without scruple, as containing the principles upon which the poems immediately before us have been composed.[7]

On glancing the eye over Mr. Wordsworth's poems, the first thing that strikes the reader is, the extreme simplicity of their language: he may peruse page after page without meeting with any of those figures of speech which distinguish we do not say verse from prose, but a plain style from one that may be called cultured, or ornate. Should he however attribute this peculiarity to indolence or deficiency of skill, Mr. W. would complain of injustice, for he has anticipated the charge, and in the preface to "Lyrical Ballads" has endeavoured to repel it. The highly metaphysical language employed in this preface, and the spirit of mysticism by which it is pervaded, render it somewhat difficult of comprehension, but this, as well as we can collect, is the substance of that portion of it which is to our present purpose.

It was his intention, he says, in his poems to take incidents and situations from humble life, and describe them in the real language of men in that

---

[5]   The article concludes with extracts from Edgeworth's book.

[6]   *Annual Review* 6 (1807): 521–9.

[7]   Aikin refers to the preface added to the 1800 edition and expanded in subsequent editions of *Lyrical Ballads*, (originally published in 1798), which stands as a key manifesto of British Romanticism. With allowance for her slight silent alterations of her source, Aikin appears to quote from an 1802 edition for her discussion of Wordsworth's theory.

class, only freed from its grosser vulgarisms. He has preferred such incidents and situations, because the feelings of persons in low life are stronger, less complex, and therefore more easy to be developed, than those of persons who move in a wider circle—their language he has preferred for similar reasons, and also because he thought that any departure from nature in this respect must weaken the interest of his poems, both as being a departure from nature, and because the language which the imagination of even the greatest poet suggests to him, must, in liveliness and truth, fall far short of that which is uttered by men in real life, and under the pressure of actual passions. All that is called poetic diction, he therefore despises, and has shunned with the same care that others seek it, convinced that a poet may give all the pleasure he wishes to do without its assistance. At the same time he has "endeavoured to throw over his draughts a certain colouring of the imagination, whereby ordinary things should be presented to the mind in an unusual way, and further, and above all, to make these incidents and situations interesting by tracing in them, truly though not ostentatiously, the primary laws of our nature chiefly as far as regards the manner in which we associate ideas in a state of excitement." This last expression savours to us of a jargon with which the public has long been surfeited, and it is evident that not a position is here advanced which might not easily be combated; but as the practical success of a poet is the true test of the justness of his principles, we shall reserve our remarks on this head till we come to extracts. Anticipating an obvious question, why with his sentiments did he write in rhyme and measure? Mr. W. now proceeds sensibly enough to defend his practice in this respect on the ground of the pleasure which the experience of ages has proved these devices to be capable of affording—he adds, that "from the tendency of metre to divest language in a certain degree of its reality, and throw a kind of half consciousness of unsubstantial existence over the whole composition, there is little doubt that more painfully pathetic incidents and situations may be endured in verse, especially in rhymed verse, than in prose"—He brings in proof, "the reluctance with which we recur to the more distressing parts of the Gamester and Clarissa Harlowe, while Shakespeare's writings in the most pathetic scenes never act upon us as pathetic beyond the bounds of pleasure."[8] Is not Mr. W. aware that these arguments might equally be urged in favour of that poetic diction which he is so anxious to banish from his pages, and that the same instances might be adduced in its support that he here brings in favour of metre? It is not poetical diction, much more than mere verse, which produces the difference here pointed out between the writings of Shakespeare, and those of More and Richardson? But Mr. W. is persuaded that he has absolutely established it as a principle that in the dramatic parts of his compositions a poet should employ no other language than such as nature would suggest

---

[8]   *The Gamester* (1753) is a sentimental remorse tragedy by Edward Moore (1712–1757).

to his characters, (which after all is a very vague direction, since nature is by no means uniform in her promptings of this kind, and education and local circumstances produce endless diversities of style and expression,) and he endeavours to show that even where the poet speaks in his own character, he should employ no other diction than that of good and select prose. He begins by defining a poet as a man "endued with more lively sensibilities, more enthusiasm and tenderness, who has a greater knowledge of human nature, and a more comprehensive soul, than are supposed to be common among mankind," and in fine, as one chiefly distinguished from others, "by a greater promptness to think and feel without immediate external excitement, and a greater power in expressing such thoughts and feelings as are thus excited in him." These "passions and thoughts, and feelings," he affirms to be the same as those of other men; but even if they were not, he proceeds to insist, that as a poet does not write for poets, but for men in general, in order to excite rational sympathy, he must still express himself as other men do. Now it appears to us in the first place, that this definition of a poet is both imperfect and incorrect. It is only that of a person of strong sympathies, who possesses in an unusual degree the power of imagining and describing the feelings of other human beings. A good novel writer must be all this—a descriptive or lyric poet, though perfect in his kind, need not. But one who really deserves the name of a poet, must certainly add another faculty which is not even hinted at in this definition—we scarcely know how to name it, but it is that kind of fancy, akin to wit, which "glancing from heaven to earth, from earth to heaven,"[9] pervading, as it were, the whole world of nature and art, snatches from each its beauteous images combines, adapts, arranges them by a magic of its own, peoples with them its newcreations [*sic*], and at length pours forth in one striking, brilliant, yet harmonious whole.

This faculty, which Mr. W. overlooks, is doubtless the true parent of that diction which he despises; nor will either the frigid reasonings of metaphysicians, or the still more frigid caricaturas [*sic*] and miserable apings of mere versifiers, ever deter the genuine poet from employing it; it is his native tongue, and he must speak it, or be dumb. It is idle and sophistical to contend that because he does not write to poets he must not write like a poet. Many there are who are capable of being moved to rapture by a picture of Raphael or Titian, though they themselves could never guide a pencil—many there are who can follow with their eye the boldest soarings of the Theban eagle, though nature has not lent to them even the rudiments of a wing. If men in general are to be supposed incapable of understanding any expressions but what they would themselves have used in similar circumstances, rich and figurative diction must indeed, on most occasions be proscribed, but let it be remembered that such an interdiction would curtail

---

[9]   Shakespeare, *A Midsummer Night's Dream* IV.i.12–13.

the eloquence of Burke no less than the poetry of Shakespeare; so sweeping a clause is this, so fatal to the scintillations of wit, and the sports of fancy.[10] Our author afterwards speaks of poetry as a thing too high and sacred to be profaned by the addition of trifling ornaments of style: we cannot well understand what his notion of poetry is, after all, for he here plunges into the very depths of mysticism, but we suppose Virgil and Milton must have had some idea of its power and dignity, and it does appear to us somewhat ridiculous, not to say arrogant, in Mr. Wordsworth, to imagine that he has discovered any thing, either in the trivial incidents which he usually makes the subjects of his narrations, or in the moral feelings and deductions which he endeavours to associate with them, too sublime for the admission of such decorations as these masters have not deemed derogatory from the highest themes they ever touched. But we believe one great source of what we consider as the errors of this writer to be his failing to observe the distinction between rhetorical and poetical diction; the former it is that offends; but in his blind zeal he confounds both under the same note of reprobation. He quotes Dr. Johnson's paraphrase of, "Go to the ant thou sluggard," and justly stigmatizes it as "a hubbub of words;" but is this a specimen of poetical diction?[11] Surely not. It contains not one of those figures of speech, —similes, metaphors, allusions, and the like—which take their birth from that inventive, or combining, faculty which we mentioned above, but is tediously lengthened out by that accumulation of idle epithets, frivolous circumstances, and pompous and abstract terms, with which the rhetorician never fails, in prose or verse, to load his feeble and high sounding pages. It is this, this spirit of paraphrase and periphrasis, this idle parade of fine words, that is the bane of modern verse writing; let it be once thoroughly weeded of this, and it will be easy for the pruning hand of taste to lop away any redundancy of metaphor, personification, &c. which may still remain. Thus much for the system of Mr. Wordsworth, which appears to us a frigid and at the same time an extravagant one; we now proceed to examine what its practical application has produced; and whether our author has succeeded according to his intention, by giving us in plain rhymed and measured prose, matter so valuable and interesting as to be capable of affording pleasure equal, or superior, to that usually produced by poems of a similar class composed in a more ornate and polished style. We shall also examine how far the principle of association, on which many of the pieces are composed, appears to have been productive of beauties or defects [...][12]

---

[10] Burke was known for florid diction in his speeches before Parliament and even more so his writing, especially *Reflections on the Revolution in France*.

[11] Wordsworth argued this about Samuel Johnson's "Paraphrase of Proverbs, Chapter IV, Verses 6–11," which opens "Turn on the prudent ant thy heedless eyes,/Observe her labours, sluggard! and be wise."

[12] The critical remarks that follow are interspersed with extracts including poems such as "Fidelity," "Alice Fell," "To a Skylark," and others.

[In "Fidelity"] Mr. W. has certainly been fortunate in his subject; the incident is affecting, the scenery picturesque, but has he made a good poem of it, even on his own principles? Surely not. The language is not only prosaic, but generally flat, and in some parts absolutely mean; as in the two last lines of the first verse. The elipsis, "For sake of which" is a vulgarism which cannot but offend the cultivated reader; and to call the noise of a fish leaping "a lonely chear," is certainly an absurdity which could never pass in prose —but, what is worse still, is the coldness and tameness of the sentiments; on the unfortunate man, scarcely one expression of commiseration is bestowed; and even the dog, the hero of the tale, is presented to the mind in so unimpassioned a manner that he excites little or no interest. On the whole, in verse or prose, we know not how the tale could have been more flatly related […].

We may here take occasion to remark that these pieces in general are extremely ill rhymed. Forced, imperfect, and double rhymes abounding to an offensive and sometimes ludicrous degree. We may also observe, that one who trusts so much to mere metre, should take a little more pains with it […].

The Sonnets, a portion of which are dedicated to liberty, are formed on the model of Milton's and have a certain stiffness—but they hold a severe and manly tone which cannot be in times like these too much listened to —they bear strong traces of feeling and of thought, and convince us that on worthy subjects this man can write worthily […].

One of the Odes to Duty, is a meanly written piece, with some good thoughts, the other is a highly mystical effusion, in which the doctrine of pre-existence is maintained. The pieces entitled Moods of my own Mind, are some of them very happy, some quite the reverse. When a man endeavours to make his reader enter into an association that exists in his own mind between daffodils waving in the wind, and laughter—or to teach him to see something very fine in the fancy of crowning a little rock with snow-drops; he fails, and is sure to fail; for it would be strange indeed if any one besides himself ever formed associations so capricious and entirely arbitrary. But when he takes for his theme the youthful feelings connected with the sight of a butterfly, and the song of the cuckoo, he has struck a right key, and will wake an answering note in the bosoms of all who have mimicked the bird or chaced the insect. There is an exquisiteness of feeling in some of these little poems that disarms criticism […].

There are likewise some "Elegiac Stanzas" of great pathos, and a perfectly original turn, which increase our regret at the quantity of mere gossip that this author has allowed to escape him.

We have now bestowed upon these volumes a survey more detailed and laborious than our usual practice, or, in some respects, their importance, might seem to require; but we were anxious to combat a system which appears to us so injurious to its author, and so dangerous to public taste.

Mr. W. doubtless possesses a reflecting mind, and a feeling heart; but nature seems to have bestowed on him little of the fancy of the poet, and a foolish theory deters him from displaying even that little. In addition to this, he appears to us to starve his mind in solitude.—Hence the undue importance he attaches to trivial incidents—hence the mysterious kind of view that he takes of human nature and human life—and hence, finally, the unfortunate habit he has acquired of attaching exquisite emotions to objects which excite none in any other human breast […].

Sydney Owenson
(Lady Morgan; 1776?–1859)

Sydney Owenson's Irish-born father moved to London at age seventeen, where he Anglicized his name from MacOwen to Owenson and became an actor. There he met and eloped with Jane Mill, a genteel young woman who brought her husband a comfortable inheritance. After returning to Dublin for an engagement at the Theatre Royal, Robert Owenson decided to remain and sent for his wife. Sydney was probably born either during her mother's journey or shortly after her arrival in Ireland but because she went to great lengths to conceal her age, even her birth year remains uncertain.

Though she attended two elite schools for girls, much of Sydney's education came from her own voracious reading, including Irish history and lore, philosophy, British and continental literature, and even chemistry. Meanwhile, Robert Owenson invested heavily in his own theater, which was soon shut down as seditious for its efforts to develop a national drama. The family never financially recovered, and in 1798 Sydney, disregarding her father's objections, accepted employment as a governess, a position that allowed her to contribute to the family income while affording her leisure to write poetry and fiction. Her first publication, *Poems, Dedicated by Permission to the Countess of Moira* (1801) appeared the same year that the Act of Union shattered nationalist hopes for Irish independence.

Sydney Owenson's first novel, *St. Claire, or First Love* (1802), was republished the following year under the title *St. Clair, or, the Heiress of Desmond*. Its strong female protagonist and themes of Irish patriotism and regional detail recur in much of her later work. The novel sold well enough that Owenson left her governess position to pursue writing full time, and other publications soon followed. On a trip to England, Owenson encountered extreme anti-Irish prejudice, and she intended *The Wild Irish Girl* (1806) to present an alternate vision of Ireland's history and its people. Ironically, the English drive at the time to incorporate Irish cultural history as a part of native British cultural heritage ensured the novel's success, definitively establishing Owenson's literary reputation. The enormously popular *O'Donnel. A National Tale* (1814) and *The O'Briens and the O'Flahertys; a National Tale* (1827), which many regard as her best work, differ considerably in the solutions they envision for Ireland's difficulties, but share the distinction of

155

standing as two exceptionally powerfully political works of Irish fiction. Both novels succeeded despite being savaged in the Tory review periodicals.

Sydney Owenson became Lady Morgan in 1812, when she married physician Thomas Charles Morgan, who was knighted during the couple's courtship. In need of income, both Sir Charles and Lady Morgan authored literary journalism for a variety of periodicals, including the *Athenæum*, to which she contributed well over one hundred identifiable reviews on an extraordinary variety of topics. Despite their often explicitly political content, these reviews were, like most at the time, published anonymously as reflecting the editorial opinion of the periodical as a whole. In 1837 Lady Morgan was awarded a government pension for her literary work, and soon after, she and her husband moved from Dublin to London, where they established permanent residence. Although deeply grieved by Sir Charles's unexpected death in 1843, she remained active both socially and in the world of letters until shortly before her own death in 1859. A versatile professional writer, Sydney Owenson became in the course of her career not only a productive critic, but a popular novelist, poet, translator, travel and historical writer, and playwright, and a key figure in the development of the national tale.

■ Preface to *O'Donnel. A National Tale.*[1]

LITERARY fiction, whether directed to the purpose of transient amusement, or adopted as an indirect medium of instruction, has always in its most genuine form exhibited a mirror of the times in which it is composed: reflecting morals, customs, manners, peculiarity of character, and prevalence of opinion. Thus, perhaps, after all, it forms the best history of nations, the rest being but the dry chronicles of facts and events, which in the same stages of society occur under the operations of the same passions, and tend to the same consequences.

But, though such be the primary character of fictitious narrative, we find it, in its progress, producing arbitrary models, derived from conventional modes of thinking amongst writers, and influenced by the doctrines of the learned, and the opinions of the refined. Ideal beauties, and ideal perfection, take the place of nature, and approbation is sought rather by a description of *what is not*, than a faithful portraiture of *what is*. He, however, who soars beyond the line of general knowledge, and common feelings, must be content to remain within the exclusive pale of particular approbation. It is the interest, therefore, of the *novelist*, who is, *par etat*,[2] the servant of the *many*, not the *minister* of the FEW, to abandon pure abstractions, and "thick coming fancies,"[3] to philosophers and to poets; to adopt, rather than create; to combine, rather than invent; and to take nature and manners for the

---

[1]   London: Henry Colburn, 1814.
[2]   by definition.

THE ATHENÆUM

Journal of English and Foreign Literature, Science, and the Fine Arts.

No. 368.   LONDON, SATURDAY, NOVEMBER 15, 1834.   PRICE FOURPENCE.

[✥ This Journal is published every Saturday Morning, and is received, by the early Coaches, at Birmingham, Manchester, Liverpool, Dublin, Glasgow, Edinburgh, and all other large Towns; but for the convenience of persons residing in remote places, or abroad, the weekly numbers are issued in Monthly Parts, stitched in a wrapper, and forwarded with the Magazines to all parts of the World.   [J. HOLMES, TOOK'S COURT.]

REVIEWS

A Journey throughout Ireland, during the Spring, Summer, and Autumn of 1834. By Henry D. Inglis. 2 vols. London: Whittaker & Co.

THE most striking, and the most valuable characteristic of this work is its strict honesty; we have often had to lament the difficulty of obtaining accurate information respecting the state of Ireland, most writers on the subject having yielded to the prejudices of party, if not to the extent of uttering falsehood, at least to the scarcely less culpable suppression of the truth. We rejoice, then, to have before us the evidence of a traveller like Mr. Inglis, whose work bears in every page the stamp and impress of veracity. We shall pass over, for the present, all that is merely descriptive of scenery in these volumes, though thus we must deprive our readers of some admirable delineations which evince great graphic power, and confine ourselves to an examination of the state and condition of the Irish peasantry, and of the causes that have rendered and still keep so large a portion of British subjects miserable themselves, and the authors of misery to others. We say *causes*, for it is worse than idle to lay the charge of Ireland's accumulated evils on any isolated part of the system of society in that unhappy country; the entire is unsound; there is much to be censured, much to be condemned in every thing and every person;—there is also something to be praised. We have more than once stated that the worst evils of Ireland are those beyond the reach of any direct legislative remedy: acts of parliament cannot render landlords humane, tradesmen provident, and factions peaceable; the great reform of Ireland must be the work of the Irish themselves; and until they become sensible of this truth, until they banish the delusion that parliament possesses the attributes of omnipotence, and that a change in the form of government will be a panacea for all diseases in the social constitution, they will remain ignorant of the nature of the ills they suffer, and incapable of devising a remedy. Valuable as this work is to Englishmen, because it contains a faithful description of a country with whose prosperity that of England is identified, it will, if read aright, be infinitely more valuable to Irishmen, for it shows them in true colours to themselves. Would to Heaven that they could be persuaded of the accuracy of the portraiture, even though forced to exclaim with Phaeton,

We feel these charges galling to our pride,
And worse, we feel they cannot be denied.

The state of the poor, even in Dublin, may be estimated by the following account of what Mr. Inglis saw at a cattle-show:—

" I was very favourably situated for observing among the crowd collected, some of those little traits which throw light upon character and condition. I remarked in particular, the great eagerness of every one to get a little employment, and earn a penny or two. I observed another less equivocal proof of low condition. After the cattle had been fed, the half-eaten turnips became the perquisite of the crowd of ragged boys and girls without. Many and fierce were the scrambles for these precious relics; and a half-gnawed turnip, when once secured, was guarded with the most vigilant jealousy, and was lent for a mouthful to another longing tatterdemalian, as much apparently as an act of extraordinary favour, as if the root had been a pine-apple. Yet these mouthfuls were freely given; and I have seen, that where two boys contended who should take charge of a gentleman's horse, the boy who obtained the preference and got the penny or twopence, divided it with his rival. These were pleasing traits; and were indicative of that generosity of character which displays itself in so many kindly shapes; but which is perhaps also in some degree the parent of that improvidence, to which the evils of absenteeism are partly to be ascribed."

We must also extract the account of the Mendicity Institution:—

" When I visited the Dublin Mendicity Society, there were 2145 persons on the charity, of whom 200 were Protestants. The finances were then at a very low ebb; and the directors of the institution were threatening a procession of the mendicants through the streets, by way of warning the charity of the spectators. This, I understand, has once or twice been resorted to; and I confess, I cannot conceive any thing more disgraceful to a civilised community. The English reader, who has never visited Ireland, can have no conception of a spectacle such as this. What a contrast to the gaiety of Grafton-street, would be the filth, and rags, and absolute nakedness, which I saw concentrated in the court of the institution! The support of this charity is a heavy tax upon the benevolent feelings of the Protestant population: 50*l.* is subscribed by the Protestant, for 1*l.* that is subscribed by the Catholic population. I am sorry to learn this; for although it be true that wealth lies chiefly amongst the Protestants, yet it is the middle classes, rather than the wealthy, who support this institution; and 50*l.* for 1*l.* is surely out of proportion."

It was once our fate to witness one of these processions of the mendicants, and never shall we forget the exhibition. Helpless infancy tottered near still more helpless age, the victim of disease was by the side of an iron frame broken down by hunger, and looked the less pitiable object; on one brow was despair, on another the scowl of suppressed vengeance; curses, not loud, but deep, were the only sounds in the procession; and when alms were asked, it was in a tone of mockery that sounded like " Moody madness laughing wild amid severest woe." But we will quit the city for the country. At the very first step Mr. Inglis found one of the worst evils that afflicts the south and west of Ireland:—

" High rent was the universal complaint; and the complaint was fully borne out, by the wretched manner in which I found the people—Catholic and Protestant—living. And if the question be put to them, why they take land at a rent which they know it will not bear,—the reply is always the same: how were they to live? what could they do? From which answer we at once arrive at the truth,—that competition for land in Ireland, is but the outbiddings of desperate circumstances."

One would suppose that the landlords of Ireland, if for no other purpose than to keep up their rents, would encourage the establishment of manufactories, but Irish landlords have a logic peculiarly their own. David Malcomson, a truly benevolent and enterprising gentleman of Clonmel, established a cotton manufactory near the village of Mayfield, which is conducted with great skill, and greater liberality. A father could scarcely be more solicitous for the welfare of his children than this worthy member of the Society of Friends for the comfort of every one in his employment. His factory has proved a national blessing.

" The most marked improvement has taken place in the neighbourhood, since the establishment of this manufactory: not in lodging only, but in food also, a great change has taken place; and although high wages, which leave a surplus, are some incentive to intoxication, it is a fact, that not an hour's labour is ever lost in the factory, owing to the dissipated habits of those employed in it."

Now let us see how he has been rewarded by those whose tenantry he has benefited:—

" I regretted deeply to learn, not from the proprietor of the mill only, but from other sources, that Lord Waterford's family have thrown every obstacle in the way of this establishment; and that, only the other day, an attempt had been made to take advantage of some manorial rights, and to demolish the mill dams. Pity it is, that the aristocracy should, even by open acts, separate themselves from the interests of the people around them. The enterprising Quaker who has established this factory, has done more for the neighbourhood, than Lord Waterford and all the Beresfords have ever done; and his lordship's pride ought to be, less in his magnificent domain, and fine stud, than in the comfortable condition of the surrounding peasantry, and in the establishment which has produced it."

And yet people speak of the ingratitude that deprived the Beresfords of the representation of the county of Waterford;—by the way, we are glad to find that good effects have resulted from that lesson:—

" The defeat of the Waterford family in the election for the county, was felt by them as a severe blow; but it has had its uses: more attention is now paid to the interests and comforts of the tenantry; and it is universally admitted, that the property has recently been, and is at present, under excellent management."

We must now see another specimen of the benevolence and wisdom of Irish land-owners:—

" I had heard, even in England, of the wretched condition of a town in the county of Kilkenny, called Callen; and finding that this town was but eight miles from Kilkenny, I devoted a day to Callen. I never travelled through a more pleasing and smiling country, than that which lies between Kilkenny and Callen; and I never entered a town reflecting so much disgrace

Fig. 11.1   The Athenæum no. 368 (15 November 1834)

grounds and groupings of works, which are professedly addressed to popular feelings and ideas.

Influenced by this impression, I have for the first time ventured on that style of novel, which simply bears upon the "flat realities of life." Having determined upon taking Ireland as my theme, I sought in its records and chronicles for the ground-work of a story, and the character of an hero. The romantic adventures, and unsubdued valor of O'DONNEL *the Red*, Chief of Tirconnel,[4] in the reign of Elizabeth, promised at the first glance all I wished, and seemed happily adapted to my purpose. I had already advanced as far as the second volume of my MS. and had expended much time and labor in arduous research and dry study, when I found it necessary to forego my original plan. The character of my sex, no less than my own feelings, urged me, in touching those parts of Irish history which were connected with my tale, to turn them to the purposes of conciliation, and to incorporate the leaven of favorable opinion with that heavy mass of bitter prejudice, which writers, both grave and trifling, have delighted to raise against my country. But when I fondly thought to send forth a dove bearing the olive of peace, I found I was on the point of flinging an arrow winged with discord. I *had* hoped, as far as *my feeble efforts could go*, to extenuate the errors attributed to Ireland, by an exposition of their causes, drawn from historic facts; but I found that, like the spirit in *Macbeth*, I should at the same moment hold up a glass to my countrymen, reflecting but *too* many fearful images,

To "*shew their eyes and grieve their hearts:*"[5]

for I discovered, far beyond my expectation, that I had fallen upon "evil men, and evil days;" and that, in proceeding, I must raise a veil which ought never to be drawn, and renew the memory of events which the interests of humanity require to be for ever buried in oblivion.

I abandoned, therefore, my original plan, took up a happier view of things, advanced my story to more modern and more liberal times, and exchanged the rude chief of the days of old, for his polished descendant in a more refined age: and I trust the various branches of the ancient house with whose name I have honored him will not find reason to disown their newly discovered kinsman.

---

3   Shakespeare, *Macbeth* V.iii.38.
4   Modern Donegal, in the province of Ulster [Owenson's note]. "Red" Hugh O'Donnell (1572–1602) led a tenacious but ultimately unsuccessful revolt against the English occupation of Ireland.
5   Shakespeare, *Macbeth* IV.i.110, slightly altered.

■ Selected Reviews from the *Athenæum*

The Betrothed. From the Italian of Alessandro Manzoni.[6]

[…] Down to the French Revolution, the nations of Europe may be considered as having abstained from all literary co-operation, and as having wandered in search of the beautiful and the true, in neglect, if not in ignorance, of each other's proceedings; for if the literature of France obtained a certain partial pre-eminence in some foreign courts, imitation was rather exerted in adopting its systems in their integrity, than in grafting them upon the several national stocks; and their influence therefore rarely extended to the people. Notwithstanding then the tendency to uniformity, produced by a common religious faith, and a common veneration for classical monuments, each different centre of knowledge gave birth to its own models of taste and beauty; and the literature of every nation was peculiar and distinct. England, more especially, attained to a greater vigour and originality of thought and style, through the limitation of its intercourse with the continent; and Germany, from the same cause, has derived the same effect.

Within the last half century, however, the march of events has given civilization an opposite direction. Commerce and war, the steam-engine and the Macadamized road, have brought nations into closer and more frequent contact; and leave has been given to *litterati*, in common with all other classes, to import improvements, to imitate foreign models, and to adopt the peculiarities of style and matter which are popular in other countries. It is thus that Shakspeare and Goethe have made their way to Paris; that German metaphysics have become popular in France; that Romanticism has found its proselytes in London; and that Byron and Walter Scott are known and imitated wherever there is leisure to read and intellects to write.

From the last author, in particular, the continent has borrowed much, and largely; and from his pages Italy derived a new and sudden inspiration in the department of fictitious narrative. The early Italians, (whose short and pithy *novelle* are little more than brief anecdotes,) with all the warmth of their poetic imagination, have produced scarcely one prose work of imagination; and the greatest story-tellers out of the East have dealt the least in tales of passion, character, or romantic and adventurous interest. Yet the history of the small Italian states, their wars and civil dissensions, have all the passionate violence of personal disputes; they teem with materials for the novelist, and seem to invite him to embody their striking situations, and to delineate their bold and deeply-shaded Protagonists. Nothing of this sort, however, exists in the original literature of the country; and with the exception of a few obscure and almost abortive imitations of the

---

[6]　*Athenæum* no. 368 (15 November 1834): 835–6.

how, indeed, are they to gain their knowledge, unless they specially seek it? They do not themselves hire labourers; they do not call on the small farmer for rent; they do not themselves eject or drive for rent;—and it is not to the hall, but to the farm-house, that the mendicant, and the mendicant's wife, and the orphan child, and the unemployed labourer, carry their sack, and their petition. The landlord has his gate-house, beyond which the vigilant porter permits no unwelcome visitor to pass."

We must conclude for the present with the description of a grievance, for the continued existence of which the rulers of the country are in a great degree responsible:—

"Trading magistrates are not yet extinct in the county Longford: value is still occasionally received for magisterial protection, in the shape of labour,—such as, a winter-cutting of turf being brought to a man's door. Neither is there much co-operation among the magistracy. They take pleasure in thwarting each other; and it is not unusual for persons imprisoned by the warrant of one magistrate, to be forthwith liberated by the warrant of another. This, I think, ought not to be possible. Crime can never be effectually repressed, where such a state of things exists; and every week's new experience in Ireland, more and more convinced me, that the establishment of a general stipendiary magistracy, would be one great step towards the civilization and pacification of the country."

We have passed over many passages worthy of remark, though our quotations have been confined to the first volume; but next week we trust to resume our examination of this excellent work.

The Betrothed. From the Italian of Alessandro Manzoni. London: Bentley.

The literature and science of modern Europe stand deeply indebted to the accident of the great conquering horde of the north having, on its triumph over the Roman empire, been split into many separate and independent states. The Romans, when their borrowings from the Greek are deducted, exhibited, in their best days, few tokens of a diversified genius, or an inventive faculty; and when, in the fulness of their conquests, they had given the impress of their own mind to the subdued nations of the then civilized world, they only enthralled its energies by the uniformity of mediocrity which they induced. For several centuries before the ultimate destruction of their empire the human intellect was stationary, and even retrograde. These were the true *bassi tempi*, in which nothing was created, in which language was corrupted, and thought unproductive. But when the Roman sway was utterly overthrown, and the independent nations of England, France, Italy, and Germany started into existence, the work of regeneration, conducted simultaneously by each, proceeded from many different centres; and mind, left to its own resources, was emancipated from authority. The earlier steps of the process, it is true, may have been rendered slower and less certain by that cause; but the ultimate results have been richer and more exuberant.

Down to the French Revolution, the nations of Europe may be considered as having abstained from all literary co-operation, and as having wandered in search of the beautiful and the true, in neglect, if not in ignorance, of each other's proceedings; for if the literature of France obtained a certain partial pre-eminence in some foreign courts, imitation was rather exerted in adopting its systems in their integrity, than in grafting them upon the several national stocks; and their influence therefore rarely extended to the people. Notwithstanding then the tendency to uniformity, produced by a common religious faith, and a common veneration for classical monuments, each different centre of knowledge gave birth to its own models of taste and beauty; and the literature of every nation was peculiar and distinct. England, more especially, attained to a greater vigour and originality of thought and style, through the limitation of its intercourse with the continent; and Germany, from the same cause, has derived the same effect.

Within the last half century, however, the march of events has given civilization an opposite direction. Commerce and war, the steam-engine and the Macadamized road, have brought nations into closer and more frequent contact; and leave has been given to *litterati*, in common with all other classes, to import improvements, to imitate foreign models, and to adopt the peculiarities of style and matter which are popular in other countries. It is thus that Shakspeare and Goethe have made their way to Paris; that German metaphysics have become popular in France; that Romanticism has found its proselytes in London; and that Byron and Walter Scott are known and imitated wherever there is leisure to read and intellects to write.

From the last author, in particular, the continent has borrowed much, and largely; and from his pages Italy derived a new and sudden inspiration in the department of fictitious narrative. The early Italians, (whose short *novelle* are little more than brief anecdotes,) with all the warmth of their poetic imagination, have produced scarcely one prose work of imagination; and the greatest story-tellers out of the East have dealt the least in tales of passion, character, or romantic and adventurous interest. Yet the history of the small Italian states, their wars and civil dissensions, have all the passionate violence of personal disputes; they teem with materials for the novelist, and seem to invite him to embody their striking situations, and to delineate their bold and deeply-shaded Protagonists. Nothing of this sort, however, exists in the original literature of the country; and with the exception of a few obscure and almost abortive imitations of the Minerva-Press school, 'Giacopo Ortis' is, we believe, the first readable novel in the Italian language.

For this peculiarity many concurring causes may be cited. One, perhaps, of the most leading will be acknowledged in the singular disposition of the people, who, all-ardent and excitable as they are, yet want that reflective temperament which delights in abstractions. Children of impulse and of sense, they are too eager to enjoy, to waste their time on the refinements and metaphysics of love.

Again, the Italians live much in the open air; and they are further prevented by the reigning despotisms from a frank reciprocation of thought and expansion of feeling, which develope the domesticity of the northerns. Italian character therefore shows few of those shades of difference which imaginative writers delight to paint. Of this verity, the comedies of Goldoni and of Nota are striking illustrations—the characters being all conventional, and the personages mutually interchangeable through the several pieces.

At length, however, the success and reputation of the English historic novel crossed the Alps; and the example of Sir Walter Scott roused the ambition of Manzoni to compete with him on his own field, and to add a new leaf to the garland of the Italian muses. 'I Promessi Sposi,' the original of the translated volume now before us, was the first fruit of this impulse; and the applause which it has gained, both from natives and foreigners, has at once domiciliated the class to which it belongs as a favourite branch of Italian literature.

The great object of this novel, like those of the school from which it is derived, is to paint a particular epoch of society, and to preserve the traits of a combination fast passing into oblivion before the refinement of the nineteenth century and the growing spirit of equality of revolutionized Europe. The moment selected is that in which feudality had received its great check, and in which the overbearing and self-willed barons were compelled to confine the exercise of their despotism to the villagers huddled round their cretuelled towers; or if they venture to indulge their insolence in the great cities, obtained only a cramped and limited licence from the supreme authority. It is curious, however, to observe, that these *Prepotenti*, these lawless and insolent contemners of humanity, who made their will avouch their most tyrannical caprices, still lingered in the society of the smaller Italian towns to a very recent date. Da Ponte, the once well-known *Poeta del teatro* of the London Opera House, whose Memoirs are full of amusing anecdotes, and deserve to be better known than they are, describes a rencontre he had with a specimen of the genus in Padua, from whose vengeance he had some difficulty in escaping.

'The Betrothed,' written by an Italian, and for Italians, is yet a novel possessing powerful resources for interesting the English reader. It is a novel of romance and adventure; and it depicts with vigour a state of society wholly new to the generality of English readers. To the Englishman it is further interesting, as the first reflection of a light kindled at the flames of English genius. Worked up, too, in the story, there is an elaborate and appalling description of the great plague at Milan, which alone would make the fortune of a modern novel, and would stand a comparison with Boccaccio's Florentine Pestilence, or Defoe's Plague of London. We mention these things for the sake of those among our readers, to whom the stores of Italian literature are not accessible, and for whose especial use this translation has been made. To those conversant with the language in which the original is written, 'I Promessi Sposi' and its author, Manzoni, are familiar as household words. It will not be expected that we should enter upon the details of a story so long before the public; and, truth to tell, we want the courage to wade through a translation, which, in its style and execution, is not the most inviting. To those whose ears have not been opened to the music of the *dolce favella Italiana*, but who love a stirring romance, and are curious concerning humanity in all its phases, 'The Betrothed'

Fig. 11.2   The Athenæum no. 368 (15 November 1834): p. 835

Minerva-Press school, 'Giacopo Ortis' is, we believe, the first readable novel in the Italian language[7] […].

Italian character therefore shows few of those shades of difference which imaginative writers delight to paint. Of this verity, the comedies of Goldoni and of Nota are striking illustrations—the characters being all conventional, and the personages mutually interchangeable through the several pieces.[8]

At length, however, the success and reputation of the English historic novel crossed the Alps; and the example of Sir Walter Scott roused the ambition of Manzoni to compete with him on his own field, and to add a new leaf to the garland of the Italian muses. 'I Promessi Sposi,' [1825–1827] the original of the translated volume now before us, was the first fruit of this impulse; and the applause which it has gained, both from natives and foreigners, has at once domiciliated the class to which it belongs as a favourite branch of Italian literature […].

'The Betrothed,' written by an Italian, and for Italians, is yet a novel possessing powerful resources for interesting the English reader. It is a novel of romance and adventure; and it depicts with vigour a state of society wholly new to the generality of English readers. To the Englishman it is further interesting, as the first reflection of a light kindled at the flames of English genius. Worked up, too, in the story, there is an elaborate and appalling description of the great plague at Milan, which alone would make the fortune of a modern novel, and would stand a comparison with Boccaccio's Florentine Pestilence, or Defoe's Plague of London.[9] We mention these things for the sake of those among our readers, to whom the stores of Italian literature are not accessible, and for whose especial use this translation has been made. To those conversant with the language in which the original is written, 'I Promessi Sposi' and its author, Manzoni, are familiar as household words. It will not be expected that we should enter upon the details of a story so long before the public; and, truth to tell, we want the courage to wade through a translation, which, in its style and execution, is not the most inviting. To those whose ears have not been opened to the music of the *dolce favella Italiana*,[10] but who love a stirring romance, and are curious con-

---

[7] *The Last Letters of Giacopo Ortis* (1802) by Ugo Foscolo (1778–1827) is an epistolary novel of an Italian patriot disillusioned by his country's social and political situation in the era of the French Revolution and Napoleonic wars. The omitted portion aligns qualities of Italian literature with characteristics of the Italian people.

[8] Alberto Nota (1775–1847) and Carlo Goldoni (1707–1793). Ironically, Goldoni is known for making Italian commedia dell'arte more realistic.

[9] Giovanni Boccaccio (1313–1375) describes the Florentine bubonic plague of 1348 in *The Decameron* (1349–1352), while Daniel Defoe's *Journal of the Plague Year* (1722) depicts the 1665 outbreak of plague in London.

[10] Sweet or gentle Italian speech.

cerning humanity in all its phases, 'The Betrothed' will doubtless prove an acceptable present; and Mr. Bentley has, we think, done the public good service in adding it to his STANDARD NOVELS.[11]

Chartism. By Thomas Carlyle.[12]

[... Mr. Carlyle][13] thinks that the condition of the working class is of paramount importance; and it is so: for, as the Italian satirist says, no matter what calamity befalls a nation, the poor constantly bear the largest share of the evil. The poor, indeed, as a body, scarcely ever permanently suffer but from something wrong in the condition of the upper classes. If the one class be ignorant, it is because the other is prejudiced and ill-informed; if employment with the former is precarious and ill-remunerated, it is because the latter mismanage their own resources; and if the one is politically oppressed, it is because the other is dishonest. But it needs no ghost, we think, to teach us that all these causes are at work, and have long been increasing the sum of social malady, of which Chartism is but one of the external symptoms. Proceeding from this starting point, the author expresses surprise at the little attention given to the condition of the great body of the people by Parliament [...].

These several minor questions, which are said to usurp public attention, are, with one or two exceptions, parts and parcels of the very question which the author states to be neglected; but he might have added others. There are the Corn question, the Ballot question, the Bribery question, the Education question, the Currency question, each involving one of the many phases of "the condition-of-England question," each of the greatest importance to the desired change; while every debate on them turns more or less cogently on the misery of the poor and their social disorganization. The fact is, that if talk would do the business, it would have been done long ago. Mr. Carlyle, indeed, has invented a new name for his question; but the thing itself is as old as parliamentary history. What he calls "condition-of-England question," is that worn-out and solemn farce, a debate on "the state of the nation," a farce again and again played off, as often as it has pleased the minister of the day to do nothing. It is perhaps one among the realized reforms of the age, that it does grapple with the general subject piecemeal, and by this isolation aims at some practical and attainable good, however trifling.

---

[11] Richard Bentley's reprint series began in the 1830s and included both British and several continental novels in translation. In *The Reading Nation*, William St. Clair examines the series's impact on book availability, price, and copyright using Mary Shelley's *Frankenstein* as his example (361–4).

[12] *Athenæum* no. 637 (11 January 1840): 27–9.

[13] The article opens with several paragraphs on Carlyle's impenetrable writing style.

The truth really at the bottom of the remark is this: that with all the signs of the times alluded to, staring the man of property and political influence in the face, the parliamentary majorities are composed of men too ill-educated for their task, or too ill-affected towards reforms, to enable them to conceive the extent, the bearings, or the necessary results to themselves of the national position. It is indeed the parliament alone, so much as the nation itself, that is in fault. The classes above immediate want, well fed and contented themselves, have not the energy nor the honesty to care for the misery of the labouring poor, or for the crises that are the ruin of the manufacturing capitalist; they will find out the import of these things to themselves when it is too late. But this defective state of the public mind is daily denounced, we repeat it, by journalists and parliamentary orators, and in language far more convincing than that of the pamphlet before us […].

The truth, the whole truth of Mr. Carlyle's doctrine, is this:—All classes and all conditions of Englishmen are out of their proper place. The ancient institutions of the country are worn out, and insufficient to its new necessities; the morals and the habits of the nation have broken down under new physical combinations and their moral consequences, and there is neither the knowledge nor the energy necessary to meet the emergency. We can neither go on with the old state of things, nor build up for ourselves a new one more adequate to our necessities. The most plenary representation would, under existing circumstances, be that which reflected the thoughtlessness, the ignorance, and the apathy of the people; and, in such a state, the education of events is that which most probably will be called into play. Suffering and calamity alone will awaken and illuminate; too happy, if its teachings are sufficiently opportune to avert the last of national misfortunes.

These are the legitimate conclusions to be drawn from Mr. Carlyle's premises; but they are either hidden beneath an accumulation of words, or undreamed of in his philosophy. Whether they contain the sum of all that is to be said of the subject, and whether they be philosophy or madness, it is not for us, as literary journalists, to decide. It is enough for us to point out the defects which detract from the author's argument, and leave the physical force men among the Chartists, and the physical force men of the high-pressure restriction party in the country, to settle their disputes on some more appropriate arena. In the meantime, we recommend the work, such as it is, to the perusal of all who feel an honest interest in the welfare of Old England, and are capable of independent reasoning on the facts which it lays before them.

Maria Jane Jewsbury
(1800–1833)

During her short life, Maria Jane Jewsbury earned the respect of the literary world for work ranging from poetry, fiction, and satire to reflective essays and literary criticism. In addition to her four books, Jewsbury's work appeared in literary annuals and periodicals, especially the prominent *Athenæum*, one of the leading literary reviews of her day.

Jewsbury was the eldest child of a successful Derbyshire businessman and his intelligent and his artistically inclined wife, who encouraged their daughter's early literary aspirations. Her boarding school education cut short by illness, Jewsbury spent much of her teens experimenting with writing poetry, drama and fiction. Her first publication, a poem which appeared in a local newspaper, shows the satirical bent that marks much of her writing throughout her career.

In 1818, business setbacks forced the family's removal to Manchester, and the following year, when Jewsbury was nineteen, her mother died, leaving Jewsbury to assume the household responsibilities, including care of five younger children. Yet despite these demands, she still published occasionally. In 1825 she anonymously brought out *Phantasmagoria; or, Sketches of Life and Literature*, a two volume collection of verse, literary sketches, and short fiction, which she dedicated to William Wordsworth. Wordsworth praised the work, and Jewsbury soon traveled to the lake district to meet him and his family. The close friendship she began with Wordsworth's daughter Dora endured for the remainder of Jewsbury's life.

The following year, Jewsbury suffered from a life-threatening bout of illness, during which she underwent a religious conversion experience. During her convalescence she resided at a girls' boarding school, and there she produced *Letters for the Young* (1828), a conduct book with an evangelical tone which remained popular through much of the nineteenth century.

At about the same time she met the Wordsworths, Jewsbury also began corresponding with Felicia Hemans, who invited Jewsbury and her sister Geraldine for an extended visit to Wales. Hemans and Jewsbury became very close, and Jewsbury dedicated her next volume, *Lays for Leisure Hours*

(1829), to Hemans. Jewsbury's last full-length publication, *The Three Histories: The History of an Enthusiast. The History of a Nonchalant. The History of a Realist* (1830), also contains a tribute to Hemans in the form of a portrait of a gifted woman artist.

In 1830 Jewsbury began living part-time in London for professional reasons, where she began publishing more frequently, especially in *The Athenæum*. There, too, Jewsbury developed a friendship with Letitia Landon, whose work, like both Jewsbury's and Hemans's, features frequent meditations on the problem of fame for women artists and writers. Jewsbury's contributions to *The Athenæum*, a sampling of which appear below, began in 1831 and continued for eighteen months. Including over fifty articles, they show astute and sometimes forward-thinking critical judgments and strong interest in women writers, including her own immediate forebears.

In 1832 Jewsbury married William Kew Fletcher, a chaplain with the East India Company, and the couple sailed for India. "The Oceanides," Jewsbury's series of poems published in the *Athenæum* during 1832–1833, were written during the voyage. Seven months after arriving in Bombay and just a few weeks short of her thirty-third birthday, Jewsbury died of cholera, cutting short a most promising literary career.

▪ Selected Contributions to the *Athenæum*

LITERARY SKETCHES.

NO. I.[1]

FELICIA HEMANS.

WERE there to be a feminine literary house of commons, Felicia Hemans might very worthily be called to fill the chair as the speaker—a representative of the whole body, as distinguished from the other estates of the intellectual realm. If she wrote, or rather published prose, for write it we know she does very charmingly, it would be characterised by the same qualities that mark her poetry, and by some that in poetry cannot well appear:—wit, for instance; but then it would be poetical wit, dealing chiefly in fanciful allusion and brilliant remark, but no puns, not even upon ideas. The wit of society is sparkling repartee, intellectual snap-dragon; poetical wit is essentially imaginative—spiritual rather than satiric—and female wit differs as much from a man's, as Cœur de Lion chopping the iron mace by a single blow of his straight ponderous sword, differed from Sultan Saladin severing the down pillow with his thin shining scimitar.[2] But to return to Mrs. Hemans. The remark that genius always gives its best first is by no means worthy of invariable credit. Inferior minds may, by throwing all their

---

[1]   *Athenæum* 12, no. 172 (February 1831): 104–5.
[2]   Saladin of Egypt and Richard I, the Lion-hearted were adversaries during the twelfth century Crusades.

energies into a first effort, achieve more than they ever do afterwards;—but it is because, in that first effort, they overleaped and exhausted themselves. Genius of a higher order generally developes gradually, passing through a regular gradation of bud, blossom, and fruit. If a first production evidence the sudden maturity of Siberian summer, it is not improbable but the creative power may be as short-lived. The best writers have all been improving writers—so have the best painters. We have at this moment before our eyes a very interesting document in proof of our assertion—a MS. copy of various poems, the composition, and in the handwriting of Felicia Hemans, when *thirteen years old*. There is not a greater disparity between the texthand of the child, and the formed, delicate, flowing autograph of the woman, than exists between their compositions. The oak is not in the acorn; and, except remarkable smoothness of versification, these poems contain nothing of the promise that has since been so splendidly fulfilled [...].[3]

That the childhood of our poetess was no common thing—that she had, from its dawn, gleams and visitings of the imagination that has since won for her such high fame—that from very early years she walked in the light of her own spirit, is true; but she has yet manifested more *progression* than any one who has written as much, and whose course we can as faithfully follow. Leaving her childhood wholly out of the question, and examining those works which have at intervals issued from the press during the last fifteen years, even they may be divided into two distinct styles—the classic and the romantic. Within the time specified, Mrs. Hemans has differed as materially from herself as from any other writer; and not in minor points merely, but in very essential ones. Up to the publication of the "Siege of Valencia," her poetry was correct, classical, and highly polished—but it wanted warmth; it partook more of the nature of statuary than of painting. She fettered her mind with facts and authorities, and drew upon her memory when she should have relied upon her imagination:—she did not possess too much knowledge, but she made too much use of it. She was diffident of herself, and to quote her own admission, "loved to repose under the shadow of mighty names:"—Since then she has acquired the courage which leads to simplicity. Those were the days when she translated, and when her own poetry had somewhat the air of translation:—see the "Restoration of the Works of Art to Italy"—the "Tales and Historic Scenes"—"Modern Greece"—"The Greek Songs"—"The Last Constantine"—and "Dartmoor."[4] But now this is no longer the case. The sun of feeling has risen upon her song—noon has followed morning—the Promethean touch has been given

---

3   Jewsbury includes "To the Muse" from *Poems* (1808) by Felicia Dorothea Browne (later Hemans). Barbauld authored a short review of the volume for the *Monthly Review* 60 (November 1809): 323.

4   The poems listed here and below are by Hemans. Most were first published in periodicals, with the *New Monthly Magazine* and *Blackwood's Edinburgh Magazine* as the most common venues.

to the statue—the Memnon yields its music.[5] She writes from and to the heart, putting her memory to its fitting use—that of supplying materials for imagination to fashion and build with. It is ridiculous to compare poets who have no points in common—equally vain to settle their priority of rank: each has his own character and his own station without reference to others. There will always be a difference between the poetry of men and women—so let it be; we have two kinds of excellence instead of one; we have also the pleasure of contrast: we discover that power is the element of man's genius—beauty that of woman's;—and occasionally we reciprocate their respective influence, by discerning the beauty of power, and feeling the power of beauty.

Mrs. Hemans has written pieces that combine power and beauty in an equal degree:—"Cœur de Lion at the Bier of his Father"—"England's Dead"—"The Pilgrim Fathers"—"The Lady of Provence"—"The Vaudois Wife"—and numbers of the same stamp, are "lumps of pure gold:"[6] poems full of heroism, full of strength, and full of spirit; but the most distinctive feature in the mind and poetry of Mrs. Hemans, is their bias towards the supernatural of thought. Most of her later poems breathe of midnight fancies and lone questionings—of a spirit that muses much and mournfully on the grave, not as for ever shrouding beloved objects from the living, but as a shrine whence high unearthly oracles may be won; and all the magnificence of this universal frame, the stars, the mountains, the deep forest, and the ever-sounding sea, are made ministrants to this form of imagination.

"The Address to a Departed Spirit"—"The Message to the Dead"—"The Spirit's Return," are express embodyings of this longing after visible signs of immortality—this turning inward and looking outward for proof that the dead dream in their long sleep, and dream of *us;* whilst incidental breathings of the same nature continually occur through her volumes.

As poetry, the productions thus characterized are exquisite; but we deeply regret the habit of thought they embody and display. With the dead we have nothing to do: we shall go to them, but they shall not return to us; and to invest anything like a wish for such return—anything like belief in its possibility—with the charms and subtleties of imagination, fancy, or feeling, is neither wise nor safe. The field of human feeling is large and varied; well has Mrs. Hemans availed herself of its resources! "Others," says an

---

5   One of two colossal statues of Amenophis III built at Thebes. After an earthquake in the first century BCE caused cracks in the statue, wind or changes in temperature caused it to intermittently "sing." The colossus was henceforth dubbed the Oracle of Memnon, after an Ethiopian king and hero in the Trojan War who, legend holds, was granted immortality by Zeus for his service to the Greeks.

6   The phrase had previously been applied to Hemans in "The Living Poets of England: Mrs. Hemans," *Literary Magnet* n.s. 1 (March 1826): 114.

American critic, "have had more dramatic power, more eloquence, more manly strength, but no woman had ever so much true poetry in her heart."[7] This is saying much; but only look in confirmation at the feelings she loves to pourtray—they are the purest, most profound, or, in other words, the most poetic of our nature:—look again at the characters she delights to honour—the wise, the virtuous, the heroic, the self-devoted, the single-hearted; those who have been faithful unto death in a noble cause; those who have triumphed over suffering and led on to holy deeds; those who have lived, and those who have died for others. PASSION is a poetical watchword of the day;—unfortunately, it is also something worse—a species of literary Goule that preys upon good sense, good feeling, and good taste. Nothing now is considered to be said strongly that is said simply—every line must produce "effect"—every word must "tell"; in fact,

Who peppers the highest is surest to please.[8]

The human heart is to be treated like Lord Peter's coat, in the Tale of a Tub: authors need "mind nothing, so they do but tear away."[9] POWERFUL is another watchword, which palms off every delineation that is monstrous and absurd. Thus, language is powerful when epithets succeed each other as fast and heavily as the strokes of a blacksmith's hammer; ideas are powerful when, like Ossian's ghosts, they reveal themselves in mists and shadow; and characters and incidents are powerful when they are worthy of the Newgate Calendar. Those who catered for the nursery in olden times had very correct notions on these points: Jack the Giant-killer is truly " powerful"; Blue Beard is fraught with "passion."[10]

The admirable taste possessed by Mrs. Hemans has entirely preserved her from these, the besetting sins of our imaginative literature; she always writes like one who feels that the heart is a sacred thing, not rashly to be wounded; whilst she scorns to lower her own intellectual dignity by an ambitious straining after effect. Her matronly delicacy of thought, her chastened style of expression, her hallowed ideas of happiness as connected with home, and home-enjoyments;—to condense all in one emphatic word,

---

[7]   Apparently John Neal (1793–1876). See "American Writers no. V," *Blackwood's Edinburgh Magazine* (February 1825): 195 and "The Living Poets of England: Mrs. Hemans," *Literary Magnet* n.s. 1 (March 1826): 113.

[8]   Oliver Goldsmith (1730–1774), "Retaliation" (1774), slightly altered.

[9]   Swift, *Tale of a Tub* (1704) Section VI.

[10] Scottish poet James MacPherson (1736–1796) claimed to have "discovered" Ossian, the fictitious third century Caledonian poet, supposed author of *Fingal* (1761) and *Temora* (1763), both by MacPherson himself. Scandal over the poems' inauthenticity did not interfere with their popularity for their heroic language and proto-Romantic themes. Sensational true crime accounts in the *Newgate Calendar*, first appearing in 1773, inspired several nineteenth-century "Newgate novels." Jack the Giant Killer and Bluebeard figure in two popular folk tales.

her *womanliness* is to her intellectual qualities as the morning mist to the landscape, or the evening dew to the flower—that which enhances loveliness without diminishing lustre. To speak confidentially to our trusted friend the public, Mrs. Hemans throws herself into her poetry, and the said self is an English gentlewoman. Now this proves the exceeding good sense of Imagination, a faculty that Utilitarians[11] are so apt to libel: Imagination says, that a poetess ought to be ladylike, claiming acquaintance with the Graces no less than with the Muses; and if it were not so, Imagination would conceive he had a right to be sulky. We appeal to any one who is imaginative. If, after sighing away your soul over some poetic effusion of female genius, a personal introduction took place, and you found the fair author a dashing dragoon-kind of woman—one who could with ease rid her house of a couple of robbers—would you not be startled? Or, if she called upon you to listen to a discussion on Petrarch's love in a voice that brayed upon your sense of hearing, would you not feel that nature had made a mistake?[12] Without a doubt you would. Your understanding might in time be converted; you might bow at the very feet, and solicit the very hand, the proportions of which at first inspired terror, but your Imagination, a recreant to the last, would die maintaining that a poetess ought to be feminine. All that we know are so; and Mrs. Hemans especially. Her Italian extraction somewhat accounts for the passion which, even in childhood, she displayed for sculpture and melody; but her taste for the beautiful, so fastidious, so universal, so unsleeping—(we are not discussing how far such a taste contributes to happiness, but in what way it modifies genius,)—is that, to which may mainly be attributed Mrs. Hemans's separation from all other sisters of the lyre. One or two might be named who excel her in some things, but not one who equals her in *this* point. Beauty of sound, natural spectacle, form and colour, is to her a life and presence—the spirit that deifies existence—the dial that records time in sunbeams.

All who remember "The Voice of Spring"—"Bring Flowers"—"The Death-Song of the Nightingale"—the "Music of Yesterday"—"The Song of Night," and others of this class, will agree, that "the imperfection of language, the embarrassment of versification, all that is material and mechanical, disappears, and the vision floats before us 'an aery stream.'"[13] They seem like some of Shelley's—less written than dreamed.

We must adventure a general remark on the subject of poetry as connected or unconnected with moral truth. It is not necessary that every poem should

---

11 Nineteenth century utilitarianism emphasized consequences of actions and the good of the many over moral absolutism and individual fulfillment. Popularized as an approach to literary criticism by journals such as the *Westminster Review*, the philosophy emphasized "thought" and social purpose over imagination or affective appeal in literary works.

12 On Petrarch, see Chapter 5, note 2.

13 Review of Hemans's *Forest Sanctuary* in the *Christian Examiner and Theological Review* 3 (September and October 1826): 403. "An aery stream" comes from Milton's "Il Penseroso" 148.

be a homily in verse, or a sermon written for music; but it *is* necessary that the bias of a poet's own mind should be towards the beneficial. It has been finely said, that the intention of poetry, like that of christianity, is, "to spiritualize our nature;"[14] if so, every poet should emulate the birds that ministered to the prophet in the wilderness, and bring us food from heaven. Such a poet may pourtray the passions, the joys, the griefs, and the affections of earth—but he will not rest among them. Like the angel who appeared to the Hebrew chief, he will touch the offerings with his staff, and there will rise from them, a pure, a heavenly, an aspiring flame.[15] Great improvement has taken place in this respect; there is a holier spirit abroad in our poetry of an imaginative nature; and, in common with some other poets, Mrs. Hemans has given us many poems destined, we trust, in better than a human sense, to "shine as the stars for ever:"[16]—"The Hebrew Mother"—the "Cross in the Wilderness"—"The Trumpet"—"The Fountain of Marah"—"The Penitent"—"The Graves of the Martyrs"—&c. We look for yet more like these, and entreat that we may not look in vain. To our minds Mrs. Hemans always succeeds best when her "strain is of a higher" mood; when she sings to us of "melancholy fear subdued by faith"; and, when, through the tender gloom that habitually hangs over her poetry (twilight on a rose-bed) we have glimpses of that future which alone can "make us less forlorn."[17] For this reason the "Forest Sanctuary" is our first favourite. But

Time is, our tedious *prose* should here have ending.[18]

Had Felicia Hemans belonged to antiquity, it is probable that some of her lyrics might have descended to us, and been considered now as perfect specimens of song. That word reminds us that we have not mentioned one branch of composition in which our poetess especially excels, and to which she appears recently to have given particular attention—we mean songwriting. Our musical readers are probably familiar with many so sweetly set to music by her sister. In songs there should be *one* thought or *one* feeling flowing out in simple, natural, melodious words. Mrs. Hemans's best, whilst full of melody, are remarkable for their variety of subject; avoiding sentiment, they contrive to embody knowledge, description, affection; and we hope she will continue this species of writing. Good Mr. Printer's black spirit, and worthy Mr. Editor's angelic spirit, be so good as make room for

---

[14]   A common phrase, but possibly adopted from an essay on Milton by William Ellery Channing (1780–1842). See the *Christian Examiner and Theological Review* 3 (1826): 33.

[15]   See Judges 6: 17–21.

[16]   Daniel 12: 3.

[17]   "strain is of a higher mood" (Milton, *Lycidas* 87); "melancholy fear subdued by faith" (Wordsworth, *The Recluse* Part First, Book First, Home at Grasmere); "make us less forlorn" (Wordsworth, *Miscellaneous Sonnets* Pt 1, xxxiii.); slightly altered.

[18]   Milton, *On the Morning of Christ's Nativity* (1629), stanza 27, slightly altered.

the following one of six, about to be published (if not already published) by Power—[…]¹⁹

Long may Mr. Power's *Strand* be strewn with such gems!²⁰ But to conclude at last: Mrs. Hemans often partakes, it is true, of the modern faults of diffuseness, over-ornament, and want of force; but, taken for all in all, and judged by her best productions, she is a permanent accession to the literature of her country; she has strengthened intellectual refinement, and beautified the cause of virtue. The superb creeping-plants of America often fling themselves across the arms of mighty rivers, uniting the opposite banks by a blooming arch: so should every poet do to truth and goodness —so has Felicia Hemans often done, and been, poetically speaking, a Bridge of Flowers.

LITERARY WOMEN. No. II.
JANE AUSTEN.²¹

[… Jane Austen]²² compares her productions to a little bit of ivory two inches wide, worked upon with a brush so fine that little effect is produced after much labour.²³ It is so; her portraits are perfect likenesses, admirably finished, many of them gems, but it is all miniature-painting; and, satisfied with being inimitable in one line, she never essayed canvas and oils—never tried her hand at a majestic daub. Her "two inches of ivory" just describes her preparations for a tale of three volumes. A village—two families connected together—three or four interlopers, out of whom are to spring a little *tracasserie*²⁴—a village or a country town, and by means of village and country town visiting and gossiping, a real plot shall thicken, and its "rear of darkness"²⁵ never be scattered till six pages off *Finis*.²⁶ The plots are simple in construction, and yet intricate in developement;—the main characters, those that the reader feels sure are to love, marry, and make mischief, are introduced in the first or second chapter; the work is all done by half a dozen people; no person, scene, or sentence, is ever introduced needless to the matter in hand—no catastrophes, or discoveries, or surprises of a grand

¹⁹ Jewsbury reproduces "The Lyre and the Flower," one of seven "Words for Melodies," *New Monthly Magazine* 39 (December 1832): 412.
²⁰ I thank Susan J. Wolfson, ed., *Felicia Hemans: Selected Poems, Letters, Reception Materials* (Princeton: Princeton UP, 2000) for explaining that John Power's publishing house was located at 34 The Strand, London.
²¹ *Athenæum* no. 200 (27 August 1831): 553–4.
²² The article opens with biographical remarks.
²³ Austen's famous description, which so powerfully influenced the reception of her work, appears in her 16–17 December 1816 letter to James Edward Austen.
²⁴ Bustle or vexation.
²⁵ Milton, "L'Allegro" (1645) 50.
²⁶ Compare the phrasing with Austen's declaration that "3 or 4 Families in a Country Village is the very thing to work on" (Letter to Anna Austen, 9–18 September 1814).

nature are allowed—neither children nor fortunes are lost or found by acci-dent—the mind is never taken off the level surface of life—the reader break-fasts, dines, walks, and gossips, with the various worthies, till a process of transmutation takes place in him, and he absolutely fancies himself one of the company. Yet the winding up of the plots involves a surprise; a few incidents are entangled at the beginning in the most simple and natural manner, and till the close one never feels quite sure how they are to be dis-entangled. Disentangled, however, they are, and that in a most satisfactory manner. The secret is, Miss Austen was a thorough mistress in the know-ledge of human character; how it is acted upon by education and circum-stance; and how, when once formed, it shows itself through every hour of every day, and in every speech to every person. Her conversations would be tiresome but for this; and her personages, the fellows to whom may be met in the streets or drank tea with at half an hour's notice, would excite no interest. But in Miss Austen's hands we see into their hearts and hopes, their motives, their struggles within themselves; and a sympathy is induced, which, if extended to daily life and the world at large, would make the reader a more amiable person. We think some of Miss Austen's works deficient in delineations of a high cast of character, in an exalted tone of thought and feeling, a religious bias that can be seen as well as understood; Miss Austen seemed afraid of imparting imagination to her favourites, and conceived good sense the *ultima Thule*[27] of moral possessions. Good sense *is* very good, but St. Leon's Marguerite, and Rebecca, and Desdemona,[28] and many other glorious shadows of the brain, possessed something more. However, the author of 'Pride and Prejudice,' &c., limited herself to this every-day world; and to return to the point of view in which her books yield moral benefit, we must think it a reader's own fault who does not close her pages with more charity in his heart towards unpretending, if prosing worth—with a higher estimation of simple kindness and sincere good-will—with a quickened sense of the duty of bearing and forbearing in domestic intercourse, and of the pleasure of adding to the little com-forts even of persons who are neither wits nor beauties—who, in a word, does not feel more disposed to be benevolent. Miss Bates and her mother, Mrs. Jennings, old Mrs. Musgrave, all the foils who with half, or at most three quarters of an idea, are humble in their ignorance and happy in their simplicity—then the fools, who are only too life-like, from Mr. Rushworth and his "forty-two speeches" out of "Lovers Vows," to Sir Walter Elliot, who hates the naval profession because it enables plebeians to fight their way to a title, and makes a man mahogany-colour before he is forty—then her worldly selfish people, who are delightful and benevolent everywhere but where it

---

27 The boundary of the known world.
28 Characters from William Godwin's *St. Leon* (1799), Sir Walter Scott's *Ivanhoe* (1819), and Shakespeare's *Othello*, respectively.

is their first duty, or at every one's expense but their own—Mrs. Elton's pretension, Aunt Norris's second-hand charity, all are inimitable. Characters of another grade, those very troublesome persons to draw, heroes and heroines, have in Miss Austen's pages spirit and reality. The hero is not a suit of fashionable clothes, and a set of fashionable phrases; the heroine is not a ball-dress, a fainting fit, and a volume of poetry; they too are taken from life, and are distinguished one from another. Caroline Morland,[29] artless and sometimes a little awkward; Emma Woodhouse, clever, spoiled, candid, faulty, and yet delightful; Fanny Price, with her meekness and humility, her loving, loveable, and most forgiving temper, her weeping-willow spirit that principle strengthens into decision and self-dependence—none of these are alike, and none appeal to our good graces by virtue of any qualities that sisters and cousins in real life may not and do not possess. We sometimes feel that Miss Austen's works deal rather too largely with the commonplace, petty, and disagreeable side of human nature—that we should enjoy more frequent sketches of the wise and high-hearted—that some of the books are too completely pages out of the world. In the last posthumous tale ('Persuasion') there is a strain of a higher mood;[30] there is still the exquisite delineation of common life, such life as we hear, and see, and make part of, with the addition of a finer, more poetic, yet equally real tone of thought and action in the principals. Miss Austen was sparing in her introduction of nobler characters, for they are scattered sparingly in life, but the books in which she describes them most we like most; they may not amuse so much at the moment, but they interest more deeply and more happily. In many respects Miss Austen resembled Crabbe:[31] she had not his genius for grappling with the passions, and forcing them to pass before the reader in living, suffering, bodily forms—but Crabbe in his lighter moods, unveiling the surface of things, playing with the follies of man, and even dealing seriously with such of his minor faults as all flesh is heir to. Crabbe himself, when not describing the terrible, is scarcely superior to the accomplished subject of this article. Her death has made a chasm in our light literature, the domestic novel with its home-borne incidents, its "familiar matter of to-day,"[32] its slight array of names and great cognizance of people and things, its confinement to country life, and total oblivion of costume, manners, the great world, and "the mirror of fashion."[33] Every species of composition, is, when good, to be admired in its way; but the revival of the domestic novel would make a pleasant interlude to the showy, sketchy, novels of high life. Hampshire (Miss Austen's county) still possesses a female writer richly endowed with

---

[29] Austen's character is actually named Catherine Morland.

[30] See Jewsbury's use of the same phrase in her article on Hemans.

[31] George Crabbe (1754–1832) was known for realistic verse depictions of rural life.

[32] Wordsworth, "The Solitary Reaper" 22.

[33] The commonplace phrase served as the title for fashion or society sections of such popular ladies periodicals as *La Belle Assemblée* and *Ladies' Monthly Museum*.

some of her predecessor's qualifications for this species of writing, and possessing on her own account a higher faculty of imagination. We allude to Caroline Bowles.[34]

Romance and Reality. By L.E.L., Author of ' The Improvisatrice,' &c. [Letitia Landon][35]

WE were always of opinion that Miss Landon's poetry failed in giving a just estimate of Miss Landon's powers. Glowing with imagery, radiant with bright words, seductive with fond fancies,

> Full of carving strange and sweet,
> All made out of the carver's brain,
> For a lady's chamber meet,—[36]

picturesque, arabesque, and romanesque, it yet lacked vigour and variety —often abounded in carelessness, and dealt too much in the superficial. It bore too great a resemblance to Thalaba's palace in the desert, a structure that Mr. Canning probably had in his mind when he said of all splendid but unsubstantial creations, "they rose in the mists of the morning, but dissolved in the noonday sun."[37] Sand often contains gold, yet sand makes a sorry foundation, and we have often wished that L.E.L. would dig till she reached the rock. So far from agreeing with the objections brought by many grave and corporate critics against the superabundance of "Love" in her verses, we have wished for more that could really deserve the name,—taking leave to think that the sparkling sentiment which has idleness and self-will for its parents, and an impersonation of moonlight and a serenade for bridemaids, bore passing small resemblance to intense yet rational feeling; real, yet not ungovernable energy of soul. Again, without going the length of other "robustious periwigged"[38] objections raised against her landscape drawing, we have ventured to wish her on more familiar terms with lady Nature; and, finally, as she has undoubtedly founded a poetic school, we have unfeignedly wished that she would whip some dozen of her scholars. The faults of an original may be merged in the light of his beauties; but the faults of a copyist call for the wet sponge of annihilation. What made us think that Miss Landon possessed "powers that she had never used," were

---

34   Poet and fiction writer Caroline Anne Bowles (1786–1854).
35   *Athenæum* no. 215 (10 December 1831): 793–7.
36   Samuel Taylor Coleridge *Christabel* (1816): 173–5.
37   George Canning (1770–1827), who served as foreign secretary and, briefly, prime minister, used this phrase (here slightly altered) in a speech reproduced in John Styles, *Memoirs of the Life of the Right Honourable George Canning* (1828). Thalaba is the central character in Robert Southey's *Thalaba the Destroyer* (1801).
38   Shakespeare, *Hamlet* III.ii.9.

occasional lines and passages manifesting, not merely thought, but a capacity for speculating upon thought—a deeper looking into man's heart and destiny—and loftier aspirations after all "that is very far off,"[39] than might beseem troubadours and improvisatrici. 'Erinna,' notwithstanding its incorrect versification, proved that there was iron in the rose; the 'Lines on Life' breathed wisdom born of tears and nursed of truth; whilst the majority of her later poems have proved her in possession not only of the genii of the lamp, but of the master of the genii; not only of fancy, that builds with gold and gems, but of truth and thought, that bring the living spirit to inhabit.[40] In that most convenient of places—*somewhere*, we remember to have read an apologue, which, as not inapplicable, we shall narrate. When the Queen of Sheba went to prove King Solomon with hard questions, she appeared one day before him with two wreaths of flowers, the one natural, the other artificial, but both so apparently alike as to render her request that he would distinguish them at a distance somewhat difficult of performance. The wisest of men and best of botanists was puzzled—but, observing a bee outside one of the palace windows, he ordered its admission and watched is movements. The little honey merchant was neither to be deceived nor allured by the bright hues of the artificial wreath, but guided the monarch's decision by settling instantly on one really composed of the roses of Sharon and the lilies of the valley.[41] Would that all poets allowed a bee (sympathy) to discern for them the difference between the false and true—Miss Landon has done so of late, and if her verses have not glittered quite so much with diamond dust, or exhaled so much of the spice islands, the absence has been well supplied by fresh dews and natural brightness. It is a flower-garden beside a fairy tale.

But it was to the prose work intended to proceed from her pen that we looked with most expectations, as the test, trial, and, if the truth must be told, triumph of Miss Landon, and of our own particular opinion of her mind. The work is here; we have read it with as much attention as if it had been theology, and as much excitement as if it had been treason. To call it a novel is incorrect; plot, incident, and narrative of all kinds, would go into a nut, or, to be literally correct, into a walnut-shell. Let no lover of history and mystery, no demander of event and catastrophe, no old-fashioned believer in its being equally the duty of governments to put down plots, and of novelists to purvey them—no person who reads a book merely to know what happens in it, sit down to 'Romance and Reality.' If they inquire of us, "who or what is the Romance?"—"who or what is the Reality?" we cannot

---

[39] Probably alluding to Isaiah 33:17. "Powers that she had never used" remains unidentified.

[40] Landon's "Erinna" was included in *The Golden Violet* (1827). "Lines of Life" appeared in *The Venetian Bracelet* (1829).

[41] A popularized expansion of the Queen of Sheba's visit to Solomon recounted in I Kings 10, 1–10.

answer, for the very primitive reason of not knowing. Those who care little about story, or who can wait for it till the third volume, will find real and delightful occupation in its pages. The correct title of the work would have been 'Maxims and Characters'—for it is composed of essays, criticisms, sketches of life, portraits living and dead, opinions on manners, descriptions of feeling, all served up with so much wit that the authoress might never have been sad,—with so much poetic and moral feeling that she might never have been gay. Perused as a work of fiction, it is too desultory and incorrect to be satisfactory; it must be read as a brilliant, and sometimes profound commentary on the life of this "century of crowds"[42]—as the result of keen and varied observation and reflection: in this view we cannot but esteem it a remarkable evidence of talent. We ask the poetry of the authoress, where, till now, dwelt the brave good sense—the sarcasm bitter with medicine, not poison—the remarks that, beginning in levity, die off into reflection—the *persiflage* that is only a feint to conceal love of the beautiful and longing after the true? and the 'Improvisatrice,' the 'Troubadour,' and the 'Venetian Bracelet,'[43] answer—"Where?" How much there is that poetry cannot or must not convey. As the Ettrick Shepherd says, "Blessings on the man who first invented sleep"[44]—so we say, "Honour to the patriarchs, who undoubtedly all wrote in prose!" But for 'Romance and Reality' in prose, half our island might never have awoke from their dream that L.E.L, was an avatar of blue eyes, flaxen ringlets, and a susceptible heart! The counter conviction, that her genius is infinitely more like an arrow, barbed at one end and feathered at the other, will dismay a thousand fancies, the cherished growth of albums […].[45]

Certainly, reading the two first volumes of 'Romance and Reality' is exceedingly like reading a volume of Horace Walpole's Letters (only that the names and news are newer), or, if acquainted with literary London, like passing an evening with half your acquaintance. In this respect the book answers to a magazine, saves postage, and, if carried on extensively, might do away with the necessity of newspapers […].

L.E.L.'s "takings" are for the most part "friendly and complimentary" —nevertheless, some are so caustic, that, unless she omits them in a second edition, it might be well to publish a literary copy of the advertisement to Rowland's Kalydor, particularly that part which states its soothing qualities

---

[42]   The phrase from Horace Walpole's letter to George Montagu, September 24, 1761 was often quoted.

[43]   Like *The Venetian Bracelet*, *The Improvisatrice* (1824) and *The Troubadour* (1825) were Landon's volumes.

[44]   Poet and novelist James Hogg (1770–1835) was known as The Ettrick Shepherd, but Don Quixote also speaks the line Cervantes's novel.

[45]   Jewsbury refers to gift annuals, where many of her own and Landon's poems appeared. Several sections of lengthy extract are omitted. See p. 179.

for "gentlemen whose chins are tender after shaving."[46] Against her second edition, too, or, rather against her next work, we would remind her, that what has been said of bagpipe music may be said of witticisms where too numerous—"the one half would sound better for the other half not being heard." The first volume is as full of points as a packet of needles, and, as the writer says of some one's attitude, fails of being easy by being elaborate. This over-abundance of repartees, similes, and epigrams, becomes tiresome to the dull, and teazing to the quick; makes wit look too like hard work, and the author too much resemble a vivacious juggler […].

An author of the *beau monde* puts wit in his first volume to purchase leave to throw heart, truth, and sentiment into his last. Miss Landon's third volume is exempt from all the faults of the two others; there is no want of story, which is so concentrated in its pages, that, with a little introduction, and the entire smothering of the Higgs' family, it might be printed separately, a perfectly true, pure, pleasant specimen of fiction. It is effective, without effect being strained after, and contains passages full of power, beauty, and simplicity. The epigrammatic style is dropped; the narrative flows sweetly yet sadly along; and the history of the grave and noble Beatrice—of the self-will and repentings of the less firmly strung Emily, would redeem an Almack's of young ladies, and "a wilderness of monkeys"[47] […].

---

[46] Rowland's Kalydor, a patent preparation for the skin, was advertised as dispelling irritability.

[47] Shakespeare, *The Merchant of Venice* III.i.122–3.

Letitia Elizabeth Landon
(1802–1838)

Best known by the signature "L.E.L.," Letitia Landon was one of the most widely read poets of her day. Born into a moderately genteel middle-class family, Landon briefly attended a nearby day school, but most of her education took place at home. She first began writing poetry for entertainment, but when her father's business losses plunged her family into financial crisis, her mother showed some poems to their neighbor, William Jerdan, editor of *The Literary Gazette*, in hopes that publication might bring in some much-needed income. Jerdan was impressed, and Landon's poems began appearing signed "L." Soon shifting to her better known signature, Landon intrigued the British reading public with her romantic subject matter and luxuriant, sentimental verse style. *The Fate of Adelaide, A Swiss Romantic Tale; and Other Poems* (1821), her first volume of poetry, met with only moderate interest, but it was followed by *The Improvisatrice; and Other Poems* (1824), which quickly sold out multiple editions. The success was crucial, for when Landon's father died that same year, her literary earnings became her and her mother's only income, and her brother relied on her as well.

Landon had discovered an irresistible formula in the tantalizing cocktail of her own feminine beauty, the coy veiling of her signature, and the erotic connotations of her poetic themes and language, and to these she now coupled a seemingly indefatigable energy for work. She kept her name before readers in the *Literary Gazette* as well as several other periodicals, while a rapid sequence of poetry volumes included *The Troubadour; Catalogue of Pictures, and Historical Sketches* (1825), *The Golden Violet, with its Tales of Romance and Chivalry; and Other Poems* (1827), and *The Venetian Bracelet, The Lost Pleiad, A History of the Lyre, and Other Poems* (1829). Despite a sometimes contested critical reception, Landon rocketed to celebrity status and became one of the best selling poets of the time.

Landon's fame derived not only from her verse, however. Her unmarried status together with her poetic preoccupation over disappointed love left her vulnerable to malicious gossip about her relationships with several prominent literary men who assisted her career. This gossip turns out to be more than rumor; Landon apparently bore children to Jerdan and may have had affairs with others as well.[1] These scandals seemed inextricably linked with her critical reception, which, by the time *The Venetian Bracelet* appeared, had become at times quite harsh as reviewers conflated Landon with her fallen verse heroines. Landon's poetry, novels, and criticism meditate on challenges faced by the celebrity artist in a commercialized culture, where public scrutiny of private emotion excludes the personal sympathy so yearned for in her verse. The shift in reception may explain the interval between publication of *The Venetian Bracelet* and *The Vow of the Peacock, and Other Poems* (1835), Landon's last poetry volume published during her lifetime.

Yet despite recurrent themes in her content, Landon was an exceptionally versatile literary professional. In addition to publishing poetry in her own collections and in several literary journals, she contributed to a number of gift annuals, a new and profitable genre just taking hold, which often paired sentimental poetry with lavish engravings in costly volumes produced in the most fashionable style. Landon edited several of the most important annuals, and in some cases wrote the entire contents of these volumes as well. She also authored three novels. Her first, *Romance and Reality* (1831), provides one of the more important examples of the popular "silver fork" fiction satirizing late Regency British aristocracy. *Francesca Carrara* (1834) capitalizes on the growing popularity of historical fiction. *Ethel Churchill; or The Two Brides* (1837), her last novel, is generally considered her best. She also wrote a play, several translations, and some children's literature. Besides all these accomplishments, Landon authored a prodigious body of literary criticism, most of which can no longer be identified. She quickly became chief reviewer at the *Literary Gazette*, and contributed unsigned as well as signed articles to the *New Monthly Magazine* as well.

In June 1938 Landon married George Maclean, governor of the Cape Coast settlement on the African Gold Coast, after a short and troubled engagement. Days later the couple sailed for Africa, where Landon died the following October. The inquest officially assigned the cause of death to accidental prussic acid poisoning, but Landon's romantic public image and the stormy course of her relationship with Maclean have left doubts about the verdict to this day. The article on Sir Walter Scott reproduced here represents part of an extensive series intended to examine all of Scott's major female characters that Landon was working on at the time of her death.

---

1   See Cynthia Lawford, "Diary," *London Review of Books* 21 (Sept. 2000): 36–7.

■ Preface to *The Venetian Bracelet*.[2]

DIFFIDENCE of their own abilities, and fear, which heightens the anxiety for public favour, are pleas usually urged by the youthful writer: may I, while venturing for the first time to speak of myself, be permitted to say they far more truly belong to one who has had experience of both praise and censure. The feelings which attended the publication of the "Improvisatrice" are very different from those that accompany the present volume. I believe I *then* felt little beyond hope, vague as the timidity which subdued it, and that excitement which every author must know: *now* mine is a "farther looking hope;"[3] and the timidity which apprehended the verdict of others, is now deepened by distrust of my own powers. Or, to claim my poetical privilege, and express my meaning by a simile, I should say, I am no longer one who springs forward in the mere energy of exercise and enjoyment; but rather like the Olympian racer, who strains his utmost vigour, with the distant goal and crown in view. I have devoted my whole life to one object: in society I have but sought the material for solitude. I can imagine but one interest in existence,—that which has filled my past, and haunts my future, —the perhaps vain desire, when I am nothing, of leaving one of those memories at once a good and a glory. Believing as I do in the great and excellent influence of poetry, may I hazard the expression of what I have myself sometimes trusted to do? A highly-cultivated state of society must ever have for concomitant evils, that selfishness, the result of indolent indulgence; and that heartlessness attendant on refinement, which too often hardens while it polishes. Aware that to elevate I must first soften, and that if I wished to purify I must first touch, I have ever endeavoured to bring forward grief, disappointment, the fallen leaf, the faded flower, the broken heart, and the early grave. Surely we must be less worldly, less interested, from this sympathy with the sorrow in which our unselfish feelings alone can take part. And now a few words on a subject, where the variety of the opinions offered have left me somewhat in the situation of the prince in the fairy tale, who, when in the vicinity of the magic fountain, found himself so distracted by the multitude of voices that directed his way, as to be quite incapable of deciding which was the right path. I allude to the blame and eulogy which have been equally bestowed on my frequent choice of Love as my source of song. I can only say, that for a woman, whose influence and whose sphere must be in the affections, what subject can be more fitting than one which it is her peculiar province to refine, spiritualise, and exalt? I have always sought to paint it self-denying, devoted, and making an almost religion of its truth; and I must add, that such as I would wish to draw her,

---

2   *The Venetian Bracelet, The Lost Pleiad, A History of the Lyre, and Other Poems* (London: Longman, Rees, Orme, Brown, and Green, 1829) iii–viii.

3   From "The Force of Prayer; or, the Founding of Bolton Priory," a traditional ballad that Wordsworth published in *The White Doe of Rylstone* (1815).

woman actuated by an attachment as intense as it is true, as pure as it is deep, is not only more admirable as a heroine, but also in actual life, than one whose idea of love is that of light amusement, or at worst of vain mortification. With regard to the frequent application of my works to myself, considering that I sometimes pourtrayed love unrequited, then betrayed, and again destroyed by death—may I hint the conclusions are not quite logically drawn, as assuredly the same mind cannot have suffered such varied modes of misery. However, if I must have an unhappy passion, I can only console myself with my own perfect unconsciousness of so great a misfortune. I now leave the following Poems to their fate: they must speak for themselves. I could but express my anxiety, an anxiety only increased by a popularity beyond my most sanguine dreams.

With regard to those whose former praise encouraged, their best recompense is the happiness they bestowed. And to those whose differing opinion expressed itself in censure, I own, after the first chagrin was past, I never laid down a criticism by which I did not benefit, or trust to benefit. I will conclude by apostrophizing the hopes and fears they excited, in the words of the Mexican king—"Ye have been the feathers of my wings."[4]

■ Selected Essays from the *New Monthly Magazine*

ON THE ANCIENT AND MODERN INFLUENCE OF POETRY.[5]

IT is curious to observe how little one period resembles another. Centuries are the children of one mighty family, but there is no family-likeness between them. We ourselves are standing on the threshold of a new era, and we are already hastening to make as wide a space, mark as vast a difference as possible, between our own age and its predecessor. Whatever follies we may go back upon, whatever opinions we may re-adopt, they are never those which have gone *immediately* before us. Already there is a wide gulph between the last century and the present. In religion, in philosophy, in politics, in manners, there has passed a great change; but in none has been worked a greater change than in poetry, whether as it regards the art itself, or the general feeling towards it. The decline and fall of that Roman empire of the mind seems now advanced as an historical fact; while we are equally ready to admit that some twenty years since the republic was in its plenitude of power. In the meantime a new set of aspirants have arisen, and a new set of opinions are to be won. But it is from the past that we best judge of the present; and perhaps we shall more accurately say what poetry is by referring to what it has been.

---

4   See Isaac D'Israeli, *The Literary Character, Illustrated by the History of Men of Genius, Drawn from Their Own Feelings and Confessions*, 3rd ed. (1822) 22. The anecdote constitutes one of several examples of traitorous councilors.

5   *New Monthly Magazine and Literary Journal* (2nd series) 35 (November 1832): 466–71.

Poetry in every country has had its origin in three sources, connected with the strongest feelings belonging to the human mind—Religion, War, and Love. The mysteries of the present; the still greater mysteries of the future; the confession of some superior power so deeply felt; higher impulses speaking so strongly of some spiritual influence of a purer order than those of our common wants and wishes;—these all found words and existence in poetry. The vainest fictions of mythology were the strongest possible evidence how necessary to the ignorance of humanity was the belief of a superior power; so entire was the interior conviction, that sooner than believe in nothing no belief was too absurd for adoption. The imagination, which is the source of poetry, has in every country been the beginning as well as the ornament of civilization. It civilizes because it refines. A general view of its influence in the various quarters of the globe will place this in the most striking point of view […].[6]

The whole origin and use of poetry may be expressed in a few brief words: it originates in that idea of superior beauty and excellence inherent in every nature—and it is employed to keep that idea alive; and the very belief in excellence is one cause of its existence. When we speak of poetry as the fountain whence youth draws enthusiasm for its hopes,—where the warrior strengthens his courage, and the lover his faith,—the treasury where the noblest thoughts are garnered,—the archives where the noblest deeds are recorded,—we but express an old belief. One of our great reviews —the "Westminster"—in speaking of the fine arts, &c. says, "The aristocracy do well to encourage poetry: it is by fiction themselves exist—and what is poetry but fiction?"[7] We deny that poetry is fiction; its merit and its power lie alike in its truth: to one heart the aspiring and elevated will come home; to another the simple and natural: the keynote to one will be the voice of memory, which brings back young affections—early confidence,—hill and valley yet glad with the buoyant step which once past over them,—flowers thrice lovely from thoughts indelibly associated with their leaf or breath: such as these are touched by all that restores, while it recalls, days whose enjoyment would have been happiness, could they but have had the knowledge of experience without its weariness. To another, poetry will be a vision and a delight, because the virtue of which he dreams is there realized—and because the "love which his spirit has painted"[8] is to be found in its pages. But in each and all cases the deep well of sympathy is only to be found when the hazel rod is poised by the hand of truth. And, till some moral steam is discovered as potent as that now so active in the physical world, vain will be the effort to regulate mankind like machinery: there will ever be spiritual awakenings, and deep and tender thoughts, to turn away from

---

[6] The omitted section argues three sources for poetic inspiration: Religion, War, and Love.
[7] *The Westminster Review* (1824–1900). The quote is unidentified.
[8] Byron, "Stanzas to [Augusta] 7.

the hurry and highways of life, and whose place of refuge will still be the green paths and pleasant waters of poesy. That tribes of worse than idle followers have crowded the temple, and cast the dust they brought around the soiled altar,—that many have profaned their high gift to base use—that poetry has often turned aside from its divine origin and diviner end,—is what must be equally admitted and lamented; but who will deny that our best and most popular (indeed in this case best and popular are equivalent terms) poetry makes its appeal to the higher and better feelings of our nature, and not a poet but owes his fame to that which best deserves it? What a code of pure and beautiful morality, applicable to almost every circumstance, might be drawn from Shakspeare!

The influence of poetry has two eras,—first as it tends to civilize; secondly as it tends to prevent that very civilization from growing too cold and too selfish. Its first is its period of action; its second is that of feeling and reflection: it is that second period which at present exists. On the mere principle of utility, in our wide and weary world, with its many sorrows and more cares, how anxiously we ought to keep open every source of happiness! and who among us does not recollect some hour when a favourite poet spread before us a page like that of a magician's; when some expression has seemed like the very echo of our feelings; how often and with what a sensation of pleasure have long-remembered passages sprang to our lips; how every natural beauty has caught a fresh charm from being linked with some associate verse! Who that has these or similar recollections but would keep the ear open, and the heart alive, to the "song that lightens the languid way!"[9]

Why one age should be more productive in poetry than another is one of those questions—a calculation of the mental longitude—likely to remain unanswered. That peculiar circumstances do not create the poet is proved by the fact, that only one individual is so affected: if it were mere circumstance, it would affect alike all who are brought within its contact. What confirmation of this theory (if theory it be) is to be found in the history of all poets!—where are we to seek the cause which made them such, if not in their own minds? We daily see men living amid beautiful scenery; and scenery is much dwelt upon by the advocates of circumstance. Switzerland is a most beautiful country, yet what great poet has it ever produced? The spirit which in ancient days peopled grove and mountain with Dryad and Oread,[10] or, in modern times, with associations, must be in him who sees, not in the object seen. How many there are, leading a life of literary leisure, living in a romantic country, and writing poetry all their days, who yet go down to their unremembered graves no more poets than if they had never turned a stanza! While, on the other hand, we see men with every obstacle

---

9   Thomas Moore, "Boat Glee" 1.
10   Nymphs from classical mythology.

before them, with little leisure and less encouragement, yet force their upward way, make their voice heard, and leave their memory in imperishable song. Take Burns for an example:[11] much stress has been laid on the legendary ballads he was accustomed to hear from infancy; but if these were so potent, why did they not inspire his brother as well as himself? Mr. Gilbert Burns is recorded, by every biographer, to have been a sensible, and even a superior man; he dwelt in the same country—he heard the same songs—why was he not a poet too? There can be but one answer,—there was not that inherent quality in his mind which there was in his brother's. Many young men are born to a higher name than fortune—many spend their youth amid the most exciting scenes—yet why do none of these turn out a Byron, but for some innate first cause? What made Milton in old age,—in sickness, in poverty—depressed by all that would have weighed to the very dust an ordinary man—without one of man's ordinary encouragements,—what could have made him turn to the future as to a home, collect his glorious energies, and finish a work, the noblest aid ever given to the immortality of a language? What, but that indefinable spirit, whose enthusiasm is nature's own gift to the poet. *Poeta nascitur non fit*[12] is, like many other old truths, the very truth after all.

We cannot but consider that, though some be still among us, our own great poets belong to another age. Their fame is established, and their horde of imitators have dispersed; those wearying followers who, to use the happy expression of a contemporary writer, "think that breaking the string is bending the bow of Ulysses."[13] We heard daily complaints of the want of present taste and talent for poetry: we are more prepared to admit the latter than the former. In the most sterile times of the imagination, love of poetry has never been lacking; the taste may have been bad, but still the taste existed. Wordsworth truly says, "that, with the young, poetry is a passion;"[14] and there will always be youth in the world to indulge the hopes, and feel the warm and fresh emotions, which their fathers have found to be vain, or have utterly exhausted. To these, poetry will ever be a natural language; and it is the young who make the reputation of a poet. We soon lose that keen delight, which marvels if others share not in it: the faculty of appreciation is the first which leaves us. It is tact rather than feeling which enables experience to foresee the popularity of a new poet. As to the alleged want of taste, we only refer to the editions of established authors which still find

---

[11]   Scottish poet Robert Burns (1759–1796).
[12]   The poet is born, not made.
[13]   Origin uncertain, but the phrase also describes imitators of Sir Walter Scott in William Jerdan's *National Portrait Gallery of Illustrious and Eminent Personages of the Nineteenth Century* (London, 1832). Beyond this echo, the essay in Jerdan's book shows other indications that it may have been written or at least co-written by Landon.
[14]   Essay, Supplementary to the Preface" to *Lyrical Ballads* (1815) paraphrased.

purchasers: one has just appeared of Scott, another of Byron. With what enthusiasm do some set up Wordsworth for an idol, and others Shelley! But this taste is quite another feeling to that which creates; and the little now written possesses beauty not originality. The writers do not set their own mark on their property: one might have put forth the work of the other, or it might be that of their predecessors. This was not the case some few years ago. Who could have mistaken the picturesque and chivalric pages of Scott for the impassioned one of Byron? or who could for a moment have hesitated as to whether a poem was marked with the actual and benevolent philosophy of Wordsworth, or the beautiful but ideal theory of Shelley? We are now producing no great or original (the words are synonymous) poet. We have graceful singing in the bower, but no voice that startles us into wonder, and hurries us forth to see whose trumpet is awakening the land. We know that when the snow has long lain, warming and fertilizing the ground, and when the late summer comes, hot and clear, the rich harvest will be abundant under such genial influences. Perhaps poetry too may have its atmosphere; and a long cold winter may be needed for its glad and glorious summer. The soil of song, like that of earth, may need rest for renewal. Again we repeat, that though the taste be not, the spirit of the day is, adverse to the production of poetry. Selfishness is its principle, indifference its affectation, and ridicule its commonplace. We allow no appeals save to our reason, or to our fear of laughter. We must either be convinced or sneered into things. Neither calculation nor sarcasm are the elements for poetry. A remark made by Scott to one of his great compeers shows how he knew the age in which he was fated to end his glorious career:—"Ah—it is well that we have made our reputation!"[15] The personal is the destroyer of the spiritual; and to the former everything is now referred. We talk of the author's self more than his works, and we know his name rather than his writings. There is a base macadamizing spirit in literature; we seek to level all the high places of old. But till we can deny that fine "farther looking hope"[16] which gives such a charm to Shakspeare's confessional sonnets; till we can deny that "The Paradise Lost" was the work of old age, poverty, and neglect, roused into delightful exertion by a bright futurity; till we can deny the existence of those redeemers of humanity—we must admit, also, the existence of a higher, more prophetic, more devoted and self-relying spirit than is to be accounted for on the principles either

---

[15] In *Memoirs of the Life of Sir Walter Scott, Bart.*, John Gibson Lockhart (1794–1854) retails an anecdote in which, in response to poet Thomas Moore's (1779–1852) observation that contemporary magazines routinely contain poetry that "some thirty years ago would have made a reputation," Scott replied "Ecod, we were in the luck of it to come before these fellows" (1837) II.427.

[16] Wordsworth, "The Force of Prayer, or, The Founding of Boulton Priory, A Tradition" 47.

of vanity or of lucre: we shall be compelled to admit that its inspiration is, indeed,

> "A heavenly breath
> Along an earthly lyre."[17]

Methinks there are some mysteries in the soul on whose precincts it were well to "tread with unsandalled foot."[18] Poetry like religion requires faith, and we are the better and happier for yielding it. The imagination is to the mind what life is to the body—its vivifying and active part. In antiquity, poetry had to create, it now has to preserve. Its first effort was against barbarism, its last is against selfishness. A world of generous emotions, of kindly awakenings, those

> "Which bid the perished pleasures move
> In mournful mockery o'er the soul of love;"[19]

a world of thought and feeling, now lies in the guardianship of the poet. These are they who sit in the gate called the beautiful, which leads to the temple. Its meanest priests should feel that their office is sacred. Enthusiasm is no passion of the drawing-room, or of the pence-table: its home is the heart, and its hope is afar. This is too little the creed of our generation; yet, without such creed, poetry has neither present life nor future immortality [...].[20] He is only a true poet, who can say, in the words of Coleridge, "My task has been my delight; I have not looked either to guerdon or praise, and to me Poetry is its own exceeding great reward."[21]

ON THE CHARACTER OF MRS. HEMANS'S WRITINGS[22]

"OH! mes amis, rapellez-vous quelquefois mes vers; mon ame y est empreinte."[23] "Mon ame y est empreinte." Such is the secret of poetry. There

---

[17]   Samuel Laman Blanchard (1804–1845), "The Spirit of Poesy" 5–6.
[18]   The phrase had appeared in a variety of contexts, and Landon herself reuses it in "The Castle of Chillon" (1835).
[19]   Apparently Coleridge's "Lines on an Autumnal Evening" (7–8), inaccurately reproduced from memory.
[20]   Landon quotes Charles Whitehead (1804–1862), *The Solitary* 397–414.
[21]   Preface to *The Poetical Works of S. T. Coleridge* (London: William Pickering, 1828).
[22]   *New Monthly Magazine and Literary Journal* (2nd series) 44 (August 1835): 425–33.
[23]   "Oh! my friends, remember my verses sometimes; my soul is stamped there." The quotation, from Germaine de Staël's "Dernier Chant de Corinne" at the conclusion of *Corinne; ou l'Italie* (1807), appears as an epigraph to Hemans's "A Parting Song." In Isabel Hill's (1800–1842) translation of the novel, Landon supplied the metrical arrangements of Staël's odes. There the lines appear as "Oh ye/ Who may survive me [...]/ I pray you sometimes to recall a line/ From out my songs—my soul is written there" (72–7).

cannot be a greater error than to suppose that the poet does not feel what he writes. What an extraordinary, I might say, impossible view, is this to take of an art more connected with emotion than any of its sister sciences. What—the depths of the heart are to be sounded, its mysteries unveiled, and its beatings numbered by those whose own heart is made by this strange doctrine—a mere machine wound up by the clock-work of rhythm! No; poetry is even more a passion than a power, and nothing is so strongly impressed on composition as the character of the writer. I should almost define poetry to be the necessity of feeling strongly in the first instance, and the as strong necessity of confiding in the second.

It is curious to observe the intimate relation that subsists between the poet and the public. "Distance lends enchantment to the view,"[24] and those who would shrink from avowing what and how much they feel to even the most trusted friend, yet rely upon and crave for the sympathy of the many. The belief that it exists in the far off and the unknown is inherent as love or death. Under what pressure of the most discouraging circumstances has it existed, given enjoyment, and stimulated to exertion. The ill-fated and yet gifted being, steeped to the lips in poverty—that bitterest closer of the human heart—surrounded by the cold and the careless—shrinking from his immediate circle, who neglect and misunderstand him, has yet faith in the far away. Suffering discourses eloquent music, and it believes that such music will find an echo and reply where the music only is known, and the maker loved for its sake.

Fame, which the Greeks idealized so nobly, is but the fulfillment of that desire for sympathy which can never be brought home to the individual. It is the essence of such a nature to ask too much. It expects to be divined where its too shy to express. Praise—actual personal praise—oftener frets and embarrasses than it encourages. It is too small when too near. There is also the fear of mistaking the false Florimel flattery for the true Florimel praise.[25] Hence Hope takes the wings of the morning, and seeks an atmosphere, warm, kindly, and congenial, and where it is not ashamed. Without such timidity, without such irritability, without a proneness to exaggeration, the poetical temperament could not exist. Nor is its reliance on distance and on solitude in vain. We talk, and can never be sure but that our hearers listen as much from kindness as from interest. Their mood may or may not be in unison with our own. If this be the case even in ordinary intercourse, how much more must it be felt where the most shrinking, subtle, and sorrowful ideas are to be expressed. But the poet relies on having his written page opened when the spirit is attuned to its melody. He asks to be read in the long summer-mornings, when the green is golden on the

---

[24] Thomas Campbell (1777–1844), *The Pleasures of Hope* (1799) 7.
[25] Florimel appears in John Dryden's *Secret Love, or the Maiden Queen* (1667).

trees, when the bird sings on the boughs, and the insect in the grass; and yet when the weight of the past presses heavily upon the present, when—

"memory makes the sky
Seem all too joyous for the shrinking eye."[26]

In such a mood the voice of passionate complaining is both understood and welcome. There is a well of melancholy poetry in every human bosom. We have all mourned over the destroyed illusion and the betrayed hope. We have quarrelled in some embittered moment with an early friend, and when too late lamented the estrangement. We have all stood beside the grave, and asked of the long grass and ever-springing wild flowers why they should have life, while that of the beloved has long since gone down to the dust. How many have

"laid their youth as in a burial urn,
Where sunshine may not find it."[27]

I remember to have read of an Hanoverian chorister, who, having lost by an early death the young village girl to whom he was betrothed, rudely carved upon her tomb a rose-bud broken on its stem, with the words beneath, "C'est ainsi qu'elle fût."[28] This might be emblem and inscription for all the loveliest emotions of the soul. While such recollections remain garnered, poetry will always have its own appointed hour. Its haunted words will be to us even as our own. Solitude and sorrow reveal to us its secrets, even as they first revealed themselves to those

"Who learnt in suffering what they taught in song."[29]

I believe that no poet ever made his readers feel unless he had himself felt. The many touching poems which most memories keep as favourites originated in some strong personal sensation. I do not mean to say that the fact is set down, but if any feeling is marked in the writing, that feeling has been keenly and painfully experienced. No indication of its existence would probably be shown in ordinary life: first, because the relief of expression has already been found in poetry, and secondly, from that extreme sensitiveness which shrinks from contact with the actual. Moreover, the habit has so grown up with us,—so grown with our growth, and strengthened

---

[26]   Hemans, "The Lady of the Castle" from the "Portrait Gallery," an unfinished poem 35–6.
[27]   Hemans, "Arabella Stuart" 98–9.
[28]   "It is thus that she was."
[29]   The quotation, from Percy Bysshe Shelley (1792–1822), "Julian and Maddalo, A Conversation" (546), appears as an epigram to Hemans's "The Diver."

with our strength, that we scarcely know the extraordinary system of dis-simulation carried on in our present state of society.

In childhood, the impetus of conversation is curiosity. The child talks to ask questions. But one of its first lessons, as it advances, is that a question is an intrusion, and an answer a deceit. Ridicule parts social life like an invisible paling; and we are all of us afraid of the other. To this may be in great measure attributed the difference that exists between an author's writings and his con-versation. The one is often sad and thoughtful, while the other is lively and careless. The fact is, that the real character is shown in the first instance, and the assumed in the second. Besides the impulses of an imaginative tem-perament are eager and easily excited, and gaiety has its impulses as well as despondency, but it is less shy of showing them. Only those in the habit of seclusion, occupied with their own thoughts, can know what a relief it is some-times to spring, as it were, out of themselves. The fertile wit, the sunny vivacity, belong to a nature which must be what the French so happily term *impression-able* to be poetical. The writer of a recent memoir of Mrs. Hemans deems it nec-essary almost to apologize for her occasional fits of buoyant spirits:—

> "Oh, gentle friend,
> Blame not her mirth who was sad yesterday,
> And may be sad to-morrow."[30]

The most intense sunshine casts the deepest shadow. Such mirth does not disprove the melancholy which belonged to Mrs. Hemans's character. She herself alludes to the times when

> "Sudden glee
> Bears my quick heart along
> On wings that struggle to be free
> As bursts of skylark song."[31]

Society might make her say—

> "Thou canst not wake the spirit
> That in me slumbering lies,
> Thou strikest not forth the electric fire
> Of buried melodies."[32]

But it might very well strike the sparkles from the surface.

---

[30] Joanna Baillie, *Orra: A Tragedy in Five Acts* I.iii.90–2 (*Plays on the Passions* vol. 3 [1812]). Hemans uses the lines as an epigraph to "Sadness and Mirth."
[31] Hemans, "The Charmed Picture" 21–4.
[32] Hemans, "The Lyre's Lament" 5–8.

I have said that the writer's character is in his writings: Mrs. Hemans's is strongly impressed upon hers. The sensitiveness of the poet is deepened by the tenderness of the woman. You see the original glad, frank, and eager nature.

> "Blest, for the beautiful is in it dwelling."[33]

Soon feeling that the weight of this world is too heavy upon it—

> "The shadow of departed hours
> Hangs dim upon its early flowers."[34]

Soon, too, does she feel that

> "A mournful lot is mine, dear friends,
> A mournful lot is mine."[35]

The fate of the pearl-diver is even as her own:—

> "A sad and weary life is thine,
>   A wasting task and lone,
> Though treasure-grots for thee may shine
>   To all beside unknown.
>
> Woe for the wealth thus dearly bought!
>   And are not those like thee
> Who win for earth the gems of thought,
>   Oh wrestler with the sea?
>
> But oh! the price of bitter tears
>   Paid for the lonely power,
> That throws at last o'er desert years
>   A darkly-glorious dower.
>
> And who will think, when the strain is sung,
>   Till a thousand hearts are stirr'd,
> What life-drops from the minstrel wrung
>   Have gush'd at every word."[36]

Imagine a girl, lovely and gifted as Mrs. Hemans was, beginning life,—conscious, for genius must be conscious of itself,—full of hope and of belief;

---

[33] Hemans, "The Image in the Heart" 31.
[34] Hemans, "The Deserted House" 5–6.
[35] Hemans, "Second Sight" 1–2.
[36] Hemans, "The Diver" 9–12, 29–32, 41–4, 49–52.

—gradually the hope darkens into fear, and the belief into doubt; one illusion perishes after another, "and love grown too sorrowful,"

"Asks for its youth again."[37]

No emotion is more truly, or more often pictured in her song, than that craving for affection which answers not unto the call. The very power that she possesses, and which, in early youth, she perhaps deemed would both attract and keep, is, in reality, a drawback. Nothing can stand its test. The love which the spirit hath painted has too much of its native heaven for earth. In how many and exquisite shapes is this vain longing introduced on her page. Some slight incident gives the framework, but she casts her own colour upon the picture. In this consists the difference between painting and poetry: the painter reproduces others,—the poet reproduces himself. We would draw attention especially to one or two poems in which the sentiment is too true for Mrs. Hemans not to have been her own inspiration. Is it not the heart's long-suppressed bitterness that exclaims—

> "Tell me no more—no more
> Of my soul's lofty gifts! are they not vain
> To quench its panting thirst for happiness?
> Have I not tried, and striven, and failed to bind
> One true heart unto me, whereon my own
> Might find a resting-place—a home for all
> Its burden of affections? I depart
> Unknown, though fame goes with me; I must leave
> The earth unknown. Yet it may be that death
> Shall give my name a power to win such tears
> As might have made life precious."[38]

How exquisitely is the doom of a woman, in whose being pride, genius, and tenderness contend for mastery, shadowed in the lines that succeed! The pride bows to the very dust; for genius is like an astrologer whose power fails when the mighty spell is tried for himself; and the tenderness turns away with a crushed heart to perish in neglect. We proceed to mark what appears to bear the deep impress of individual suffering:—

> "One dream of passion and of beauty more:
> And in its bright fulfilment [*sic*] let me pour
> My soul away! Let earth retain a trace
> Of that which lit my being, though its race

---

[37] "Come Home" 27–8.
[38] Epigraph to "Properzia Rossi," probably by Hemans herself.

Might have been loftier far....
...... For thee alone, for thee!
May this last work, this farewell triumph be—
Thou loved so vainly! I would leave enshrined
Something immortal of my heart and mind,
That yet may speak to thee when I am gone,
Shaking thine inmost bosom with a tone
Of best affection—something that may prove
What she hath been, whose melancholy love
On thee was lavished; silent love and tear,
And fervent song that gushed when none were near,
And dream by night, and weary thought by day,
Stealing the brightness from her life away."

"And thou, oh! thou on whom my spirit cast
Unvalued wealth—who knew not what was given
In that devotedness, the sad and deep
And unrepaid farewell! If I could weep
Once, only once, beloved one! on thy breast,
Pouring my heart forth ere I sink to rest!
But that were happiness, and unto me
Earth's gift is fame."
                              "I have been
Too much alone."[39]

With the same sympathy does she stand beside the grave of the author of
"Psyche"—

"And mournful grew my heart for thee—
   Thou in whose woman's mind
The ray that brightens earth and sea,
   The light of song was shrined."

"Thou hast left sorrow in thy song,
   A voice not loud but deep!
The glorious bowers of earth among
   How often didst thou weep!"[40]

Did we not know this world to be but a place of trial—our bitter probation
for another and for a better—how strange in its severity would seem the lot

---

[39] Hemans, "Properzia Rossi" 1–18; 103–10; 65–6.
[40] Hemans, "The Grave of a Poetess" 13–16, 45–8. Mary Tighe (1772–1810) published *Psyche; or The Legend of Love* in 1811.

of genius in a woman. The keen feeling—the generous enthusiasm—the lofty aspiration—and the delicate perception—are given but to make the possessor unfitted for her actual position. It is well; such gifts, in their very contrast to the selfishness and the evil with which they are surrounded, inform us of another world—they breathe of their home, which is Heaven; the spiritual and the inspired in this life but fit us to believe in that which is to come. With what a sublime faith is this divine reliance expressed in all Mrs. Hemans's later writings. As the clouds towards nightfall melt away on a fine summer evening in to the clear amber of the west, leaving a soft and unbroken azure whereon the stars may shine through; so the troubles of life, its vain regrets and vainer desires, vanished before the calm close of existence—the hopes of Heaven rose steadfast at last—the light shone from the windows of her home as she approached unto it.

> "No tears for thee, though light be from us gone
> With thy soul's radiance, bright and restless one—
>   No tears for thee.
> They that have loved an exile must not mourn
> To see him parting for his native bourn,
>   O'er the dark sea."[41]

We have noticed this yearning for affection—unsatisfied, but still unsubdued—as one characteristic of Mrs. Hemans's poetry: the rich picturesque was another. Highly accomplished, the varied stores that she possessed were all subservient to one master science. Mistress both of German and Spanish, the latter country appears to have peculiarly captivated her imagination. At that period when the fancy is peculiarly alive to impression—when girlhood is so new, that the eagerness of childhood is still in its delights—Spain was, of all others, the country on which public attention was fixed: victory after victory carried the British flag from the ocean to the Pyrenees; but, with that craving for the ideal which is so great a feature in her writings, the present was insufficient, and she went back upon the past;—the romantic history of the Moors was like a storehouse, with treasures gorgeous like those of its own Alhambra.

It is observable in her minor poems that they turn upon an incident rather than a feeling. Feelings, true and deep, are developed; but one single emotion is never the original subject. Some graceful or touching anecdote or situation catches her attention, and its poetry is developed in a strain of mourning melody, and a vein of gentle moralizing. I always wish, in reading my favourite poets, to know what first suggested my favourite poems. Few things would be more interesting than to know under what circumstances they were composed,—how much of individual sentiment there was

---

[41] Hemans, "The Requiem of Genius" 1–6.

in each, or how, on some incident seemingly even opposed, they had contrived to ingraft their own associations. What a history of the heart would such annals reveal! Every poem is in itself an impulse.

Besides the ideal and the picturesque, Mrs. Hemans is distinguished by her harmony. I use the word harmony advisedly, in contradistinction to melody. Melody implies something more careless, more simple, than belongs to her style: it is song by snatches; our English ballads are remarkable for it. To quote an instance or two. There is a verse in that of "Yarrow Water:"—

> "O wind that wandereth from the south,
>   Seek where my love repaireth,
> And blow a kiss to his dear mouth,
>   And tell me how he fareth."[42]

Nothing can exceed the tender sweetness of these lines; but there is no skill. Again, in "Faire Rosamonde," the verse that describes the cruelty of Eleanor,—

> "With that she struck her on the mouth,
>   So dyed double red:
> Hard was the heart that gave the blow,
>   Soft were the lips that bled."[43]

How musical is the alliteration; but it is music which, like that of the singing brook, has sprung up of itself. Now, Mrs. Hemans has the most perfect skill in her science; nothing can be more polished than her versification. Every poem is like a piece of music, with its eloquent pauses, its rich combinations, and its swelling chords. Who that has ever heard can forget the exquisite flow of "The Voice of Spring?"—

> "I come! I come!—ye have call'd me long;
>   I come o'er the mountains with light and song!
> Ye may trace my step o'er the wakening earth,
> By the winds that tell of the violet's birth,
> By the primrose stars in the shadowy grass,
> By the green leaves opening as I pass."[44]

It is like the finest order of Italian singing—pure, high, and scientific.

---

[42] "Willy Drowned in Yarrow" 9–12, a traditional ballad.
[43] William Warner (1558–1609), *Albion's England* (1586): Book VIII, chapter xli, stanza 53.
[44] Hemans, "The Voice of Spring" 1–6.

I can never sufficiently regret that it was not my good fortune to know Mrs. Hemans personally; it was an honour I should have estimated so highly—a happiness that I should have enjoyed so keenly. I never even met with an acquaintance of hers but once; that once, however, was much. I knew Miss Jewsbury, the late lamented Mrs. Fletcher.[45] She delighted in speaking of Mrs. Hemans: she spoke of her with the appreciation of one fine mind comprehending another, and with the earnest affection of a woman and a friend. She described her conversation as singularly fascinating—full of poetry, very felicitous in illustration by anecdote, happy, too, in quotation, and very rich in imagery; "in short, her own poem on 'The Treasures of the Deep' would best describe it." She mentioned a very striking simile to which a conversation on Mrs. Hemans's own poem of "The Sceptic[46]" had led:—"Like Sindbad, the sailor, we are often shipwrecked on a strange shore. We despair; but hope comes when least expected. We pass through the gloomy caverns of doubt into the free air and blessed sunshine of conviction and belief." I asked her if she thought Mrs. Hemans a happy person; and she said, "No; her enjoyment is feverish, and she desponds. She is like a lamp whose oil is consumed by the very light which it yields." What a cruel thing is the weakness of memory! How little can its utmost efforts recall of conversation that was once an instruction and a delight!

To the three characteristics of Mrs. Hemans's poetry which have already been mentioned—viz., the ideal, the picturesque, and the harmonious—a fourth must be added,—the moral. Nothing can be more pure, more feminine and exalted, than the spirit which pervades the whole: it is the intuitive sense of right, elevated and strengthened into a principle. It is a glorious and a beautiful memory to bequeath; but she who left it is little to be envied. Open the volumes which she has left, legacies from many various hours, and what a record of wasted feelings and disappointed hopes may be traced in their sad and sweet complainings! Yet Mrs. Hemans was spared some of the keenest mortifications of a literary career. She knew nothing of it as a profession which has to make its way through poverty, neglect, and obstacles: she lived apart in a small, affectionate circle of friends. The high road of life, with its crowds and contention—its heat, its noise, and its dust that rests on all—was for her happily at a distance; yet even in such green nest, the bird could not fold its wings, and sleep to its own music. There came the aspiring, the unrest, the aching sense of being misunderstood, the consciousness that those a thousand times inferior were yet more beloved. Genius places a woman in an unnatural position; notoriety frightens away affection; and superiority has for its attendant

---

45 See the contributions by Maria Jane Jewsbury in the present volume.
46 The Sceptic. Murray. [*New Monthly Magazine* note]. The poem was published in 1820. "The Treasures of the Deep" appeared as one of the "Miscellaneous Pieces" included in Hemans's *Forest Sanctuary; with Other Poems* (1825).

fear, not love. Its pleasantest emotions are too vivid to be lasting: hopes may sometimes,

> "Raising its bright face,
> With a free gush of sunny tears, erase
> The characters of anguish;"[47]

but, like the azure glimpses between thunder-showers, the clouds gather more darkly around for the passing sunshine. The heart sinks back on its solitary desolation. In every page of Mrs. Hemans's writings is this sentiment impressed; what is the conclusion of "Corinne crowned at the Capitol?"

> "Radiant daughter of the sun!
> Now thy living wreath is won.
> Crown'd of Rome! Oh, art thou not
> Happy in that glorious lot?
> Happier, happier far than thou
> With the laurel on thy brow,
> She that makes the humblest hearth
> Lovely but to one on earth."[48]

What is poetry, and what is a poetical career? The first is to have an organization of extreme sensibility, which the second exposes bareheaded to the rudest weather. The original impulse is irresistible—all professions are engrossing when once began; and acting with perpetual stimulus, nothing takes more complete possession of its follower than literature. But never can success repay its cost. The work appears—it lives in the light of popular applause; but truly might the writer exclaim—

> "It is my youth—it is my bloom—it is my glad free heart
> I cast away for thee—for thee—ill fated as thou art."[49]

If this be true even of one sex, how much more true of the other. Ah! Fame to a woman is indeed but a royal mourning in purple for happiness.

———

NOTE.—I have alluded to Miss Jewsbury (Mrs. Fletcher), and cannot resist a brief recollection of one who was equally amiable and accomplished. I

47 Hemans, "Arabella Stuart" 37–9.
48 Hemans, "Corinne at the Capitol" 41–8.
49 Hemans, "The Chamois Hunter's Love" 17–18.

never met with any woman who possessed her powers of conversation. If her language had a fault, it was its extreme perfection. It was like reading an eloquent book—full of thought and poetry. She died too soon; and what noble aspirings, what generous enthusiasm, what kindly emotions went down the grave with her unfulfilled destiny. There is no word that will so thoroughly describe her as "high-minded;" she was such in every sense of the word. There was no envy, no bitterness about her; and it must be a lofty nature that delights in admiration. Greatly impressed as I was with her powers, it surprised me to note how much she desponded over them.

> "Day by day,
> Gliding, like some dark mournful stream away,
> My silent youth flows from me."[50]

Alas! it was the shadow of the early grave that rested upon her. Her letters were very brilliant, and I believe her correspondence was extensive; what a pity that they should not be collected. Speaking of Wordsworth she said, "There is about him a grand and noble plainness, a dignified simplicity—a something of high ideal Paganism, that I never saw in anyone else. He is not so much a rock covered with flowers, as a rock crowned with a castle. He is a dweller on the heights—he would have made a friend for Phocion.[51] He reminds me of the Druidical oaks, strong and sacred." Again, while discussing the intercourse of society,—"You consider society something like a honeycomb—sweet, but hollow; so do I. But you seemed also to consider it expedient for every one by right or courtesy termed 'distinguished' to play truant—laying aside all habits of thought or feeling by which such distinction had been acquired. As if the earnestness of genius were less endurable than the heartlessness of the world; nay, as if the polished chain-mail of the latter were the only garb fit to be worn by the former. Personally speaking, I should be sorry to go into public with any other disposition than one anxious to give and willing to receive pleasure. Very high or very deep conversation, anything like communion of heart, would be out of place; but I do not see that we are called upon to pay so costly a compliment to society, as to assume a character diametrically opposed to our real world; to utter sentiments we secretly disbelieve—to be as angry with our better nature for their bursting from restraint, as at other times with our inferior nature for refusing submission. I think that wisdom may wear 'motley,' and truth, unlike man, be born laughing; and that until we go into society thus determined to seek for more than mere amusement in pleasure, we must not be surprised to find ourselves living in Thalaba's palace of the desert—a

---

50   Hemans, "Arabella Stuart" 125–7.
51   An esteemed statesman from fourth century BCE Greece.

creation of clouds.[52] Genius ought everywhere to be true to itself—to its origin, the divine mind—to its home, the undying spirit—to its power, that of being a blessing—to its reward, that of being remembered. If genius be not true to itself, if in reckless sport it flings around the flowers and tendrils, how are we ever to look for a fruitage time?"

I need not dwell on the eloquence and beauty of such passages, and her letters were filled with them. Mrs. Fletcher went to India, full of hope and belief—she thought she might do much good. These anticipations were fated to disappointment. The tomb has closed upon her warm and kindly heart. Better it should be thus.

> "Where couldst thou fix on mortal ground
>   Thy tender thoughts and high?
> Now peace the woman's heart hath found,
>   And joy the poet's eye[53]."

L.E.L.

Female Portrait Gallery, From Sir Walter Scott.
BY THE AUTHOR OF "THE IMPROVISATRICE."

No. I.—FLORA M'IVOR AND ROSE BRADWARDINE.[54]

SIR WALTER SCOTT was the Luther of literature. He reformed and he regenerated. To say that he founded a new school is not saying the whole truth; for there is something narrow in the idea of a school, and his influence has been universal. Indeed, there is no such thing as a school in literature; each great writer is his own original, and "none but himself can be his parallel."[55] We hear of the school of Dryden and of Pope, but where and what are their imitators? Parnassus is the very reverse of Mont Blanc. There the summit is gained by treading closely in the steps of the guides; but in the first, the height is only to be reached by a pathway of our own. The influence of a genius like Scott's is shown by the fresh and new spirit he pours into literature.

No merely literary man ever before exercised the power over his age exercised by Scott. It is curious to note the wealth circulated through his

---

[52] On Thalaba, see Jewsbury's review of Landon's *Romance and Reality* Chapter 12, note 37.
[53] It is almost needless to say, that all the poetical quotations are from Mrs. Hemans's own writings [Landon's note]. The quotation is from Hemans's "The Grave of a Poetess" 49–52.
[54] *New Monthly Magazine and Literary Journal* (2nd series) 52 (January 1838): 35–9. In Scott's novel *Waverley* (1814), Flora Mac-Ivor and Rose Bradwardine represent the contrast of ideals and loyalties between lowland and highland Scottish nobility.
[55] A frequently recurring expression used or quoted by Seneca (*Hercules Furens*), Virgil, and, perhaps the source for Landon's citation, Pope in his *Peri Bathous*.

means, and the industry and intelligence to which he gave the impetus. The innkeepers of Scotland ought to have no sign but his head. When Waverley appeared, a tour through Scotland was an achievement: now, how few there are but have passed an autumn at least amid its now classic scenery. I own it gave my picturesque fancies at first a shock, to hear of a steam-boat on Loch Katrine; but I was wrong. Nothing could be a more decisive proof of the increased communication between England and Scotland—and communication is the regal road to improvement of every kind. How many prejudices have floated away on the tremulous line of vapour following the steam-vessel; and what a store of poetical enjoyment must the voyagers have carried home! More than one touch of that sly humour, which seems to me peculiarly and solely marking the *Scotch*, has been bestowed on the cockney invaders of the "land of brown heath and shaggy wood"[56] […].

But the dwellers in the country have little understanding of, and therefore little sympathy with, the longing for green fields which haunts the dweller in towns. The secret dream of almost every inhabitant in those dusky streets where even a fresh thought would scarcely seem to enter, is to realise an independence, and go and live in the country. Where is every holiday spent but in the country! What do the smoky geraniums, so carefully tended in many a narrow street and blind alley attest, but the inherent love of the country! To whom do the blooming and sheltered villas, which are a national feature in English landscape, belong, but to men who pass the greater part of their lives in small dim counting-houses! This love of nature is divinely given to keep alive, even in the most toiling and world-worn existence, something of the imaginative and the apart. It is a positive good quality; and one good quality has some direct, or indirect tendency to produce another. It were an unphilosophical creation, that of a human being—

"Linked with one virtue, and a thousand crimes."[57]

That virtue would have been a sweet lure to better companions. Schiller is nearer truth when he says—

"Never, believe me, appear the immortals—
Never alone."[58]

Scott has a peculiar faculty of awakening this love of the country, and of idealising it into a love of the picturesque. Who can wonder then, that when such descriptions came accompanied with all the associations of romance

---

[56] Scott's *The Lay of the Last Minstrel* canto VI, st. 2, followed with a quote from Scott, *Lady of the Lake* canto VI, 372–4, here omitted.
[57] Byron, *The Corsair* canto III, st. 24.
[58] Samuel Taylor Coleridge, *The Visit of the Gods* (Imitated from Schiller).

—all the interest of stirring narrative—that a visit to "Caledonia, stern and wild,"[59] became the day-dream of all who looked to their summer excursion as the delight and reward of the year. I have never visited Scotland—in all human probability I never shall; but were a fairy, that pleasant remover of all ordinary difficulties, to give me the choice of what country I wished to see, my answer would be—Scotland; and that solely to realise the pictures, which reading Scott has made part of my memory.

Another noticeable fact is, the number of books which have grown out of the Waverley novels. How many local and antiquarian tomes have brought forth a world of curious and attractive information, in which no one before took an interest! And here I may be allowed to allude to the prejudice, for such it is, that the historical novel is likely to be taken for, and to interfere with history. Not such novels as Scott wrote, certainly. In the first place, his picture of the time is as exact as it is striking: the reader must inevitably add to his stock of knowledge, as well as of amusement: he must acquire a general notion of the time; its good and its evil are brought in a popular shape before him; while the estimate of individual character is as true as it is forcible. Secondly, there must be something inherently vacant and unproductive in the mind which his pages stimulate to no further inquiry.

In such hands it would be of little consequence whether a fictitious or an actual chronicle were placed—either would lead to no result. Scott's works have done more towards awakening a rational curiosity, than a whole world of catechisms and abridgments would ever have accomplished. History has been read owing to his stimulus.

Prose fiction was at its lowest ebb when Waverley appeared. Scott gives in his preface a most amusing picture of the supply then in the market: a castle was no castle without a ghost, or at least what seemed one till the last chapter, and the heroine was a less actual creation than the harp which ever accompanied her. These heroines were always faultless: the heroes were divided into two classes; either as perfect as their impossible mistresses, or else rakes who were reformed in the desperate extremity of a third volume. Waverley must have taken the populace of novel readers quite by surprise: there is in its pages the germ of every excellence, afterwards so fully developed—the description, like a painting; the skill in giving the quaint and peculiar in character; the dramatic narrative, and above all, that tone of romance before unknown to English prose literature. Flora M'Ivor is the first conception of female character in which the highly imaginative is the element.

Perhaps we must except the Clementina of Richardson[60]—a poetical creation, which only genius could have conceived amid the formal and narrow-motived circle which surrounded her. Clarissa is more domestic

---

[59]   Scott, *Lay of the Last Minstrel* canto VI, st. 2.
[60]   One of four rivals for the affection of the eponymous hero of *Sir Charles Grandison*.

and pathetic; though in the whole range of our dramatic poetry, so fertile in touching situation, there is nothing more heart-rending than the visit of her cousin to her in the last volume. He finds the happy and blooming girl whom he left the idol of her home circle, accustomed to affection and attention, surrounded by cheerful pleasures and graceful duties—he finds her in a miserable lodging, among strangers, faded, heart-broken, and for daily employ making her shroud. A French critic says: "Even Richardson himself did not dare hazard making Clarissa in love with his hero."[61] Richardson had far too fine a perception of character to do any such thing. What was there in Lovelace that Clarissa should love him? He is witty; but wit is the last quality to excite passion, or to secure affection. Liberty is the element of love; and from the first he surrounds her with restraint, and inspires her with distrust. Moreover, he makes no appeal to the generosity of her nature; and to interest those generous feelings, so active in the feminine temperament, is the first step in gaining the citadel of her heart. To have loved, would not have detracted one touch from the delicate colouring of Clarissa's character; to have loved a man like Lovelace would. In nothing, more than in attachment is "the nature subdued to what it works in."[62] But Lovelace is now an historical picture; it represents a class long since passed away, and originally of foreign importation. It belonged to the French *régime*, when the young men of birth and fortune had no sphere of activity but the camp; all more honourable and useful occupation shut, and when, as regarded his country, he was a civil cipher. The Lovelace or the Lauzun[63] could never have been more than an exception in our stirring country, where pursuits and responsibility are in the lot of all. They may, however, be noted as proofs that where the political standard is low, the moral standard will be still lower.

Excepting, therefore, the impassioned Italian of Sir Charles Grandison, Flora M'Ivor is the first female character of our novels in which poetry is the basis of the composition. She has all Clementine wants; picturesque accessories, and the strong moral purpose. Generally speaking, the mind of a woman is developed by the heart; the being is incomplete till love brings out either its strength or its weakness. This is not the case with the beautiful Highlander; and Scott is the first who has drawn a heroine, and put the usual master-passion aside. We believe few women go down to the grave without at some time or other feeling the full force of the affections. Flora, had not her career been cut short in the very fulness of its flower, would have loved, loved with all the force of a character formed before it loved.

---

[61] Probably Chateaubriand (1768–1848), whose *Sketches of English Literature* Landon had reviewed two years before.

[62] Shakespeare, Sonnet CXI.

[63] Armand Louis de Gontaut-Biron, Duc de Lauzun (1747–1793), a supporter of the French Revolution who had been a notable gallant during his youthful travels in Europe. His *Memoirs* were published in England in 1822.

Scott's picture is, at the time when she is introduced, as full of truth as of beauty. The strong mind has less immediate need of an object than the weak one. Rose Bradwardine falls in love at once, compelled by "the sweet necessity of loving."[64] Flora M'Ivor feels no such necessity; her imagination is occupied; her on-lookings to the future, excited by the fortunes of the ill-fated House to which her best sympathies and most earnest hopes are given. The House of Stuart[65] has at once her sense of justice and of generosity on its side; it is connected with the legends of her earliest years; she is impelled towards it with true female adherence to the unfortunate. Moreover, her affections have already an object in her brother. There is no attachment stronger, more unselfish, than the love between brother and sister, thrown on the world orphans at an early age, with none to love them save each other. They feel how much they stand alone, and this draws them more together. Constant intercourse has given that perfect understanding which only familiarity can do; hopes, interests, sorrows, are alike in common. Each is to either a source of pride; it is the tenderness of love without its fears, and the confidence of marriage, without its grave and more anxious character. The fresh impulses of youth are all warm about the heart.

It would have been an impossibility for Flora to have attached herself to Edward Waverley. A woman must look up to love: she may deceive herself, but she must devoutly believe in the superiority of her lover. With one so constituted as Flora—proud, high-minded, with that tendency to idealise inseparable from the imagination, Flora must have admired before she could have loved. The object of her attachment must have had something to mark him out from "the undistinguishable many."[66] Now, Edward Waverley is just like nine-tenths of our acquaintance, or at least what they seem to us—pleasant, amiable, and gentlemanlike, but without one atom of the picturesque or the poetical about them. Flora is rather the idol of his imagination than of his heart, and it might well be made a question whether he be most in love with the rocky torrent, the Highland harp, the Gaelic ballad, or the lovely singer. They would have been unhappy had they married. Flora's decision of temper would have deepened into harshness, when placed in the unnatural position of exercising it for a husband; while Edward would have had too much quickness of perception not to know the influence to which he submitted—he would have been mortified even while too indolent to resist. Respect and reserve would have become their household deities; and where these alone reign, the hearth is but cold.

---

64 Unidentified.
65 Scott's novel depicts the Jacobite uprising of 1745. Scottish forces loyal to Charles Edward Stuart, grandson of the Catholic King James II (James VII of Scotland), who was driven from the English throne by the "Glorious" Protestant Revolution of 1688, advanced south to restore the Stuart lineage, presenting a serious threat to the English Hanoverian throne before their defeat.
66 Coleridge's rendering of Schiller's *The Death of Wallenstein* V.v.

Rose Bradwardine is just the ideal of a girl—simple, affectionate, ready to please and to be pleased—likely to be formed by her associates, ill-fitted to be placed in difficult situations; but whose sweet and kindly nature is brought out by happiness and sunshine. She would be content to gaze on the plans her husband drew for "ornamental grottoes and temples,"[67] and, content that they were his, ask not if his talents did not need a more useful range and a higher purpose. Rose would have kept her husband for ever at Waverley Honour—Flora would have held

> "Shame to the coward thought that ere betrayed
> The noon of manhood to a myrtle shade.[68]

But, alas! to such—the decided and the daring—Fate deals a terrible measure of retribution. I know nothing in the whole range of fiction—that fiction whose truth is life—so deeply affecting as "Flora in a large gloomy apartment, seated by a latticed window, sewing what seemed to be a garment of white flannel." It is the shroud of her brother—the last of his ancient line—the brave—the generous—the dearly-loved Fergus! How bitter is her anguish when she exclaims, "The strength of mind on which Flora prided herself has murdered her brother! Volatile and ardent, he would have divided his energies amid a thousand objects. It was I who taught him to concentrate them. Oh! that I could recollect that I had but once said to him 'He that striketh with the sword shall die by the sword!'"[69] [...].

L.E.L.

---

[67] Paraphrase of Flora's prediction for Waverley's future married life. See Chapter 12.
[68] Campbell, "The Pleasures of Hope" Pt II, 53–4.
[69] This quote and the previous one come from *Waverley*, Chapter 68.

Harriet Martineau (1802–1876)

The versatile Harriet Martineau launched her long career during the Romantic era through literary criticism. She was born to a family of emotionally austere but intellectually and politically progressive Norwich religious dissenters who believed in rigorous education for both boys and girls. Martineau received a solid home education, and enrolled for a time in a local grammar school primarily for boys. She was an early and avid reader of a broad range of literature as well as more "unfeminine" subjects such as philosophy, theology, social theory, and political economy. While visiting an aunt in Bristol, Martineau came under the influence of philosopher and Unitarian minister Lant Carpenter (1780–1840), who encouraged her intellectual growth. Martineau's physical health, however, was weak, and before she reached age twenty, illness had left her virtually deaf.

Martineau's literary career began with "Female Writers on Practical Divinity," composed on the encouragement of her brother James and submitted pseudonymously to the *Monthly Repository*, a small, struggling Unitarian periodical. The essay outshone recent contributions, and both Martineau's family and the periodical's editor encouraged her to further efforts. Only after setbacks in her father's business permanently deprived the Martineaus of their middle-class status, however, was she able to pursue writing professionally. Moving to London, she contributed to the *Monthly Repository*, becoming one of its must important reviewers through most of its remaining life, as well as authoring fiction, children's literature, and tracts, but only with *Illustrations of Political Economy* (1832–1834) did she achieve the success that secured her professional standing.

Though controversial for both her political and social positions and the masculine subject matter of much of her work, Martineau became one of the most prominent literary figures of Victorian England. Of her fiction, *Deerbrook* (1839) and *The Crofton Boys* (a novel for adolescents from her collection *The Playfellow* [1841–1843]) are the most significant today. Martineau invariably turned life events to literary account. *Society in America* (1837) and *Retrospect of Western Travel* (1838) emerged from travels to the US. Several years of severe illness yielded *Life in the Sick-Room* (1844). *Letters on Mesmerism* (1845) describe her experiences with this approach to her cure. A residence on a farm in the Lake District engendered *Health, Husbandry and Handicraft* (1861). She related experiences from a trip to the Middle East in *Eastern Life, Present and Past* (1848). Meanwhile, she remained politically active, working with Florence Nightingale for the repeal of the Contagious Diseases Act, legislation which provided for control of venereal disease through forced physical examination of women suspected of prostitution. Though the acts were not repealed for another decade, Martineau's "Appeal to the Women of England," (1869) proved a vital influence. Her *Autobiography* (1877) is one of the crowning achievements in nineteenth-century life writing.

Periodical reviewing launched Martineau on her literary career, and proved vital to her intellectual development. Reviewing allowed her to write on a broad range of topics, many of them traditionally the province of men, including religion and metaphysics, aesthetics, prison reform, the condition of women, even the British empire. Through her articles in the *Monthly Repository* Martineau participated in the early nineteenth-century secularization of Unitarianism and the widespread shift toward Utilitarian views, and her later work for other periodicals only extended her influence. In her case, Romantic period literary criticism made possible one of the most eminent careers among Victorian professional women writers.

■ **Selected Essays from the *Monthly Repository* and *Tait's Edinburgh Magazine***

Female Writers on Practical Divinity.
No. I.
Mrs. MORE[1].

I DO not know whether it has been remarked by others as well as myself, that some of the finest and most useful English works on the subject of Practical Divinity are by female authors. I suppose it is owing to the peculiar susceptibility of the female mind, and its consequent warmth of feeling, that its productions, when they are really valuable, find a more ready way to the heart than those of the other sex; and it gives me great pleasure to see women gifted with superior talents, applying those talents to promote the cause of religion and virtue. As I think this a subject which it may be useful to consider, both as doing justice to those whose names are before the public, and as exciting the emulation of those of their sex who are capable of imitating such bright examples, I wish to devote this and some future articles to the consideration of some of the works of the English female authors of the day on Practical Divinity, and further to examine some of the prejudices which still exist on the subject of female education.

---

[1]   *Monthly Repository* 1st series 17 (October 1822): 593–6. On More, see Wollstonecraft Chapter 6 note 22.

It is a proof (if any were needed) of the value of our religion, purified from the degrading superstitions of the Romish Church, that England has produced in one age so many female writers on morals and divinity, whose works are conspicuous for their force of argument, for their simplicity, and for that earnestness which can be expressed only because it is felt, and which can be felt only because the truths which it declares are as evident to the understanding as they are interesting to the heart. While, if we turn our attention to authors of the same sex in Catholic countries, and consider the services which they have rendered to the cause of religion, what a contrast will they form with our countrywomen! Whatever their religion may be as exemplified in their lives, in their writings it is cold, artificial, made use of to display talents by unnatural refinements, at the same time that it evinces the grossest inconsistencies. If in reading their works we find any religious observation which pleases us, how soon is our pleasure alloyed by discovering some defective morality, some hidden licentiousness, or at least some artificial sentiment, which proves that they have drawn their ideas from that source which is tainted by the foul admixtures of superstition, instead of from that well-spring of life which, under the influence of a pure religion, springs up in every bosom! Compare the elevated and noble works of Mrs. Hannah More with the qualified morality, the affected feeling, the long-drawn-out sentiments of Madame Genlis; though I believe both to be women of great talents and sincere piety. It is the difference of the religions that has raised one to such an eminence above the other. Compare the brilliant imagination, the warm feelings, the conversational accomplishments of Madame de Staël, with the similar qualities of our first female poet, Mrs. Barbauld.[2] What has given to the productions of the latter their irresistible force, their universal interest? Surely, the spirit of pure and simple devotion which breathes through every line. For genius, Madame de Staël stands pre-eminent, for goodness of heart scarcely less so; but our countrywoman has been taught to fix her standard higher, and has consequently made the greatest advances […].[3]

DISCIPULUS.[4]

Female Writers on Practical Divinity.
No. II.
Mrs. MORE AND Mrs. BARBAULD.[5]

[…]It is now my duty to take a cursory view of some of the few—too few fruits of the genius of our first living female poet, Mrs. Barbauld. Her

---

[2]   Stéphanie-Félicité Ducrest, Comtesse de Genlis (1746–1830). On Staël, see Barbauld Chapter 2, note 6.
[3]   Extracts from More's *Practical Piety* (1811) and remarks on doctrinal differences are omitted.
[4]   On the signature, see Wollstonecraft Chapter 6, note 4.
[5]   *Monthly Repository* 1st series 17 (December 1822): 746–50. Martineau opens with remarks on More's *Essay on the Character and Practical Writings of Saint Paul* (1815) before turning to Barbauld.

powerful eloquence, her chaste enthusiasm, and her devotional feelings, make such an impression on her readers, that deep is the regret they feel, that her powers of writing should not have been more frequently employed. [...][6]

I must not quit this subject without stating that [Barbauld's *Thoughts on Devotional Taste*] has not my entire approbation. I think that though it professes to treat of devotional *taste*, and not religious principle, it is still too imaginative. Though I do not believe that Mrs. Barbauld could approach such an awful subject with improper familiarity, yet there is too much of the language of poetry and romance, instead of that calm, though warm, that sedate, though animated tone of feeling, which the theme demands.

It is curious to observe the difference in the style of writing of Mrs. Barbauld and Mrs. More. Both have the same end in view, both are forcible and eloquent, and yet this force and eloquence are of totally different kinds. Mrs. More awakens and impresses us, and we listen to her warnings with an awe which would make us believe that we are on no equality with her. We stand reproved under her solemn exhortations. But with Mrs. Barbauld it is different. She meets our ideas, and seems to express what had passed through our own minds, much more forcibly than we ourselves could have done. We have a fellow-feeling with her in all that she says, and it is thus that we are carried away by her fervour of feeling, and are tempted to overlook all errors, and all that borders on extravagance, in consideration of the justice with which she paints our passions and emotions, and touches every chord of feeling in our bosoms [...].[7]

DISCIPULUS.

THE ACHIEVEMENTS OF THE GENIUS OF SCOTT.[8]

[...] There is little reason to question that Scott has done more for the morals of society, taking the expression in its largest sense, than all the divines, and other express moral teachers, of a century past [...].[9] Our dissenting preachers may obtain a hold on the hearts of their people, and employ it to good purpose, but they cannot send their voices east and west to wake up the echoes of the world. Let all these classes unite in a missionary scheme,

---

[6] Several extracts and paraphrases omitted.
[7] Martineau concludes with mention of poet Elizabeth Smith (1776–1806), who translated the Book of Job (1810).
[8] *Tait's Edinburgh Magazine* 2 (January 1833): 445–60. This installment continues an article from December 1832 (301–14), where Martineau discusses Scott's biography. Her opening declaration here that she will consider Scott in terms of his social benefit rather than his artistic achievement is omitted.
[9] Omitted section compares Scott's moral influence to that of clergy, moral philosophers, educators, and political figures. As a literary figure, Scott's influence is broader and more powerful.

and encompass the globe, and still Scott will teach morals more effectually than them all. They will not find audiences at every turn who will take to heart all they say, and bear it in mind for ever; and if they attempt it now, they will find that Scott has been before them everywhere […]. And all this in addition to what has been done in his native kingdom, where he has exalted the tastes, ameliorated the tempers, enriched the associations, and exercised the intellects of millions. This is already done in the short space of eighteen years; a mere span in comparison with the time that it is to be hoped our language and literature, will last. We may assume the influence of Scott, as we have described it, to be just beginning its course of a thousand years; and now, what class of moral teachers (except politicians, who are not too ready to regard themselves in this light,) will venture to bring their influence into comparison with that of this great lay preacher? […].

His grateful countrymen, of all ranks, acknowledge that he has benefited Scotland, as much morally as in respect of her worldly prosperity. Not only has he carried civilization into the retreats of the mountains and made the harmonious voices of society float over those lakes where the human war-cry once alternated with the scream of the eagle; not only has he introduced decency and comfort among the wilder classes of his countrymen, a full half century before they could have been anticipated, and led many thousands more into communion with nature, who would not, but for him, have dreamed of such an intercourse; not only has he quickened industry and created wealth, and cherished intelligence within the borders of his native land; he has also exercised a direct moral influence over the minds of those on whom Scotland's welfare largely depends; softening their prejudices, widening their social views, animating their love of country while drawing them into closer sympathy with men of other countries […].[10]

To do his next work of beneficence, this great moralist stepped beyond the Border, and over continents and seas. He implanted or nourished pure tastes, not only in a thousand homes, but among the homeless in every land. How many indolent have been roused to thought and feeling, how many licentious have been charmed into the temporary love of purity, how many vacant minds have become occupied with objects of interest and affection, it would be impossible to estimate, unless we could converse with every Briton, from the Factory Terrace at Canton round the world to the shores of the Pacific, and with every foreigner on the Continent of Europe whose countenance lights up at the name of Scott. If one representative only of every class which have been thus benefited were to repair to his grave, the mourning train would be of a length that kings might envy. There would be the lisping child, weeping that there should be no more tales of the Sherwood Foresters and the Disinherited Knight; there would be the

---

[10] Martineau argues that Scott's pecuniary stresses indicate insufficient gratitude for his contribution to society.

school-boy, with his heart full of the heroic deeds of Cœur de Lion in Palestine; and the girl, glowing with the loyalty of Flora, and saddening over the griefs of Rebecca; and the artizan who foregoes his pipe and pot for the adventures of Jeanie Deans;[11] and the clerk and apprentice, who refresh their better part from the toils of the counting-house amidst the wild scenery of Scotland; and soldier and sailor relieved of the tedium of barracks and cabin by the interest of more stirring scenes presented to the mind's eye; and rambling youth chained to the fireside by the links of a pleasant fiction; and sober manhood made to grow young again; and sickness beguiled, and age cheered, and domestic jars forgotten, and domestic sympathies enhanced;—all who have thus had pure tastes gratified by the creations of his genius, should join the pilgrim train which will be passing in spirit by his grave for centuries to come. Of these, how many have turned from the voice of the preacher, have cast aside "good books," have no ear for music, no taste for drawing, no knowledge of any domestic accomplishment which might keep them out of harm's way, but have found that they have a heart and mind which Scott could touch and awaken! How many have thus to thank him, not only for the solace of their leisure, but for the ennobling of their toils!

Another great service rendered is one which could be administered only by means of fiction—a service respecting which it matters not to decide whether it was afforded designedly or unconsciously. We mean the introduction of the conception of nature […]. There is little use in assuring people of middling ranks, that kings eat beef and mutton, and queens ride on horseback: they believe, but they do not realize. And this is the case, not only with the child who pictures a monarch with the crown on his head, on a throne, or with the maid-servant who gazes with awe on the Lord Mayor's coach; but, to a much greater degree than is commonly supposed, with the father of the child, the master of the maid,—with him whose interests have to do with kings and courts, and who ought, therefore, to know what is passing there. It would be impossible to calculate how much patriotism has lain dormant, through the ignorance of the plain citizen, of what is felt and thought in the higher regions of society, to which his voice of complaint or suggestion ought to reach, if he had but the courage to lift it up. The ignorance may be called voluntary: it may be truly said that every one ought to know that human hearts answer to one another as a reflection in water, whether this reflection be of a glow-worm on the brink, or of the loftiest resplendent star. This is true; but it is not a truth easy in the use; and its use is all-important. The divine preaches it, as is his duty, to humble courtly pride, and to remind the lowly of their manhood: but the divine himself realizes the doctrine better while reading Kenilworth [1821], or the

---

11 Characters and situations from Scott's *Ivanhoe* (1819), *Waverley* (1814), and *The Heart of Midlothian* (1818).

Abbot [1820], than while writing his sermon; and his hearers use this same sermon as a text, of which Nigel and Peveril are the exposition.[12] Is this a slight service to have rendered?—to have, perhaps unconsciously, taught human equality, while professing to exhibit human inequality?—to have displayed, in its full proportion, the distance which separates man from man, and to have shewn that the very same interests are being transacted as one and the other end of the line? Walter Scott was exactly the man to render this great service; and how well he rendered it, he was little aware. A man, born of the people, and therefore knowing man, and at the same time a Tory antiquarian, and therefore knowing courts, he was the fit person to show the one to the other. At once a benevolent interpreter of the heart, and a worshipper of royalty, he might be trusted for doing honour to both parties; though not, we must allow, equal honour. We cannot award him the praise of a perfect impartiality in his interpretations. We cannot but see a leaning towards regal weaknesses, and a toleration of courtly vices. We cannot but observe, that the same licentiousness which would have been rendered disgusting under equal temptation in humble life, is made large allowance for when diverting itself within palace walls […].[13]

The fictions of Scott have done more towards exposing priestcraft and fanaticism than any influence of our own time, short of actual observation […]. It is, we allow, no new thing to meet with exposures of spiritual domination; but the question is, not of the newness, but of the extent of the service. These things are condemned in the abstract by books on morals; they are disclaimed from the pulpit, and every Christian church demonstrates its odiousness by the example of every other; but these exposures do not effect half so much good as exemplification from the hand of a philosophical observer, and disinterested peace-maker. Men may go on for centuries bandying reproaches of priestcraft and superstition on the one hand, and irreligion on the other; […] and less will be done by recrimination towards finding a remedy, than by the illustrations of a master-hand, choosing a bygone age for the chronology, orders long overthrown for the instruments, and institutions that have passed away, for the subjects of his satire […].[14]

The rich variety of Scott's assemblage of oddities, and the exquisite mirth and good-humour with which they are shown off, are among the most remarkable particulars of his achievements. There is not only a strong cast of individuality (as there ought to be) about all his best characters; but his best characters are none of them representatives of a class. As soon as he attempted to make his personages such representatives, he failed. His

---

12   From *The Fortunes of Nigel* (1822) and *Peveril of the Peak* (1822).
13   In the omitted section, Martineau lauds Scott's realism in portraying the aristocratic classes and regrets that he portrayed the lower classes with less accuracy.
14   Omitted section includes an excerpt from Scott's *Quentin Durward* (1823) and examples of satirical characters from a number of Scott's works.

ostensible heroes, his statesman and leaders, his magistrates, his adventurers, his womankind, whether mistresses or maids, leave little impression of individuality; while his sovereigns, real heroes, and oddities, are inimitable […]. The result is, that Walter Scott is not only one of the most amiable, but one of the most effective satirists that ever helped to sweep the path of life clear of the strewn follies under which many a thorn is hidden.

In ascending the scale of social services, for which gratitude is due to the illustrious departed, we next arrive at one which is so great that we cannot but mourn that it was not yet greater. There can be no need to enlarge upon the beauty and excellence of the spirit of kindliness which breathes through the whole of Scott's compositions; a spirit which not only shames the Mala-growthers[15] of society, just spoken of, but charms the restless to repose, exhilarates the melancholy, rouses the apathetic, and establishes a good understanding among all who contemplate one another in these books. It is as impossible for any one to remain cynical, or moody, or desponding, over these books, as for an infant to look dismally in the face of a smiling nurse. As face answers to face, so does heart to heart; and as Walter Scott's over-flowed with love and cheerfulness, the hearts of his readers catch its brim-mings. […] If it be true, as no readers of Scott will deny, that it exhilarates the spirits, and animates the affections, to follow the leadings of this great Enchanter, it is certain that he has achieved a great moral work of incite-ment and amelioration. The test of his merits here is, that his works are for the innocent and kindly-hearted to enjoy; and if any others enjoy them, it is by becoming innocent and kindly for the time, in like manner as it is for the waking flocks and choirs to welcome the sunrise: if the fox and the bat choose to remain abroad, the one must abstain from its prey, and the other hush its hootings.

This kindliness of spirit being of so bright a quality, makes us lament all the more, as we have said that it had not the other excellence of being uni-versally diffused. We know how unreasonable it is to expect every thing from one man, and are far from saying or believing that Walter Scott looked otherwise than benignantly on all classes and all individuals that came under his observation. What we lament is, that there were extensive classes of men, and they the most important to society, that were secluded from the light of his embellishing genius. […] What is there of humble life in his nar-ratives? What did he know of those who live and move in that region? Nothing. There is not a *character* from humble life in all his library of vol-umes; nor had he any conception that character is to be found there. By humble life we do not mean Edie Ochiltree's lot of privileged mendicity, nor Dirk Hatteraick's smuggling adventures, nor the Saxon slavery of Gurth, nor the feudal adherence of Dougal, and Caleb Balderstone, and Adam Wood-

---

15   Scott's fictive persona created in 1826 as a vehicle for publishing satirical letters promoting Scottish autonomy in the *Edinburgh Review*.

cock, nor the privileged dependence of Caxon and Fairservice.[16] None of
these had anything to do with humble life; each and all formed part of the
aristocratic system in which Walter Scott's affections were bound up. Jeanie
Deans herself, besides being no original conception of Sir Walter's, derives
none of her character or interest from her station in life, any farther than as
it was the occasion of the peculiarity of her pilgrimage. We never think of
Jeanie as poor, or low in station. Her simplicity is that which might pertain
to a secluded young woman of any rank; and it is difficult to bear in mind
—it is like an extraneous circumstance, that her sister was at service, the
only attempt made throughout at realizing the social position of the parties.
We do not mention this as any drawback upon the performance, but merely
as saving the only apparent exception to our remarks, that Sir Walter rendered no service to humble life in the way of delineating its society. Faithful
butlers and barbers, tricky lady's maids, eccentric falconers and gamekeepers,
are not those among whom we should look for the strength of character, the
sternness of passion, the practical heroism, the inexhaustible patience, the
unassuming self-denial, the unconscious beneficence—in a word, the *true-
heartedness* which is to be found in its perfection in humble life. Of all this
Walter Scott knew nothing. While discriminating, with the nicest acumen,
the shades of character, the modifications of passion, among those whom he
did understand, he was wholly unaware that he bounded himself within
a small circle, beyond which lay a larger, and a larger; that which he represented being found in each, in a more distinct outline, in more vivid colouring, and in striking and various combinations, with other characteristics of
humanity which had never presented themselves to him. He knew not that
the strength of soul, which he represents as growing up in his heroes amidst
the struggles of the crusade, is of the same kind with that which is nourished in our neighbours of the next alley, by conflicts of a less romantic,
but not less heroic cast. [… H]e knew not that all passions, and all natural
movements of society, that he has found in the higher, exist in the humbler
ranks; and all magnified and deepened in proportion as reality prevails
over convention, as there is less mixture of the adventitious with the true.
The effect of this partial knowledge is not only the obliteration to himself and to his readers, as far as connected with him, of more than half
the facts and interests of humanity, but that his benevolence was stinted in
its play. We find no philanthropists among his characters; because he had
not the means of forming the conception of philanthropy in its larges sense.
He loved men, all men whom he knew; but that love was not based
on knowledge as extensive as his observation was penetrating; and it
did not therefore deserve the high title of philanthropy. We have no sins
of commission to charge him with, no breaches of charity, not a thought or

---

16   Characters from *Guy Mannering* (1815), *The Antiquary* (1816), *Rob Roy* (1818), *Ivanhoe, The
      Bride of Lammermoor*(1819), and *The Abbot*.

expression which is tinged with bitterness against man, collectively or individually; but we charge him with omission of which he was unconscious, and which he would, perhaps, scarcely have wished to repair, as it must have been done at the expense of his Toryism, to which the omission and unconsciousness were owing. How should a man be a philanthropist who knows not what freedom is?—not the mere freedom from foreign domination, but the exemption from misrule at home, the liberty of watching over and renovating institutions, that the progression of man and of states may proceed together. Of this kind of freedom Sir Walter had no conception, and neither, therefore, are there any patriots in his *dramatis personæ*. There are abundance of soldiers to light up beacons and fly to arms at the first notice of invasion; many to drink the healths and fight the battles of their chiefs, to testify their fidelity to their persons, and peril life and liberty in their cause; plenty to vindicate the honour of England abroad, and to exult in her glory at home. But this is not patriotism, any more than kindliness is philanthropy. We have no long-sighted views respecting the permanent improvement of society,—no extensive regards to the interests of an entire nation; and therefore, no simple self-sacrifice, no stedfastness of devotion to country and people. The noble class of virtues, which go to make up patriotism, are not even touched upon by Scott. The sufferings of his heroes are represented to arise from wounded pride, and from the laceration of personal, or domestic, or feudal feelings and prepossessions; and in no single instance from sympathy with the race, or any large body of them. The courage of his heroes is, in like manner, compounded of instincts and of conventional stimuli; and in no one case derived from principles of philanthropy, or of patriotism, which is one direction of philanthropy. Their fortitude, howsoever stedfast, when arising from self-devotion at all, arises only from that unreasoning acquiescence in established forms, which is as inferior to the self-sacrifice of philanthropy as the implicit obedience of a child is inferior to the concurrence of the reasoning man. None of Scott's personages act and suffer as members and servants of society. Each is for his own; whether it be his family, his chief, his king, or his country, in a warlike sense. The weal or woe of many, or of all, is the only consideration which does not occur to them—the only motive to enterprise and endurance, which is not so much as alluded to. There is no talk of freedom, as respects any thing but brute force,—no suspicion that one class is in a state of privilege, and another in a state of subjugation, and that these things ought not to be. Gurth, indeed, is relieved from Saxon bondage, and Adam Woodcock is as imperious and meddling as he pleases, and the ladies' maids have abundant liberty to play pranks; but this sort of freedom has nothing to do with the right of manhood, and with what ought to be, and will be, the right of womanhood—it is the privilege of slavery, won by encroachment, and preserved by favour. Gurth got rid of his collar, but in our days he would be called a slave; and Adam Woodcock and Mistress Lilias lived by the breath of their lady's nostrils, in the same manner as the courtiers of Cœur de Lion gained an unusual length of tether from their lord's knightly courtesy, and those of the second Charles from his careless clemency. There is no freedom in all this. *Slave* is written on the knightly crest of the master, and on the liveried garb of the servitor, as plainly as even on the branded shoulder of the negro. But it must be so, it is urged, when times, and scenes of slavery, are chosen as the groundwork of the fiction. We answer, Nay: the spirit of freedom may breathe through the delineation of slavery. However far back we may revert to the usages of the feudal system, there may be,—there must be, if they exist in the mind of the author,—aspirations after a state of society more worthy of humanity. In displaying all the pomp of chivalry, the heart ought to mourn the woes of inequality it inflicted, while the imagination revels in its splendours. But this could not be the case with Scott, who knew about as much of the real condition and character of the humbler classes of each age as of the Japanese; perhaps less, as he was a reader of Basil Hall.[17] Beyond that which seemed to him the outermost circle, that of the domestics of the great, all was a blank; save a few vague outlines of beggar-women with seven small children, and other such groups that have by some chance found their way into works of fiction. His benignity, therefore, alloyed by no bitterness of disposition in himself, was so far restricted by the imperfection of his knowledge of life, as to prevent his conveying the conception of philanthropy in its largest sense. His services to freedom are of a negative, rather than a positive character; rendered by showing how things work in a state of slavery, rather than how they should work in a condition of rational freedom; and it follows, that his incitements to benevolence are also tendered unconsciously. Through an exhibition of the softening and brightening influence of benignity shed over the early movements of society, he indicates what must be the meridian splendour of philanthropy, penetrating everywhere, irradiating where it penetrates, and fertilizing, as well as embellishing whatever it shines upon.

Much has Walter Scott also done, and done it also unconsciously, for woman. Neither Mary Wollstonecraft, nor Thompson of Cork,[18] nor any other advocate of the rights of woman, has pleaded so eloquently to the thoughtful, —and the thoughtful alone will entertain the subject,—as Walter Scott, by his exhibition of what women are, and by two or three indications of what they might be. He has been found fault with for the poverty of character of the women of his tales; a species of blame against which we have always protested. If he had made as long a list of oddities among his women as his men, he would have exposed himself to the reproach of quitting nature, and

---

[17] British naval officer Basil Hall (1788–1844) published accounts of his travels, including voyages to the orient.
[18] Among his utilitarian-based views, Irish political philosopher and social reformer William Thompson (1775–1833) advocated the extension of women's rights, particularly the vote and access to contraception.

deserting classes for extravagant individualities; since there is much less scope for eccentricity among women, in the present state of society, than among men. But, it is alleged, he has made so few of his female characters representatives of a class. True; for the plain reason, that there are scarcely any classes to represent. We thank him for the forcible exhibition of this truth: we thank him for the very term *womankind*; and can well bear its insulting use in the mouth of the scoffer, for the sake of the process it may set to work in the mind of the meditative and the just […].[19] The best argument for Negro Emancipation lies in the vices and subservience of slaves: the best argument for female emancipation lies in the folly and contentedness of women under the present system,—an argument to which Walter Scott has done the fullest justice; for a set of more passionless, frivolous, uninteresting beings was never assembled at morning auction, or evening tea-table, than he has presented us with in his novels. The few exceptions are made so by the strong workings of instinct, or of superstition (the offspring of strong instinct and weak reason combined;) save in the two or three instances where the female mind had been exposed to manly discipline. Scott's female characters are easily arranged under these divisions: —Three-fourths are *womankind* merely: pretty, insignificant ladies, with their pert waiting maids. A few are viragoes, in whom instinct is strong, whose souls are to migrate hereafter into the she-eagle or bear,—Helen M'Gregor, Ulrica, Magdalen Græme, and the Highland Mother. A few are superstitious,—Elspeth, Alice, Norna, Mother Nieneven. A few exhibit the same tendencies, modified by some one passion; as Lady Ashton, Lady Derby, and Lady Douglas. Mary and Elizabeth are womankind modified by royalty. There only remain Flora M'Ivor, Die Vernon, Rebecca, and Jeannie Deans.[20] For these four, and their glorious significance, womankind are as much obliged to Walter Scott, as for the insignificance of all the rest; not because they are what women might be, and therefore ought to be; but because they afford indications of this, and that these indications are owing to their having escaped from the management of man, and been trained by the discipline of circumstance. If common methods yield no such women as these; if such women occasionally come forth from the school of experience, what an argument is this against the common methods,—what a plea in favour of a change of system! Woman cannot be too grateful to him who has furnished it. Henceforth, when men fire at the name of Flora M'Ivor, let woman

---

19   Martineau suggests that fictional representation of female flaws may work toward women's emancipation by prompting readers to consider the sources of those flaws. The ideas that follow contain strong echoes of Mary Wollstonecraft as well as lesser-known women's rights advocates.

20   Female characters from *Rob Roy, Ivanhoe, The Abbot, The Antiquary, The Monastery* (1820), *Waverley, The Pirate* (1822), *The Bride of Lammermoor, Peveril of the Peak, Kenilworth,* and *The Heart of Midlothian*. Several, like many of Scott's male characters, are based with varying accuracy on historical or legendary personages.

say, "There will be more Floras when women feel that they have political power and duties." When men worship the image of Die Vernon, let them be reminded, that there will be other Die Vernons when women are impelled to self-reliance. When Jeanie is spoken of with tender esteem, let it be suggested, that strength of motive makes heroism of action; and that as long as motive is confined and weakened, the very activity which should accomplish high aims must degenerate into puerile restlessness. When Rebecca is sighed for, as a lofty presence that has passed away, it should be asked, how she should possibly remain or reappear in a society which alike denies the discipline by which her high powers and sensibilities might be matured, and the objects on which they might be worthily employed? As a woman, no less than as a Jewess, she is the representative of the wrongs of a degraded and despised class: there is no abiding-place for her among foes to her caste; she wanders unemployed (as regards her peculiar capabilities) through the world; and when she dies, there has been, not only a deep injury inflicted, but a waste made of the resources of human greatness and happiness. Yes, women may choose Rebecca as the representative of their capabilities: first despised, then wondered at, and involuntarily admired; tempted, made use of, then persecuted, and finally banished—not by a formal decree, but by being refused honourable occupation, and a safe abiding place. Let women not only take her for their model, but make her speak for them to society, till they have obtained the educational discipline which beseems them; the rights, political and social, which are their due; and that equal regard with the other sex in the eye of man, which it requires the faith of Rebecca to assure them they have in the eye of Heaven. Meantime, while still suffering under injustice, let them lay to heart, for strength and consolation, the beautiful commentary which Walter Scott has given on the lot of the representative of their wrongs. If duly treasured, it may prove by its effects, that our author has contributed, in more ways than one, to female emancipation; by supplying a principle of renovation to the enslaved, as well as by exposing their condition; by pointing out the ends for which freedom and power are desirable, as well as the disastrous effects of withholding them [...].[21]

These, then, are the moral services,—many and great,—which Scott has rendered,—positively and negatively,—consciously and unconsciously, to society. He has softened national prejudices; he has encouraged innocent tastes in every region of the world; he has imparted to certain influential classes the conviction that human nature works alike in all; he has exposed priestcraft and fanaticism; he has effectively satirized eccentricities, unamiablenesses and follies; he has irresistibly recommended benignity in the survey of life, and indicated the glory of a higher kind of benevolence; and finally, he has advocated the rights of woman with a force all the greater for his

---

[21]   Omitted section quotes Scott on reader response to the character Rebecca of York from his introduction to the Magnum Opus edition of *Ivanhoe* (1830).

being unaware of the import and tendency of what he was saying.—The one other achievement which we attribute to him, is also not the less magnificent for being overlooked by himself.

By achieving so much within narrow bounds, he has taught how more may be achieved in a wider space. He has taught us the power of fiction as an agent of morals and philosophy; "and it shall go hard with us but we will better the instruction."[22] Every agent of these master spirits is wanted in an age like this; and he who has placed a new one at their service, is a benefactor of society. Scott might have written, as he declared he wrote, for the passing of his time, the improvement of his fortunes, and the amusement of his readers: he might have believed, as he declared he believed, that little moral utility arises out of works of fiction: we are not bound to estimate his works as lightly as he did, or to agree in his opinions of their influences. We rather learn from him how much may be impressed by exemplification which would be rejected in the form of reasoning, and how there may be more extensive *embodiments* of truth in fiction than the world was before thoroughly aware of. It matters not that the truth he exemplified was taken up at random, like that of all his predecessors in the walks of fiction. Others may systematize, having learned from him how extensively they may embody. There is a boundless field open before them; no less than the whole region of moral science, politics, political economy, social rights and duties. All these, and more, are as fit for the process of exemplification as the varieties of life and character illustrated by Scott. And not only has he left the great mass of material unwrought, but, with all his richness of variety, has made but scanty use of the best instruments of illustration. The grandest manifestations of passion remain to be displayed; the finest elements of the poetry of human emotion are yet uncombined; the most various dramatic exhibition of events and characters is yet unwrought; for there has yet been no recorder of the poor; at least, none but those who write as mere observers; who describe, but do not dramatize humble life. The widest interests being thus still untouched, the richest materials unemployed, what may not prove the ultimate obligations of society to him who did so much, and pointed the way towards doing infinitely more; and whose vast achievements are, above all, valuable as indications of what remains to be achieved? That this, his strongest claim to gratitude, has not yet been fully recognised, is evident from the fact, that though he has had many imitators, there have been yet none to take suggestion from him; to employ his method of procedure upon new doctrine and other materials. There have been many found to construct fiction within his range of morals, character, incident, and scenery; but none to carry the process out of his range. We have yet to wait for the philosophical romance, for the novels which shall relate to other classes than the aristocracy; we have yet to look

---

[22] Shakespeare, *Merchant of Venice* III.i.73, slightly altered.

for this legitimate offspring of the productions of Scott, though wearied with the intrusions of their spurious brethren.

The progression of the age requires something better than this imitation; —requires that the above-mentioned suggestion should be used. If an author of equal genius with Scott were to arise to-morrow, he would not meet with an equal reception; not only because novelty is worn off, but because the serious temper of the times requires a new direction of the genius of the age. Under the pressure of difficulty, in the prospect of extensive change, armed with expectation, or filled with determination as the general mind now is, it has not leisure or disposition to receive even its amusements unmixed with what is solid and has a bearing upon its engrossing interests. There may still be the thoughtless and indolent, to whom mere fiction is necessary as a pastime; but these are not they who can guarantee an author's influence, or secure his popularity. The bulk of the reading public, whether or not on the scent of utility, cannot be interested without a larger share of philosophy, or a graver purpose in fiction, than formerly; and the writer who would effect most for himself and others in this department must take his heroes and heroines from a different class than any which has yet been adequately represented […].

It appears, then, from the inquiry we have pursued, that the services for which society has to be eternally grateful to Walter Scott are of three distinct kinds. He has vindicated the character of genius by the healthiness of his own. He has achieved marvels in the province of art, and stupendous benefits in that of morals. He has indicated, by his own achievements, the way to larger and higher achievements.—What a lot for a man,—to be thus a threefold benefactor to his race! […].[23]

---

[23] The omitted conclusion affirms that Scott's social achievements are no less laudable for sometimes being unintentional.

Appendix: Featured Periodicals[1]

The Analytical Review

Dissenter Thomas Christie founded *The Analytical Review; or, History of Literature, Domestic and Foreign, on an Enlarged Plan* as a monthly publication in May 1778 with radical bookseller Joseph Johnson as editor. Aspiring to encyclopedic coverage of all new works, Christie planned "to give such an account of new publications as may enable the reader to judge of them for himself."[2] This goal meant that as was also the case with many of its contemporaries, summary and extract featured prominently in longer articles, with shorter ones often consisting of one or two lines of description. Mary Wollstonecraft was an important contributor from nearly the first issue. During its relatively short lifetime, it also published criticism by other women writers, including Lucy Aikin, Anna Letitia Barbauld, and Mary Hays. The most radical among important literary reviews, the *Analytical Review* gave favorable notice to creative writers whose work experimented with new literary forms that rejected neoclassical aesthetic strictures and to works espousing progressive viewpoints on topics such as parliamentary reform, personal liberty, the condition of women, religious tolerance, and the slave trade. It also brought much foreign literature to the attention of the British public, an object to which Wollstonecraft lent noteworthy assistance. The publication was introduced as evidence at Johnson's trial for sedition, presumably as an illustration of Johnson's radical publishing practices.

[1]   Further information on Romantic-era periodicals and assistance with locating reviews can be found in Walter Edwards Houghton, ed., *The Wellesley Index to Victorian Periodicals, 1824–1900*, 5 vols. (Toronto: U of Toronto P, 1965–1988); Alvin Sullivan, ed., *British Literary Magazines*, 4 vols. Historical Guides to the World's Periodicals and Newspapers (Westport, CN: Greenwood P, 1983–1986); and William S. Ward's two compilations, *Literary Reviews in British Periodicals 1798–1820: A Bibliography*, 2 vols. (New York: Garland, 1972) and *Literary Reviews in British Periodicals 1821–1826: A Bibliography* (New York: Garland, 1977).

[2]   *Analytical Review* 1 (1788): iv.

Though Johnson was convicted and, in November 1798, imprisoned, he tried to continue running the review from King's Bench Prison, but the January–June 1799 issue, published under a new editor, was the *Analytical Review*'s last.

The Annual Review; or, Register of Literature

Founded in 1803 by publishing magnate Thomas Longman III and his Unitarian partner, Owen Rees, the *Annual Review* promoted critical values strongly supported by the London and Norwich dissenting middle class. Lucy Aikin's brother Arthur Aikin was editor for most of the *Annual Review*'s life, and he drew for contributions on his father John Aikin, his sister, and his aunt Anna Letitia Barbauld. Other important contributors included William Taylor of Norwich, a former pupil of Barbauld and her husband at their school in Palgrave, and Lant Carpenter, the dissenting minister under whose guidance Harriet Martineau undertook the broad reading and developed the intellectual skills that later boosted her into a literary career. After a name change to *The Annual Review, and History of Literature* in 1804, the periodical continued until 1809.

The Artist

The Artist: A Collection of Essays Relative to Painting, Poetry, Sculpture, Architecture, the Drama, Discoveries of Science, and Various Other Subjects was founded by Prince Hoare, painter, dramatist, art critic, and Secretary for Foreign Correspondence of the Royal Academy. Published weekly by John Murray, *The Artist* was inaugurated in March 1807 and ran through August of the same year, reappearing in 1809 to continue through 1810. Under its ambitious title, Hoare aimed to publish "professional information on the subject of the liberal Arts [...] in a familiar garb."[3] The paper featured belletristic essays by noted artists, writers, and politicians, often in the form of letters to the publication. To emphasize and substantiate the professional qualifications of contributors, articles were signed with initials, and authors' full names were supplied in the index to the bound volume version, a significant break with common periodical practice. Besides Hoare, who wrote much of the content himself, dramatist Richard Cumberland and painter John Hoppner were among the most important contributors to the first (1807) volume, with painter James Northcote and scientist Tiberius Cavallo prominent in the second. Its circulation was small, and apparently for the most part limited to the same intellectual and artistic circles from which Hoare drew his writers.

---

3   *Artist* 1 (14 May 1807): 10.

The Athenæum

Founded in 1828 as a weekly literary review, the *Athenæum* operated under several names during the later Romantic period, including *The Athenæum* (1828), *The Athenæum and London Literary Chronicle* (1828), *The Athenæum and Literary Chronicle* (1828–1830), and *The Athenæum and Weekly Review of English and Foreign Literature, Fine Arts and Works of Embellishment* (1830–1921). After a rough start, it became the most successful literary weekly through the end of the century, respected for its wide range of topics, sound judgments, and extensive extracts, and attractive for its modest price. The journal employed several women contributors in a variety of fields, including both Maria Jane and her sister Geraldine Jewsbury, Sydney Owenson (Lady Morgan), and occasionally Elizabeth Barrett Browning, with the number of women contributors and the frequency of their contributions increasing through most of the century. A marked copy survives at the City University in London, providing the attributions for The Athenæum *Index of Reviews and Reviewers*, maintained at http://web.soi.city.ac.uk/%7Easp/v2/home.html.

Fraser's Magazine for Town and Country

Edited first by William Maginn, a former *Blackwood's Edinburgh Magazine* contributor, and published by James Fraser of Regent Street, *Fraser's* ran in its original series from 1830–1869 with a new series continuing into 1882. During its first decade its sarcastic, humorous tone attracted a following that rivaled the major review quarterlies and exceeded that of *Blackwood's*, its most direct competitor. Contributions included fiction, essays, and reviews by such notables as William Makepeace Thackeray and Thomas Carlyle. Its "Gallery of Illustrious Literary Characters," authored by Maginn and illustrated by Daniel Maclise, features Letitia Landon, Harriet Martineau, and Sydney Owenson (Lady Morgan) among the nine women included in the series. No marked copy exists, and signed contributions constituted a minority, so that Baillie's signed discussion of her own play constitutes one of the comparatively few *Fraser's* contributions that can be attributed with confidence.

The Monthly Magazine

In 1796 with some help from Joseph Johnson, Richard Phillips founded his literary miscellany, the *Monthly Magazine and British Register*, employing Anna Barbauld's brother, John Aikin, as editor. With such a start, it should not be surprising that contributors included most of the important literary figures from the British dissenting community, including Joseph Priestley, William Enfield, Gilbert Wakefield, and William Taylor. Under Phillips's direction, it attained circulation numbers among the largest of any periodical in its day. Its articles ranged from economic and social concerns to scientific and technological advancements to domestic and foreign literature, including translations. Though the attention it gave to fiction was minimal, it featured original verse, including poems by Barbauld, Mary Robinson, and Amelia Opie, as well as Coleridge and Lamb. Articles on poetry and fiction such as the contributions from Wollstonecraft and Hays also appeared, and while her brother was editor Barbauld probably authored articles as well. In 1806 John Aikin resigned, apparently over a dispute with Phillips, and George Gregory, another dissenter, took over for two years, until 1808. Phillips sold the magazine to George Whittaker in 1824. In 1826, after incorporating the *European Magazine*, it began a second series under the name *The Monthly Magazine: or British register of literature, science, and belles letters*, and a third series was inaugurated in 1839 as *The Monthly Magazine of politics, literature, science, and belles lettres*. Though it continued into 1843, its quality and profitability declined steadily from its prime under Phillips.

The Monthly Repository

Originally a struggling Unitarian publication under the proprietorship of Robert Aspland, *The Monthly Repository* was sold in 1826 to an organization partly founded by William Johnson Fox, who took over editorship in 1828. Shortly thereafter, Fox published a call for contributors to which Harriet Martineau responded. Under Fox's mentorship Martineau became over the next decade one of the *Monthly Repository's* most important contributors, central to its turn away from Unitarianism to staunch utilitarianism. As was the growing trend among literary reviews, *Monthly Repository* articles usually take the new publications as a starting point for an article that offers a general discussion of a topic that often overshadowed its treatment of the books reviewed. Martineau's articles reviewed publications on such varied topics as religion, metaphysics, the legal profession, criminal justice, imperialism, and witchcraft. She was the only woman known to contribute major articles, but several other women supplied brief critical notices, including Harriet Taylor Mill and Eliza Flower, and Barbauld occasionally numbered among the contributing poets.

The Monthly Review

The first true literary review, the *Monthly Review; or Literary Journal* was founded in 1749 by dissenting publisher Ralph Griffiths "to register all the new Things in general, without exception to any, on account of their lowness of rank, or price."[4] As the leading review for the half century when Griffiths served as editor, it provided summary and extract of all but the most specialized publications, converting only slowly to the evaluative program of competitors like the *Edinburgh Review* and the *Quarterly Review*

---

[4]   *The Monthly Review* 1st series 1 (1749): 238.

after Griffiths' death in 1803. Griffiths assembled an expert staff of contributors to produce a journal respected for its high intellectual standards and appealing as well for its Whig, antiestablishment perspective. After his death, his son George Edward Griffiths took over management, but though his standards remained high, he failed to adequately adapt to a changing critical environment. The younger Griffiths relinquished control in 1825, after which the publication survived another two decades. Benjamin Nangle has assembled indexes of *Monthly Review* articles from marked copies running up to 1815.[5] Elizabeth Moody and Anna Letitia Barbauld are the only known regular women *Monthly* reviewers.

The New Monthly Magazine and Literary Journal

Launched in 1814 under the title *New Monthly Magazine and Universal Register* by Henry Coburn, *The New Monthly Magazine* continued with several name changes until 1884. Though Coburn was notorious for literary puffing and often used the magazine accordingly, the second series (1821–1871) enjoyed, at least for its first two decades, respect and consequently strong circulation despite a comparatively high price. Contributions included work by some of the most distinguished literary figures of the age, including Hazlitt's "Table Talk" series, Stendhal's "Sketches of Parisian Society," essays by Charles Lamb, letters from Coleridge, a dramatic sketch by Matthew Lewis, and Mary Shelley's "Byron and Shelley on the Character of Hamlet." Sydney Owenson contributed travel articles while Letitia Landon, Felicia Hemans, and Elizabeth Barrett Browning were among the poets featured. In later years work by Harriet Martineau appeared there as well. Ann Radcliffe's "On the Supernatural in Poetry" was published posthumously under the editorship of the first new series editor, Thomas Campbell. Landon's first known critical article was an installment in the "Living Literary Characters" series on her friend Edward Bulwer-Lytton, published shortly before his tenure as editor began[6]. In addition to her poetry and the essays included in the present volume, Landon contributed satirical social commentary and sketches and probably authored many of the short "Critical Notices" dated during the years before her death.

Tait's Edinburgh Magazine

A liberal competitor to the conservative *Blackwood's Edinburgh Magazine*, *Tait's* appeared in 1832 with William Tait as both proprietor and editor. In 1834 Tait incorporated *Johnstone's Edinburgh Magazine*, placing its proprietor/editor

---

5   *The Monthly Review, 1ˢᵗ Series, 1749–1789: Indexes of Contributors and Articles* (Oxford, Clarendon P, 1934) and *The Monthly Review, 2ⁿᵈ Series, 1790–1815: Indexes of Contributors and Articles* (Oxford: Clarendon P, 1955).

6   *New Monthly Magazine* 2ⁿᵈ series 31 (May 1831): 437–50.

Christian Johnstone as editor of *Tait's* with Mrs. Johnstone as literary editor and writer of much of the literary copy. This fruitful partnership lasted until Tait sold the periodical in 1846 and George Troup took over until the magazine closed in 1861. A true miscellany, with original fiction and poetry and articles on topics such as politics, social criticism, and the arts, *Tait's* emphasized a utilitarian perspective, and boasted John Stuart Mill among its contributors. Utilitarian influence can be seen in Martineau's article on Scott featured in this volume, and is reflected in a laudatory review of her "Illustrations of Political Economy"[7] which was scorned in more conservative publications. In addition to Mill and Martineau, especially noteworthy contributors included Leigh Hunt and Thomas De Quincey. The literary quality, humor, and, after a price reduction in its early years, affordability of *Tait's* made it the best selling magazine in Scotland and it was widely read in England as well.

---

[7]   *Tait's Edinburgh Magazine* 1 (Aug. 1832): 612–18.

Selected Bibliography

Adburgham, Alison. *Women in Print: Writing Women and Women's Magazines From the Restoration to the Accession of Victoria*. London: George Allen and Unwin, 1972.

Aikin, Lucy, ed. *The Works of Anna Lætitia Barbauld; with a Memoir by Lucy Aikin*. 2 vols. London: Longman, Hurst, Rees, Orme, Brown and Green, 1825.

Analytical Review; or, History of Literature, Domestic and Foreign, on an Enlarged Plan, The. London: J. Johnson, 1788–1799.

Andrews, Stuart. *The British Periodical Press and the French Revolution, 1789–99*. Houndmills, Hampshire: Palgrave, 2000.

Annual Review, and History of Literature, The. London, 1803–1809.

Artist: A Collection of Essays Relative to Painting, Poetry, Sculpture, Architecture, the Drama, Discoveries of Science, and Various Other Subjects, The. London, 1807–1810.

Athenæum and Weekly Review of English and Foreign Literature, Fine Arts and Works of Embellishment, The. London, 1828–1921.

Athenæum *Index of Reviews and Reviewers: 1830–1870, The*. http://web.soi.city.ac.uk/%7Easp/v2/home.html.

Baillie, Joanna. *A Series of Plays*. London: T. Cadell, Jun. and W. Davies, 1798–1812.

Barbauld, Anna Letitia. "On the Origin and Progress of Novel-Writing." *The British Novelists; with an Essay, and Prefaces Biographical and Critical, by Mrs. Barbauld*. ed. Anna Letitia Barbauld. 50 vols. London: F.C. and J. Rivington, 1810. 1:1–62.

Barker-Benfield, G.J. *The Culture of Sensibility: Sex and Society in Eighteenth-Century Britain*. Chicago and London: U of Chicago P, 1992.

Basker, James. "Criticism and the Rise of Periodical Literature." *The Eighteenth Century*. ed. H.B. Nisbet and Claude Rawson. Cambridge: Cambridge UP, 1997. Vol. 4 of *The Cambridge History of Literary Criticism*. 8 vols. 316–32.

Blank, Antje and Janet Todd, eds. *Desmond* by Charlotte Smith. Peterborough, ON: Broadview P, 2001.

Boaden, James, ed. *Memoirs of Mrs. Inchbald: Including Her Familiar Correspondence with the Most Distinguished Persons of Her Time. To Which Are Added* The Massacre *and* A Case of Conscience; *Now First Published from Her Autograph Copies*. 2 vols. London: Richard Bentley, 1833.

Bonnell, Thomas F. "Bookselling and Canon-Making: The Trade Rivalry over the English Poets, 1776–83." *Studies in Eighteenth-Century Culture* 19 (1989): 53–69.

Braithwaite, Helen. *Romanticism, Publishing and Dissent: Joseph Johnson and the Cause of Liberty*. Houndmills, Basingstoke: Palgrave Macmillan, 2003.

Brewer, William D. "The Prefaces of Joanna Baillie and William Wordsworth." *The Friend: Comments on Romanticism* 1 (1991–1992): 34–47.

Brigham, Linda. "Joanna Baillie's Reflections on the Passions: The 'Introductory Discourse' and the Properties of Authorship." *Studies in Romanticism* 43 (2004): 417–37.

Brock, Claire. *The Feminization of Fame, 1750-1830*. Basingstoke: Palgrave Macmillan, 2006.

Burroughs, Catherine B. *Closet Stages: Joanna Baillie and the Theater Theory of British Romantic Women Writers*. Philadelphia: U of Pennsylvania P, 1997.

——. "English Romantic Women Writers and Theatre Theory: Joanna Baillie's Prefaces to the *Plays on the Passions*." *Re-Visioning Romanticism: British Women Writers, 1776–1837*. ed. Carol Shiner Wilson and Joel Haefner. Philadelphia: U of Pennsylvania P, 1994. 274–96.

Butler, Marilyn. "Culture's Medium: The Role of the Review." *The Cambridge Companion to British Romanticism*. ed. Stuart Curran. Cambridge: Cambridge UP, 1993. 120–47.

——. *Romantics, Rebels and Reactionaries: English Literature and Its Background 1760–1830*. Oxford: Oxford UP, 1981.

Byrne, Paula. *Perdita: The Life of Mary Robinson*. London: Harper Collins, 2005.

Carlson, Marvin. "Elizabeth Inchbald: A Woman Critic in Her Theatrical Culture." *Women in British Romantic Theatre: Drama, Performance, and Society, 1790-1840*. Ed. Catherine Burroughs. Cambridge, Cambridge UP, 2000. 207–22.

Carnall, Geoffrey. "The *Monthly Magazine*." *Review of English Studies: A Quarterly Journal of English Literature and the English Language* 5 (1954): 158–64.

Castle, Terry. "Women and Literary Criticism." *The Eighteenth Century*. ed. H.B. Nisbet and Claude Rawson. Cambridge: Cambridge UP, 1997. Vol. 4 of *The Cambridge History of Literary Criticism*. 8 vols. 434–55.

Chandler, Anne. "The 'Seeds of Order and Taste': Wollstonecraft, the *Analytical Review*, and Critical Idiom." *European Romantic Review* 15 (2005): 1–21.

Chandler, David. "'A Sort of Bird's Eye View of the British Land of Letters': The *Monthly Magazine* and its Reviewers, 1796–1811." *Studies in Bibliography: Papers of the Bibliographical Society of the University of Virginia* 52 (1999): 169–79.

Chandler, James. "The Pope Controversy: Romantic Poetics and the English Canon." *Critical Inquiry* 10 (March 1984): 481–509.

Christie, Thomas. "To the Public." *Analytical Review* 1 (May 1788): i–vi.

Clarke, Norma. *The Rise and Fall of the Woman Writer*. London: Pimlico, 2004.

Conger, Syndy McMillen. *Mary Wollstonecraft and the Language of Sensibility*. Rutherford: Fairleigh Dickinson UP, 1994.

Craciun, Adriana. "Mary Robinson, the *Monthly Magazine*, and the Free Press." *Prose Studies* 25 (2002): 19–40.

Craciun, Adriana, ed. *Women Romantic-Era Writers*. http://www.bbk.ac.uk/english/ac/wrew.htm.

Critical Review; or Annals of Literature, The. London, 1756–1817.

Curran, Eileen M., ed. "The Curran Index: Additions to and Corrections of *The Wellesley Index to Victorian Periodicals*. http://victorianresearch.org/curranindex.html.

de Brouwer, Walter. "Mary Imlay, Analytical Reviewer." *Notes and Queries* 29 (227) (1982): 204–6.

Donaghue, Frank. *The Fame Machine: Book Reviewing and Eighteenth-Century Literary Careers*. Stanford, CA: Stanford UP, 1996.

Edinburgh Review, or Critical Journal, The. Edinburgh, 1802–1929.

Eger, Elizabeth, Charlotte Grant, Clíona Ó Gallchoir, and Penny Warburton, eds. *Women, Writing and the Public Sphere, 1700–1830*. Cambridge: Cambridge UP, 2001.

Folger Collective on Early Women Critics, ed. *Women Critics 1600–1820: An Anthology*. Bloomington: U of Indiana P, 1995.

Flexner, Eleanor. *Mary Wollstonecraft: A Biography*. New York: Coward, McCann & Geoghegan, 1972.

Forrer, Sally Stewart. "The Literary Criticism of Mary Wollstonecraft." Diss. U of Colorado, 1979.

Fraser's Magazine for Town and Country. London, 1830–1882.

Fryckstedt, Monica Correa. "The Hidden Rill: The Life and Career of Maria Jane Jewsbury." *Bulletin of the John Rylands University Library of Manchester* 66 (1984): 177–203; continued in 67 (1984): 450–73.

Gilson, David. "Jane Austen and the *Athenæum* Again." *Persuasions: Journal of the Jane Austen Society of North America* 19 (1997): 20–2.

Gordon, Lyndall. *Vindication: A Life of Mary Wollstonecraft*. New York: HarperCollins, 2005.

Graham, Walter James. *English Literary Periodicals*. New York: T. Nelson and Sons, 1930.

Greenfield, John R., ed. *British Romantic Prose Writers, 1789–1832: Second Series*. Detroit, MI: Gale, 1991.

Harris, Michael. "Periodicals and the Book Trade." *Development of the English Book Trade, 1700–1899*. ed. Robin Myers and Michael Harris. Oxford: Oxford Polytechnic, 1981. 66–94.

Hayden, John O. *The Romantic Reviewers, 1802–1824*. Chicago: U of Chicago P, 1968.

Hays, Mary. *The Love-Letters of Mary Hays (1779–1780)*. ed. A. F. Wedd. London: Methuen, 1925.

——. *Memoirs of Emma Courtney*. London: G.G. and J. Robinson, 1796.

——. ["On Novel Writing"]. *Monthly Magazine* 4 (September 1797): 180–1.

Henderson, Andrea. "Passion and Fashion in Joanna Baillie's 'Introductory Discourse.'" *PMLA* 112 (1997): 198–213.

Herzog, Don. *Poisoning the Minds of the Lower Orders*. Princeton: Princeton UP, 1998.

Houghton, Walter Edwards, ed. *The Wellesley Index to Victorian Periodicals, 1824–1900*. 5 vols. Toronto: U of Toronto P, 1965–1988.

Inchbald, Elizabeth. "On Novel Writing." *The Artist* 1 (June 13, 1807): 9–19.

——., ed. *The British Theatre; or, A Collection of Plays, Which Are Acted at the Theatres Royal, Drury-Lane, Covent-Garden, and Haymarket, With Biographical and Critical Remarks, by Mrs. Inchbald.* 25 vol. London: Longman, Hurst, Rees, and Orme, 1808.

Jeffrey, Francis. Review of *The Excursion; being a portion of The Recluse,* a Poem. By William Wordsworth. *Edinburgh Review* 24 (November 1814): 1–30.

Jenkins, Annibel. *I'll Tell You What: The Life of Elizabeth Inchbald.* Lexington, KY: UP of Kentucky, 2003.

Jewsbury, Maria Jane. "Literary Sketches I: Felicia Hemans." *Athenæum* no. 172 (February 1831): 104–5.

——. "Literary Women II: Jane Austen." *Athenæum* no. 200 (August 1831): 553–4.

Johnson, Claudia L. "'Let me make the novels of a country': Barbauld's *The British Novelists* (1810/1820)." *Novel: A Forum on Fiction* 34 (2001): 163–79.

Johnson, Samuel. *The Rambler 1750–1752.* 6 vols. London: Payne, 1752.

Jones, Robert W. *Gender and the Formation of Taste in Eighteenth-Century Britain: The Analysis of Beauty.* Cambridge: Cambridge UP, 1998.

Jump, Harriet Devine. *Mary Wollstonecraft: Writer.* New York: Harvester Wheatsheaf, 1994.

Kelley, Theresa M. "Women, Gender, and Literary Criticism." *The Cambridge History of Literary Criticism.* Vol. 5. Romanticism. ed. Marshall Brown. Cambridge: Cambridge UP, 2000. 320–37.

Kelly, Gary. "Bluestocking Feminism." *Women, Writing and the Public Sphere, 1700–1830.* ed. Elizabeth Eger, Charlotte Grant, Clíona Ó Gallchoir, and Penny Warburton. Cambridge: Cambridge UP, 2001. 163–80.

——. *Revolutionary Feminism: The Mind and Career of Mary Wollstonecraft.* London: Macmillan, 1992.

Klancher, Jon P. *The Making of English Reading Audiences, 1790–1832.* Madison: U of Wisconsin P, 1987.

Kramnick, Jonathan Brody. *Making the English Canon: Print-Capitalism and the Cultural Past, 1700–1770.* Cambridge: Cambridge UP, 1998.

Labbe, Jacqueline M. *Charlotte Smith: Romanticism, Poetry and the Culture of Gender.* Manchester: Manchester UP, 2003.

Labbe, Jacqueline M., ed. *Mary Robinson.* Spec. issue of *Women's Writing* 9 (2002): 3–151.

Landon, Letitia (L.E.L.). "Female Portrait Gallery, from Sir Walter Scott, No. 1: Flora M'Ivor and Rose Bradwardine." *New Monthly Magazine* 2nd series 52 (January 1838): 35–9.

——. "On the Ancient and Modern Influence of Poetry." *New Monthly Magazine* 2nd series 35 (November 1832): 466–71.

——. "On the Character of Mrs. Hemans's Writings." *New Monthly Magazine* 2nd series 44 (August 1835): 425–33.

——. *The Venetian Bracelet, the Lost Pleiad, A History of the Lyre, and Other Poems.* (London: Longman, Rees, Orme, Brown & Green, 1829).

Lanser, Susan Sniader, and Evelyn Torton Beck. "[Why] Are There No Great Women Critics?: And What Difference Does It Make?" *The Prism of Sex: Essays in the*

Sociology of Knowledge. ed. Julia A. Sherman and Evelyn Torton Beck. Madison: U of Wisconsin P, 1977. 79–91.

Lawford, Cynthia. "Diary." *London Review of Books* 21 (September 2000): 36–7.

Levin, Susan M. "Romantic Prose and Feminine Romanticism." *Prose Studies* 10 (1987): 178–95.

Lott, Anna. "Sexual Politics in Elizabeth Inchbald." *SEL: Studies in English Literature, 1500–1900* 34 (1994): 635–48.

MacDermott, Kathy. "Literature and the Grub Street Myth." *Literature and History* 8 (1982): 159–69.

Macheski, Cecilia, ed., *Remarks for the British Theatre (1806–1809) by Elizabeth Inchbald*. Delmar, NY: Scholars' Facsimiles & Reprints, 1990.

Mandell, Laura, ed., *The Poetess Archive*. http://unixgen.muohio.edu/~poetess/.

Manini, Luca. "Charlotte Smith and the Voice of Petrarch." *British Romanticism and Italian Literature: Translating , Reviewing, Rewriting*. ed. Laura Bandiera and Diego Saglia. New York: Rodopi, 2005. 97–108.

Manvell, Roger. *Elizabeth Inchbald: England's Principal Woman Dramatist and Independent Woman of Letters in 18th Century London, a Biographical Study*. Lanham, NY: UP of America, 1987.

Marchand, Leslie A. The Athenæum: *A Mirror of Victorian Culture*. Chapel Hill: U of North Carolina P, 1941.

Martineau, Harriet. "The Achievements of the Genius of Scott." *Tait's Edinburgh Magazine* 2 (December 1832): 301–14; continued in (January 1833): 445–60.

——. [Discipulus, pseudo.] "Female Writers on Practical Divinity: No. I, Mrs. More" *Monthly Repository* 17 (1822): 593–6 and "No. II, Mrs. More and Mrs. Barbauld" *Monthly Repository* 17 (1822): 746–50.

——. *Harriet Martineau's Autobiography*. ed. Maria Weston Chapman. 3 vols. London: Smith, Elder, 1877.

——. *Harriet Martineau: Selected Letters*. ed. Valerie Sanders. Oxford: Clarendon P, 1990.

Mason, Nicholas. "'The Quack has Become God': Puffery, Print, and the 'Death' of Literature in Romantic-Era Britain." *Nineteenth-Century Literature* 60 (2005): 1–31.

McCarthy, William and Elizabeth Kraft, eds., *Anna Letitia Barbauld: Selected Poetry and Prose*. Peterborough, ON: Broadview, 2002.

McCarthy, William. "What Did Anna Barbauld Do to Samuel Richardson's Correspondence? A Study of Her Editing." *Studies in Bibliography* 54 (2001): 191–223.

McDowell, Paula. *The Women of Grub Street: Press, Politics, and Gender in the London Literary Marketplace, 1678–1730*. Oxford: Clarendon P, 1998.

McGann, Jerome. *The Poetics of Sensibility: A Revolution in Literary Style*. Oxford: Clarendon P, 1996.

McGann, Jerome and Daniel Riess, eds *Letitia Elizabeth Landon: Selected Writings*. Peterborough, ON: Broadview, 1997.

Mellor, Anne K. "A Criticism of Their Own: Romantic Women Literary Critics." *Questioning Romanticism*. ed. John Beer. Baltimore: Johns Hopkins UP, 1995. 29–48.

——. *Mothers of the Nation: Women's Political Writing in England, 1780–1830*. Women of Letters. ed. Sandra M. Gilbert and Susan Gubar. Bloomington: Indiana UP, 2000.

Miles, Robert. *Ann Radcliffe: The Great Enchantress*. Manchester: Manchester UP, 1995.

Mineka, Francis E. *The Dissidence of Dissent: The* Monthly Repository, *1806–1838; under the Editorship of Robert Aspland, W.J. Fox, R.H. Horne, & Leigh Hunt; with a Chapter on Religious Periodicals, 1700–1825*. Chapel Hill: U of North Carolina P, 1944.

Monthly Magazine and British Register, The. London, 1796–1843.

Monthly Repository, The. London, 1806–1838.

Monthly Review; or Literary Journal, The. London, 1749–1844.

Moore, Catherine E. "'Ladies … Taking the Pen in Hand': Mrs. Barbauld's Criticism of Eighteenth-Century Women Novelists." *Fetter'd or Free: British Women Novelists 1670–1815*. ed. Mary Anne Schofield and Cecilia Macheski. Athens, OH: U of Ohio P, 1986. 383–97.

Mullan, John. *Sentiment and Sociability: The Language of Feeling in the Eighteenth Century*. Oxford: Clarendon P, 1988.

Myers, Mitzi. "Mary Wollstonecraft's Literary Reviews." *The Cambridge Companion to Mary Wollstonecraft*. ed. Claudia L. Johnson. Cambridge, England: Cambridge UP, 2002. 82–98.

———. "Sensibility and the 'Walk of Reason': Mary Wollstonecraft's Literary Reviews as Cultural Critique." *Sensibility in Transformation: Creative Resistance to Sentiment from the Augustans to the Romantics*. ed. Syndy McMillen Conger. Rutherford: Fairleigh Dickinson UP; London: Associated UP, 1990. 120–44.

Myers, Sylvia Harcstark. *The Bluestocking Circle: Women, Friendship, and the Life of the Mind in Eighteenth-Century England*. Oxford: Clarendon P, 1990.

Nangle, Benjamin Christie. *The Monthly Review, First Series, 1749–1789: Indexes of Contributors and Articles*. Oxford: Clarendon P, 1934.

———. *The Monthly Review, Second Series, 1790–1815: Indexes of Contributors and Articles*. Oxford: Clarendon P, 1955.

The New Monthly Magazine and Literary Journal. London, 1814–71.

Newman, Gerald. *The Rise of English Nationalism: A Cultural History 1740–1830*. 1987. New York: St. Martin's P, 1997.

Norton, Rictor. *Mistress of Udolpho: The Life of Ann Radcliffe*. London, England: Leicester UP, 1999.

Owenson, Sydney (Lady Morgan). *O'Donnel: A National Tale*. London: Colburn, 1814.

Parker, Mark. *Literary Magazines and British Romanticism*. Cambridge Studies in Romanticism 45. Cambridge: Cambridge UP, 2000.

Peterson, Linda. "(Re)inventing Authorship: Harriet Martineau in the Literary Marketplace of the 1820s." *Women's Writing* 9 (2002): 337–50.

Pichanick, Valerie Kossew. *Harriet Martineau: The Woman and Her Work, 1802–1876*. Ann Arbor: U of Michigan P, 1980.

Pinch, Adela. *Strange Fits of Passion: Epistemologies of Emotion, Hume to Austen*. Stanford: Stanford UP, 1996.

Quarterly Review, The. London, 1809–1962.

Radcliffe, Ann. "On the Supernatural in Poetry." *New Monthly Magazine* 16 (February 1826): 145–52.

Reiss, Daniel. "Laetitia Landon and the Dawn of English Post-Romanticism," *SEL: Studies in English Literature* 36 (1996): 807–27.

Rizzo, Betty. "Isabella Griffiths." *A Dictionary of British and American Women Writers, 1660–1800*. ed. Janet Todd. Totowa, NJ: Roan and Allanheld, 1985. 143.

Robinson, Mary. *Sappho and Phaon, in a Series of Legitimate Sonnets*. London: Hookham and Carpenter, 1796.

Robinson, Solveig C., ed. *A Serious Occupation: Literary Criticism by Victorian Women Writers*. Peterborough, ON: Broadview, 2003.

Rogers, Katherine M. "Anna Barbauld's Criticism of Fiction—Johnsonian Mode, Female Vision." *Studies in Eighteenth-Century Culture* 21 (1991): 27–41.

——. "Britain's First Woman Drama Critic: Elizabeth Inchbald," *Curtain Calls: British and American Women and the Theater, 1660–1820*. ed. Mary Anne Schofield and Cecilia Macheski. Athens, OH: U of Ohio P, 1991. 277–90.

Roper, Derek. "Mary Wollstonecraft's Reviews." *Notes and Queries* 203 (1958): 37–8.

——. "The Politics of the *Critical Review*, 1766–1817." *Durham University Journal* 53 (1961): 117–22.

——. *Reviewing before the* Edinburgh*: 1788–1802*. Newark: U of Delaware P, 1978.

Saggini, Francesca. "The Art of Fine Drama: Inchbald's *Remarks for The British Theatre* and the Aesthetic Experience of the Late Eighteenth-Century Theatre-Goer. *Textus* 18 (2005): 133–52.

St. Clair, William. *The Reading Nation in the Romantic Period*. Cambridge: Cambridge UP, 2004.

Sanders, Valerie. "'Meteor Wreaths': Harriet Martineau, 'L.E.L.' Fame and *Fraser's Magazine*." *Critical Survey* 13 (2001): 42–60.

Seward, Anna. *The Letters of Anna Seward*. 6 vols. Edinburgh: Constable; London: Longman, 1811.

Sigl, Patricia. "Prince Hoare's *Artist* and Anti-Theatrical Polemics in the Early 1800s: Mrs Inchbald's Contribution." *Theatre Notebook* 44 (1990): 62–73.

Smith, Charlotte. *Desmond*. London: G.G.J. and J. Robinson, 1792.

——. *Elegiac Sonnets, and Other Essays*. London: Cadell and Davies, 1797.

——. *Letters of a Solitary Wanderer*. London: Low, 1802.

Stephenson, Glennis. *Letitia Landon: The Woman Behind L.E.L.*. Manchester: Manchester UP, 1995.

Stewart, Sally N. "Mary Wollstonecraft's Contributions to the *Analytical Review*." *Essays in Literature* 11 (1984): 187–99.

Sullivan, Alvin, ed. *British Literary Magazines*. 4 vols. Historical Guides to the World's Periodicals and Newspapers. Westport, CN: Greenwood P, 1983–1986.

Sweet, Nanora. "The *New Monthly Magazine* and the Liberalism of the 1820s." *Prose Studies* 25 (2002): 147–62.

Tait's Edinburgh Magazine. Edinburgh, 1832–1855.

Taylor, Barbara. *Mary Wollstonecraft and the Feminist Imagination*. Cambridge Studies in Romanticism 56. Cambridge: Cambridge UP, 2003.

Thompson, Ann, and Sasha Roberts, ed. *Women Reading Shakespeare, 1660–1900: An Anthology of Criticism*. Manchester: Manchester UP, 1997.

Todd, Janet. *Mary Wollstonecraft: A Revolutionary Life*. London: Weidenfeld & Nicholson, 2000.

———. *Sensibility: An Introduction*. London: Methuen, 1986.

Trela, D.J. "Introduction: Nineteenth Century Women and Periodicals." *Nineteenth Century Women and Periodicals*. Spec. issue of *Victorian Periodicals Review* 29 (1996): 89–94.

Trolander, Paul and Zeynep Tenger. *Sociable Criticism in England, 1625–1725*. Newark, DE: U of Delaware P, 2007.

Turner, Cheryl. *Living by the Pen: Women Writers in the Eighteenth Century*. London: Routledge, 1992.

Vargo, Lisa, ed. *Anna Laetitia Barbauld Web Site*. http://www.usask.ca/english/barbauld/.

Walker, Gina Luria. *Mary Hays (1759–1843): The Growth of a Woman's Mind*. Aldershot, Hampshire: Ashgate, 2006.

Walker, Gina Luria, ed. *The Idea of Being Free: A Mary Hays Reader*. Peterborough, ON: Broadview, 2005.

Ward, William S. *Literary Reviews in British Periodicals 1798–1820: A Bibliography*. 2 vols. New York: Garland, 1972.

Ward, William S. *Literary Reviews in British Periodicals 1821–1826: A Bibliography*. New York: Garland, 1977).

Wardle, Ralph M. "Mary Wollstonecraft, *Analytical Reviewer*." *PMLA* 62 (1947): 1000–9.

———. *Mary Wollstonecraft: A Critical Biography*. Lawrence, KS: U of Kansas P, 1951.

Waters, Mary A. *British Women Writers and the Profession of Literary Criticism, 1789–1832*. Palgrave Studies in the Enlightenment, Romanticism and the Cultures of Print. Houndmills, Basingstoke, UK: Palgrave Macmillan, 2004.

———. "'The First of a New Genus': Mary Wollstonecraft as a Literary Critic and Mentor to Mary Hays." *Eighteenth-Century Studies* 37 (2004): 415–34.

———. "'Slovenly Monthly Catalogues': The *Monthly Review* and Anna Letitia Barbauld's Periodical Literary Criticism." *Nineteenth-Century Prose* 31 (2004): 53–81.

Weir, Zach, and Laura Mandell, eds. *Anna Letitia Barbauld Prose Works*. http://www.orgs.muohio.edu/womenpoets/barbauld.

Wellington, Jan. *The Poems and Prose of Elizabeth Moody*. Diss. University of New Mexico, 1997.

Wilkes, Joanne. "'Only the Broken Music'? The Critical Writings of Maria Jane Jewsbury." *Women's Writing* 7 (2000): 105–18.

———. "'Without Impropriety': Maria Jane Jewsbury on Jane Austen." *Persuasions: Journal of the Jane Austen Society of North America* 13 (1991): 33–8.

Wolfson, Susan J., ed. *Felicia Hemans: Selected Poems, Letters, Reception Materials* (Princeton: Princeton UP, 2000).

Wollstonecraft, Mary. *The Collected Letters of Mary Wollstonecraft*. ed. Janet Todd. New York: Columbia UP, 2003.

———. [W.Q., pseudo.] "On Artificial Taste." *Monthly Magazine* 3 (April 1797): 279–82.

——. *The Works of Mary Wollstonecraft*. ed. Janet Todd and Marilyn Butler. Vol. 5. London: William Pickering, 1989.

Yudin, Mary F. "Joanna Baillie's Introductory Discourse As a Precursor to Wordsworth's Preface to *Lyrical Ballads*." *Compar(a)ison: An International Journal of Comparative Literature* 1 (1994): 101–11.

Index

Abelard, Peter (1079–1142), 83
ability, 2, 90, 100, 101, 103, 106, 119, 180
absurdity, 21, 36, 38, 54, 93, 96, 100, 111, 123, 132, 153, 168, 182
affectation, 18, 32, 45, 58, 59, 63, 92, 96, 98, 102, 113, 131, 185, 206
Aikin, Anna Letitia; *see* Barbauld, Anna Letitia
Aikin, Arthur (1773–1854), 220
Aikin, John (1747–1822), 23, 220, 221–2
Aikin, Lucy (1781–1864), 10, 24, 146–7, 219, 220; criticism by, 147–54
amusement; 18, 19, 29, 31, 66, 72, 73, 76, 95, 98, 112, 124, 131, 147, 156, 198, 200, 217, 218; *see also* entertainment
Analytical Review, The (1788–1789), 4 n. 6, 10, 13–14, 23, 31 n. 35, 59 n. 15, 86–7, 107, 109 n. 3, 147, 219–20; criticism from, 92–106, 110–11
Annual Review, The (1803–1809), 23, 146, 220; criticism from, 147–54
Artist, The (1807–1810), 220; criticism from, 61–5
Athenæum, The (1828–1921), 10, 156, 157, 160, 164, 221; criticism from, 159–63, 165–77
Austen, Jane (1775–1817), 1, 12 n. 20, 14, 15, 60, 136, 171–4; *Sense and Sensibility* (1811), 172; *Pride and Prejudice* (1813), 172; *Mansfield Park* (1814), 60, 172–3; *Emma* (1816), 172–3; *Northanger Abbey* (1818), 1, 173; *Persuasion* (1818), 172, 173

Baillie, Joanna (1762–1851), 3, 5, 23, 37 n. 28, 77–8, 115–16, 189 n. 30, 221; criticism by, 116–35; *Plays on the Passions*, 3, 5, 37 n. 28, 77–8, 115–16, 189 n. 30, 221; excerpts from, 116–33
Barbauld, Anna Letitia Aikin (1743–1825), 3–6, 10, 12, 15, 23–4, 115, 136, 146, 166 n. 3, 206–7, 219, 220, 221–2, 223; criticism by, 24–50; *The British Novelists* (ed.), 3–6, 12, 15, 23–4, excerpts from, 24–50; 25; "On the Origin and Progress of

Novel-Writing," 3–6, 12, 15, 23–4, 24–37; *Thoughts on Devotional Taste*, 207
Barker-Benfield, G.J., 12 n. 20
Barrett, Elizabeth; *see* Browning, Elizabeth Barrett
Basker, James, 7, 13 n. 22
Beattie, James (1735–1803), 144
Behn, Aphra (1640–1689), 8
Bible, The, Judges, 170 n. 15; I Kings, 135 n. 41; Job, 207 n. 7; Proverbs, 54 n. 3, 152 n. 11; Isaiah, 175 n. 39; Daniel, 170 n. 16; Matthew, 56 n. 7, 110 n. 4
Blanchard, Samuel Laman (1804–1845), 186 n. 17
Blank, Antje, 54 n. 5
Boccaccio, Giovanni (1313–1375), 161
Boileau, Nicolas (1636–1711), 38
Bowles, Caroline Anne (1786–1854), 15, 174
Bowles, William Lisle (1762–1850), 51
Brooke, Frances (1724?–1789), 6, 39; *The Old Maid*, 6, 39; *The History of Lady Julia Mandeville*, 39 n. 36
Brooke, Henry (1703?–1783), 32 n. 17; *The Fool of Quality*, 72
Browning, Elizabeth Barrett, (1806–1861), 1, 221, 223
Burke, Edmund (1729–1797), 36 n. 27, 49, 87, 136, 142–4, 152; *Philosophical Enquiry into the Origin of Our Ideas of the Sublime and Beautiful* (1757), 49, 137, 138 n. 1, 142–4; *Reflections on the Revolution in France* (1790), 36 n. 27, 87, 152 n. 10
Burney, Fanny (Frances, Mme. D'Arblay; 1752–1840), 1, 31–2, 42–6, 104; *Evelina* (1778), 31 n. 16, 42–3, 101; *Cecilia* (1782), 31, 32 n. 18, n. 19, 42, 43–5, 46, 50; *Camilla* (1796); 45–6, 104
Burns, Robert (1759–1796), 184
Burroughs, Catherine, 3 n. 4
Burton, Robert (1577–1640), *Anatomy of Melancholy* (1621), 30
Butler, Marilyn, 7, 92 n. 5
Byron, George Gordon (1788–1824), 136, 159, 182 n. 8, 184, 185, 199 n. 57

Calprénede, Gautier de Costes La (1610?–1663), 38

Campbell, Thomas (1777–1844), 187 n. 24, 223

Canning, George (1770–1827), 174

Carlyle, Thomas (1795–1881), *Chartism* (1839), 162–3, 221

Carter, Elizabeth (1717–1806), 47 n. 47

Castle, Terry, 8

Catholicism, 206, 210, 216; *see also* superstition, religious

Centlivre, Susannah (1667?–1723), 8, 74, 76

Channing, William Ellery (1780–1842), 170 n. 14

Chateaubriand, Franc[,]ois-Auguste, Viscount de (1768–1848), 201 n. 61

Christie, Thomas (1761–1796), 13–14, 92 n. 6, 219

Cibber, Colley (1671–1757), 74

Clarke, Norma, 8–9

Coleridge, Samuel Taylor (1772–1834), 2, 51, 52, 136, 174 n. 36, 186, 199 n. 58, 202 n. 66, 222, 223

Collins, William (1721–1759), 23, 84, 144

Cooper, Elizabeth, 8

Cowley, Hannah (1743–1809), 76

Cowper, William (1731–1800), 83 n. 5

Crabbe, George (1754–1832), 173

Crébillon, Claude-Prosper Jolyot de (Crébillon fils; 1707–1777), 36

Cumberland, Richard (1732–1811), 75–6, 220

D'Arblay, Madame; *see* Burney, Fanny

Defoe, Daniel (1660–1731), 29; *Robinson Crusoe* (1719), 29; *A Journal of the Plague Year* (1722), 161

delicacy, 2 n. 3, 18, 27–8, 29, 30, 31–2, 33–4, 38 n. 33, 43, 44, 61, 63, 67, 68, 74, 76, 95, 98, 99, 101, 104, 106, 107, 110, 117, 121, 124, 127, 134, 144, 147, 148, 168, 193, 201; *see also* elegance; polish; refinement; softness; indelicacy

dialogue, 14, 40, 67, 72, 74, 75, 77, 101, 124, 126, 137, 140–1, 148

dissent, religious; *see* religious dissent

Dodd, L.L.D, William (1729–1777), 88 n. 2

Donaghue, Frank, 11 n. 19

Dryden, John (1631–1700), 72, 73, 144–5, 198

Edgeworth, Maria (1768–1849), 1, 32, 36, 50 n. 57, 61, 115, 147–9

Eger, Elizabeth, 2 n. 3, 8 n. 11

elegance, 18, 20, 27, 37, 39, 41–2, 43, 50, 61, 63, 67, 82–3, 89, 90, 94, 101, 103, 124, 128, 148; *see also* delicacy; polish; refinement; softness; vulgarity

Eloisa; *see* Héloïse

entertainment, 4, 12, 14, 24, 29, 30–2, 54, 59, 67, 68, 72, 75, 76, 127; *see also* amusement

epic, 21, 26, 117; *see also* Milton, *Paradise Lost*

fame, 26, 99, 114, 165, 166, 178–9, 184, 187–98

fancy, 30, 32, 37, 42, 45, 50, 63, 67, 69, 74, 80, 88–90, 95, 97, 105, 106, 111, 113, 124, 129, 151–2, 153, 154, 156, 165, 167, 172, 174, 175, 176, 193, 199; *see also* imagination

Fénelon, Franc[,]ois (1651–1715), 26

Field, Michael (Katherine Harris Bradley [1846–1914] and Edith Emma Cooper [1862–1913]), 1 n. 1

Fielding, Henry (1707–1754), 18, 26 n. 3, 29, 35 n. 24, 36, 113, *Tom Jones* (1749), 26 n. 3, 35, 50

Fielding, Sarah (1710–1768), 8

Fletcher, Andrew Laird of Saltoun (1655–1716), 36–7, 127

Foscolo, Ugo (1778–1827), 161 n. 7

Fraser's Magazine for Town and Country (1830–1882), 221; criticism from, 133–5

French literature, 2, 17, 20–2, 26–8, 33, 36, 38, 41, 43, 44, 74, 93–4, 95–6, 98, 99, 108, 159, 186 n. 23, 201, 206

French Revolution, 2, 28, 36 n. 27, 52, 54–5, 87, 96, 99, 102, 131, 136, 159, 161 n. 7, 201 n. 63

Gainsborough, Thomas, (1727–1788), 80, 94–5

Garrick, David (1717–1779), 70 n. 5, 79

genius, 2, 18, 26, 29, 31, 41, 43, 46, 47, 55, 62, 67, 72, 76, 77, 84, 90, 90, 91, 94, 95, 101, 102, 104, 105, 111, 113, 119, 134, 144, 161, 165–6, 167, 169, 173, 176, 190, 191, 193, 195, 197, 198, 200, 206, 207, 209, 211, 218

Genlis, Stéphanie-Félicité, Comtesse de (1746–1830), 20, 206

German literature, 28–9, 159, 199, 202 n. 66; *see also* individual authors

Godwin, William (1756–1836), 87, 88 n. 1, 107–8, 114 n. 11, 172 n. 28; *Caleb Williams* (1794), 109, 113–14; *St. Leon* (1799), 172

Goethe, Johann Wolfgang von (1749–1832), 28, 159; *The Sorrows of Young Werther* (1774), 28
Goldoni, Carlo (1707–1793), 161
Goldsmith, Oliver (1730–1774), 168 n. 8; *Vicar of Wakefield* (1766), 32
Grant, Charlotte, 2 n. 3, 8 n. 11
Gray, Thomas (1716–1771), 27 n. 4, 35 n. 23, 144–5
Griffiths, Ralph (1720–1803), 6, 17, 222–3
Griffiths, Isabella (1713?–1764), 6

Hall, Basil (1788–1844), 214
Hamilton, Elizabeth (1758–1816), 36 n. 27; *Memoirs of Modern Philosophers* (1800), 36
Hayley, William (1745–1820), 55, 82 n. 4
Hays, Mary (1760–1843), 4 n. 6, 10 n. 16, 12, 31 n. 15, 36 n. 27, 52, 59 n. 15, 92 n. 4, 93 n. 7, 107–8; criticism by, 108–14, 219, 222; *Memoirs of Emma Courtney* (1796), 108–10; *The Victim of Prejudice* (1799), 108
Haywood, Eliza (1693?–1756), 6
heart, 26, 27, 29, 31, 40, 44, 45, 54, 55, 62, 63, 66, 68, 69, 71, 73, 74, 78, 84, 89, 91, 93–104, 109, 110, 113, 117, 119, 122–5, 127, 128, 134–5, 144, 154, 167–8, 172, 175, 177, 180, 186–7, 191–4, 196–8, 201–2, 205–6, 209–12, 216; *see also* sensibility
Héloïse (Eloisa; 1101–1164), 83
Helvétius, Claude-Arien (1715–1771), 108
Hemans, Felicia (1793–1835), 1, 164–5, 165–71, 173 n. 30, 186–98, 223
Herzog, Don, 11 n. 19
Hill, Isabel (1800–1842), 186 n. 23
historical fiction or drama, 27, 38, 70, 94, 111, 129, 156–62, 179, 200; *see also* individual authors and titles
Hogg, James (1770–1835), 176 n. 44
Holcroft, Thomas (1745–1809), 36, 77; *Anna St. Ives* (1792), 36, 102; *The Road to Ruin* (1792), 77
Houghton, Walter Edwards, 219
Hume, David (1711–1776), 2 n. 3, 27, 69

imagination, 27, 29, 37, 41, 42, 47, 48, 59, 66, 69, 74, 84, 89–91, 94, 95, 97, 99, 104–5, 110, 112, 113, 117, 129, 130, 137, 139, 141–4, 150, 159, 165, 166–7, 169–70, 172, 174, 182, 184, 186, 189, 193, 199, 200, 202, 206, 207, 214; *see also* fancy

imitation, 17, 21, 38, 61, 65, 74, 81, 89, 90, 101, 106, 112, 120, 123, 133, 136, 159, 184, 198, 205, 217–18; *see also* innovation; invention; originality; novelty
Inchbald, Elizabeth (1753–1821), 5–6, 10 n. 16, 18, 36, 39–41, 60–1, 100–1, 115; criticism by, 61–78; *A Simple Story* (1791), 39–40, 60, 100–1, 103; *Nature and Art* (1796), 40–1, 60, 103–4; *The British Theatre* (1808–1810), 5–6, 60–1, 65–78
indelicacy, 29, 73, 94; *see also* delicacy
innovation, 2–3, 64, 82, 198; *see also* invention; originality; imitation; novelty
Italian literature, 17, 21, 55, 81, 82, 84, 159–62, 169
invention, 26, 29, 37, 45, 62, 67, 68, 74, 75, 84, 101, 106, 113, 118, 125, 130, 152, 156, 162; *see also* innovation; originality; imitation

Jewsbury, Maria Jane (Mrs. Fletcher; 1800–1833), 14–15, 164–5, 195, 196–8, 221; criticism by, 165–77
Johnson, Claudia, 4 n. 5
Johnson, Joseph (1758–1809), 10, 13, 36 n. 27, 86–7, 107, 113 n. 10, 147, 219–20, 221
Johnson, Samuel (1709–1784), 4, 12, 13, 17, 31 n. 15, 44, 59 n. 15, 81–2, 91, 93 n. 7, 109 n. 3, 111–12, 152; *The Rambler* (1750–1752), 4, 13, 111
Johnstone, Charles (1719–1800), 105 n. 31
Jones, Robert W., 2 n. 3

Kelly, Gary, 2 n. 3
Kemble, Charles (1775–1854), 70 n. 5
Kemble, Frances (1809–1893), 1 n. 1
Kemble, John Philip (1757–1823), 60, 70, 71

L.E.L.; *see* Landon, Letitia Elizabeth
Landon, Letitia Elizabeth (L.E.L.; 1802–1838), 1, 10, 165, 174–7, 178–9, 221, 223; criticism by, 180–203
Lauzun, Armand Louis de Gontaut-Biron, Duc de (1747–1793), 201
Lavater, Johann Kaspar (1741–1801), 113
Lawford, Cynthia, 179 n. 1
Lee, Nathaniel (c. 1645–1692), 73
Lennox, Charlotte (1729–1804), 38–9, 98–9; *The Female Quixote* (1752), 38–9; *Euphemia* (1790), 98–9
Lewis, Matthew (1775–1818), 110 n. 5, 223; *The Monk* (1796), 110 n. 5

Lockhart, John Gibson (1794–1854), 185 n. 15
Louvet, Jean-Baptiste (1760–1797), 36

Macheski, Cecilia, 4 n. 5, 65 n. 3
Macklin, Charles (1699–1797), 75
MacPherson, James (1736–1796), 168 n. 10
Madan, Judith (1702–1781), 8
Manzoni, Alessandro (1785–1873), 159–62
Marivaux, Pierre Carlet de (1688–1763), 44
Martineau, Harriet (1802–1876), 10, 92 n. 4, 204–5; criticism by, 205–18, 220, 221, 222, 223, 224
McDowell, Paula, 9
McGann, Jerome, 12 n. 20
Milton, John (1608–1674), 2, 15, 21, 81 n. 3, 81, 82, 84, 88, 143–5, 152, 153, 169 n. 13, 170 n. 14, 171 n. 25, 184; *Paradise Lost* (1667), 17, 29 n. 11, 48 n. 52, 49 n. 54, 81, 143–5, 184, 185; *Lycidas* (1638), 170 n. 17; "L'Allegro" (1645), 171 n. 25; "Il Penseroso" (1645), 169 n. 13; sonnets, 81–2, 153
Molière (Jean Baptiste Poquelin; 1622–1673), 38, 43
Monthly Magazine, The (1796–1843), 3, 107–8, 221–2; criticism from, 88–92, 111–14
Monthly Repository (1806–1838), 92 n. 4, 204–5, 222; criticism from, 205–7
Monthly Review, The (1749–1844), 5 n. 7, 6, 13, 17, 23, 166 n. 3, 222–3; criticism from, 18–22
Moody, Elizabeth (1737–1814), 10, 14, 17–18, 223; criticism by, 18–22
Moore, Catherine, 4 n. 5
Moore, Edward (1712–1757), 150
Moore, Thomas (1779–1852), 183 n. 9, 185 n. 15
morality; moral effect; 4, 12, 18, 22, 26–7, 28, 30, 31, 32, 33, 35–6, 40, 42, 44, , 46, 53, 64, 70, 76–7, 82, 97, 100, 102, 103, 106, 109–10, 111–13, 116, 122, 124, 125–7, 144–5, 147, 148–9, 152, 156, 163, 169, 172, 176, 183, 195, 201, 206, 207–8, 210, 211, 216–17, 218; *see also* propriety; vulgarity
More, Hannah (1745–1833), 23, 79, 99 n. 21, 205–7
Morgan, Lady; *see* Sydney Owenson
Mullan, John, 12 n. 20
Myers, Sylvia Harcstark, 8 n. 12

national character, 2, 4, 6, 15, 17, 20, 21, 24, 27–8, 35–7, 47, 54–5, 67, 74, 127, 155–7, 158, 159–62, 161, 169, 201, 213, 216
Neal, John (1793–1876), 168 n. 7
New Monthly Magazine, The (1814–1871), 137 n. 2, 166 n. 4, 171 n. 19, 179, 223; criticism from, 137–45, 181–203
Newgate Calendar, The, 168
Newgate Novels, 168 n. 10
Norton, Caroline (1808–1877), 1 n. 1
Nota, Alberto (1775–1847), 161
novelty, 29, 40, 44, 45, 46, 62, 71, 77, 104, 130, 149, 159–61, 162, 218; *see also* innovation; originality

Ó Gallchoir, Clíona 2 n. 3, 8 n. 11
"On the Origin and Progress of Novel-Writing," *see* Barbauld, Anna Letitia (Aikin)
O'Neill, Henrietta (1753–1793), 54 n. 5
Opie, Amelia Alderson (1769–1853), 41, 222; *Father and Daughter* (1801), 41
originality, 2, 14, 19, 29–30, 39, 43, 45, 62, 64, 76, 78, 90, 97, 101, 109, 119, 153, 159, 174, 185, 196, 198, 212; *see also* imitation; invention; innovation; novelty
Otway, Thomas (1652–1685), 66
Owenson, Sydney (Lady Morgan; 1776?–1859), 10, 155–7, 221, 223; criticism by, 156–63

Paradise Lost (1667); *see* Milton, John
Parker, Mark, 11 n. 18
passion, 18, 26, 27, 28, 29, 31, 33–4, 35, 44, 45, 46, 52–3, 66, 67, 69, 71–2, 73, 76, 78, 89, 90, 91, 92, 93, 95,97, 98, 101, 103, 104, 105, 108–9, 112–13, 117–35, 137–9, 144, 150–1, 153, 156, 159, 168–70, 184, 185–6, 186–91, 201, 207, 212, 215, 217; *see also* sensibility
pathos, 28, 29, 41–4, 49, 58, 66, 71, 120 n. 2, 147, 150, 153, 201
Petrarch (Francesco Petrarca; 1304–1374), 81, 84, 169
Pinch, Adela, 12 n. 20
Philips, Ambrose (1675–1749), 74
Phillips, Richard (1767–1840), 52, 221–2
picturesque, 50, 91, 94, 100, 102, 104–5, 113, 136, 144–5, 153, 174, 185, 193–5, 199, 201, 202; *see also* sublime
Pitt, William "the Younger" (1759–1806), 75
Plumptre, Anne (1760–1818), 131

polish, 27, 29, 39, 41, 83, 91, 152, 166, 180, 194; *see also* delicacy; elegance; refinement; softness
Pope, Alexander (1688–1744), 33, 47 n. 49, 57 n. 11, 74 n. 9, 83 n. 7, 97, 99, 198
predictability, 35, 37, 62, 122; *see also* suspense
Prior, Matthew (1664–1721), 34 n. 21
probability, 35, 37, 39, 40, 46, 65, 67, 68, 73–4, 102, 104–5, 110, 113, 134, 141–2, 148
Procter, Adelaide (1825–1864), 1 n. 1
prolixity, 110, 148
propriety, 34, 37, 54, 60, 63, 67, 70; *see also* moral effect; vulgarity

Quarterly Review, The, 133 n. 13, 134, 222

Racine, Jean (1639–1699), 74 n. 9
Radcliffe, Ann (1764–1823), 14, 36, 46–50, 61, 104–5, 106, 108–9, 136–7, 223; criticism by, 137–45; *Romance of the Forest* (1791), 46–50, 136; *A Sicilian Romance* (1790), 47 n. 50, 49 136; *The Mysteries of Udolpho* (1794), 48–9, 50, 136, 137 n. 2; *The Italian* (1797), 47 n. 50, 49–50, 104–5, 136
Rapin, Paul de (1661–1725), 27
Reeve, Clara (1729–1807), 37, 137; *The Old English Baron* (1778), 37
refinement, 22, 27–8, 31, 63, 67, 72, 74, 77, 83, 88, 92, 93, 97, 98, 107, 117, 120 n. 2, 124, 128, 140, 156, 158, 171, 180, 182, 206; *see also* delicacy; elegance; polish; softness; vulgarity
Reiss, Daniel, 14 n. 4
religious dissent, 10, 12–13, 17, 23, 86, 107, 136, 146, 204–5, 207, 219, 220, 221, 222
Reynolds, Frederick (1764–1841), 76–7
Richardson, Samuel (1689–1761), 18, 23–4, 29, 36, 111, 150, 200–1; *Clarissa* (1747–1748), 8 n. 11, 29, 31, 34, 46, 111–12, 150, 200–1; *Sir Charles Grandison* (1753–4), 34, 44, 200–1
Rizzo, Betty, 6 n. 8
Robinson, Mary (1758–1800), 10 n. 16, 52, 79–80, 103, 106, 222; criticism by, 80–5; *Angelina* (1796), 103; *Hubert de Sevrac* (1796), 106
Rosa, Salvator (1615–1673), 47
Rossetti, Christina (1830–1894), 1 n. 1
Rousseau, Jean-Jacques (1712–1778), 26–7, 33, 41, 93–4, 95–6

St. Clair, William, 11 n. 18, 11 n. 19, 162 n. 11
Saltoun, Andrew Fletcher, Laird of (1653–1716); *see* Fletcher, Andrew Laird of Saltoun
Schiller, Johann Christoph Friedrich von (1759–1805), 28–9, 199, 202 n. 66
Schofield, Mary Anne, 4 n. 5
Scott, Walter (1771–1832), 114, 136, 159–61, 179, 184–5, 198–203, 207–18, 224; *Waverley* (1814), 198–203, 209, 215–16; *The Heart of Midlothian* (1818), 209, 212, 215–16; *Rob Roy* (1818), 212, 215–16; *Ivanhoe* (1819), 172, 209, 211, 213, 215–16
Scudéry, Madeleine de (1607–1701), 38
sensibility, 26, 29, 32–3, 39, 40, 55, 61, 68, 73, 88, 92, 93, 94, 96, 100, 107, 109, 113, 117, 140–1, 144, 151, 196, 216; *see also* delicacy; heart; softness; sympathy
Sévigné, Marie de Rabutin-Chantal, Marquise de (1626–1696), 99
Seward, Anna (1742–1809), 1, 51
Shakespeare, William (1564–1616), 2, 5, 15, 27, 47–8, 50, 60, 76, 78, 79, 88 n. 2, 101, 128–9, 132–3, 134, 137–45, 150, 151, 152, 159, 183, 185; *The Comedy of Errors* (c. 1592–1594), 65–6; *King John* (c. 1594–1596), 47–8, 148 n. 51; *Romeo and Juliet* (c. 1595–1596), 66, 79; *A Midsummer Night's Dream* (c. 1595–1596), 151; *Merchant of Venice*, (c. 1596–1597), 67, 177 n. 47, 217 n. 22; *Henry IV, pt. 1* (c. 1596–1597), 66–7; *Much Ado About Nothing* (c. 1598–1599), 68; *Henry V* (1599?), 67–8; *Julius Caesar* (1599), 58 n. 13, 70, 138; *As You Like It* (c. 1599–1600), 54 n. 4; *Hamlet* (c. 1600–1601), 19, 53 n. 2, 65, 140–3, 145, 174 n. 38, 223; *Twelfth Night* (c. 1601–1602), 72–3; *Measure for Measure* (1604), 68–9; *Othello* (1604), 69, 71–2, 134–5, 172; *King Lear* (1606), 68, 69; *Macbeth* (1606), 19, 65, 70, 138–40, 142, 158; *Coriolanus* (c. 1607–1608), 70–1; *Cymbeline* (1609), 138; *The Winter's Tale* (1611), 69, 80; *The Tempest* (1611), 50, 65, 72, 145; sonnets, 185, 201 n. 62
Shelley, Mary Wollstonecraft (1797–1851), 87, 107, 162 n. 11, 223
Shelley, Percy Bysshe (1792–1822), 2, 136, 169, 185, 188 n. 29
Sheridan, Frances (1724–1766), 30

Sheridan, Richard Brinsley (1751–1816), 30 n 14, 79

Siddons, Sarah (1755–1831), 60, 70, 78, 133, 139–40

Simplicity, 39, 43, 44, 55, 63, 73, 88, 94, 97, 98, 100, 102, 110–11, 112, 113, 117, 118, 122, 124, 125, 127–8, 131, 138, 145, 148, 149, 166, 168, 170, 171, 172, 177, 182, 194, 197, 203, 206, 212; *see also* affectation

Smith, Charlotte (1749–1806), 4 n. 6, 9, 10 n. 16, 15, 31 n. 15, 41–2, 51–2 , 82 n. 4, 92–3, 93 n. 7, 94–5, 97, 101, 102, 105–6, 108, 109 n. 3; criticism by, 52–9; *Emmeline* (1788), 92–3; *Ethelinde* (1789), 94–5; *Celestina* (1791), 101; *Desmond* (1792), 42, 52–5, 102; *The Old Manor House* (1793), 42; *Marchmont* (1796), 105–6

Smith, Elizabeth (1776–1806), 207 n. 7

Smollett, Tobias (1721–1771), 29, 113

softness, 12, 31–2, 89, 98, 99, 100, 109, 113, 119, 120 n. 2, 138, 140, 180, 193, 208, 214, 216; *see also* delicacy; elegance; polish; refinement

sonnet, 9, 41–2, 51–2, 55–8, 80–5, 93, 94, 153, 185

Southerne, Thomas (1660–1746), 73

Southey, Robert (1774–1843), 174 n. 37; *Thalaba the Destroyer* (1801), 174, 197–8

Spenser, Edmund (c. 1552–1599), 84

Staël, Anne Louise Germaine Necker de (1766–1817), 27–8, 33, 93–4, 206; 186 n. 23; *Corinne* (1807), 27–8, 186 n. 23, 196

Stephenson, Glennis, 10 n. 17

Sterne, Laurence (1713–1768), 29–30; *Tristram Shandy* (1760–1767), 29–30

style, 18, 20, 24, 39, 40, 41, 42, 43, 93, 97, 101, 104, 113, 118, 148, 149, 151, 152, 159, 161, 162 n. 13, 166, 168, 177, 194, 207

sublime, 21, 46, 47 n. 48, 49, 70, 73, 81, 84, 89–90, 117, 136, 137–45, 152, 193; *see also* picturesque; transport

Sullivan, Alvin, 219

superstition
  irrational beliefs, 83, 85, 111, 139–41, 215
  religious superstition, 206, 210; *see also* Catholicism

suspense, 19, 34, 46–8, 49, 62; *see also* predictability

Swift, Jonathan (1667–1745), 26, 168 n. 9; *Gulliver's Travels* (1726), 26

sympathy, 12, 40, 45, 48, 63, 66, 68, 71, 72, 73, 89, 95, 97, 107, 113, 114, 116 n. 1, 118, 124, 129–30, 135, 138, 151, 172, 175, 179, 180, 182, 187, 192, 202, 208, 209, 213; *see also* sensibility

system, 26, 36

Tait's Edinburgh Magazine (1832–1855), 223–4; criticism from, 207–18

talent, 26, 83, 84, 85, 93, 94, 99, 103, 104, 108, 114, 124, 144, 148, 176, 184, 203, 205, 206; *see also* ability

taste, 2 n. 3, 6, 11, 13–14, 27, 29, 30, 31, 36, 39, 41, 46, 55, 58, 59, 62, 64, 72, 74, 77, 81, 82 n. 4, 88, 89–91, 94, 95, 96, 97, 101, 105, 128, 132–3, 144, 152, 153, 159, 168, 169, 184–5, 207–9, 216

Tenger, Zeynep, 8 n. 12

Thompson, William (1775–1833), 214

Thomson, James (1700–1748), 18–19, 91, 144, 145 n. 11

Tighe, Mary (1772–1810), 192

Todd, Janet, 6 n. 8, 12 n. 20, 54 n. 5, 92 n. 5

transport; 26, 63, 72; *see also* sublime

Trolander, Paul, 8 n. 12

unnatural, 19, 20, 22, 90, 101, 104, 116–18, 206

Utilitarianism, 169, 183, 205, 214 n. 18, 218, 222, 224

usefulness, 59, 96, 100, 108, 113, 128, 131, 147, 201, 203, 205, 217

variety, 18, 28, 30, 42–3, 45, 53, 62, 69, 74, 75, 82 n. 4, 83, 95, 109, 113, 118, 119, 120, 121, 123, 124, 125–6, 127, 128, 131, 133, 147, 170, 174, 210, 212, 217

Voltaire, François Marie Arouet de (1694–1778), 26

vulgarity, 43, 45, 150, 153; *see also* delicacy; refinement

Waller, Edmund (1606–87), 83

Walpole, Horace (1717–97), 37 n. 30, 176; *The Castle of Otranto* (1764), 37

Warburton, Penny, 2 n. 3, 8 n. 11

Ward, William S., 219

Warner, William (1558–1609), 194 n. 43

Wellington, Jan, 14 n. 25

West, Jane (1758–1832), 36, 110–11; *The Gossip's Story* (1796), 110–11

Waters, Mary A., 5 n. 7, 10 n. 17, 92 n. 5

Whitehead, Charles (1804–1862), 186 n. 20

Wilde, Jane, Lady (1826–1896), 1 n. 1

Williams, Helen Maria (1762–1827), 96–8, 99; *Julia* (1790), 96–8; *Letters Written in France in the Summer of 1790*, (1790)

Wolfson, Susan J., 171 n. 20

Wollstonecraft, Mary (1759–1797), 3, 4 n. 6, 10, 13–14, 15, 31 n. 15, 59 n. 15, 80, 86–7, 107, 109 n. 3, 214, 215 n. 19, 219, 222; criticism by, 88–106; *A Vindication of the Rights of Woman* (1792), 80, 87, 107; "On Artificial Taste" (1797), 3, 88–92

women writers, 18, 30, 53, 77, 85, 99, 100, 108, 165, 169, 205–6; *see also* names of individual writers

Wordsworth, William (1770–1850), 2, 3, 4, 15, 52, 116, 147, 149–54, 164, 170 n. 17, 173 n. 32, 179 n. 3, 184, 185, 197; *Lyrical Ballads* (1798; prefaces to the 1800 and subsequent editions), 2, 3, 149–52, 116, 154, 184 n. 14; *Poems; in Two Volumes* (1807), 149–54

Yearsley, Ann Cromartie (1753–1806), 99–100, 101–2